Schizophrenia

NEW DIRECTIONS

for

CLINICAL RESEARCH

and

TREATMENT

EDITORS

Charles A. Kaufmann, M.D.
Associate Professor of Clinical Psychiatry
College of Physicians & Surgeons of Columbia University

Jack M. Gorman, M.D.
Professor of Clinical Psychiatry
College of Physicians & Surgeons of Columbia University

Mary Ann Liebert, Inc. ❧*publishers*

Table of Contents

CONTENTS

List of Contributors

Xavier F. Amador, Ph.D.
Associate Professor of Clinical Psychology, Columbia University

Alan S. Brown, M.D.
Assistant Professor of Clinical Psychiatry, Columbia University

Gerard E. Bruder, Ph.D.
Associate Professor of Clinical Psychology, Columbia University

Scott C. Clark, M.D.
Assistant Clinical Professor of Psychiatry, Columbia University

Andrew J. Dwork, M.D.
Associate Professor of Clinical Pathology (in Psychiatry), Columbia University

Alan Felix, M.D.
Assistant Clinical Professor of Psychiatry, Columbia University

Kelly L. George, B.A.
Research Assistant, Developing Clinical Research Center for the Study of Schizophrenia

Jack M. Gorman, M.D.
Professor of Clinical Psychiatry, Columbia University

Jill M. Harkavy Friedman, Ph.D.
Assistant Professor of Clinical Psychology, Columbia University

Luanne Holsinger, B.S.
State Board Member, Virginia Alliance for the Mentally Ill

Janet E. Johnson, M.D.
Postdoctoral Clinical Fellow/Assistant in Clinical Psychiatry, Columbia University

Charles A. Kaufmann, M.D.
Associate Professor of Clinical Psychiatry, Columbia University

Lawrence S. Kegeles, M.D., Ph.D.
Postdoctoral Clinical Fellow/Assistant in Clinical Psychiatry, Columbia University

Ellen Lukens, M.S.W., Ph.D.
Assistant Clinical Professor of Psychiatry, Columbia University

Dolores Malaspina, M.D.
Assistant Professor of Clinical Psychiatry, Columbia University

Lewis A. Opler, M.D., Ph.D.
Clinical Professor of Psychiatry, Columbia University

David J. Printz, M.D.
Postdoctoral Clinical Fellow/Assistant in Clinical Psychiatry, Columbia University

Esther Rabinowicz, Ph.D.
Postdoctoral Research Fellow in Psychiatry, Columbia University

Santhi Ratakonda, M.D.
Postdoctoral Clinical Fellow/Assistant in Clinical Psychiatry, Columbia University

Zafar Sharif, M.D.
Assistant Professor of Clinical Psychiatry, Columbia University

David H. Strauss, M.D.
Assistant Clinical Professor of Psychiatry, Columbia University

Ezra S. Susser, M.D., Dr.P.H.
Associate Professor of Clinical Psychiatry, Columbia University

Craig E. Tenke, Ph.D.
Research Scientist, New York State Psychiatric Institute

Helle Thorning, M.S.W.
Assistant Clinical Professor of Psychiatric Social Work, Columbia University

James P. Towey, Ph.D.
Research Scientist II, New York State Psychiatric Institute

Elie Valencia, J.D., M.A.
Assistant Clinical Professor of Public Health (in Psychiatry), Columbia University

Ronald L. Van Heertum, M.D.
Professor of Clinical Radiology, Columbia University

Martin S. Willick, M.D.
Lecturer in Psychiatry, Columbia University

Preface

This volume celebrates an important event, not only for people involved in psychiatric research at Columbia University, but for those involved in the struggle against schizophrenia. Ten years ago, Dr. Martin Willick, Mr. Jerry Modell, and Mr. John Rosenthal decided that consumers of psychiatric services—most notably those involved with people who have schizophrenia—needed and deserved more information about the state of research into this serious and sometimes life-threatening illness. They began what has become a tradition, the annual Schizophrenia Research Conference, sponsored jointly by Columbia's Department of Psychiatry, the New York State Psychiatric Institute, and the National Alliance for the Mentally Ill (NAMI). The original conference, as has been the case for the nine succeeding conferences, brought together hundreds of family members, people with schizophrenia, scientists, and clinicians to hear about research progress.

That progress has been substantial and is a major reason that people with schizophrenia and their families now legitimately maintain hope that more effective treatments are near. For the first time in 20 years there are new medications for schizophrenia and psychosocial researchers have learned much about the role of stress and the benefits of nonmedication treatments for patients with schizophrenia. At the same time, new technologies in molecular biology, immunology and brain imaging along with better epidemiology and diagnostic ability have brought us much closer to understanding what causes schizophrenia in the first place.

This book, based on the tenth annual conference, highlights the progress that has been made in the last decade and predicts where schizophrenia research is going in the next decade. It is an impressive compilation by people who are dedicated—perhaps obsessed—with getting the answers we need to improve the lives of people who suffer with schizophrenia and to make the lives of their families easier as well. But the book is also a testament to the persistence and dedication of several individuals who have made schizophrenia research at Columbia University and within the New York State Office of Mental Health system a successful enterprise.

We thank Dr. Willick who has done as much as any individual to highlight the needs of consumers in dealing with schizophrenia. He is both a great physician, father, and friend to us at Columbia. And we thank his colleagues who worked at his side to start these annual conferences, Mr. Modell and Mr. Rosenthal. We thank Constance and Stephen Lieber, who have stuck by us for many years as friends, supporters, and patrons. What they have done for psychiatric research in general and for schizophrenia research in particular sets an example for all caring people to follow.

Much of our work is made possible by the foresight and support of the government of New York State. The New York State Psychiatric Institute is the nation's oldest psychiatric research facility, brought into existence by state legislators 100 years ago. Today, we see the same high level of commitment to finding answers for schizophrenia from our current state government. We thank Ms. Charlotte Seltzer, director of Creedmoor Psychiatric

PREFACE

Center, and Dr. William Fischer, clinical director, for their continued help in establishing and maintaining a schizophrenia research unit at Creedmoor.

Our work is made possible by the patients and families who agree to participate in research projects. We value your opinions and input and applaud your patience and help as we fight this awful disorder. We thank the dedicated staffs at both sites of the Schizophrenia Research Unit (Creedmoor and the Psychiatric Institute) who exhibit the highest level of professionalism and scientific curiosity.

Finally, our deepest thanks go to two individuals who have worked tirelessly to ensure that research about schizophrenia continues at Columbia, throughout New York State's mental health system, and around the country. These two are dedicated psychiatrists whose vision and energy are an inspiration to all of us. They are Dr. Herbert Pardes, Vice President for Health Sciences, Dean of the Faculty of Medicine, and Chairman of the Department of Psychiatry at Columbia University and Dr. John Oldham, Director of the New York State Psychiatric Institute, Chief Medical Officer for the Office of Mental Health of New York State, and Vice Chairman of the Department of Psychiatry at Columbia University. It is a pleasure to work for both of them.

Jack M. Gorman, M.D.

Prologue

CHARLES A. KAUFMANN, M.D., and KELLY L. GEORGE, B.A.

Respice, adspice, prospice!
(Look to the past, look to the present, look to the future!)
Motto of the City College of New York (1847)

1896 was a memorable year. In Munich, Emil Kraepelin was completing the 5th edition of *Psychiatrie* (1896) in which he developed "the line of thought . . . (leading) to dementia praecox (schizophrenia) being regarded as a distinct disease" (Kraepelin, 1919). In New York, Ira Van Gieson was establishing the New York State Psychiaric Institute, an institute for the "study of the causes and conditions that underlie (such) mental diseases" (Van Gieson, 1896). During the ensuing 100 years, the paths of schizophrenia research, of the Psychiatric Institute, and of the affiliated Department of Psychiatry of Columbia University have been intricately intertwined (Kolb and Roizin, 1993): JW Moore collaborating with Hideoye Noguchi of the Rockefeller Institute for Medical Research, discovered the spirochetal cause of perhaps the then most prevalent form of "symptomatic" schizophrenia—general paresis (Noguchi and Moore, 1913); Franz Kallmann (himself an emigré from Munich) conducted the first comprehensive studies of the genetic etiology of schizophrenia (Kallmann, 1946); his successor, Nikki Erlenmeyer-Kimling, went on to describe the earliest manifestations of the schizophrenia genotype (Erlenmeyer-Kimling and Cornblatt, 1992); and Joseph Zubin (and later Robert Spitzer and Jean Endicott) made seminal contributions to the nosology of schizophrenia, culminating in the development of DSM III, DSM III-R, and DSM IV. Moreover, the Psychiatric Institute/Columbia University was the site of the earliest demonstration in the United States of the efficacy of phenothiazines in the treatment of schizophrenia (Malitz et al., 1956), as well as the site of the discovery of the first neurophysiologic correlate of cognitive activity, the P300 brain potential, providing an important investigative approach to brain function in those with the disorder (Sutton et al., 1965)

This volume celebrates this century of synergy between schizophrenia research and the Psychiatric Institute/Columbia University. Each contributor has looked to the past and present, taking stock of developments in schizophrenia research in their respective field. To make their presentations more comprehensible and timely, each has focused primarily on advances during the past decade, a period that has witnessed remarkable progress in our understanding of schizophrenia, and in the expansion of schizophrenia efforts on campus. These efforts have included establishing inpatient psychiatric research units at the Psychiatric Institute and nearby Creedmoor Psychiatric Center, funding by the National Institute of Mental Health (NIMH) of two research centers devoted to schizophrenia (the Schizophrenia Developing Clinical Research Center and the Diagnostic Center for Schizophrenia Linkage Studies), and creation of the first academic psychiatric presence in a shelter for homeless mentally ill persons. They have also included instituting an annual meeting which highlights research developments for both professional and lay audiences, the tenth of which provided the motivation for this monograph. Each contributor to this book also has looked to the future, speculating on the directions schizophrenia research may take as we move into a new decade and a new century.

Kraepelin adopted Morel's term "dementia praecox" (démence précoce, Morel, 1860) to reflect his appreciation that this disorder, despite "the most varied initial clinical symptoms," resulted in "states of dementia" and to reinforce Hecker's (and Clouston's) observation (Hecker, 1871; Clouston, 1891) that its onset "seemed to stand in near relation to the period of youth" (Kraepelin, op cit.). This "simple, fairly high-grade state of mental impairment accompanied by an acute or subacute mental disturbance" was differentiated from periodic insanity (manic-depressive psychosis), paranoia, and organic psychosis (due to a recognizable physical illness) primarily through symptoms, associated features, and course of illness (Kraepelein, 1896).

Many who were present at the first formal presentation of this concept, the 29th Congress on Southwestern German Psychiatry (Heidelberg, 1898), objected to the delineation of a new disorder in the absence of an established pathophysiology or etiology (described in Lehmann, 1975). Kraepelin opined that dementia praecox arose from "a tangible morbid process occurring in the brain," but recognized that "morbid anatomy (theretofore, had) been quite unable to help" in clarifying the nature of this morbid process (Kraepelein, 1896). Nonetheless, he also realized that "reliable methods (had) not yet been employed in a serious search for morbid changes." Thus, from the time schizophrenia was first considered a distinct disease, its students have held that neither symptomatology nor course of illness were *sufficient* to account for it. Some have even suggested that a clinical state beginning in adolescence and ending in dementia might not be *necessary* to the diagnosis of schizophrenia (Bleuler, 1903). Cases with late onset and/or favorable outcome prompted Bleuler (1911) to shift attention from manifest phenomenology to underlying pathophysiology, to focus on what Kraepelin (1919) had identified as "the peculiar destruction of internal connections of the psychic personality," and to rename the disorder "schizophrenia" (from the Greek *schizein*, to split, and *phren*, the mind).

Contemporary nosologists would argue that Kraepelinian notions of dementia praecox were destined to fall short of providing the detail necessary and sufficient to define a distinct disease entity (Kaufmann et al., 1995). Continuing with the previously articulated theme, the clinical perspective available to Kraepelin at the end of the 19th Century allowed him a clear look only at the present, permitting clinical distinctions to be made on the basis of signs and symptoms. His view of the future was necessarily less distinct; he could refer to an uncertain course of illness, but could not avail himself of other outcome data, such as treatment-response. And for Kraepelin, lacking our contemporary (neurophysiologic, neuroradiologic, and neuroanatomic) windows on brain function and structure and our contemporary (epidemiologic, genetic, and immunologic) windows on brain pathology, etiologic and pathophysiologic events in the past were hopelessly shrouded in mystery.

Grounded in the present, Kraepelin could at best hope to observe a syndrome; we, who can simultaneously focus on etiology, pathophysiology, signs, symptoms, course of illness, and treatment response, can hope to discern a disease. Thus, in the chapters which follow, the contributors guide us through current concepts of the phenomenology, pathophysiology, and etiology of schizophrenia, and touch on treatment response, in an effort to move beyond Bleuler's "group of schizophrenias" (Bleuler, 1911) to definable diseases.

PROLOGUE

Schizophrenia is not only a disease, affecting the brain, but an illness that befalls the individual, and a sickness influencing and influenced by the family and society. General systems theory (von Bertalanffy, 1968; also see Engel, 1980) provides a theoretical framework for viewing schizophrenia as an affliction of a hierarchically organized biologic system. Once again, the aforementioned theme applies. To fully understand schizophrenia, first we must look backward, presumably at the most elemental level, to molecules, thence to synapses, cells, nuclei, brain networks, and the brain itself. We must then examine the individual with schizophrenia *sui generis*, and ultimately, we must look forward to the familial and social setting in which he/she exists. Axiomatic to systems theory is that each hierarchically organized level interacts with, and consequently influences, each other level: molecular pathology can best be understood (and addressed) in the context of social forces, and vice versa.

This volume has been written within such a hierarchical framework, which is reflected in its four sections: Schizophrenia and the Brain, Schizophrenia and the Self, Schizophrenia and the Family, and Schizophrenia and Society. Beginning with the phenomenon of schizophrenia, the authors look backwards, at ever greater levels of magnification, to abnormalities in brain networks, macroscopic brain structure, microscopic brain structure, and molecular regulation in schizophrenia. They look to the present, to the experience of patients with schizophrenia and to pharmacotherapeutic and psychotherapeutic approaches to treating individual psychopathology. Also, they look forward to the experience of families and society coping with this disorder and to psychotherapeutic and psychosocial approaches to ameliorating the impact of schizophrenia.

More has been learned about schizophrenia in the past 10 years than in the preceding 100 years. We ardently hope that the next decade will bring us even closer to identifying the "morbid process" inferred by Kraepelin which underlies this devastating disorder, and to bringing lasting relief to our patients, their families, and their communities.

REFERENCES

Bleuler E. Dementia praecox. *J Ment Pathol* 3:113–120, 1903.

Bleuler E. 1911. *Dementia Praecox or the Group of Schizophrenias.* New York: International Universities Press; 1950.

Clouston TS. *The Neuroses of Development; Being the Morison Lectures for 1890.* Edinburgh: Oliver & Boyd; 1891.

Engel GL. The clinical application of the biopsychosocial model. *Am J Psychiatry* 137:535–544, 1980.

Erlenmeyer-Kimling L, Cornblatt B. A summary of attentional findings in the New York High Risk Project. *J Psych Res* 26:405–426, 1992.

Hecker E. Die Hebephrenie. *Virchows Archiv für pathologische Anatomie* 53:392–449, 1871.

Kallmann FJ. The genetic theory of schizophrenia. *Am J Psychiatry* 103:309–322, 1946.

Kaufmann CA, Johnson JE, Pardes H. Evolution and revolution in psychiatric genetics. In: Hall LL, ed. Genetics and Mental Illness: Evolving Issues for Research and Society. New York: Plenum Medical Book Company; 1995.

Kolb LC, Roizin L. *The First Psychiatric Institute: How Research and Education Changed Practice.* Washington, DC: American Psychiatric Press, Inc.; 1993.

Kraepelin E. 1896 *Psychiatrie*, 5th edition, Leipzig Barth, pp. 426–441, Translated in: Cutting J, Shepherd M, *The Clinical Roots of the Schizophrenia: Translations of Seminal European Contributions on Schizophrenia Concept*. Cambridge, MA: Cambridge University Press; 1987.

Kraepelin E. *Dementia Praecox*. Edinburgh: Livingstone; 1919, p. 1.

Lehmann HE. Schizophrenia: Introduction and history. In: Freedman AM, Kaplan HI, Sadock BJ, eds. *Comprehensive Textbook of Psychiatry—II*. 2nd ed. Baltimore: The Williams & Wilkins Company, 1975:851–860

Morel BA. *Traité des maladies mentales*. Paris: Librarie V. Masson, 1860: p. 566.

Noguchi H, Moore JW. A demonstration of *Treponema pallidum* in the brain of cases of general paralysis. *J Exp Med* 17:232–238, 1913.

Sutton S, Barren M, Zubin J, John EK. Evoked-potential correlates of stimulus uncertainty. *Science* 150:1187–1188, 1965.

Van Gieson I. Remarks on the scope and organization of the Pathological Institute of the New York State Hospitals, part II: The toxic basis of neural diseases. *State Hospitals Bull* 1:407–488, 1896.

von Bertalanffy L. *General Systems Theory*. New York: Braziler, 1968.

The Diagnosis of Schizophrenia:
Past, Present, and Future

XAVIER F. AMADOR, Ph.D., and SANTHI RATAKONDA, M.D.

What can be gained, at this point in time, from reevaluating the diagnosis of schizo-phrenia? After all, this diagnostic category in one form or another has been with us for nearly 100 years. In its various manifestations, the category has proven to be useful in everyday clinical practice with respect to treatment decisions and predicting the course of illness. Given this observation, one could rightly ask, "if it's not broke, why fix it?" Alternatively, since the precise etiology and pathophysiology of schizophrenia continue to elude us, it could be argued effectively that all of the existing diagnostic criteria for schizo-phrenia leave us completely empty handed. In fact, depending on what we ask of the cat-egory, the concept of schizophrenia and its many offspring in the form of diagnostic crite-ria, has proven to be successful in some ways while unsuccessful in others.

In this chapter we will begin by providing a historical context from which our present day diagnostic system came and continues to draw upon. We will then turn to recent ad-vances in the nosology of schizophrenia during the past decade. This will include a de-scription of the revision of the DSM and ICD and a discussion of the rationale given for many of the changes made. In addition, a review of recent work aimed at developing more valid subtypes of schizophrenia will be presented. We will argue that new subtyping schemes are leading to increased predictive power with respect to the unfolding course of illness and to identifying more specific brain regions implicated in the etiology of this disorder. The last part of this chapter will focus on the future of the concept of schizophrenia. We will argue that a broader net will likely be cast with respect to phenomenologic features. In addition, studies using neuropsychologic, neuroimaging, brain mapping, genetic linkage, and molecular biologic techniques to identify homogeneous subgroups will likely succeed in reducing the heterogeneity of this disorder in increasingly meaningful ways. This may or may not always lead to specific information about etiology, but will constitute an im-portant step toward achieving that goal.

THE PAST

Toward the end of the nineteenth century, Kraepelin (1896) grouped together the then pre-existing diagnostic categories of hebephrenia, catatonia and paranoid psychosis into a sin-gle disease entity which he termed "*dementia praecox*." This formulation was modified by

Bleuler (1911) and renamed the *"group of schizophrenias."*[1] During the century following Kraepelin's initial formulation, several sets of criteria have been proposed for diagnosing the condition that have received various degrees of attention and clinical acceptance (Schneider 1959; Langfelt 1969; WHO 1978, 1992; Feighner et al. 1972; Wing et al. 1974; Spitzer et al. 1978; APA 1980, 1987, 1994, etc.). The latest in this succession of modified diagnostic formulations is the DSM IV (APA 1994), but few would believe that it is the final word in the endeavor to develop a valid diagnostic category for what we have come to know as schizophrenia.

These diagnostic formulations differed from one another in their relative emphasis on one or more aspects of the concept of schizophrenia: broad vs. narrow definitions, monothetic vs. polythetic concepts, cross sectional vs. longitudinal symptoms, experiential vs. behavioral symptoms, and objective vs. inferential assessments. Each new diagnostic formulation was meant to be an improvement on the ones already in existence. The fact that so many attempts at improvement have been made during the past 99 years indicates that the diagnostic system has not been able to fully accomplish what it was meant to accomplish. To understand the deficiencies of this system and to improve on it, first it is necessary to examine the purpose of making a diagnostic classification as well as the unique nature of psychiatric diagnoses in this context.

The two main components of a good diagnostic system are *reliability* and *validity*. *Reliability* of a diagnostic system refers to the consistency with which subjects are classified. Application of a reliable diagnostic system to the same data at different times or by different clinicians should yield the same diagnosis. In other words, high reliability would minimize diagnostic inconsistencies stemming from variation in clinicians' backgrounds, theoretical orientations, personal preferences, or emotional state. Reliability is of great importance for facilitating communication and for research, since it ensures that everyone using the same diagnosis is referring to the same clinical condition. *Validity* of a diagnostic category refers to its meaningfulness and utility. A valid diagnostic category would help predict future course of the illness, estimate prognosis and clarify treatment needs. Moreover, a valid clinical diagnosis of an illness would be informative with respect to etiology and/or pathophysiology. While reliability is required to ensure validity, all reliable systems are not necessarily valid.

Achieving validity for diagnostic categories in psychiatry is much more complex than for diagnostic categories in the rest of medicine. In medicine, diagnoses are usually validated by etiologic and pathophysiologic mechanisms and serve as guides to predicting treatment response and outcome. In psychiatry, the etiologic and/or pathophysiologic mechanisms of most conditions are unknown. Consequently, it is necessary to formulate a diagnosis by selecting patients with similar clinical pictures and then attempt to validate the diagnosis based on other measures such as treatment response, family "loading" for the disorder, and outcome. It is assumed that patients so diagnosed, by virtue of similarities in

---

[1]Throughout this chapter references will be made to "the diagnosis of schizophrenia" or to "criteria for schizophrenia." To make our prose less cumbersome and to conform to convention, we have chosen to label what we believe to likely be several different illnesses, under a single rubric. Nonetheless, we agree with Bleuler (and most modern nosologists) that until we have definitive evidence to the contrary, we are most likely talking about a group of disorders with similar and overlapping presentations.

clinical presentation, familial history, course of the illness, and treatment response would have the same underlying etiologic and/or pathophysiologic condition.

While reliability and validity are the two most important issues in constructing a diagnostic system, other factors may also play a role, depending on the purpose for which the diagnostic system is to be used. For example, diagnostic systems used for research purposes need to be narrow to minimize false-positives and decrease contamination of the study population with subjects who do not have the illness (i.e., that do not share the same etiology and/or pathophysiology). Meanwhile, diagnostic systems meant for use in clinical practice need to be less complex, more acceptable to clinicians of differing theoretical orientations, contain criteria limited to symptoms that occur relatively frequently, and may be broader so as not to exclude too many patients who really have the illness (false-negatives).

During the past 25 years, modifications to the criteria used for diagnosing schizophrenia have greatly improved the reliability of the diagnosis. However, these modifications have also significantly altered the concepts of schizophrenia as used in clinical practice. In describing dementia praecox, Kraepelin (1896) used the chronic course and poor outcome of the condition to both define and validate the concept. Although Kraepelin described a number of signs and symptoms occurring in dementia praecox, it was acknowledged that these manifestations can vary widely and that the essential characteristic of the disorder was the longitudinal downhill course of the illness.

In an attempt to integrate the diverse clinical presentations covered by Kraepelin's dementia praecox, Bleuler (1911) introduced the concept of basic and accessory symptoms of schizophrenia. The basic symptoms (which included Bleuler's four As) were thought to derive from the fundamental disease process and were considered to be permanent and pathognomonic of schizophrenia. When present, they precluded the diagnosis of any other functional psychiatric disorder. Bleuler's criteria allowed a diagnosis of schizophrenia to be made cross-sectionally and de-emphasized the longitudinal course of the illness. Application of Bleuler's basic symptoms required relatively greater subjective and inferential judgement, and was less amenable to formulation of operational criteria. The concept significantly influenced diagnostic practices and broadened the scope of schizophrenia to cover a large spectrum of clinical states. This resulted in a lack of reliability which was shown by a striking difference in the definitions of schizophrenia used by clinicians in the United States and United Kingdom (Cooper et al. 1972; Kendell et al. 1971).

The 1970s saw an increased emphasis being placed on improving the reliability of the diagnosis. This was achieved in part by formulating operational criteria and by relying more on observable (or "objective") symptoms to make up the diagnosis. A major influence on these efforts was the description of first rank symptoms by Kurt Schneider (1959). Schneider described eight first rank symptoms, all of which are disturbances of experiences reported by the patient and which were easy to comprehend and identify in clinical practice. Schneider considered these symptoms as being pathognomonic for diagnosing schizophrenia once known organic factors were excluded, although their presence was not an obligatory requirement for making the diagnosis. These first rank symptoms were the first implements for an operational definition of schizophrenia, and played an important role in many subsequent elaborations of diagnostic criteria and in the construction of interviewing instruments such as the Present State Examination (PSE; Wing et al. 1974) and the Schedule for Affective Disorders and Schizophrenia (SADS). Indeed, cross-sectional evaluations and Schneider's first rank symptoms were given prominence in the PSE which was used in the US/UK project mentioned above and in the International Pilot study of Schizophrenia (WHO 1973).

Moreover, this conceptualization of schizophrenia influenced the way the disorder was conceptualized by mental health professionals throughout the world. This was followed by development of operational criteria by Feighner et al. in 1972 (the St. Louis Criteria) and by Spitzer et al. in 1978 (the Research Diagnostic Criteria or RDC). The Feighner and RDC diagnostic systems were the forerunners of the DSM III (APA 1980). The third edition of the DSM set up unambiguous diagnostic criteria which required an illness duration of at least six months, provided exclusion criteria for similar disorders (i.e., affective disorders), and emphasized the presence of psychotic symptoms, which were similar to Schneider's first rank symptoms, during the active phases of the illness. This helped to narrow the definition and increase the reliability of the diagnosis.

Relatively minor changes were made for the next version of this criteria (DSM III-R; APA 1987). Essentially, this revision entailed a simplification of the criteria and a clearer definition of the boundary between schizophrenia and delusional disorder. Although the definitions of schizophrenia published in the DSM III and DSM III-R improved reliability by emphasizing the easily identifiable positive psychotic symptoms, they have been criticized for neglecting negative symptoms which are often the cause for significant functional disability. Studies have shown that negative symptoms have predictive power and that they can be identified and measured reliably (Andreasen 1982; Kay et al. 1989).

To summarize, in the years following the early work of Kraepelin and Bleuler, psychiatrists continued to focus on many of the same symptoms and course of illness features. The diagnostic process also continued in essentially the same way. However, as described above, important modifications in diagnostic criteria and in the process of making diagnoses have occurred, especially so in the past two decades. Two issues were considered separately in our review: the first involved the choice of *what* symptoms the category's creators considered to be necessary and sufficient to make a diagnosis of schizophrenia; the second involved *how* such symptoms were assessed and the diagnostic criteria implemented. With few exceptions, the choice of symptoms (the "what") has been driven by concepts rather than validating data. The question of what constitutes "validation" of a criterion will be discussed further in the last section of this chapter.

We also reviewed the issue of reliability. We raised the question of how these categories have been used, and argued that this is an essential question that must be addressed when developing new diagnostic categories. Before the advent of the DSM III, diagnostic criteria for schizophrenia differed dramatically in their rates of diagnosing schizophrenia. In large part, the revision of the DSM II was motivated by the discovery that clinicians and researchers alike had relatively poor diagnostic reliability. This low reliability was hindering progress in both the clinical and research realms. For example, when faced with a failure to replicate a particular finding, an investigator has to know with certainty that he or she studied the same "type" of patients as were studied previously. Without this knowledge, it is impossible to know how to compare, much less replicate, results. In short, it is impossible to know if the same type of patients (e.g., schizophrenia vs. bipolar disorder) are being studied or treated. In the past 15 years reliability has improved for the most part. This change came about through the use of explicitly stated criteria. In addition, each criterion was designed to emphasize observable objective behavior and characteristics and to minimize the need for the examiner to rely on inference. This type of criteria was ultimately incorporated into the DSM and the International Classification of Diseases (ICD) systems. These two diagnostic systems are the most widely used worldwide and have been designed to serve clinical, sociologic, and research needs.

Increased validity does not necessarily accompany increased reliability. In the remainder of this chapter, we will discuss the most recent changes to the DSM system and several new validation schemes aimed at increasing the meaningfulness of diagnostic criteria.

THE PRESENT

During the past several years the DSM and ICD criteria for schizophrenia and related disorders have been revised again. In both instances, the overarching goal was to increase the descriptive validity of these criteria. The revision of the DSM criteria was additionally driven by the desire to make the criteria more consistent with the ICD system, to incorporate signs and symptoms with demonstrated criterion validity (i.e., symptoms with predictive power), and to make the criteria easier to implement (i.e., "user friendly").

The main differences between the previous DSM criteria and those published in the DSM IV center on both symptom type and duration. Specifically, two negative symptoms (alogia and avolition) have been added to the A criteria and the duration of active phase symptoms has been increased from 1 week to 1 month, to reduce the possibility of false-positives. In addition, the definition of the prodromal and residual phases has been simplified by eliminating the list of specific symptoms. Finally, new course specifiers have been added that were adapted from the ICD-10. These changes provide increased descriptive validity, particularly with respect to the negative symptoms of schizophrenia and with the inclusion of such symptoms, increased criterion validity. Similarly, the course specifiers offer a more detailed description of symptoms over time, and as such, are inherently more valid with respect to their predictive power (i.e., since past course is one of the best predictors of the future course). It was hoped that by simplifying various aspects of the criteria, it would become easier to use, resulting in increased reliability. This feature of the new criteria has not been formally tested yet. However, it is likely that with increased ease of implementation, there will be a reduced likelihood of errors and resulting decrease in reliability.

In summary, there are numerous sets of diagnostic criteria for schizophrenia in use today. No single set has proven to be more valid than the others with respect to identifying specific etiologies. The DSM III-R and its predecessors the DSM III, the RDC, Feigner criteria, etc. were devised to improve upon various aspects of the diagnostic endeavor. Most notably, significant gains have been made in increasing the reliability of diagnoses (e.g., Endicott et al. 1982). The development of many criteria sets has also been guided by the desire to better characterize what is an extremely hetereogeneous disorder. Diagnostic criteria continue to change rapidly. Both the DSM and International Classification of Disease (ICD) criteria have very recently been revised. Nonetheless, the problem of the validity of the diagnosis of schizophrenia persists. We have no pathognomonic symptom and the diagnosis is based entirely on the phenomenology and course of the disorder. In this context, it can be argued that any nosology of schizophrenia should not rely solely on traditional signs and symptoms if other valid characterizations are available. There are many domains of psychopathology with proven criterion validity which can be used to enhance the characterization of patients with the disorder. This approach involves characterizing patients diagnosed with schizophrenia across multiple domains of psychopathology (e.g., trait-related psychobiologic markers, neurobiologic deficits, structural abnormalities of the brain, course of illness dimensions). In the next section, we briefly review two domains of psychopathology that we believe to be promising (i.e., with respect to enhancing the validity of the diagnosis) and representative of this approach.

THE FUTURE

Current and previous research and clinical criteria for schizophrenia-related disorders have essentially followed the approach to establishing diagnostic validity described by Robins and Guze (1970). Five phases are described. Each phase involves identifying validators for the criteria under development. The first involves the development of descriptive validity. In other words, there should be a consensus in the field with respect to the signs and symptoms required by the criteria to meet the diagnosis. This follows from the tradition of Kraepelin and Bleuler.

The second phase, still not incorporated into any modern criteria, casts a broader net with respect to the signs and symptoms of the disorder. Here, the goal is to link the manifest syndrome to underlying pathophysiology and cognitive processes. It was hoped that this would be achieved through the use of laboratory (i.e., radiologic, chemical, etc.) and psychologic tests.

The third phase involves delimitation from other disorders. This strategy is one of the more evolving ones in modern criteria as the etiology of other disorders are identified. The fourth phase essentially focuses on the long-term course of the disorder. As mentioned at the outset, course of illness has long been a feature, although not always a prominent one, of diagnostic criteria for schizophrenia in the last century. Finally, Robins and Guze recommend family studies of patients with the disorder to better validate with respect to genetic versus environmental factors. More recently, Andreasen (1995) has "made more conscious" the modern nosologists' shift in emphasis toward uncovering underlying etiologies and pathophysiologies. This shift has occurred, in part, as a consequence of emerging technologies such as restriction length polymorphism analyses, neuroimaging, and brain-mapping. The rapid development of more sophisticated functional and structural imaging techniques will undoubtedly yield information as to underlying pathophysiology. However, for this to succeed, the manifest or descriptive heterogeneity of the disorder will very likely need to be reduced further. One way to achieve this involves broadening the scope of what we consider to be the manifest symptoms of schizophrenia to other domains of psychopathology.

We agree with Carpenter and his associates (1985) who have argued that schizophrenia, in the absence of evidence of valid disease entities, should be conceptualized as expressing itself across several domains of psychopathology. This conceptualization has encouraged researchers (ourselves included) to adopt a "multi-trait" approach to studies of the phenomenology of schizophrenia. This strategy has been encouraged by the research literature which has many reports of trait-related deficits in schizophrenia coming from seemingly diverse domains of psychopathology (e.g., trait-related clinical, course of illness, social, psychophysiologic and neuropsychologic deficits). This approach has yielded important data that are relevant to the diagnostic endeavor. We will briefly discuss the recent literature representative of this approach, focusing in particular on the deficit syndrome and disorders of awareness in schizophrenia.

The deficit syndrome

Many patients with schizophrenia have enduring negative or "deficit symptoms" that have been conceptualized as being primary to the disorder (Carpenter et al., 1988). Recent reports show that deficit symptoms can be reliably diagnosed and that patients with a deficit syndrome differ from those without one on measures of premorbid adjustment, severity of affective symptoms, saccadic eye movement latency, and brain structure, glucose metabolism, and function (Carpenter et al. 1991, 1992, Amador et al. 1996). Assessment of the deficit syndrome involves measuring negative symptoms longitudinally rather than cross-sectionally. A strength to this approach is that trait-related negative symptoms are identified rather than transient symptoms that may be due to neuroleptics, depression, or other nonschizophrenia related causes. Recently, we found that the deficit syndrome is in fact stable when studied prospectively over 3 to 5 years. This finding confirmed the descriptive validity of this categorization in that the deficit symptoms originally assessed were proven to be enduring and unrelated to transient factors (Amador et al. 1996). This approach to characterizing patients with schizophrenia has yielded syndromal data which indicate that the deficit syndrome also has predictive, in addition to descriptive, validity.

The notion of a deficit syndrome in schizophrenia has obvious descriptive validity. Patients with schizophrenia, by definition, have marked deterioration in their ability to function in many arenas of life (e.g., work, education, relationships). We are particularly interested in this conceptualization as it is consistent with our hypotheses regarding enduring self-awareness deficits and attentional abnormalities in schizophrenia (discussed in more detail later in this chapter). However, our interest as nosologists is not only in descriptive validity, but also in predictive, or "criterion" validity. In other words, our second main concern should be to answer the question, what does the dimension we are assessing predict?

As it turns out, patients with the deficit syndrome appear to differ from nondeficit patients in a number of clinically meaningful ways. For example, deficit patients have been found to have significantly worse neuropsychologic dysfunction of the frontal and parietal lobes relative to nondeficit patients. With respect to the course of illness, deficit patients have been found to also have a poorer course and poorer premorbid functioning. In addition, we have completed three independent empirical studies that confirmed our clinical impression that deficit patients have significantly worse self-awareness deficits than do nondeficit patients (Amador et al. 1996, Amador et al., unpublished data). As will be discussed in the next section, self-awareness deficits also have powerful predictive, or criterion, validity in patients with schizophrenia.

Self-awareness deficits in schizophrenia

There has been a recent resurgence of interest in the study of poor insight, or what we have called more broadly, self-awareness deficits in schizophrenia. We have conceptualized self-awareness deficits as spanning a broad range of domains, e.g., awareness of particular signs and symptoms, of having an illness more generally, of medication efficacy, etc. We also believe that the more severe forms of self-awareness deficit stem from a more general neuropsychologic deficit state (Amador et al., 1991). Recent studies strongly support this conceptualization (Young et al., 1993, Kasapis et al. 1995, Lyskaer and Bell, in press). There is compelling evidence in the research literature indicating that level of insight, or awareness of illness, is an important dimension on which patients with schizophrenia can be meaningfully subtyped. For example, self-awareness deficits have been implicated in a poorer course of illness, poorer psychosocial functioning, and poor compliance with treatment, and has demonstrated validity as a factor on which patients can be subtyped based on cluster analytic analyses of the signs and symptoms of schizophrenia (WHO, 1973;

Carpenter et al., 1976; Van Putten et al. 1976; McGlashan and Carpenter, 1981; Wilson et al., 1986, McEvoy et al., 1989a, 1989b; Amador, et al., 1991).

We recently published data relevant to the question of how specific self-awareness deficits are to patients with schizophrenia when compared with individuals who have other psychotic disorders (Amador et al., 1994). These data were collected in collaboration with the Schizophrenia and Psychotic Disorders Work Group empaneled by the American Psychiatric Association to revise the diagnostic criteria for schizophrenia in the DSM. An abbreviated version of the Scale to assess Unawareness of Mental Disorder (SUMD) (Amador et al., 1993) was used in the assessment procedure for the DSM-IV field trial. In this study, 412 patients from geographically diverse regions of the USA were evaluated for a wide range of symptoms. A total of 221 patients with DSM III-R-defined schizophrenia were identified.

The main objective of our study of insight was to determine the prevalence of poor insight in psychotic disorders and to examine its specificity to schizophrenia. The assessment of insight was both highly reliable and demonstrated criterion validity (i.e., was associated with poorer overall functioning and the deficit syndrome). The results indicated that nearly 60% of the patients with schizophrenia had moderate to severe unawareness of having a mental disorder. This finding agrees with results from the International Pilot Study of Schizophrenia and the Classification of Chronic Hospitalized Schizophrenics study (WHO, 1973, Wilson et al., 1986). Both of these studies indicated that a majority of patients with schizophrenia believe they do not have a mental disorder. In addition, proportions of the DSM sample of schizophrenic patients who were unaware of particular signs and symptoms (e.g., delusions, thought disorder, blunt affect, anhedonia, asociality and other symptoms) ranged from 27.8% to 57.6%. The prevalence of unawareness of symptoms in patients with schizophrenia had not previously been reported in the literature.

The most noteworthy result, with respect to this discussion, was the finding that patients with schizophrenia were significantly less aware of having a mental disorder, the efficacy of medication, and of having various signs and symptoms (e.g., hallucinations, delusions, flat affect) than were schizoaffective and psychotic mood disorder patients. To our knowledge, these data are the first suggesting that particular self-awareness deficits may be unique to schizophrenia relative to other psychotic disorders. In short, the literature on insight described earlier and the field trial data support the commonly held belief that patients with schizophrenia display poor insight and that level of insight is an important dimension by which patients can be subtyped. The field trial data also provided the first evidence suggesting that pervasive and severe self-awareness deficits are more common in patients with schizophrenia than in other psychotic disorders.

We have proposed that the areas implicated in unawareness of illness in neurologic disorders (i.e., anosognosia and anosdiaphoria), the frontal and right parietal lobes, may also be involved in unawareness of illness in schizophrenia (Amador et al., 1991). The reports mentioned earlier provide empirical support for this hypothesis (Young et al., 1993, Lysaker and Bell, in press, Kasapis et al., 1995). Of particular interest to us was the recent finding that deficit syndrome patients performed more poorly than nondeficit patients on tests sensitive to frontal and parietal dysfunction (Buchannan et al., 1994). This pattern of neuropsychologic dysfunction fits with what has been observed (and predicted) in patients with increased unawareness. These data, and our clinical impressions, led us to examine the relations between self-awareness deficits and the deficit syndrome in schizophrenia. In brief, we found these two domains of psychopathology to be highly associated with one another.

The investigations described above share the strategy of assessing schizophrenia across multiple domains of psychopathology and the promise of providing useful data regarding the neuropsychology, epidemiology, course and neuropsychology of the disorder. By evaluating the interrelations among affective deficits (e.g., the deficit syndrome), self-awareness deficits (i.e., multiple dimensions of unawareness) and neuropsychologic dysfunction (i.e., frontal and right parietal lobes) in patients with schizophrenia, we can reduce the heterogeneity of the disorder in meaningful ways.

This strategy is representative of a multi-domain approach to evaluating the signs and symptoms of schizophrenia and linking them to underlying processes. In the examples described above, this approach enabled us to identify a subgroup of patients with enduring negative symptoms, deficits in self-awareness, and to link these symptoms to brain dysfunction and important course variables. Patients with the deficit/unawareness syndrome are more likely to have a poor course of illness, poor medication compliance, poor premorbid function, and increased dysfunction of the frontal and parietal lobes of the brain relative to patients without these symptoms. What remains to be seen is whether a discrete, criteria-derived syndrome, can be reliably diagnosed. We are currently testing such criteria for their reliability and validity. It is ironic perhaps that investigations of the kind just described hold the promise of reducing the heterogeneity of schizophrenia because they rely on a broader view of the disorder—one that is not tied to any preexisting diagnostic criteria.

Looking at multiple domains of psychopathology is one emerging strategy for increasing the validity of diagnosis, others have less to do with symptom content than with the process of making diagnoses. Two strategies stand out in our minds as particularly powerful. One involves the use of dimensional, rather than categorical, symptom data. The other involves using polydiagnostic approach. For example, in our studies of self-awareness we have avoided dichotomizing what we believe to be a continuous phenomenon (e.g., one can have a little awareness). This provides increased power to detect relations between self-awareness and putative etiologic variables such as neuropsychologic dysfunction. Meanwhile, a polydiagnostic approach (i.e., making diagnoses with multiple systems) gives the researcher the power to uncover phenotypes that are linked to underlying pathology. For example, if an abnormal gene(s) is found in a sample of schizophrenic patients, one could examine, provided they collected the data using a polydiagnostic approach, which phenomenologic type was associated with the pathologic genotype.

In this chapter we briefly described the evolution of the diagnosis of schizophrenia during the past 99 years. Significant improvement in the descriptive validity of the diagnosis and in reliability has been made. The original problem of how to link the diagnosis to underlying etiologic and pathophysiologic processes persists. However, with emerging technologies, a paradigmatic shift toward consideration of multiple domains of psychopathology, and the introduction of new methods for characterizing patients with the disorder, it is more likely than ever that more valid diagnostic categories can be developed.

REFERENCES

Amador XF, Andreasen NC, Flaum M, Strauss DH, Yale SA, Clark S, Gorman JM. Awareness of illness in schizophrenia, schizoaffective and mood disorders. *Arch Gen Psychiat* 51:826–836, 1994.

Amador XF, Carpenter WT, Kirkpatrik B, Marcinko L, Yale SA. The long-term stability of the deficit syndrome in schizophrenia: A follow-up study. Presentation at the Winter Workshop on Schizophrenia Research, Crans Montana, Switzerland, March 1996.

Amador XF, Strauss DH, Yale S, Gorman JM, Endicott J. The assessment of insight in psychosis. *Am J Psychiat* 150,6:873–879, 1993.

Amador XF, Strauss DH, Yale SA, Gorman JM. Awareness of illness in schizophrenia. *Schizophren Bull* 17:113–132, 1991.

American Psychiatric Association. DSM-III: Diagnostic and Statistical Manual of Mental Disorders, 3rd ed. Washington, DC: The Association, 1980.

American Psychiatric Association. DSM-III-R: Diagnostic and Statistical Manual of Mental Disorders, 3rd ed., revised. Washington, DC: The Association, 1987.

American Psychiatric Association. DSM-IV Diagnostic and Statistical Manual of Mental Disorders, 4th ed. Washington, DC: The Association, 1994.

Andreasen NC. Negative symptoms in schizophrenia: Definition and reliability. *Arch Gen Psychiat* 39:784–788, 1982.

Andreasen NC. The validation of psychiatric diagnosis: New models and approaches. *Am J Psychiat* 152:161–162, 1995.

Andreason NC, Olson S. Negative v. positive schizophrenia: Definition and validation. *Arch Gen Psychiat* 39:769–94,1982.

Bleuler E. Dementia Praecox or the Group of Schizophrenia. (1911) New York, NY: International Universities Press, 1950.

Buchanan RW, Strauss ME, Kirkpatrik B, Holstein C, Breier A, Carpenter WT Jr. Neuropsychological impairments in deficit vs nondeficit forms of schizoprenia. *Arch Gen Psychiat* 51:804–811, 1994.

Carpenter WT, Bartko JJ, Carpenter CL, Strauss JS. Another view of schizophrenic subtypes. *Arch Gen Psychiat* 33:508–516, 1976.

Carpenter WT Jr, Heinrichs DW, Alphs LD. Treatment of negative symptoms. *Schiz Bull* 11:440–452, 1985.

Carpenter WT, Heinrichs DW, Wagman AMI. Deficit and nondeficit forms of schizophrenia: The concept. *Am J Psychiat* 145:578–583, 1988.

Carpenter WT Jr, Strauss JS. The prediction of outcome in schizophrenia. IV: Eleven year follow-up of the Washington IPSS cohort. *J Nerv Ment Dis* 179:517–525, 1991.

Carpenter WT Jr. The negative symptom challenge. *Arch Gen Psychiat* 49:236–237, 1992.

Cooper JE, Kendell RE, Gurland BJ, et al. Psychiatric diagnosis in New York and London. London: Oxford University Press, 1972.

Endicott J, Nee J, Fleiss J, Cohen J, Williams JB, Simon R. Diagnostic criteria for schizophrenia: reliabilities and agreement between systems. *Arch Gen Psychiat* 39:884–889, 1982.

Feighner JP, Robins E, Guze SB, et al. Diagnostic criteria for use in psychiatric research. *Arch Gen Psychiat* 26:57–63, 1972.

Kasapis C, Amador XF, Yale SA, Strauss D, Gorman JM. Poor insight in schizophrenia: Neuropsychological and defensive aspects, in press *Schizophren Res*.

Kay SR, Opler LA, Lindenmeyer JP. The positive and negative syndrome scale (PANSS): Rationale and standardisation. *Brit J Psychiat* 1 (Suppl.):59–65, 1989.

Kendell RE, Cooper JE, Gourlay AG. Diagnostic criteria of American and British Psychiatrists. *Arch Gen Psychiat* 26:123–130, 1971.

Kraepelin E. Lehrbuch der Psychiatrie. 5th ed. Leipzig: Barth, 1896.

Langfeldt, G. Schizophrenia: Diagnosis and prognosis. *Behav Sci* 14:173–182, 1969.

Lysaker PH, Bell MD. Impaired insight in schizophrenia: Advances from psychosocial treatment research. In, Amador XF, David AS, eds, *Insight and Psychosis*, Oxford University Press (in press).

McEvoy JP, Appebaum PS, Apperson LJ, Geller JL, Freter S. Why must some schizophrenic patients be involuntarily committed? The role of insight. *Compr Psychiatry* 30:13–17, 1989a.

McEvoy JP, Apperson LJ, Applebaum PS, Ortlip P, Brecosky J, Hammill K, Geller JL, Roth L. Insight in schizophrenia. Its relationship to acute psychopathology. *J Nerv Ment Dis* 177:43–47, 1989b.

McGlashan TH, Carpenter WT Jr. Does attitude toward psychosis relate to outcome? *Am J Psychiat* 138:797–801, 1981.

Robins E, Guze SB. Establishment of diagnostic validity in psychiatric illness: Its application to schizophrenia. *Am J Psychiat* 126:983–987, 1970.

Schneider K. *Clinical Psychopathology*. New York, NY: Grune & Stratton, 1959.

Spitzer RL, Endicott J, Robins E. Research Diagnostic Criteria (RDC) for a selected group of functional disorders, 3rd ed. New York State Psychiatric Institute, 1978.

Van Putten T, Crumpton E, and Yale C. Drug refusal in schizophrenia and the wish to be crazy. *Arch Gen Psychiat* 33:1443–1446, 1976.

Wilson WH, Ban TA, Guy W. Flexible system criteria in chronic schizophrenia. *Compr Psychiat* 27:259–265, 1986.

Wing JK, Cooper JE, Sartorius N. *The Measurement and Classification of Psychiatric Symptoms*. New York: Cambridge University Press, 1974.

World Health Organization. The International Pilot Study of Schizophrenia. Geneva, World Health Organization, 1973.

World Health Organization. Mental disorders: Glossary and guide to their classification in accordance with the ninth revision of the international classification of diseases. Geneva: World Health Organization, 1978.

World Health Organization. The lCD-10 Classification of Mental and Behavioural Disorders. Geneva, Switzerland: The World Health Organization, 1992.

Young DA, Davila R, and Scher H. Unawareness of illness and neuropsychological performance in chronic schizophrenia. *Schiz Res* 10:117–124, 1993.

SCHIZOPHRENIA AND THE BRAIN: PATHOPHYSIOLOGY

Electrophysiologic Studies of Brain Activity in Schizophrenia*

GERARD E. BRUDER, Ph.D., CRAIG E. TENKE, Ph.D.,
ESTHER RABINOWICZ, Ph.D., JAMES P. TOWEY, Ph.D.,
DOLORES MALASPINA, M.D., XAVIER F. AMADOR, Ph.D.,
CHARLES A. KAUFMANN, M.D., and JACK M. GORMAN, M.D.

INTRODUCTION

Cognitive deficits are crucial features of schizophrenia in clinical or phenomenologic systems (see the previous chapter and DSM IV criteria), as well as in laboratory or experimental investigations. Despite the importance of cognitive deficits in schizophrenia, consensus regarding explanatory mechanisms or the optimal methods for studying these deficiencies is lacking. One aim of recent laboratory-based research has been elucidating the elementary processes that underlie cognitive deficits in schizophrenia and identifying their neurobiologic substrate (e.g., Goldman-Rakic 1994, Knight 1993, Nuechterlein and Dawson 1984). In this regard, it is crucial to isolate the earliest-occurring deficit process because all subsequent processing stages may be adversely affected. For instance, behavioral researchers have investigated the extent to which information processing dysfunctions in schizophrenia are related to two processes: a Stage 1 sensory/perceptual register and a Stage 2 short-term memory representation (Phillips 1974; Potter 1976).

Recent studies have suggested that schizophrenic patients are *not* deficient in early sensory processing per se, but demonstrate failures in allocation of attention (Knight 1993; Rabinowicz et al. 1994) and in maintaining representations of stimuli in working memory (Goldman-Rakic 1990; Park and Holzman 1992). However, more direct measures of the temporal course of brain activation are needed to strengthen the inference of the critical role of these attentional and memory processing dysfunctions in schizophrenia. This chapter deals with precisely this sort of methodology—electrophysiologic measures of brain activity. Measures of quantitative electroencephalogram (EEG) and event-related brain potentials (ERPs) provide an important complement to behavioral measures of cognitive processing because of their sensitivity in the temporal domain and the data they yield on the physiologic correlates of cognitive deficits in schizophrenia.

---

*This chapter is based in part on an address presented at the American Psychiatric Electrophysiology Association meeting in Miami, Florida, May, 1995.

17

We review in this chapter recent studies that have used quantitative EEG measures of "spontaneous" brain activity, but will give greatest attention to studies in which the P3 brain potential was measured during cognitive tasks. After reviewing past and current EEG and ERP findings for schizophrenia, we will discuss some promising future research directions, including recent developments for enhancing spatial resolution of brain potentials and for examining the regional distribution of brain electrical activity during cognitive tasks.

In this age of brain imaging (see chapter by Malaspina et al.), one could ask the question, why study brain potentials in schizophrenia? From a practical standpoint, EEG and ERP techniques have the advantage of being risk-free, noninvasive, and inexpensive. From a research perspective, EEG and ERP measures provide a relatively continuous record of ongoing brain activity with a temporal resolution in the millisecond range, which far exceeds that provided by current brain imaging techniques, such as positron emission tomography (PET) or magnetic resonance imaging (MRI) scans. This allows us to study the physiologic correlates of information processing as it unfolds over time.

EEG STUDIES OF SCHIZOPHRENIA

The EEG provides a record of brain potentials recorded from scalp electrodes and is typically measured while the person is resting with eyes closed or open. The resulting brain waves can be quantified by computing frequency spectra using a Fast Fourier Transform (FFT) analysis. This yields measures of the extent to which the EEG waves contain frequencies in standard bands—delta (1–3 Hz), theta (3–8 Hz), alpha (8–13 Hz) and beta (13–30 Hz).

Shagass (1991) reviewed over 50 years of EEG research in schizophrenia and we will not attempt to repeat this accomplishment, but will focus on some of the more well replicated or promising findings in this area. One of the most consistent findings has been that schizophrenic patients display an excess of low frequency EEG activity in delta or theta bands and less alpha activity when compared with controls (Flor-Henry and Koles 1984; Itil et al. 1972; John et al. 1994; Sponheim et al. 1994). Sponheim et al. showed that the pattern of augmented low frequency and reduced alpha was equally present in first-episode and chronic patients with different durations of illness, suggesting that long-term treatment has little effect on this abnormality. Moreover, it has been found in remitted schizophrenic patients (Iacono 1982) and was found to be stable during a 9-month period (Clementz et al. 1994), which supports the conclusion that the augmentation of low frequency and reduced alpha in schizophrenia represents a trait-related characteristic. While this is consistent with a report that children of schizophrenic patients have a similar abnormality of EEG frequency distribution (Itil 1977), Clementz et al. (1994) found no significant EEG band differences among first-degree biologic relatives of schizophrenic, bipolar, or nonpsychiatric probands. Also, the pattern of increased low frequency and reduced alpha was not specific to schizophrenia, but was also found for patients having bipolar psychoses. This abnormal EEG frequency pattern has been interpreted as reflecting subcortical abnormalities, possibly involving thalamic or hippocampal dysfunction (Clementz et al. 1994; Shagass 1991; Sponheim et al. 1994).

Other investigators have examined the topography of EEG abnormalities in schizophrenia. Most notable was the finding of greater low-frequency activity in frontal areas and greater high-frequency activity in posterior areas in schizophrenia, which is consistent with other evidence of hypofrontality in schizophrenia (Morstyn et al. 1983a; Morihisa and McAnulty 1985). Still others have found evidence that excessive low frequency activity (delta and theta bands) in schizophrenia is localized to left frontal and temporal regions (Abrams and Taylor 1980; Guenther and Breitling 1984; Morihisa et al. 1983). While EEG findings such as this have been cited in support of hypotheses of left hemisphere dysfunction in schizophrenia (Flor-Henry 1976), others have found evidence of bilateral EEG abnormalities in schizophrenia (Clementz et al. 1994). Reports of lateralized abnormalities of EEG alpha power have also been inconsistent, with some findings of higher left-sided alpha in schizophrenic patients when compared with controls and other findings of no difference between these groups or differences in the opposite direction (d'Elia et al. 1977; Merrin et al. 1986; Iacono 1982; Shagass et al. 1983). One possibility is that the differences in findings across studies might be due to differences in the clinical characteristics of the schizophrenic patients in these studies. Thus, it has been suggested that "active and withdrawn syndromes of schizophrenia" display opposite patterns of lateral asymmetries (Gruzelier et al. 1993).

In addition to the measurement of EEG spectral power in different frequency bands, EEG coherence has been examined, i.e., a measure of the correlation of EEG signals recorded over different regions of the brain. This index of "functional or anatomical coupling" can provide information on regions of the brain that work together under resting or activation conditions. The most consistent finding using this measure has been the *higher* interhemispheric coherence in schizophrenic patients when compared with normal controls or patients with affective disorders, which has been found for both medicated and unmedicated patients (Ford et al. 1986; Merrin et al. 1989; Nagase et al. 1992). The greater EEG coherence in schizophrenic patients was found in different frequency bands, and the interpretation of this finding is problematic. The greater coherence in schizophrenic patients has been interpreted as being due to more diffuse or undifferentiated cortical organization in schizophrenia (Merrin et al. 1989), less lateralized cerebral organization in schizophrenia (Nagase et al. 1992), or to a difference in cortical arousal (Ford et al. 1986).

One of the most promising uses of EEG coherence measures is in elucidating cortical "networks" activated during cognitive tasks that predominantly involve left or right brain function. For instance, Morrison-Stewart et al. (1991) found that normal subjects had increased EEG alpha coherence between the left frontal area and other brain regions during a continuous calculation task, which may reflect verbal/analytic superiority of the left hemisphere. Schizophrenic patients, unlike normal subjects, did not show this focal left frontal increase in coherence during the continuous calculation task, but they did show coherence increases in right posterior regions during a visuospatial task. They concluded that schizophrenic patients were unable to activate left anterior regions to the same extent as normal subjects. Further use of EEG coherence measures to study abnormalities of neural networks in schizophrenia would seem to be in order.

Studies have also been focused on the possible value of EEG measures for differential diagnosis of psychiatric disorders. The discriminant validity of quantitative EEG measures for separating schizophrenic patients and controls was originally demonstrated by Shagass et al. (1984) and later by John et al. (1994). However, it is less clear that quantitative EEG would be of value in differentiating among diagnostic entities in psychiatry. For instance, Shagass et al. found that schizophrenic patients could be discriminated from patients with personality disorders, but not from manic patients. Also, John et al. developed quantitative EEG algorithms for clustering schizophrenic patients into five subtypes, but no significant clinical differences were found among the five clusters.

A more clinically promising approach is suggested by several studies of the value of quantitative EEG indices as predictors of therapeutic response to neuroleptics. Thus, more fast EEG activity has been reported among treatment-responsive patients, whereas a predominance of alpha activity was associated with poor response to neuroleptics (Czobor and Volavka 1991; Galderisi et al. 1994; Itil et al. 1981; Small et al. 1989). Most recently, Galderisi et al. found less slow activity (5.7–9.5 Hz) and more high alpha activity (9.7–12.5 Hz) in responders than nonresponders to 4 weeks of haloperidol treatment. There was, however, considerable overlap in the distribution of baseline EEG data for responders and nonresponders, suggesting that this may be inadequate as a clinical predictor. A better predictor of treatment outcome was provided by the change in quantitative EEG following a single dose of neuroleptic. Treatment responders showed an increase in slow alpha activity (7.7–9.5 Hz), whereas nonresponders showed a decrease. The increase in alpha at the left central site (C3) was the best predictor of treatment outcome. Although this finding needs replication, it suggests the value of further study of the clinical utility of the "test dose" procedure as a predictor of treatment outcome in schizophrenia.

In summary, differences have been found consistently between schizophrenic patients and controls in both EEG frequency spectra and interhemispheric coherence. The possible value of quantitative EEG measures for differential diagnosis or for predicting therapeutic response to antipsychotic medication also shows some promise, and suggests the need for additional studies of the potential clinical utility of EEG measures in psychiatry.

There are several limitations in early EEG research in schizophrenia, which were discussed by Shagass (1991), that continue to be a problem. One of the main limitations is reliance on measurement of EEG during a resting state. This procedure allows no control of the patient's cognitive, emotional or arousal state during EEG measurement. While resting EEG provides adequate baseline measures, it would be best to compare these to EEG measures recorded during cognitive tasks that demand active attention and behavioral responses. Tasks that involve specific cognitive processes, e.g., working memory, language processing, or affective discrimination, and are thought to activate localized brain regions might be of particular value in EEG studies of schizophrenia.

ERP STUDIES IN SCHIZOPHRENIA

One of the major advantages of ERPs is that they are time-locked to the onset of stimuli in cognitive tasks. By averaging the EEG over many trials, spontaneous background activity that is not time-locked to stimulus onset will tend to cancel out and ERP components linked to the ongoing sensory or cognitive processing of the stimulus will be enhanced. Figure 1 illustrates average ERP waveforms for normal adults (n = 20) recorded at right frontal (F4), central (C4), parietal (P4) and occipital (O2) sites to tones in a Complex Tone Test (see below). The two most prominent ERP components evident in Figure 1 are: (1) a negative component peaking at about 100 msec after stimulus onset, i.e., the N1 component, which is known to be associated with early sensory and attentional processing; and (2) a positive component peaking at about 550 msec, i.e., the classical P3 component, which is associated with later cognitive processes such as stimulus evaluation. The application of these ERPs in the study of schizophrenia can, therefore, provide evidence concerning the stage of information processing that may be altered in this disorder. Also, the measurement of ERPs at corresponding electrode sites over the right and left hemispheres (Figure 1) can

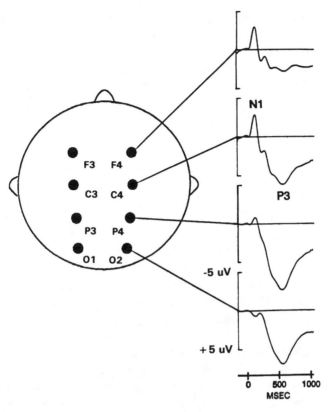

FIG. 1. Average ERP waveforms for 20 normal adults recorded over right hemisphere sites (F4, C4, P4, O2) to binaural complex tones.

help evaluate theories concerning possible left hemisphere dysfunction in schizophrenia (Flor-Henry 1976, Crow 1990, McCarley et al. 1991).

Studies have consistently demonstrated that ERPs to tones, including both N1 and P3, are reduced in schizophrenic patients when compared to normal controls (for reviews see Shagass et al. 1977, Roth et al. 1986, Pfefferbaum et al. 1989, McCarley et al. 1991). We focus below on a review of recent P3 findings for schizophrenia, which suggest that reduced P3 amplitude and abnormal hemispheric asymmetry of P3 in schizophrenia are related to asymmetric temporal lobe pathology.

P3 FINDINGS IN SCHIZOPHRENIA

This year marks the 30th anniversary of the discovery of the P3 brain potential by the late Samuel Sutton and his colleagues (Sutton et al. 1965). The importance of this component is that it gives researchers a means of measuring physiologic activity of the brain that is correlated with ongoing cognitive processing. This makes it possible, for the first time, to simultaneously study alterations of cognitive function in schizophrenia and their relation to underlying electrophysiologic events.

21

P3 has clearly been the most thoroughly studied brain ERP in schizophrenia. An excellent review of the early studies of P3 in schizophrenia is given in Roth et al. (1986). We review more recent studies, with emphasis on what is known about the importance of task demands (e.g., silent counting vs reaction time), stimulus conditions (e.g., auditory vs visual modality), medication, and diagnostic features. Particular attention is also given to recent studies of the topographic asymmetry of P3 in schizophrenia and its possible relation to pathophysiology of temporal lobe sites.

Reduction of P3 amplitude in schizophrenia is one of the most robust and well replicated findings in psychiatry. In most studies, P3 has been recorded during an "oddball" task. The oddball task consists of presenting a sequence of two different tones, i.e., a frequent standard tone of a given pitch (e.g., 1000 Hz) and an infrequent target tone of a different pitch (e.g., 1500 Hz). The subject's task is either to count silently the target tones or to press a button as quickly as possible when they hear the target tone. In the studies reviewed by Roth et al. (1986), P3 amplitude to target stimuli was smaller in schizophrenic patients when compared with normal controls in 19 of 23 comparisons.

More recent studies have found that smaller P3 amplitude in schizophrenic patients was evident not only to target tones in oddball tasks, i.e., for the classical P3b component, but also to task-irrelevant "novel" sounds, i.e., for the P3a component (Grillon et al. 1990, Merrin and Floyd 1994). For instance, Grillon et al. (1990) measured ERPs to infrequent target tones in oddball tasks with and without "distractor" stimuli consisting of novel sounds (buzzes, filtered noises, etc.). Schizophrenic patients (n = 15) showed an overall reduction of amplitude of P3b to target tones and P3a to novel sounds when compared to normal controls (n = 15). Moreover, distractor stimuli resulted in a shift of attention away from the central oddball task, as indicated by a reduction in P3b amplitude to tones, and this distractor effect was most evident among schizophrenic patients. Grillon et al. concluded that P3 findings for schizophrenia were suggestive of a misallocation of attentional resources to distractor as opposed to task-relevant stimuli. Merrin and Floyd (1994) reported that medication-free schizophrenic patients (n = 12) failed to show the more anterior scalp distribution of P3a for novel stimuli, consistent with less prefrontal input. However, this conflicts with the findings of Grillon et al. who found an anterior augmentation of P3a in schizo-phrenic and normal subjects, and Ohta et al. (1995) who found schizophrenic patients (n = 14) to show an anterior scalp distribution for both P3a and P3b in a novelty paradigm.

The reduction of P3 amplitude to tones in oddball tasks has been found for both medicated and unmedicated schizophrenic patients and is not likely to be due to medication effects (Pfefferbaum et al. 1989, Faux et al. 1993, Ford et al. 1994). P3 amplitude to tones in schizophrenic patients is not normalized by antipsychotic treatment or clinical improvement, and has, therefore, been thought to be a stable trait characteristic (Blackwood et al. 1987, Duncan et al. 1987, Ford et al. 1994). Duncan et al. (1987) did, however, find P3 increases to visual stimuli in clinically improved patients, and Ford et al. (1995) found small increases in both auditory and visual P3 amplitude during clinical improvement, suggesting that clinical state does have some influence on P3 in schizophrenia.

There is evidence that P3 reduction in schizophrenia is less evident for visual than auditory tasks (Egan et al. 1994; Ford et al. 1994). For instance, Egan et al. found markedly smaller P3 amplitude in unmedicated schizophrenic patients (n = 16) when compared with normal controls (n = 16) in a tone discrimination task, but only a small nonsignificant P3 reduction in a visual letter discrimination task. The importance of this "modality effect" is what it might tell us about the source of the P3 reduction in schizophrenia. It could point to involvement of auditory processing centers in the posterior temporal lobe, which are among the regions that have been implicated in the generation of P3 to tones (Knight et al. 1989, Lovrich et al. 1988).

Additional support for the involvement of temporal lobe sites has come from studies that found the P3 reduction in schizophrenia to be larger at electrode sites over left (T3) than right (T4) temporal lobe (Morstyn et al. 1983b, McCarley et al. 1991). However, this hemispheric asymmetry of P3 in schizophrenic patients was not found in some studies (Pfefferbaum et al. 1989; Ford et al. 1994). There are a number of methodologic differences between the studies by the McCarley et al. and Pfefferbaum et al. groups, which could have contributed to this difference in findings. One of the likely candidates is the different oddball tasks used in these studies. The McCarley et al. group have primarily used silent counting oddball tasks in which the patient keeps a running count of the number of oddball tones, but no overt response is required to each tone. In contrast, the Pfefferbaum et al. group used a reaction time task in which the patient presses a response key with the preferred hand to each oddball tone.

Table 1 summarizes the findings for more recent studies that recorded ERPs of schizophrenic patients during a silent counting task. All five studies that used lateral electrode placements confirmed the essential findings of Morstyn et al. (1983b). Two studies by this same group of researchers (Faux et al. 1988, 1990) replicated their finding of greater reduction of P3 amplitude in schizophrenic patients at left than right temporal sites. Although the Muir et al. (1991) study used only a midline electrode (Cz), this study is of importance

TABLE 1. ERP STUDIES USING ODDBALL TASKS: SILENT COUNTING

Study	Subjects	Stimuli	Findings
Faux et al. (1988)	11 Chronic Sch 9 Nor	960 Hz (P = .85) 1070 Hz (P = .15)	P3 reductions in Sch greatest at left temporal sites (T3, T5)
Faux et al. (1990)	20 Chronic Sch 20 Nor	1000 Hz (P = .85) 1500 Hz (P = .15)	Confirmed asymmetric P3 reductions in Sch using linked-ears and nose references
Muir et al. (1991)	96 Sch, 88 BP, 46 MDD, 213 Nor	1000 Hz (P = .90) 1500 Hz (P = .10)	Sch and BP patients had smaller P3 than MDD or Nor at Cz
Strik et al. (1994)	41 Sch, 31 Nor (in remission)	100 Hz (P = .80) 2000 Hz (P = .20)	Right lateralized P3 peak in Sch due to lower left amplitudes
Souza et al. (1995)	26 Sch, 19 BP, 27 Nor	1000 Hz (P = .90) 1500 Hz (P = .10)	Sch had reduced P3 at left temporal (T3) site but BP did not
Salisbury et al. (1995)	1st Episode 12 Sch-like 20 Manic-like	1000 Hz (P = .85) 1500 Hz (P = .15)	Smaller P3 at left than right temporal site in Sch but not in manic

Sch, schizophrenic; BP, bipolar disorder; MDD, major depressive disorder; Nor, normal.

because it recorded ERPs of large samples of patients having a schizophrenic or affective disorder. Both schizophrenic patients and patients having bipolar disorders had smaller P3 amplitude than normal controls or depressed patients. This is a clear demonstration that P3 reductions are not specific to schizophrenia, but occur in affective disorders as well.

A subsequent study by this group (Souza et al. 1995) used a larger array of electrodes in smaller samples. Schizophrenic patients had significantly smaller P3 amplitude than controls at the left temporal (T3) but not right temporal site (T4), whereas patients having bipolar disorders did not differ significantly from either of these groups. This raises the possibility that the asymmetric P3 reduction may be specific to schizophrenia, which is also supported by the recent findings of Salisbury et al. (1995). They recorded ERPs of first episode patients having a schizophrenia-like psychosis or a mania-like psychosis. The schizophrenia-like group had smaller P3 amplitude over the left than right temporal sites, whereas the mania-like group tended to have the opposite direction of P3 asymmetry. These findings are also noteworthy because they indicate that abnormal P3 asymmetry is present in first-episode patients and is not a byproduct of chronicity.

Lastly, Strik et al. (1994) tested schizophrenic patients after remission of acute psychosis and found both an overall reduction in P3 amplitude and an asymmetric P3 with a right lateralized peak. This confirms other evidence that P3 abnormalities in schizophrenia are not normalized after clinical remission, and are, therefore, likely to reflect a state-independent abnormality. In summary, all six studies, including Morstyn et al. (1983b), that measured ERPs at lateral electrodes during a silent counting oddball task found greater P3 reduction over left than right temporal lobe sites in schizophrenia.

In contrast, only two of five studies in which ERPs were measured in a reaction time task have found a P3 asymmetry in schizophrenia (Table 2). The findings of three studies (Pfefferbaum et al. 1989, Ford et al. 1994, Egan et al. 1994), which tested unmedicated schizophrenic patients in both auditory and visual reaction time tasks, were highly similar. Schizophrenic patients had significantly smaller P3 amplitude than normal controls for auditory but *not* visual stimuli, and they showed no P3 asymmetry. It is not likely that the lack of a P3 asymmetry in these studies was due merely to the testing of *unmedicated* schizophrenic patients because Faux et al. (1993) showed that their prior findings of P3 asymmetry in medicated patients was also present in a sample of unmedicated patients. It is also not likely that a difference in task difficulty could account for the difference in P3 asymmetry findings for the silent counting and reaction time paradigms. Salisbury et al. (1994) varied stimulus discriminability in an auditory oddball task and found that P3 reduction and asymmetry in schizophrenia were not alleviated under conditions of increased stimulus discriminability.

The difference in findings for the silent counting and reaction time paradigms suggests that some aspect of the reaction time task might interfere with the demonstration of P3 asymmetry in schizophrenia. One possibility would be movement-related potentials, which are negative in polarity and larger over the hemisphere contralateral to the hand movement. In reaction time tasks, in particular when the right hand was the predominant mode of response (e.g., Pfefferbaum et al. 1989, Ford et al. 1994), movement-related potentials might have interfered with the demonstration of a P3 asymmetry difference between schizophrenic patients and normal controls. There is evidence that movement-related potentials differ in schizophrenic patients and normal controls. Singh et al. (1992) measured movement-related potentials in chronic schizophrenic patients (n = 9) and matched normal controls (n = 9) during a self-paced button press with the right or left hand. Schizophrenic patients had

TABLE 2. ERP STUDIES USING REACTION TIME TASKS

Study	Subjects	Stimuli	Findings
Pfefferbaum et al. (1989)	18 Unmed Sch 13 Med Sch 37 Nor	*Auditory:* 500/ 1000 Hz *Visual:* ± signs	Reduced P3 in Sch for auditory but not visual task; No P3 asymmetry
Ford et al. (1994)	30 Unmed Sch 29 Nor	Same as above	Replicated above findings; No change in P3 following treatment
Faux et al. (1993)	14 Unmed Sch 14 Nor	1000 Hz (P = .85) 1500 Hz (P = .15)	P3 asymmetry with L < R at temporal sites in unmed Sch
Salisbury et al. (1994)	8 Chronic Sch 8 Nor	1000 Hz/1500 Hz (soft/Loud) 1400 Hz/1500 Hz (soft/Loud)	P3 reduction and asymmetry (L < R) in all but least discriminable condition
Egan et al. (1994)	16 Unmed Sch 16 Nor	*Auditory:* 600/ 1500 Hz *Visual:* S/L letters	Reduced P3 in Sch for auditory but not visual task; No P3 asymmetry

Unmed, unmedicated; Sch, schizophrenic; Med, medicated; Nor, normal.

markedly smaller movement-related potentials similar to those seen in patients with dorsolateral prefrontal lesions.

The above findings underscore the importance of controlling for possible confounding effects of movement-related potentials in ERP studies of schizophrenia. Counterbalancing the hand used during reaction time tasks is one approach for dealing with this problem (e.g., Faux et al. 1993, Egan et al. 1994), but findings obtained when subjects use their preferred hand may differ from those when they use their nonpreferred hand. The silent counting oddball task has the advantage of avoiding the problem of motor potentials, but it adds additional memory demands because the patient must keep a running total of the number of oddballs. It is possible that this added memory load may enhance the demonstration of P3 asymmetry in schizophrenia, which in itself might account for the difference in findings for the silent counting and reaction time oddball tasks.

ERP TO COMPLEX TONES IN SCHIZOPHRENIA AND MANIA

We have begun to measure ERPs of schizophrenic patients during a dichotic listening task in which no response is made until well after the occurrence of P3, thus minimizing the influence of motor potentials. ERPs were recorded during the Complex Tone Test, which uses a S1-S2-R matching paradigm (Sidtis 1981, Tenke et al. 1993). After onset of a central fixation light, a different complex tone was simultaneously presented to the two ears. This was followed 2 seconds later by a binaural probe tone, which was the same as one member of the dichotic pair or was different from both. The patient's task was to press a button if the probe matched either of the dichotic tones. The response period was signaled by the offset of the fixation light, 1.5 seconds after the probe tone. ERPs to dichotic pairs and probe tones were recorded at frontal (F3,F4), central (C3,C4), parietal (P3,P4) and occipital sites (O1,O2) sites over the left and right hemisphere (Figure 1), with a nose tip reference (see Tenke et al. 1993 for details).

ERPs were measured in 8 psychotic patients and 20 normal controls. The patients (6 males and 2 females; mean age = 27.8 yr, SD = 7.2) were from the Schizophrenia Developing Clinical Research Center at Psychiatric Institute and they met the following DSM III R criteria: 5 schizophrenic, 1 schizoaffective, 1 paranoid delusional, and 1 schizo-type/bipolar disorder. Five patients were receiving haloperidol and 3 patients were unmedicated when tested. The 20 controls (8 male and 12 females; mean age = 31.8 yr, SD = 9.1) were from our recent study (Tenke et al. 1993). All but one subject in each group were right-handed and all were screened for hearing impairments.

Figure 2 shows the average ERP waveforms to probe tones for the psychotic patients

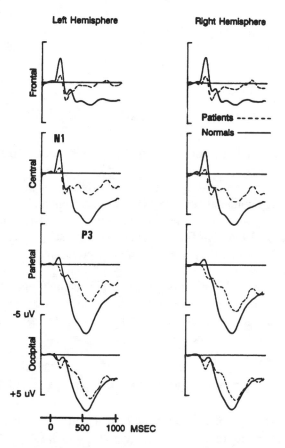

FIG. 2. Average ERP waveforms for 8 psychotic patients and 20 normal adults recorded over left and right hemisphere sites to binaural complex tones.

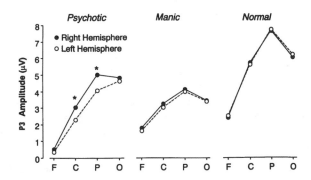

FIG. 3. Mean P3 amplitude for psychotic patients (n = 8), manic patients (n = 8), and normal controls (n = 20) at frontal (F), central (C), parietal (P), and occipital (O) sites over each hemisphere; psychotic patients showed a significant hemispheric asymmetry at central and parietal sites (p < 0.05).

and controls. Patients had significantly smaller N1 amplitude than normal controls (F = 12.10, p < 0.01), bilaterally at frontal and central sites. The marked difference in N1 amplitude between patients and controls was equally present over each hemisphere. Patients also had smaller P3 amplitude than controls (F = 5.17, p < 0.05). Most importantly, the difference in P3 amplitude between patients and controls was larger over the left than right hemisphere (Group by Hemisphere interaction: F = 4.40, p < 0.05). As can be seen in Figure 3, the psychotic patients had significantly less P3 amplitude over the left than right central site (t = 2.96, p < 0.05) and parietal site (t = 3.14, p < 0.05), whereas normal controls did not. Thus, in a dichotic pitch discrimination task, we found a P3 asymmetry similar to that observed for schizophrenic patients in the silent counting oddball task (Morstyn et al. 1983b; McCarley et al. 1991).

Figure 3 also shows the average P3 amplitudes for 8 right-handed inpatients having a bipolar disorder (6 male, 2 female; mean age = 36 yr, SD = 9.3), who were in a manic episode at the time of testing. Their scores on the Modified Manic State Rating Scale (Blackburn et al. 1977) ranged from 22 to 67 (mean = 45, SD = 17), with five patients having positive ratings on psychotic symptoms (delusions or hallucinations). The manic patients resembled the schizophrenic patients in showing overall reduction in P3 amplitude when compared to normal controls, but they showed *no* evidence of a hemispheric asymmetry of P3. In a separate study (Bruder et al. 1995a), ERPs of right-handed depressed outpatients were measured during this same Complex Tone Test. The depressed patients (n = 44) had significantly smaller P3 amplitude than normal controls (n = 19), but they showed no P3 asymmetry.

In summary, reduction of P3 amplitude to tones is found in both schizophrenic and affective disorders, whereas abnormal P3 asymmetry, with smaller P3 over left than right hemisphere, appears to be primarily found in schizophrenia-spectrum disorders.

RELATION OF P3 ABNORMALITIES TO TEMPORAL LOBE STRUCTURES

The above findings are consistent with the hypothesis that abnormalities of P3 in schizophrenia are related to pathophysiology of lateral or medial temporal lobe sites involved in the generation or modulation of auditory ERPs (McCarley et al. 1991; Salisbury et al. 1994). Further support for this hypothesis has come from studies finding relationships between P3 reduction or P3 asymmetry and temporal lobe volumes in MRI scans. McCarley et al. (1993) measured P3 amplitudes of chronic schizophrenic patients (n = 15) in an auditory oddball task and also measured in their MRIs volumes of specific temporal lobe gray matter regions of interest. Reduced amplitudes of P3 at left temporal (T3) and central (C3) sites were significantly correlated with volume reductions in the left posterior superior temporal gyrus, but not with left hippocampal volume or volume of regions of interest in the right temporal lobe. Similarly, Egan et al. (1994) found a significant relationship between reduced P3 amplitude to tones at the left central site (C3) and smaller left temporal lobe volume in schizophrenic patients. Egan et al. also found that P3 amplitude to *visual* stimuli was significantly correlated only with volume of more medial sites, in particular with right hippocampal volume, which is of interest given the modality differences observed in P3 findings for schizophrenia.

In conclusion, there is evidence linking P3 reductions and hemispheric asymmetries in schizophrenia to some of the same temporal lobe structures that appear to be involved in the generation or modulation of auditory ERPs (Lovrich et al. 1988, Knight et al. 1989, McCarthy et al. 1989), and that have also been implicated in the pathophysiology of schizophrenia (Crow 1990, McCarley et al. 1991). It is, however, recognized that structural deficits involving lateral or medial temporal lobe sites, particularly on the left side, may not be present in all schizophrenic patients but may be associated with one form of this disorder with specific clinical features, such as positive symptoms. Thus, McCarley et al. (1991) hypothesized that one form of schizophrenia involves temporal lobe pathology, which is reflected electrophysiologically in asymmetric P3 at temporal sites, and clinically in positive symptoms. This formulation is supported by correlations between left hemisphere deficits in schizophrenia and positive symptoms of thought disorder (Shenton et al. 1992) or auditory hallucinations (Barta et al. 1990, Bruder et al. 1995b).

FUTURE RESEARCH DIRECTIONS

One of the limitations of ERP studies of schizophrenia has been overreliance on the oddball tone discrimination task (Roth et al. 1986). Although we and other groups have begun to record ERPs of schizophrenic patients during more cognitively demanding tasks, there remains a lack of studies using *verbal* stimuli. This is surprising given the possible value of verbal tasks in evaluating current hypotheses of left hemisphere dysfunction in schizophrenia. One could, for instance, record ERPs of schizophrenic patients during verbal oddball or dichotic listening tasks that are likely to involve areas of the left superior temporal gyrus, which are known to be related to language dominance (Geshwind and Levitsky 1968, Foundas et al. 1994).

To evaluate function of more medial regions in the temporal lobe, particularly the hippocampus, it would also be of value to record ERPs of schizophrenic patients during word recognition tasks. Impairments of recognition memory for words have been found in patients with left-sided damage to medial temporal lobe (Milner 1972, Squire 1983), and ERP "repetition effects" for word recognition were attenuated in patients with left temporal lobectomy (Smith and Halgren 1989). If left temporal deficits in schizophrenia involve medial structures, similar abnormalities would be expected to occur in schizophrenic patients.

Lastly, the future of both EEG and ERP research clearly lies in the use of larger arrays of recording electrodes that would permit more fine-grained topographic analyses. The inadequate spatial sampling of brain electrical activity in prior studies has limited the application of "high resolution" EEG and ERP techniques in schizophrenia research. Several recent developments have dramatically improved the spatial information that can be provided by EEG recordings: 1) development of techniques for applying dense arrays of electrodes on up to 128 sites on scalp (Tucker et al. 1994); 2) development of techniques for topographic mapping of brain electrical fields in 2D and 3D projections on the head surface (Gevins et al. 1995, Nunez et al. 1991, Tucker et al. 1994); 3) development of functional mapping and regional covariance analysis techniques that can reveal relationships or interactions among spatially distributed regions of information processing networks (Alexander and Moeller 1995, Moeller et al. 1993). These techniques offer new approaches for providing spatiotemporal mapping of brain electrical activity. High-resolution EEG or ERP techniques can also be used jointly with other imaging modalities (PET or MRI scans) to increase chronometric precision and provide converging measures of regional brain activity. The application of these new high-resolution techniques should greatly enhance our understanding of brain abnormalities associated with cognitive dysfunctions in schizophrenia.

REFERENCES

Abrams R, Taylor MA. Psychopathology and the electroencephalogram. *Biol Psychiatry* 15:871–878, 1980.

Alexander GE, Moeller JR. Application of Scaled Subprofile Model analysis to functional imaging of neurological disorders: A principal component approach to modeling regional patterns of brain function in disease. *Human Brain Mapping* 2:79–94, 1995.

Barta PE, Pearlson GD, Tune LE, Powers RE, Richards SS. Superior temporal gyrus volume in schizophrenia. *Schizophr Res* 3:22, 1990.

Blackburn IM, Loudin JB, Ashworth C. A new scale for measuring mania. *Psychol Med* 7:453–458, 1977.

Blackwood DHR, Walley LJ, Christie JE, Blackburn IM, St. Clair DM, McInnes A. Changes in auditory P3 event-related potential in schizophrenia and depression. *Br J Psychiat* 150:154–160, 1987.

Bruder G, Rabinowicz E, Towey J, Brown A, Kaufmann CA, Amador X, Malaspina D, Gorman J. Smaller right ear (left hemisphere) advantage for dichotic fused words in patients with schizophrenia. *Am J Psychiat* 152:932–935, 1995b.

Bruder GE, Tenke CE, Stewart JW, Towey JP, Leite P, Voglmaier M, Quitkin FM. Brain event-related potentials to complex tones in depressed patients: relations to perceptual asymmetry and clinical features. *Psychophysiology* 32:373–381, 1995a.

Clementz BA, Sponheim SR, Iacono WG, Beiser M. Resting EEG in first-episode schizophrenia patients, bipolar psychosis patients, and their first-degree relatives. *Psychophysiology* 31:486–494, 1994.

Crow TJ. Temporal lobe asymmetries as the key to the etiology of schizophrenia. *Schizophr Bull* 16:433–443, 1990.

Czobor P, Volavka J. Pretreatment EEG predicts short-term response to haloperidol treatment. *Biol Psychiat* 30:927–942, 1991.

d'Elia G, Jacobsson L, von Knorring L, *et al.* Changes in psychopathology in relation to EEG variables and visual averaged evoked potentials. *Acta Psychiatr Scand* 55:309–318, 1977.

Duncan CC, Morihisa JM, Fawcett RW, Kirch DG. P300 in schizophrenia: State or trait marker? *Psychopharmacol Bull* 23:497–501, 1987.

Egan MF, Duncan CC, Suddath RL, Kirch DG, Mirsky AF, Wyatt RJ. Event-related potential abnoralities correlate with structural brain alterations and clinical features in patients with chronic schizophrenia. *Schizophr Res* 11:259–271,1994.

Faux SF, McCarley RW, Nestor PG, Shenton ME, Pollak SD, Penhune V, Mondrow E, Marcy B, Peterson A, Horvath T, Davis KL. P300 topographic asymmetries are present in unmedicated schizophrenics. *Electroencephalogr Clin Neurophysiol* 88:32–41, 1993.

Faux SF, Shenton M, McCarley RW, Nestor P, Marcy B, Ludwig A. Preservation of P300 event-related potential topographic asymmetries in schizophrenia with use of either linked-ear or nose reference sites. *Electroencephalogr Clin Neurophysiol* 75:378–391, 1990.

Faux SF, Torrello MW, McCarley RW, Shenton ME, Duffy FH. P300 in schizophrenia: Confirmation and statistical validation of temporal region deficit in P300 topography. *Biol Psychiat* 23:776–790, 1988.

Flor-Henry P. Lateralized temporal-limbic dysfunction and psychopathology. *Ann NY Acad Sci* 280:777–795, 1976.

Flor-Henry P, Koles ZJ. Statistical quantitative EEG studies of depression, mania, schizophrenia and normals. *Biol Psychol* 19:257–279, 1984.

Ford JM, White PM, Csernansky JG, Faustman WO, Roth WT, Pfefferbaum A. ERPs in schizophrenia: Effects of antipsychotic medication. *Biol Psychiat* 36:153–170, 1994.

Ford JM, Mathalon DH, Pfefferbaum A. P300 amplitude tracks clinical status in schizophrenic patients. *Biol Psychiat* 37:671–672, 1995.

Ford MR, Goethe JW, Dekker DK. EEG coherence and power in the discrimination of psychiatric disorders and medication effects. *Biol Psychiat* 21:1175–1188, 1986.

Foundas AL, Leonard CM, Gilmore R, Fennell E, Heilman KM. Planum temporale asymmetry and language dominance. *Neuropsychologia* 32:1225–1231, 1994.

Galderisi S, Maj M, Mucci A, Bucci P, Kemali D. QEEG alphal changes after a single dose of high-potency neuroleptics as a predictor of short-term response to treatment in schizophrenic patients. *Biol Psychiat* 35:367–374, 1994.

Geschwind N, Levitsky W. Left-right asymmetry in temporal speech region. *Science* 161:186–187, 1968.

Gevins A, Cutillo B, Smith ME. Regional modulation of high resolution evoked potentials during verbal and non-verbal matching tasks. *Electroncephalogr Clin Neurophysiol* 94:129–147, 1995.

Goldman-Rakic PS. Prefrontal cortical dysfunction in schizophrenia: The relevance of working memory. In: Carroll B, Barrett JE, eds. *Psychopathology and the Brain.* New York: Raven Press, 1990, pp. 1–23.

Goldman-Rakic PS. Working memory dysfunction in schizophrenia. *J Neuropsychiatry* 6:348–357, 1994.

Grillon C, Courchesne E, Ameli R, Geyer MA, Braff DL. Increased distractibility in schizophrenic patients. *Arch Gen Psychiat* 47:171–179, 1990.

Gruzelier JH, Jutai JW, Connolly JF, Hirsch SR. Cerebral asymmetries and stimulus intensity relationships in EEG spectra of VEPs in unmedicated schizophrenic patients:

Relationships with active and withdrawn syndromes. *Int J Psychophysiol* 15:239–246, 1993.

Guenther W, Breitling D. Predominant sensorimotor area left hemisphere dysfunction in schizophrenia measured by brain electrical activity mapping. *Biol Psychiat* 20:515–532, 1985.

Iacono WG. Bilateral electrodermal habituation-dishabituation and resting EEG in remitted schizophrenics. *J Nerv Ment Dis* 170:91–101, 1982.

Itil TM. Quantitative and qualitative EEG findings in schizophrenia. *Schizophr Bull* 3:61–79, 1977.

Itil TM, Saletu B, Davis S. EEG findings in chronic schizophrenics based on digital computer period analysis and analog power spectra. *Biol Psychiat* 5:1–13, 1972.

Itil TM, Shapiro DM, Schneider SJ, Francis IB. Computerized EEG as a predictor of drug response in treatment resistant schizophrenics. *J Nerv Ment Dis* 169:629–637, 1981.

John ER, Prichep LS, Alper KR, Mas FG, Cancro R, Easton P, Sverdlov L. Quantitative electrophysical characteristics and subtyping of schizophrenia. *Biol Psychiat* 36:801–826, 1994.

Knight RA. Comparing cognitive models of schizophrenics' input dysfunction. In: Cromwell RL, Snyder CR, eds. *Schizophrenia: Origins, Processes, Treatment, and Outcome*. Oxford, England: Oxford University Press, 1993.

Knight RT, Scabini D, Woods DL, Clayworth CC. Contribution of temporal-parietal junction to the human auditory P3. *Brain Res* 502:109–116, 1989.

Lovrich D, Novick B, Vaughan Jr HG. Topographic analysis of auditory event-related potentials associated with acoustic and semantic processing. *Electroencephalogr Clin Neurophysiol* 71:40–54, 1988.

McCarley RW, Faux SF, Shenton ME, Nestor PG, Adams J. Event-related potentials in schizophrenia: Their biological and clinical correlates and a new model of schizophrenic pathophysiology. *Schizophr Res* 4:209–231, 1991.

McCarley RW, Shenton ME, O'Donnell BF, Faux SF, Kikinis R, Nestor PG, Jolesz FA. Auditory P300 abnormalities and left posterior superior temporal gyrus volume reduction in schizophrenia. *Arch Gen Psychiat* 50:190–197, 1993.

McCarthy G, Wood CC, Williamson PD, Spencer DD. Task-dependent field potentials in human hippocampal formation. *J Neurosci* 9:4253–4268, 1989.

Merrin EL, Fein G, Floyd TC, Yingling CD. EEG asymmetry in schizophrenic patients before and during neuroleptic treatment. *Biol Psychiat* 21:455–464, 1986.

Merrin EL, Floyd TC. P300 responses to novel auditory stimuli in hospitalized schizophrenic patients. *Biol Psychiat* 36:527–542, 1994.

Merrin EL, Floyd TC, Fein G. EEG coherence in unmedicated schizophrenic patients. *Biol Psychiat* 25:60–66, 1989.

Milner B. Disorders of learning and memory after temporal lobe lesions in man. *Clin Neurosurg* 19:421–446, 1972.

Moeller JR, Luber B, Rubin E, Sackeim HA. With network modeling, topographic EEG predicts memory capacity and RT in continuous performance tasks. *Soc Neurosci Abstr* 19:1606, 1993.

Morihisa JM, Duffy FH, Wyatt RJ. Brain electrical activity mapping (BEAM) in schizophrenic patients. *Arch Gen Psychiat* 40:719–728, 1983.

Morihisa JM, McAnulty GB. Structure and function: Brain electrical activity mapping and computed tomography in schizophrenia. *Biol Psychiat* 20:3–19, 1985.

Morrison-Stewart SL, Williamson PC, Corning WC, Kutcher SP, Merskey H. Coherence on electroencephalography and aberrant functional organization of the brain in schizophrenic patients during activation tasks. *Brit J Psychiat* 159:636–644, 1991.

Morstyn R, Duffy FH, McCarley RW. Altered topography of EEG spectral content in schizophrenia. *Electroenceph Clin Neurophysiol* 56:263–271, 1983a.

Morstyn R, Duffy FH, McCarley RW. Altered P300 topography in schizophrenia. *Arch Gen Psychiat* 40:729–734, 1983b.

Muir WJ, St. Clair DM, Blackwood DHR. Long-latency auditory event-related potentials in schizophrenia and in bipolar and unipolar affective disorder. *Psychol Med* 21:867–879, 1991.

Nagase Y, Okubo Y, Matsuur M, Kojima T, Toru M. EEG coherence in unmedicated schizophrenic patients: Topographical study of predominantly never medicated cases. *Biol Psychiat* 32:1028–1034, 1992.

Nuechterlein KH, Dawson ME. Information processing and attentional functioning in the developmental course of schizophrenic disorders. *Schizophr Bull* 10:160–203, 1984.

Nunez PL, Pilgreen KL, Westdorp AF, Law SK, Nelson AV. A visual study of surface potentials and Laplacians due to distributed neocortical sources: Computer simulations and evoked potentials. *Brain Topogr* 4:151–168, 1991.

Ohta H, O'Donnell BF, McCarley RW, Hokama H, Wible CG, Shenton ME, Law SE, Karapelou ME, Nestor PG, Jolesz FA, Kikinis R. An ERP study of the auditory P3A and P3B components in schizophrenia. *Biol Psychiat* 37:630–631, 1995.

Park S, Holzman PS. Schizophrenics show spatial working memory deficits. *Arch Gen Psychiat* 49:975–982, 1992.

Pfefferbaum A, Ford JM, White PM, Roth WT. P300 in schizophrenia is affected by stimulus modality, response requirements, medication status, and negative symptoms. *Arch Gen Psychiat* 46:1035–1044, 1989.

Phillips WA. On the distinction between sensory storage and short-term visual memory. *Percept Psychophysics* 16:283–290, 1974.

Potter MC. Short-term conceptual memory for pictures. *J Exp Psych: Hum Learning Mem* 2:509–522, 1976.

Rabinowicz EF, Knight RA, Owen DR, Gorman JM. Assessing the effects of medication on schizophrenics' form and numerosity judgments. Presented at the Ninth Annual Meeting of the Society for Research in Psychopathology, Coral Gables, FL. September, 1994.

Roth WT, Duncan CC, Pfefferbaum A, Timsit-Berthier M. Applications of cognitive ERPs in psychiatric patients. In: McCallum WC, Zappoli R, Denoth F, eds. *Cerebral Psychophysiology: Studies in Event-Related Potentials* (*EEG Suppl. 38*). Amsterdam: Elsevier Science Publishing, 1986.

Salisbury DF, O'Donnell BF, McCarley RW, Nestor PG, Faux SF, Smith RS. Parametric manipulations of auditory stimuli differentially affect P3 amplitude in schizophrenics and controls. *Psychophysiology* 31:29–36, 1994.

Salisbury DF, Shenton ME, McCarley RW, Yurgelun-Todd DA, Tohen M, Sherwood AR. P3 topography differs in schizophrenia-like and mania-like first episode psychosis. *Biol Psychiat* 37:626, 1995.

Shagass C. EEG studies of schizophrenia. In: Steinhauer SR, Gruzelier JH, Zubin J, eds. *Handbook of Schizophenia, Vol 5: Neuropsychology, Psychophysiology & Information Processing*. Amsterdam: Elsevier Science Publishers, 1991.

Shagass C, Straumanis JJ, Roemer RA, Amadeo M. Evoked potentials of schizophrenics in several sensory modalities. *Biol Psychiat* 12:221–235, 1977.

Shagass C, Roemer RA, Straumanis JJ. Relationships between psychiatric diagnosis and some quantitative EEG variables. *Arch Gen Psychiat* 39:1423–1435, 1983.

Shagass C, Roemer RA, Straumanis JJ, Josiassen RC. Psychiatric diagnostic discriminations with combinations of quantitative EEG variables. *Br J Psychiat* 144:581–592, 1984.

Shenton ME, Kikinis R, Jolesz FA, Pollak SD, LeMay M, Wible CG, Hokama H, Martin J, Metcalf D, Coleman M, McCarley RW. Abnormalities of the left temporal lobe and thought disorder in schizophrenia. *New Engl J Med* 327:604–612, 1992.

Sidtis JJ. The complex tone test: Implications for the assessment of auditory laterality effects. *Neuropsychologia* 19:103–112, 1981.

Singh J, Knight RT, Rosenlicht N, Kotun JM, Beckley DJ, Woods DL. Abnormal pre-movement brain potentials in schizophrenia. *Schizophr Res* 8:31–41, 1992.

Small JG, Milstein V, Kellams JJ, Miller MJ, Boyko OB, Small IF. EEG topography in psychiatric diagnosis and drug treatment. *Ann Clin Psychiat* 1:7–17, 1989.

Smith ME, Halgren E. Dissociation of recognition memory components following temporal lobe lesions. *J Exp Psychol: Learn, Mem and Cog* 15:50–60, 1989.

Souza VBN, Muir WJ, Walker WT, Glabus MF, Roxborough HM, Sharp CW, Dunan JR, Blackwood DHR. Auditory P300 event-related potentials and neuropsychological performance in schizophrenia and bipolar affective disorder. *Biol Psychiatry* 37:300–310, 1995.

Sponheim SR, Clementz BA, Iacono WG, Beiser M. Resting EEG in first-episode and chronic schizophrenia *Psychophysiology* 31:37–43, 1994.

Squire LR. The hippocampus and the neuropsychology of memory. In: Seifert W, ed. *Neurobiology of the Hippocampus*. New York: Academic Press, 1983.

Strik WK, Dierks T, Franzek E, Stober G, Maurer K. P300 in schizophrenia: Interactions between amplitudes and topography. *Biol Psychiat* 35:850–856, 1994.

Sutton S, Braren M, Zubin J, John ER. Evoked-potential correlates of stimulus uncertainty. *Science* 150:1187–1188, 1965.

Tenke CE, Bruder GE, Towey J, Leite P, Sidtis JJ. Correspondence between ERP and behavioral asymmetries for complex tones. *Psychophysiology* 30:62–70, 1993.

Tucker DM. Spatial sampling of head electrical fields: The geodesic sensor net. *Electroencephalogr Clin Neurophysiol* 87:154–163, 1993.

Tucker DM, Liotti M, Potts GF, Russell GS, Posner MI. Spatiotemporal analysis of brain electrical fields. *Human Brain Mapping* 1:134–152, 1994.

Brain Imaging in Schizophrenia

DOLORES MALASPINA, M.D., LAWRENCE S. KEGELES, M.D., Ph.D.,
and RONALD L. VAN HEERTUM, M.D.

INTRODUCTION

The rapidly evolving techniques for imaging brain structure and function are among the most exciting advances in schizophrenia research. Newer structural brain imaging methodologies permit the resolution of smaller and smaller brain regions, and there is anticipation that neuroanatomy may soon be explored at the cellular level. Functional brain imaging capabilities are also rapidly advancing, specific neurophysiological activity can now be imaged during different behavioral conditions and an understanding of the various networks of coordinated brain activity that underlie different mental operations is evolving. These advances in imaging technology may directly reveal the aberrant neurobiology that underlies schizophrenia.

We are fortunate that the compelling questions about the neurobiology of this dreadful disease have kept it at the forefront of emerging brain imaging research methodologies. This chapter will describe the major imaging technologies being used in schizophrenia research, including their applications and major findings.

OVERVIEW

It has long been clear that schizophrenia is a brain disease. In the 1920s, researchers were already attempting to examine *brain structure* in living human beings using a process called pneumo-encephalography. The procedure was dangerous and difficult, it entailed withdrawing cerebrospinal fluid, injecting air into the brain fluid spaces, and then making radiograms. Reports suggested structural brain changes in schizophrenia, but the limitations of the methodology did not permit any firm conclusions.

Brain imaging capabilities began rapidly expanding when technology developed for space exploration research was applied to imaging the brain. The first advance in methodology occurred in the 1970s with computerized axial tomography (CT), for which Hounsfield and Cormack won the Nobel Prize in 1979. CT scans revealed, for the first time, the size and shape of brain anatomy in three dimensions. By 1976, Johnstone et al. (1976) had already published a report of enlarged cerebral ventricles in schizophrenia. The next goal in structural brain imaging was to visualize smaller and smaller portions of neuroanatomy. The past decade has seen the rapid evolution and expansion of nuclear magnetic resonance imaging (MRI), which can produce clear and detailed three-dimensional neuroanatomic images without ionizing radiation.

Most patients with schizophrenia studied by CT or MRI have brain structural images that are read as "normal" by radiologists, despite the overwhelming clinical evidence that their brain function is abnormal. Clearly then, a disease can severely compromise the function of the brain without visibly affecting the structure of the brain's anatomy. Although brain structure is relatively unchanging, brain *function* varies continuously with behavioral state and cognitive endeavor.

The first study to examine brain function in schizophrenia was performed in 1948 by Kety and Schmidt. Using a nitrous oxide technique, they found that whole brain blood flow did not differ between subjects with or without schizophrenia. Nonetheless, they predicted that advancing techniques to examine specific brain regions would show regional differences in patients with schizophrenia. Twenty-six years later, using intra-arterial [133]Xenon, Ingvar and Franzen (1974) found decreased relative frontal brain blood flow. In recent years there have been major technologic advances in the field of functional brain imaging. These new technologies include positron emission tomography (PET), single photon emission computed tomography (SPECT), and functional MRI. Nuclear magnetic resonance spectroscopy (MRS) is an emerging MRI-derived imaging technique that can assess brain chemistry and function without applied ionizing radiation. Present functional brain imaging studies continue to assess the earlier described "hypofrontality" during cognitive activations, while also exploring dopamine and other neurotransmitter systems, normal brain function, changes in brain function during development and senescence, and the relationship between regional brain function and specific symptoms.

Although our present focus is on the schizophrenia research developments of the past decade, there is another milestone that we should consider. It was nearly a century ago, in 1896, that Professor Emil Kraepelin of Munich first regarded schizophrenia ("dementia praecox") as a distinct disease. It is humbling to realize that with the technology of his day, he speculated that "the disease attacks by preference the frontal areas of the brain, the central convolutions and the temporal lobes." He believed that "clinical experience and anatomical findings in dementia praecox" could someday be "brought into agreement to some extent." With such an early and profound intuition about the brain regions that underlie schizophrenia, we may wonder why the mechanisms that cause it are still not determined, whereas the etiologies of many other medical conditions have been determined. The answer to this question probably lies in the complex heterogeneity of the schizophrenia syndrome and in our awaitment of advances in brain imaging technology. Kraepelin concluded that "it must be left to the future to decide how far (his theories could) stand the test of increasing knowledge" (Kraepelin 1919).

It seems that "the future" may now be at hand. Perhaps in this decade, science has finally advanced to the point where the theories of Kraepelin, now a century old, can be fully examined. In the following sections, we review the neuroimaging modalities and their applications to schizophrenia, with particular attention to progress during the past decade and a view of their future potential. In each section a brief discussion of the technical principles of the method is followed by a description of applications and findings relevant to schizophrenia.

STRUCTURAL BRAIN IMAGING

Computed tomography

In the early 1970s CT became available for psychiatric research and quickly yielded the first significant and highly replicable findings of abnormal brain structure in schizophrenia. The etiology of the ventricular enlargement in schizophrenia is still undetermined, but there is no disputing the importance of the finding. It led directly to the present renaissance of research into the neurobiology and neuropathology of schizophrenia.

Technology

CT images show the tissues of the brain across single planes. These images are obtained from narrow collimated radiographic beams that penetrate the brain from a source that is rotated 180° around the subject. The penetrating beams are detected by sensitive scintillation crystals, and the computer constructed image reflects the differential absorption of the beams by the various tissues. Each brain slice is based on information from thousands of intersecting radiation intensity measurements, with spatial resolution limited by the number of beam intersections. The resultant attenuation coefficients are visually displayed as light and dark areas in the scan.

Applications

Much of the published CT work in schizophrenia is based on measurements from the film images showing the domains of interest. Brain regions are traced and volumes are determined by planimeter. Both local volumes and ratios of areas can be compared among subject groups or be related to clinical features of illness. The availability of CT initiated the image processing applications that have evolved for the more advanced methodologies. Progress in CT scanning capabilities (denoted by successive "generations" of the systems) has resulted in shorter scan times with reduced radiation exposure, as well as greater contrast and spatial resolution.

Findings

Enlarged lateral ventricles. Increased ventricular cerebrospinal fluid (CSF) volume is the most replicated and robust image finding in schizophrenia. Over 50 studies have been conducted since Johnstone's 1976 report. Her findings are supported in about 75% of studies, as reviewed by many authors, including Raz and Raz (1990), Lewis (1990), and Pfefferbaum (1990). Negative symptoms, chronicity, cognitive impairments and neuroleptic non-responsivity have been variably associated with ventricular enlargement. A recent study of symptoms and CT measurements indicated a negative correlation of temporal horn size and positive symptoms (Rubin et al. 1994).

Most longitudinal studies have indicated that ventricular enlargement is present at illness onset and is not progressive with illness course or treatment (Owens 1985, Nasrallah et al. 1986). Although mild enlargement over time has been reported (Kemali et al. 1989, Woods et al. 1990), it may just be indicative of normal aging. The CT data of nonprogressive ventriculomegaly without gliosis provided some initial evidence for the hypothesized neurodevelopmental etiology of schizophrenia.

Enlarged third ventricles. The third ventricular enlargement found in schizophrenia appears to be more specific to the illness than lateral ventricular enlargement (Boronow et al. 1985). The third ventricle is surrounded by brain regions that are implicated in schizophrenia, including the thalamus, hypothalamus, and fornix.

Widened cortical sulci. This is a nonspecific, but common, CT finding in schizophrenia, suggestive of reduced cortical volumes. Shelton et al (1984) found that sulcal enlargement was only related to prominent prefrontal and temporal lobe atrophy. CT sulcal enlargement is sometimes found to be associated with cognitive impairments (Nasrallah et al. 1983), but not consistently (Weinberger et al. 1979). Within multi-generational pedigrees with schizophrenia, sulcal enlargement in the lateral temporal cortex characterized ill family members in one pedigree (Honer et al. 1994), but Jones et al. 1993 found that abnormally wide sulci were more common in family-history-negative than positive patients.

Other findings. Other inconsistent CT findings include cerebellar atrophy, cerebral asymmetry, and decreased brain density, as reviewed by Coffman (1989).

Future

CT studies consistently identified larger ventricles and cortical sulci in schizophrenic patients. As the first neuroimaging technique accessible to psychiatrists, it generated great interest and paved the way for subsequent imaging research in schizophrenia. For reasons that will become clear in the next section, CT structural imaging has now been largely supplanted by MRI for research, although it is still widely used for clinical applications. Previous CT findings in schizophrenia are being re-examined and amplified with MRI techniques, as will be described.

Magnetic resonance imaging

Technology

MRI technology may permit the identification and localization of the abnormal brain tissue suggested by increased CSF. It presents far greater neuroanatomic detail than CT and requires no external ionizing radiation. MRI technology is advancing rapidly and recent developments now also enable MR to examine brain function (described later in this chapter under magnetic resonance spectroscopy and functional MRI). Only a brief capsule of MRI methodology is presented here, but there are many excellent recent reviews, including those by Sanders (1995) and Pearlson and Marsh (1993).

MRI employs the properties of atomic nuclei having odd numbers of protons, such as ^1H, ^{13}C, ^{23}Na, ^{31}P, and ^{39}K, to generate images. Since these nuclei carry extra charges and magnetic moments, they naturally produce undetectable random magnetic fields. When a constant external magnetic field is applied, transitions between high and low energy states of the nuclei are in dynamic equilibrium. With the application of a large external magnetic field during MR imaging, the nuclear spins align parallel (or antiparallel) to the external magnet. A subsequent brief pulse of a specific electromagnetic radiation frequency then shifts the protons of interest to a high energy state. For each atomic type there is a specific resonant frequency of electromagnetic energy (the Larmor frequency) which causes the nuclear transition from low to a high energy state. Carbon and hydrogen are the most commonly used nuclei because of their biologic abundance. When the nuclei subsequently relax back to their low energy state they emit recordable radio frequency waves called free induction decay. T1 (spin lattice relaxation) reflects the restoration of the longitudinal magnetization back to equilibrium as an exponential growth constant. T2 (spin-spin relaxation) is an exponential decay constant that reflects the loss of signal strength as the spins dephase, also known as transverse relaxation. T1 is related to the molecular size and tissue mobility factors and T2 is related to the tissue state.

Inversion-recovery and spin-echo are types of pulse sequences for data acquisition in MRI. The best pulse sequences for detecting abnormal tissue are different from those best suited to examine anatomy. Inversion recovery relies heavily on T1 signals and produces good resolution of grey matter and white matter. With inversion-recovery, a 180° pulse excites the protons, causing an inverted alignment of the magnetic moment. Although the relaxation from this 180° alignment is not measurable, a second 90° pulse tips the magnetization dipole again. The time between the two pulses is the inversion time. After measurement, the tissues relax in a period that is determined by the tissue characteristics and the pulse sequence is repeated. Spin-echo pictures rely more on T2 weighting. Although they are less anatomically clear, they have higher clinical utility because they are better detectors of small focal lesions. This sequence is commonly used for screening. Fast MRI is an echo-planar technique that requires one nuclear spin excitement for each image, generating echos with a single free induction decay. It is not yet widely available, but it has many advantages consequent to very rapid data acquisition.

Applications

MRI has superior capability to CT for distinguishing grey-white matter boundaries and for image reconstruction in multiple planes. Neuroanatomy can be explored with direct visualization or by computerized methodology. Edge detection and thresholding are tools that can define regions of interest based on tissue contrast differences. In addition, T1 and T2 relaxation times can be used to probe for regional tissue abnormalities.

When reconstructed in three dimensions, image data can be reformatted into standardized stereotactic space. Such coordinated configurations allow brains to be averaged across subjects, to be superimposed on functional brain images from PET or SPECT, and to be entered into data base atlases. Studies in schizophrenia have included linear size and volume measurements of the ventricles, frontal system, corpus callosum, temporolimbic structures, thalamus, cerebellum, and other brain regions.

Findings

The organization of brain MRI findings by region in this section is more convenient than theoretical. It is likely that the brain dysfunction in schizophrenia occurs within neural networks that involve multiple neural levels. Defects in neurotransmitter modulation of networks, abnormal structure or function in specific network nodes, and dysfunctional connectivity could all account for the observed abnormalities. Such diverse etiologies may account for the heterogeneity in the disorder.

Increased cerebrospinal fluid volume. Expanded cerebrospinal fluid (CSF) furnishes evidence of neuropathology in schizophrenia, despite its nonspecificity and as yet undetermined etiology. As in CT, the ventricular enlargement appears nonprogressive (Degreef et al. 1991, DeLisi et al. 1992). Deficit schizophrenia symptoms are proposed to be associated with the enlarged ventricular brain ratios (VBRs), but associations among symptoms and VBRs are not always found (Delisi et al. 1991, Mozley et al. 1994). Perhaps ventricular enlargement needs to be more precisely defined.

In a study that divided the ventricular space into occipital, temporal, and frontal regions, all ventricular areas were enlarged compared to controls, but only temporal horn enlargement was associated with a wide array of positive and negative symptoms (Degreef et al. 1992). Gur et al. (1994) classified MRI images by brain size and CSF volumes. These authors found that patients with severe negative symptoms had decreases in brain volume proportional to increased VBR (suggesting atrophy), that patients with Schneiderian symptoms had decreased brain volume without increased CSF (suggesting neurodevelopmental lesions), and that paranoid patients had normal CSF and brain volumes (actually having reduced sulcal volumes). There are data indicating that greatly enlarged ventricles are associated with poor neuroleptic treatment response, although a meta-analysis of 33 studies did not detect a significant association of any structural brain morphology to medication responsivity (Friedman et al. 1992).

Gender effects in VBR are also considered, with most studies noting more enlargement in males (Goetz and Van Kammen 1986, Flaum et al. 1990), although females had greater CSF in other studies (Gur et al. 1994). Increased sulcal CSF, associated with reduced cortical volumes, is also reported with MRI (Pfefferbaum et al. 1988), and appears to be specific to schizophrenia vis-a-vis psychotic bipolar disorder (Harvey 1993). Mozley et al (1994) found that increased sulcal CSF ratio related to earlier age of onset.

The heterogeneity in VBR among patients has been used to examine genetic hypotheses of schizophrenia. In a series of monozygotic discordant twins, the ill twin had relatively increased VBR, reduced brain volume, and smaller hippocampi. These results were consistent with environmental antecedents to these brain changes (Suddath et al. 1990).

Frontal lobes. Diminished frontal cortical volume is a variable finding, perhaps because of methodologic limitations to defining brain region boundaries. Zipursky et al. (1992) found that reduced grey matter volumes accounted for the diminished cortical volumes in frontal as well as other cortical regions. No localized frontal abnormality was found.

The left dorsolateral area, a specific prefrontal cortical region, has been inversely associated with neurocognitive performance (Seidman et al. 1994). Some data support that deficits in prefrontal function (either primary or downstream from medial temporal abnormalities) could lead to subcortical hyperdopaminergia. This is backed by an inverse relationship between CSF homovanillic acid (a dopamine metabolite) and prefrontal cortical volume (Brier et al. 1993). Also, Lewine et al. (1991) found a reciprocal relationship between lateral ventricle size and dopamine activity relative to serotonin activity in schizophrenia patients. Several indicated found that positive symptom patients with temporal lobe abnormalities did not show frontal grey matter reductions (Shenton et al. 1992, Weibel et al. 1995).

Temporal lobe. A major emphasis in MRI studies in schizophrenia has been to examine volumes of the lateral temporal association areas and medial temporolimbic structures. Reduced volumes of the medial temporal lobe structures, including the hippocam-

pus and amygdala, are reported (Barta et al. 1990, Suddath et al. 1990) and left temporal lobe volume reductions have been correlated with thought disorder (Shenton et al.
1992).

The left posterior superior temporal lobe gyrus volume was uniquely associated with the
amplitude of the P300 evoked potential in one study (McCarley et al. 1993). The P300 amplitude represents the updating of memory systems for novel stimuli and it is a commonly
explored psychophysiologic vulnerability marker for schizophrenia (see chapter by Bruder
et al.). On the other hand, abnormal medial temporal lobe structures in schizophrenia have
also been associated with normal eye tracking, the most commonly utilized genetic vulnerability marker in schizophrenia research (Levy 1992).

Zipursky et al. (1994) also found grey matter reductions in the temporal lobe, but similar changes were present in other cortical areas, suggesting that temporal lobe sites are not
preferentially affected in schizophrenia. Hippocampal volumes did not differ between normals and schizophrenic patients in this study.

Basal ganglia. There have been contradictory volume studies of the basal ganglia volumes in schizophrenia. This may relate in part to the emerging data showing effects of
treatment on these structures. Selective hypertrophy of the caudate may occur early after
treatment begins, possibly resulting from pharmacotherapy with typical neuroleptics
(Chakos et al. 1994), but not from clozapine (Bilder et al. 1994).

Other findings. There are other intriguing MRI findings concerning total brain volume,
thalamus, corpus callosum and brain laterality in schizophrenia. Many sources suggest altered lateralization of brain function in schizophrenia. In some structural imaging studies,
schizophrenia patients do not show the expected increased left temporal lobe convolutions,
denotative of language dominance. Decreased total brain volumes have been reported by
some investigators and it is possible that this may better distinguish patients from controls
than VBR (Gur et al. 1994, Andreasen et al. 1994). In addition, Andreasen et al. (1994)
identified thalamic abnormalities in a subtraction study of averaged MRIs from schizophrenic patients and controls. Significant differences between male patients and controls in
the area of the corpus callosum that communicates between the temporal lobes have been
described (Woodruff et al. 1993).

Gunther et al. (1991) found no overall callosal differences between schizophrenia and
controls. Nonetheless, they did identify heterogeneity of callosal size in schizophrenia, such
that Crow's Type I patients (those with a preponderance of positive symptoms) had larger
callosal brain ratios than Type II patients (those with little positive but distinct negative
symptomatology). Again, enhanced neuroanatomic detail, regional considerations of large
brain structures and spaces, and reduced patient heterogeneity may enhance data from structural imaging studies.

Future

MRI is a rapidly evolving technology that is in its initial phases. Structural evidence
of neuropathology in schizophrenia from MRI is in need of larger sample sizes of
well characterized patients and advances in image analysis methodology. It may prove
to be a superb tool to resolve the etiologic heterogeneity of the schizophrenia
syndrome.

FUNCTIONAL IMAGING MODALITIES

Positron emission tomography

Technology

Positron emission tomography (PET) is a functional imaging modality based on the use of a number of positron-emitting radionuclides (Hoffman and Phelps 1986; Fowler and Wolf 1986). These nuclides (see Table 1) are isotopes of elements that naturally and frequently occur in organic molecules or are readily substitutable for such elements (such as ^{18}F for H). These radionuclides can be incorporated into a wide variety of molecules that participate in a broad spectrum of metabolic brain functions (see Table 2; see also Daniel et al. 1992), and thus give rise to a correspondingly wide range of PET applications for functionally assessing and imaging the brain.

Another major advantage of these positron nuclides is the production of dual photon coincidence detection events, which contributes to the relatively high spatial resolution (4–8 mm) of PET. The dual photon production is a direct consequence of positron emission. The positron, which is the anti-particle of the electron, travels a short distance (generally 1–2 mm) before encountering an electron. The encounter results in annihilation of the electron/positron pair with the production of two photons (gamma rays) traveling in almost exactly opposite directions, each with the same energy (511 KeV) as the electron mass-energy equivalent. It is the simultaneous coincidence detection of these pairs of oppositely aligned high-energy photons that allows reconstruction of the emission event along their line of travel; backprojection of the coincidence data results in the computer reconstruction of the tomographic functional brain image.

Characteristics:

1. PET radiotracers are diverse, allowing for the diverse applications noted.
2. PET studies are, in general, high-resolution images, a result of the image methodology, in particular the dual-photon coincidence detection technique.
3. The radionuclides listed in Table 1 have very short half-lives ranging from 2–110 minutes. This feature results in diminished patient radiation exposure compared to longer-lived tracers. Unfortunately, there is a greater expense as this feature necessitates the use of a small in-house cyclotron for local on-site production.
4. The tracers listed in Table 2 are chemically similar to the naturally occurring nonradioactive compounds. This characteristic simplifies analysis of the metabolic functions in which they participate.

TABLE 1.   PET RADIONUCLIDES AND DECAY TIMES

Nuclide	Half-life
^{15}O	2 min
^{13}N	10 min
^{11}C	20 min
^{18}F	110 min

TABLE 2. SOME PET TRACERS APPLICABLE TO THE STUDY OF SCHIZOPHRENIA

Glucose metabolism	Dopamine receptors
^{18}F-deoxyglucose	C-N-methylspiperone
^{11}C-glucose	^{11}C-raclopride
	^{18}F-haloperidol
Protein synthesis	^{11}C-nomifensine
	^{11}C-SCH 23390
^{11}C-methionine	
^{11}C-leucine	
^{11}C-valine	
Blood flow	Dopamine metabolism
C^{15}O$_2$	^{18}F-dopa
C^{15}O	^{11}C-tyrosine
H$_2$^{15}O	

5. Analysis of PET image data can yield relevant quantitative information when appropriate kinetic and physiologic modeling of the tracer's behavior in blood and brain is applied (Sokoloff et al. 1977, Huang and Phleps 1986).

Applications

The main application areas for PET scanning in schizophrenia include the assessment of glucose metabolism, protein synthesis, blood flow, neuroreceptor sites, drug studies, neurochemistry or neurotransmitter concentration, and other metabolic processes including dopamine metabolism (Holcomb et al. 1989).

Glucose metabolism. The metabolic rate of glucose, the primary cerebral energy substrate, has been widely measured in PET studies. This rate is ascertained by labeling glucose itself with ^{11}C or a glucose analog (deoxyglucose) with ^{18}F. The labeled analog, ^{18}F-deoxyglucose (FDG), has a unique advantage in studying traits or enduring states that are of 40-minute or longer duration in that it proceeds only partway along the metabolic pathway of glucose and then becomes trapped in the neuron, remaining as a marker of metabolic activity. FDG is injected prior to a patient's entry into the scanner, which occurs after a 40-minute uptake period. The technique yields high-resolution images that reflect average neuronal activity during the uptake period.

Protein synthesis/dopamine metabolism. A number of amino acids can be labeled with positron radionuclides. After intravenous administration in a human subject, these radiotracers can be followed to assess alterations in protein or neurotransmitter synthesis. This method can be used to assess alterations in overall uptake and utilization of a variety of metabolic precursors in the schizophrenic brain.

Blood flow. Regional cerebral blood flow can be studied by using the PET tracers indicated in Table 2. These tracers diffuse out of the blood and produce images of activity proportional to regional cerebral blood flow, which is of interest because of its tight coupling to neuronal activation. Because of the short half-life of the ^{15}O compounds (see Table 1) and the 1–2-minute scan time, they are useful for sequential activation studies of state-dependent blood flow, such as in a series of distinct cognitive tasks. However, image spatial resolution is poorer than other PET tracers because the more energetic positrons emitted by ^{15}O travel farther before pair annihilation and create more uncertainty in both the location of the emission event and in the dual-photon line of travel.

Receptor studies. The nuclides of Table 1 can be used to label high-affinity receptor ligands for use as PET tracers. They yield images with regional activity related to characteristics (B_{MAX} or receptor density and K_D or affinity) of the receptors under study. Quantitative models taking into account tracer transport, receptor binding affinity, receptor density, and nonspecific binding are developed and applied to quantify these receptor characteristics. Separate determination of these two quantities generally requires multiple injections of tracer with varying degrees of competitive displacement by an unlabeled ligand, often an active pharmacologic agent. Studies of this type in schizophrenia have focused on the dopaminergic systems with increasing ability to specify dopamine receptor subtypes.

Pharmacokinetic and neurotransmitter studies. Neuroleptic dose-occupancy studies can also be performed using receptor ligand methods. This approach investigates the displacement of labeled ligand by a range of doses of unlabeled neuroleptic and can provide information about dose needed for full receptor occupancy. Similarly, an approach under development has the potential to use low-affinity labeled ligands to assess synaptic neurotransmitter concentrations. In this approach, an agent is administered that causes release of endogenous neurotransmitter, which then competes in a measurable way at the receptor site with the PET tracer.

Findings

Numerous studies have used ^{11}C-glucose and FDG to investigate the issue of metabolic hypofrontality in schizophrenia, and most have confirmed the finding (Andreasen et al. 1994). Historically, the studies have progressed from "resting" states to more controlled states, including specific brain activations. FDG studies confirming hypofrontality include those of Buchsbaum et al. (1982), Bushsbaum et al. (1984), Farkas et al. (1984), Wolkin et al. (1988), Cohen et al. (1987), and Buchsbaum (1990). In some FDG studies, however, no hypofrontality was found (Jernigan et al. 1985, Kling et al. 1986, Gur et al. 1987) as did a ^{11}C-glucose study (Wiesel et al. 1987), while in some FDG studies, increased relative frontal glucose metabolism was noted (Szechtman et al. 1988; Cleghorn et al. 1989).

Frontal hypometabolism has also been found in a protein synthesis study (Bustany et al. 1985) using ^{11}C-methionine. A study of ^{11}C-tyrosine, a labeled precursor of dopamine (Wiesel et al. 1991) showed altered parameters of tyrosine uptake in the illness. Not only was plasma tyrosine abnormal in the study patients, but tyrosine influx into the CNS and net utilization of tyrosine in the brain were reduced.

^{15}O PET blood flow studies have also been used to examine hypofrontality in schizophrenia as well as to link symptom complexes in the illness to altered perfusion in predicted brain regions. The studies of Sheppard et al. (1983) and Early et al. (1987) of patients in a resting, eyes closed state failed to show differences in frontal ratio analysis, unlike many studies using other blood flow methodologies. A steady-state inhalation technique involving ^{15}O-labeled CO_2, O_2, and CO was used by Liddle et al. (1992) and confirmed their predictions of pre-frontal loci of altered perfusion associated with both psychomotor poverty and disorganization syndromes, as well as of abnormal medial temporal perfusion associated with reality distortion.

Dopamine D2 receptor study results have been inconsistent with regard to the question of elevation of striatal receptor density in the illness (Wong et al. 1986; Farde et al. 1988; Andreasen et al. 1988), with the discrepancy attributable, in part, to differing properties of the labeled ligands (^{11}C-raclopride and ^{11}C-NMSP) used in the different studies. D1 receptor studies using [^{11}C]SCH 23390 (Farde et al. 1992) have shown that some antipsychotic drugs block not only D2 but also D1 receptors, and that the atypical agent clozapine exhibits this property to a high degree, blocking the two receptor subtypes about equally in schizophrenic patients.

A dose-occupancy study of displacement of ^{11}C-NMSP by a range of doses of haloperidol (Tamminga et al. 1993) suggests that therapeutic response to this neuroleptic occurs in the linear dose range of its dopamine receptor occupancy. This method has been used by Wolkin et al. to show that neuroleptic-resistant patients have about the same degree of receptor blockade as patients with treatment response.

Future

Future developments in the area of receptor-ligand studies in schizophrenia research can be expected along the lines of: 1) improving characterization of the dopamine receptor subtypes (D1, D2, D4); 2) measurement of synaptic levels of neurotransmitter (dopamine) concentration by displacement of low-affinity ligand (e.g., [^{11}C]raclopride) through administering an agent (e.g., amphetamine) that stimulates endogenous transmitter release; and 3) continuing development of tracers for other neurotransmitter receptor systems such as the serotonin 5-HT$_2$ receptor and opiate and benzodiazepine receptors.

Single photon emission computed tomography

Technology

Single photon emission computed tomography (SPECT) was evolved as a technique that could overcome some of the limitations of PET brain imaging. PET requires highly complex instrumentation and its radio-tracers disintegrate very rapidly, usually requiring an on site cyclotron and preparation within minutes to hours of use. SPECT equipment, in contrast, is available in most hospital radiology departments and SPECT radioisotopes can be prepared days in advance. SPECT does not yet have the same resolution or quantitative abilities of PET, but it is a simple and readily accessible technique to assess brain function. Several different types of procedures and instrumentation are called SPECT. SPECT imaging methodologies all include the administration of radioisotopes, the subsequent counting of emitted photons by one or more collimated detectors, and the computerized reconstruction of three dimensional images from filtered back-projection of the acquired planar projection images. Since these technique detect single photon events, quantification in SPECT differs significantly from PET, which, as described, uses coincidence detection for more precise localization of radio-tracer activity. Noncamera based tomographic SPECT systems include: rotating detector arrays, multi detector scanners, and fixed ring detector devices. Single gamma-camera based systems are currently being rapidly replaced by multihead systems that maximize photon detection sensitivity. Multidetector SPECT, in general, improves image resolution and shortens imaging times. Currently, state-of-the-art SPECT systems can provide relatively high spatial resolution (6–9 mm) imaging of statically distributed brain radio pharmaceuticals with patient imaging times in the range of 10–20 minutes (Devous 1994).

Radiopharmaceutical development for SPECT tracers has lagged behind that of PET tracers, but several [99m]Tc- and ^{123}I ligands for the measurement of regional cerebral blood flow (rCBF) have been developed. Even though unlike PET, SPECT cannot directly measure regional cerebral metabolism, regional cerebral blood flow (rCBF) provides an excellent indirect estimate of metabolism in most clinical settings. [133]Xenon is a rapidly diffusible brain blood flow marker that has been in use for several decades. As an inert gas, it undergoes no metabolic transformation in the brain, and has rapid brain transit. For quantification, input can be determined from lung [133]Xenon measurement, and mathematical models can then be used to estimate brain blood flow. Complete scan acquisitions must occur in 10 seconds with a total study time of approximately 10 minutes. The tradeoff for the high sensitivity of the Xenon procedure is its poor spatial resolution.

Other SPECT brain perfusion radiotracers are retained in the brain by trapping or metabolic change. The longer imaging times that are possible with these perfusion agents enhance spatial resolution, but the images are not quantifiable using simple mathematical models. Iodinated agents were the first of these tracers developed: ^{123}I-IMP (^{123}I-N-isopropyl-P-iodoamphetamine), (Winchell et al. 1980), which is no longer commercially available, was soon followed by another labeled amine, HIPDM (N-N-N']-trimethyl-N'-(2-hydroxy-3-methyl-5-iodobenzyl)-1,3-propanediamine 2 Hcl (Kung et al. 1983). Of the technetium[99m]-tagged agents, HMPAO (^{99m}Tc hexamethyl-propylene-amine-oxime), was the first to be approved by the FDA (Leonard et al. 1986). It differs somewhat from other ^{99m}Tc agents in its extraction fraction, grey-to-white matter contrast, and blood clearance.

Applications

Regional cerebral blood volume. As described, SPECT can not yet be used to measure cerebral metabolism directly. Because of the usual tight coupling of cerebral blood flow to tissue metabolism, however, the SPECT derived ratio of rCBF to regional cerebral blood volume (rCBF/rCBV) can be used to estimate global and regional oxygen extraction.

Receptor imaging. SPECT radioligands under study for neuroreceptor quantification are primarily radiolabeled with ^{123}I; they currently include ligands for dopamine D1, D2, serotonergic, benzodiazepine, and muscarinic cholinergic receptors. Although the iodination process causes structural change, the affinity for the receptor is preserved (or exceeded) in useful compounds, which should be lipophilic, receptor-specific, and have high total brain uptake. The iodinated benzodiazepine receptor antagonist, iomazenil, has a tenfold higher affinity for the receptor than its parent compound, flumazenil (Innis 1992).

SPECT receptor probes in schizophrenia have centered on dopamine. ^{123}I-IBZM, (S-(−)-N-[(1-ethyl-2-pyrrolidinyl)methyl]-2-hydroxy-3-iodo-6-methoxybenzamide) is a raclopride analogue that labels D2 receptors and shows high uptake in the striatum. It is displaceable by haloperidol, a high affinity D2 antagonist (Kessler et al. 1991, Seibyl et al. 1992) and it is commercially available in Europe. A D1 receptor antagonist, TISH ([123]I-(+)-7-chloro-

8-hydroxy-1-(3′-iodophenyl)3 methyl 2,3,4,5 tetra hydro ^{1}H-3 benzapine) localizes in the prefrontal cortex, hippocampus, and the amygdala. Other PET inspired agents are being developed to study the pharmacokinetics of dopamine receptor agonists and antagonists, such as Ro-16-0154 and ^{123}I Iodolisuride (Beer et al. 1990, Chabrait et al. 1992). Other tracers are being developed to image dopamine transporter sites.

Findings

Hypofrontality. SPECT studies examining hypofrontality have reached disparate conclusions. Some investigators find an association of resting hypofrontality to chronicity and negative symptoms (Ingvar 1980, Hoyer and Oesterreich 1977, Hoyer 1982), but others do not (Gur et al. 1983, Berman et al. 1984). Ariel et al. (1983) described a reduced anterior-posterior gradient, rather than hypofrontality per se. It has also been suggested that the pattern during acute exacerbation is more consistent with a hypoparietal state (Wiesel et al. 1987), and that it is not different from normal patterns (Cleghorn et al. 1989).

More recent studies have moved toward using cognitive tasks to activate the frontal lobes for rCBF analysis (Berman et al. 1984, 1986). Lower prefrontal flow at rest, with higher left striatal flow during activation is described (Rubin et al. 1994). Impaired frontal activation has been associated with negative symptoms (Weinberger et al. 1991; Andreasen et al. 1992), and there are associated findings of increased flow in positive symptom patients (Gunther et al. 1991, 1992). Schizophrenia-related eye movements have also been associated with prefrontal ^{123}I-IMP uptake (Tsunoda et al. 1992). Catafau et al. (1994) found that physiologic dysfunction of the prefrontal cortex was present at illness onset in neuroleptic-naive patients. This dysfunction was manifest as resting left-sided hyperfrontality and hypotemporality, along with failure to show the prefrontal flow increases on activation seen in their controls.

Interhemispheric differences on SPECT imaging in schizophrenia support the presence of underlying brain lateralization defects. Task related lateralized left sided hypoperfusion is described (Kawasaki et al. 1993), as well as higher left-sided resting prefrontal flow states that do not show the expected increases with cognitive activation (Catafau et al. 1994). Gur et al (1993) reported that schizophrenia patients had opposite laterality of activation to normals, showing left, rather than right, hemispheric lateralization for spatial tasks and Matthew et al. (1981) found blood flow reduction only in the right prefrontal area.

There is, as yet, no consensus concerning the presence, meaning, and stability of hypofrontality assessed by SPECT. The effect of critical variables in these remain unclear, certainly patient factors, cognitive tasks, methodological differences, medication effects, and patient heterogeneity may all play a role.

Temporal lobe. Functional activity in the temporal lobes has also been investigated with SPECT. Rubin et al. (1994) found that symptom severity was associated with high temporal lobe and striatal rCBF during a frontal activation task. In a different study, a verbal memory task yielded equivalent medial temporal lobe activations for patients and controls, despite markedly impaired test performance in the schizophrenia sample (Busatto et al. 1994).

SPECT studies of hallucinations have yielded interesting results. Musalek et al. (1989) found associations between hallucination severity and SPECT flow in the hippocampus, parahippocampus, and amygdala and Cleghorn et al. (1990) found decreased flow in Wernicke's area. Anderson et al. (1991) found lower left temporal flow during hallucinations, but in a serial study there was increased left superior temporal activity during prominent auditory hallucinations that normalized during clinical remission (Suzuki et al. 1993), a discrepancy warranting further study. Additionally, McGuire et al. (1993), found significant blood flow increases in Broca's area during hallucinations, with nonsignificant increases in the left anterior cingulate and left temporal lobe.

Basal ganglia. A functional SPECT rCBF study found impaired striatal suppression during a prefrontal cognitive activation task, supportive of corticostriatal feedback impairments in schizophrenia (Rubin et al. 1991). Most SPECT studies of the basal ganglia have examined dopamine receptors and methodology for the absolute quantification of neuroreceptors with SPECT is being developed. Studies of striatal D2 receptors have found that poor neuroleptic responders do not differ from responders in their D2 blockade during neuroleptic treatment, that clozapine efficacy does not hinge on similar levels of D2 blockade to those of typical neuroleptics (Pilowsky et al. 1992, 1993), and that D2-receptor occupancy was correlated with extrapyramidal symptoms (Scherer et al. 1994). Similar overall D2-binding was found between controls and neuroleptic-free schizophrenia patients, although there was an absence of the expected age related decline in striatal D2-binding among schizophrenia patients and a left lateralized asymmetry in male patients (Pilowsky et al. 1992). This abnormal lateralization in striatal D2-binding has also been associated with performance on a cognitive choice task (Pedro et al. 1994). At present, a new set of studies in schizophrenia is examining dopamine transporters.

Future

SPECT has great potential as a research tool for schizophrenia, particularly as regards receptor quantification studies. SPECT is more limited than PET for quantitative analysis, but standards for image acquisition, standardized methodology, mathematical modeling of count data, and appropriate radiopharmaceutical ligands are rapidly evolving.

It is likely that SPECT measures in the future may be used to resolve disease pathogenesis, correlate symptoms with regional, cortical and subcortical circuit brain metabolism, and be utilized as an objective measure to determine rational pharmacotherapy for individuals with schizophrenia.

Functional magnetic resonance imaging

Technology

Functional MRI (fMRI) refers to a pair of newer methods of measuring regional cerebral blood flow and blood volume (Cohen et al. 1995; David et al. 1994; Rauch and Renshaw 1995). These methods are the blood-oxygen-level-dependent (BOLD) technique that relies on the paramagnetic properties of deoxyhemoglobin (Ogawa et al. 1990) and the tracer method that uses intravenous bolus injection of a paramagnetic contrast agent (Belliveau et al. 1990). Both methods can be used with or without a high-speed echo-planar imaging device; utilization of such equipment improves temporal resolution of perfusion scanning to the point where individual image planes can be acquired in 50–100 msec and multiple planes can be acquired each second. High-speed acquisition is advantageous both in allowing visualization of regional perfusion changes on a time scale appropriate for some cognitive events, and in shortening total study times, thus improving patient compliance, reducing motion artifact, and increasing cost efficiency.

The BOLD method offers the tradeoff of freedom from the need for the introduction of any foreign agent into the body, even a nonradioactive one, against the inability to quantify perfusion results as yet in terms of absolute blood flow or volume. This inability stems from the lack to date of a detailed mathematical model of the physiologic processes on which the signal depends. The method also suffers from relatively low sensitivity. In one activation paradigm where photic stimulation is known to increase occipital cortical blood flow by 70%, BOLD MR signal was found to increase by only 2%–4% (Rauch and Renshaw 1995; Kwong et al. 1992, Hathout et al. 1994). The tracer method on the other hand does produce large (20%–40%) alterations in MR signal intensity on first pass of the bolus of contrast agent (Rauch and Renshaw 1995).

As with other cerebral perfusion modalities, fMRI measurements are of interest because of the tight coupling of focal changes in neuronal activity to changes in regional blood flow and blood volume. In comparison with the established regional perfusion imaging methods of PET and SPECT, the fMRI methods have several advantages:

1. fMRI allows, in the same imaging session, functional data to be mapped onto a standard MRI structural image for high-resolution localization of regional perfusion results. In practice, coregistration of PET and SPECT images with MRI is commonly done, achieving the same goal, but two scan sessions are required;
2. temporal resolution is greater as noted, particularly with echo-planar methods;
3. spatial resolution is markedly better with fMRI, in the 1 mm range, with potential for further improvement with use of stronger magnets; and
4. fMRI is noninvasive, with BOLD requiring no intravenously injected agent, and neither BOLD nor tracer methods requiring exposure to ionizing radiation.

While these methods hold great promise for application to cerebral perfusion studies in schizophrenia and other psychiatric illness, their use to date remains limited in comparison to the established perfusion imaging modalities.

Applications

The fMRI methods are generally applicable to regional perfusion studies, with expectation of improved temporal and spatial resolution over the established modalities of PET and SPECT. Most studies to date have focused on demonstrating the validity of fMRI, and the context has most often been perceptual, motor, and cognitive activations of cerebral perfusion. However, there have been recent psychiatric applications that include presentation of the above types of activation paradigms to psychiatric patients, as well as investigation of the effects of psychotropic medication on regional cerebral perfusion in these patients.

Findings

Studies aimed at validating the fMRI methods include a number of perceptual and motor studies that show the perfusion activation expected from PET, SPECT, and clinical neuropsychology. In addition, cognitive studies have shown perfusion changes using picture memory recognition (Stern et al. 1993), mental representation of photic stimulation (Le

Bihan et al. 1992), and linguistic task activation (McCarthy et al. 1993); the latter being a replication of an earlier PET study (Peterson et al. 1988). The first psychiatric applications of fMRI have begun to be reported, some of which relate to schizophrenia. Functional MRI has shown decreased activation of the frontal cortex in schizophrenic patients during cognitive task performance (Yurgelun-Todd et al. 1994). The method has revealed other abnormalities of regional brain activation as well, including an increased response to photic stimulation (Renshaw et al. 1994). Functional MRI has been used to investigate changes in response to motor cortex stimulation with use of neuroleptic drugs (Wenz et al. 1993).

Future

The fMRI techniques hold perhaps the best promise for addressing blood flow patterns of fleeting events and for integrating structural and functional abnormalities. The technique has consistently shown a time delay between stimulation and hemodynamic response of 3–8 s as well as a delayed response to cessation of activation, which may enable investigation of the mechanism of hemodynamic response to mental activity itself. Psychiatric phenomena of brief duration such as hallucinations and thought disorder, as well as cognitive responses in psychiatric patients, may be best captured by fMRI methods. Hypothesized relationships of structural and functional deficits in schizophrenia, already studied using conventional MRI of the temporal lobes and established regional perfusion imaging methods applied to prefrontal cortex (Weinberger et al. 1992), may also be best studied by these methods, with their capability for natural integration of structure and function.

Magnetic resonance spectroscopy

Technology

Magnetic resonance spectroscopy (MRS) is a functional modality capable of revealing the concentrations of various compounds in living tissue through characteristic signals emitted by their nuclei when they undergo relaxation from excited magnetic states (Nasrallah and Pettegrew 1995). The principles, equipment, and the scanning environment experienced by study subjects are generally the same as in structural magnetic resonance imaging (MRI). However, it is the fine details of the emission signal, ignored and unnecessary for MRI, that are captured and analyzed in MRS (Shulman et al. 1993). The nuclei most often studied in MRS are hydrogen or proton (^{1}H), lithium (^{7}Li), carbon (^{13}C), fluorine (^{19}F), sodium (^{23}Na), and phosphorus (^{31}P), with the majority of studies focusing on ^{1}H or ^{31}P. In MRI, the signal used for the structural image is derived from hydrogen, and the predominant source of these nuclei in living tissue is water. In proton MRS, the same nuclei provide the signal. However, the fine spectral structure arises from protons in compounds other than water, and the major technical challenge has been to eliminate the dominant water signal while leaving intact the fine structure and its information about other compounds of interest. The spectrum itself is a graph of the amount of energy emitted in the form of radio waves as a function of frequency. It is the form of this graph with its characteristic peaks that enables the identification of compounds of interest. The locations of these peaks depend on the local chemical and electrical environment of the nuclei under study in their compound of interest.

As with MRI, the scans are obtained without the use of ionizing radiation. The major limitation of MRS is its low sensitivity and poor spatial resolution. For ^{1}H MRS the resolution is 1–10 cm^3 and for ^{31}P MRS it is 25–150 cm^3, although these figures improve with greater field strength of the MR magnet.

Applications

MRS can be used to identify endogenous cerebral compounds as well as psychotropic medications such as lithium and certain fluorinated drugs. The list of compounds visible to MRS is determined by the dual requirements that they contain one of the resonant nuclei noted above, and that their concentration be about 1 mM or greater in living tissue. Endogenous brain metabolites are most often studied by using hydrogen and phosphorus nuclei.

^{31}P-MRS can be used to investigate concentrations of high-energy phosphate compounds such as adenosine triphosphate (ATP) and adenosine diphosphate (ADP), as well as adenosine monophosphate (AMP), phosphocreatine, phospholipid metabolites such as phosphomonoesters and phosphodiesters, and inorganic phosphate. Proton MRS can be applied to compounds such as choline, the putative neuronal marker N-acetyl-aspartate, creatine and phosphocreatine, myo-inositol, lactate, and potentially to glutamine, glutamate, and gamma-amino-butyric acid (GABA). The latter three compounds, however, are difficult to distinguish because of nearly coincident spectral peaks at 1.5 Tesla clinical magnet field strength. Under suitable conditions, MRS can be used to probe state-dependent changes in neurochemistry, as in detection of increased brain lactate in hyperventilation (Dager et al. 1995) and in visual (Prichard et al. 1991) and auditory (Singh et al. 1992) stimulation.

MRS also provides a tracer method free of radioisotopes, whereby the resonant isotope of a nucleus that is uncommon in nature, e.g. ^{13}C, is used to label the molecule of the tracer compound. In this way the metabolism of biologic compounds can be studied in vivo free of the use of ionizing radiation. For example, 1-^{13}C-glucose has been used to follow lactate production in brain infarct (Rothman et al. 1991) and to measure the tricarboxylic acid cycle rate (Rothman et al. 1992).

Findings

Proton MRS has begun to reveal neurochemical abnormalities in schizophrenia. The putative neuronal marker N-acetyl-aspartate has been shown in several studies to be reduced in temporal lobes, an indication of reduction in normal neurons (Buckley et al. 1994, Nasrallah et al. 1994, Renshaw et al. 1995, Yurgelun-Todd et al. 1993). Abnormalities detected in right prefrontal white matter in schizophrenia include a decrease in the N-acetyl-aspartate to creatine ratio and an increase in the gamma-aminobutyric acid plus glutamate complex to creatine ratio (Choe et al. 1994), suggesting deficit of neuronal projections, possibly dopaminergic, with compensatory reciprocal upregulation of glutamate. Another study which examined glutamate alone found a decrease in left dorsolateral prefrontal cortex in treatment-naive patients (Stanley et al. 1995).

Pettegrew et al. (1991), using ^{31}P MRS, has shown reduced phosphomonoesters and increased phosphodiesters in schizophrenia in dorsal prefrontal cortex, with similar findings reported by Stanley et al. (1995). Abnormal laterality of the ratio of phosphocreatinine to inorganic phosphate in temporal lobes in schizophrenia has been reported by Calabrese et al. (1992). These results suggest membrane-related abnormalities in schizophrenia that may contribute to the pathophysiology of the illness. Medications whose levels and distribution have proven measurable by MRS are lithium and the fluorinated agents fluphenazine, trifluoperazine, fluoxetine, paroxetine and fluvoxamine (Durst et al. 1990, Komoroski et al. 1991, Renshaw et al. 1992, Renshaw and Wicklund 1988).

Future

It is becoming evident with the broadening scope of applications that MRS permits the opening of a new window on brain chemistry and metabolism, leading to characterization of MRS as "noninvasive biopsy" of the brain. Future developments that will enhance its usefulness include: 1) methods to distinguish neurotransmitter pools from other (general metabolic) pools of brain compounds; 2) separation of overlapping spectral peaks of compounds of great interest in psychiatry, such as glutamate, glutamine, and GABA, an area where some progress is being reported (Stanley et al. 1995, Mason et al. 1994); 3) improved quantification of concentration of compounds (Shungu et al. 1992, Tofts and Wray 1988), and 4) increased spatial resolution, which can be expected with higher field strengths and with implementation of tomographic spectroscopic imaging methods. Because of the safety of repeated scans with MR methods, MRS has potential for longitudinal studies, including studies involving populations at high risk for psychiatric disorders.

CONCLUSION

The past 10 years of progress in brain imaging research in schizophrenia have seen a gradual expansion from structural to metabolic and neurochemical studies as the functional modalities have been introduced and begun to mature. In addition, those findings, both structural (increased ventricular size) and functional (hypofrontality, basal ganglia metabolic abnormalities) that have best withstood the test of replicability have become clearer with the passage of time.

The developments that hold the most promise for future progress include a host of recent technical advances that will facilitate this research area, making the technology more widely available and the approaches wider in scope. SPECT, a more economical and widespread functional modality than PET, is approaching the latter technique in resolution and quantifiability. Together, these two techniques hold promise of increasingly refined understanding of neurotransmitter systems disorder in the illness. The rapid time resolution methods of fMRI and [15]O PET hold promise for improving understanding of fleeting cognitive, perceptual, and other mental events that often also are disordered in schizophrenia.

Coregistration methods for accurate alignment of lower-resolution functional images with sharp structural MRI scans provide finer localization of functional abnormalities, the functional MR methods of MRS and fMRI yield "built-in" coregistration with MRI. The MR methods as a group have no dosage limitations, with their freedom from ionizing radiation, and thus hold promise of a new generation of longitudinal studies both of patients and of high-risk populations. MRS and fMRI are in their infancy but have exciting potential for new and less invasive windows into neurochemistry and function, including in vivo medication studies that may guide future drug design and response monitoring. The information provided by all the MR methods will increase as higher field-strength magnets are introduced. Together, the armamentarium of neuroimaging methods will continue to bring us closer to an understanding of the brain processes and abnormalities in this puzzling and devastating illness. If earlier technical limitations to defining the brain abnormality in schizophrenia contributed to the stigma of the disorder, let us hope that new knowledge about brain function in schizophrenia will herald a next century of knowledge, treatment, and cure.

REFERENCES

Anderso, SE, Damasio H, Jones RD, Tranel D. Wisconsin Card Sorting test performance as a measure of frontal lobe damage. *J Clin Exp Neuropsychol* 13:909–922, 1991.

Andreasen NC. *Brain Imaging Applications in Psychiatry*. Washington, DC: American Psychiatric Press, 1989.

Andreasen NC, Carson R, Diksic M, et al. Workshop on schizophrenia, PET, and dopamine D2 receptors in the human neostriatum. *Schizophr Bull* 14:471–483, 1988.

Andreasen NC, Rezai K, Alliger R, et al. Hypofrontality in neuroleptic-naive patients and in-patients with chronic schizophrenia. *Arch Gen Psychiat* 49:943–958, 1992.

Andreason NC, Arndt S, Swayze II V, Cizadlo T, Flaum M, O'Leary D, Ehrhardt JC, Yuh WTC. Thalamic abnormalities in schizophrenia visualized through magnetic resonance image averaging. *Science* 266:294–297, 1994.

Andreasen NC, Swayze VW, Flaum M, O'Leary D, Alliger R. The neural mechanisms of mental phenomena. In: Andreasen NC, ed. *Schizophrenia from Mind to Molecule*. Washington, DC: American Psychiatric Press, Inc., 1994, pp. 49–91.

Ariel RN, Golden CJ, Berg RA, et al. Regional cerebral blood flow in schizophrenics: Tests using the Xenon-133 inhalation method. *Arch Gen Psychiat* 40:258–263, 1983.

Barta PE, Pearlson GD, Powers RE, Richards SS, Tune LE. Auditory hallucinations and smaller superior temporal lobe gyrus volume in schizophrenia. *Am J Psychiat* 147: 1457–1482, 1990.

Beer HF, Blauenstein PA, Hasler PH, et al. In vitro and in vivo evaluation of ^{123}I-Ro 16-0154: A new imaging agent for SPECT investigations of benzodiazepine receptors. *J Nucl Med* 31:1007–1014, 1990.

Belliveau JW, Rosen BR, Kantor HL, et al. Functional cerebral imaging by susceptibility contrast imaging. *Magn Reson Med* 14:538–546, 1990.

Berman KF, Weinberger DR, Morihisa JM, et al. Regional cerebral blood flow: applications to psychiatry research. In: Morihisa J, ed. *Brain Imaging in Psychiatry*. Washington, DC: American Psychiatric Press, 1984, pp. 41–64.

Berman KF, Zec RF, Weinberger DR. Physiologic dysfunction of dorsolateral prefrontal cortex in schizophrenia, II: Role of neuroleptic treatment, attention, and mental effort. *Arch Gen Psychiat* 43:126–135, 1986.

Besson JAO, Corrigan FM, Cherryman GR, Smith FW. Nuclear magnetic resonance brain imaging in chronic schizophrenia. *Brit J Psychiat* 150:161–163, 1987.

Bilder RM, Wu H, Chakos MH, Bogerts B, Pollack S, Aronowitz J, Ashtari M, Degreef G, Kane JM, Lieberman JA. Cerebral morphometry and clozapine treatment in schizophrenia. *J Clin Psychiat* 55(Suppl B):53–56, 1994.

Boronow J, Pickar D, Ninan RP, et al. Atrophy limited to third ventricle only in chronic schizophrenic patients: reports of a controlled series. *Arch Gen Psychiat* 42:266–271, 1985.

Brier A, Davis OR, Buchanan RW, Moricle LA, Munson RC. Effects of metabolic perturbation on plasma homovanillic acid in schizophrenia. *Arch Gen Psychiatry* 50:541–550, 1993.

Buchsbaum MS, Ingvar DH, Kessler R, et al. Cerebral glucography with positron tomography. *Arch Gen Psychiat* 39:251–259, 1982.

Buchsbaum MS, De Lisi LE, Holcomb HH, et al. Anteroposterior gradients in cerebral glucose use in schizophrenia and affective disorders. *Arch Gen Psychiat* 41:1159–1166, 1984.

Buchsbaum MS. The frontal lobes, basal ganglia, and temporal lobes as sites for schizophrenia. *Schizophr Bull* 16:379–389, 1990.

Buckley PF, Moore C, Long H, et al. [1]H magnetic resonance spectroscopy of the left temporal and frontal lobes in schizophrenia: Clinical neurodevelopmental and cognitive correlates. *Biol Psychiat* 36:792–800, 1994.

Busatto GF, Costa DC, Ell PJ, Pilowsky LS, David AS, Kerwin RW. Regional cerebral blood flow (rCBF) in schizophrenia during verbal memory activation: a 99mTc-HMPAO single photon emission tomography (SPECT) study. *Psychol Med* 24:463–472, 1994.

Bustany P, Henry JF, Rotrou JD, et al. Correlation between clinical state and positron emission tomography measurement of local brain protein synthesis in Alzheimer's dementia, Parkinson's disease, schizophrenia, and gliomas. In: Greitz T, Ingvar DH, Widen L, eds. *The Metabolism of the Human Brain Studied With Positron Emission Tomography*. New York: Raven Press, 1985, pp. 241–251.

Calabrese G, Deicken RF, Fein G, et al. 31-Phosphorus magnetic resonance spectroscopy of the temporal lobes in schizophrenia. *Biol Psychiat* 32:26–32, 1992.

Catafau AM, Parellada E, Lomena FJ, Bernardo M, Pavia J, Ros D, Setoain J, Gonzalez-Monclus E. Prefrontal and temporal blood flow in schizophrenia: Resting and activation technetium-[99m]-HMPAO SPECT patterns in young neuroleptic-naive patients with acute disease. *J Nucl Med* 35:935–941, 1994.

Chabrait H, Levasseur M, Vidailhet M, et al. In-vivo SPECT imaging of D2 receptor with iodine-iodolisuride: Results in supranuclear palsy. *J Nucl Med* 33:1481–1485, 1992.

Chakos MH, Mayerhoff DI, Loebel AD, Alvir JM, Lieberman JA. Incidence and correlates of acute extrapyramidal symptoms in first episode of schizophrenia. *Psychopharmacol Bull* 28:81–86, 1992.

Choe B-Y, Kim K-T, Suh T-S, et al. [1]H magnetic resonance spectroscopy characterization of neuronal dysfunction in drug-naive, chronic schizophrenia. *Acad Radiol* 1:211–216,1994.

Cleghorn JM, Garnett ES, Nahmias C, et al. Increased frontal and reduced parietal glucose metabolism in acute untreated schizophrenia. *Psychiatry Res* 28:119–133, 1989.

Cleghorn JM, Garnett ES, Nahmias C, Brown GM, Kaplan RD, Szechtman H, Szechtman B, Franco S, Dermer SW, Cook P. Regional brain metabolism during auditory hallucinations in chronic schizophrenia. *Brit J Psychiat* 157:562–570, 1990.

Cleghorn JM, Garnett ES, Nahmias C, Firnau G, Brown GM, Kaplan R, Szechtman H, Szechtman B. Increased frontal and reduced parietal glucose metabolism in acute untreated schizophrenia. *Psychiatry Res* 28:119–133, 1989.

Coffman JA, Schwarzkopf SB, Nasrallah HA, Bornstein RA, Olson SC. Temporal lobe asymmetry in schizophrenics by coronal MRI. *Biol Psychiat* 25:97–98, 1989.

Cohen, BM, Renshaw, PF, and Yurgelun-Todd, D Imaging the mind: magnetic resonance spectroscopy and functional brain imaging (editorial). *Am J Psychiat* 152:655–659, 1995.

Cohen RM, Gross M, Nordahl TE, et al. Dysfunction in a prefrontal substrate of sustained attention in schizophrenia. *Life Sci* 40:2031–2039, 1987.

Dager SR, Strauss WL, Marro KI, et al. Proton magnetic resonance spectroscopy investigation of hyperventilation in subjects with panic disorder and comparison subjects. *Am J Psychiat* 152:666–672, 1995.

Daniel DG, Zigun JR, Weinberger DR. Brain imaging in neuropsychiatry. In: Yudofsky SC, Hales RE, eds. *Textbook of Neuropsychiatry*. Washington, DC: American Psychiatric Press, Inc., 1992, pp. 165–186.

David A, Blamire A, Breiler H. Functional magnetic resonance imaging: a new technique with implications for psychology and psychiatry (editorial). *Br J Psychiat* 164:2–7, 1994.

Degreef G, Ashtari M, Bogerts B, Bilder RM, Jody DN, Alvir JMJ, Lieberman JA. Volumes of ventricular system subdivisions measured from magnetic resonance images in first-episode schizophrenic patients. *Arch Gen Psychiat* 49:531–537, 1992.

Degreef G, Ashtari M, Wu H, Borenstein M, Geisler S, Leiberman J. Follow-up MRI study in first-episode schizophrenia. *Schizophr Res* 5:204–205, 1991.

DeLisi LE, Stritzke P, Riordan H, Holan V, Boccio A, Kushner M, McClelland J, Van Eyl O, Anand A. The timing of brain morphological changes in schizophrenia and their relationship to clinical outcome. *Biol Psychiat* 31:241–254, 1992.

DeLisi LE, Hoff AL, Schwartz JE, Shields GW, Halthore SN, Gupta SM, Henn FA, Anand AK. Brain morphology in first episode schizophrenic-like psychotic patients: A quantitative MRI study. *Biol Psychiat* 29:159–175, 1991.

Devous MD. Instrumentation, radiopharmaceuticals, and technical factors. In: *Cerebral SPECT Imaging*. 2nd Ed. New York: Raven Press, 1994, p6.

Durst P, Schuff N, Crocq MA, et al. Non-invasive in vivo detection of a fluorinated neuroleptic in the human brain by 19F NMR spectroscopy. *Psychiat Res* 35:107–114, 1990.

Early TS, Reiman EM, Raichle ME, et al. Left globus pallidus abnormality in never-medicated patients with schizophrenia. *Proc Natl Acad Sci USA*, 84:561–563, 1987.

Farde L, Wiesel FA, Hallidin C, et al. Central D2-dopamine receptor occupancy in schizophrenic patients treated with antipsychotic drugs. *Arch Gen Psychiat* 45:71–76, 1988.

Farde L, Norstrom AL, Wiesel FA, et al. Positron emission tomographic analysis of central D_1 and D_2 dopamine receptor occupancy in patients treated with classical neuroleptics and clozapine: Relation to extrapyramidal side effect. *Arch Gen Psychiat* 49:538–544, 1992.

Farkas T, Wolf AP, Jaeger J, et al. Regional brain glucose metabolism in chronic schizophrenia: A positron emission transaxial tomographic study. *Arch Gen Psychiat* 41:293–300, 1984.

Flaum M, Arndt S, Andreasen NC. The role of gender in studies of ventricle enlargement in schizophrenia: A predominantly male effect. *Am J Psychiat* 147:1327–1332, 1990.

Fowler JS, Wolf AP. Positron emitter-labeled compounds: priorities and problems. In: Phelps ME, Mazziotta JC, Shelbert HR, eds. *Positron Emission Tomography and Autoradiography: Principles and Applications for the Brain and Heart*. New York: Raven Press, 1986, pp. 391–450.

Friedman L, Lys C, Schulz SC. The relationship of structural brain imaging parameters to antipsychotic treatment response: A review. *J Psychiat Neurosci* 17:42–54, 1992.

Goetz KL, Van Kammen DP. Computerized axial tomography scans and subtypes of schizophrenia. A review of the literature. *J Nerv Ment Dis* 174:31–41, 1986.

Gunther W, Petsch R, Steinberg R, Moser E, Streck P, Heller H, Kurtz G, Hippius H. Brain dysfunction during motor activation and corpus callosum alterations in schizophrenia measured by cerebral blood flow and magnetic resonance imaging. *Biol Psychiat* 29:535–555, 1991.

Gur RE, Mozley PD, Shtasel DL, Cannon TD, Gallacher F, Turetsky B, Grossman R, Gur RC. Clinical subtypes of schizophrenia: Differences in brain and CSF volume. *Am J Psychiat* 151:3, 1994.

Gur RE, Pearlson GD. Neuroimaging in schizophrenia research. *Schizophr Bull* 19:337–353, 1993.

Gur RE, Resnick SM, Alavi A, et al. Regional brain function in schizophrenia, I: A positron emission tomography study. *Arch Gen Psychiat* 44:119–125, 1987.

Harvey I, Ron MA, DuBoulay G, Wicks D, Lewis SW, Murray RM. Reduction of cortical volume in schizophrenia on magnetic resonance imaging. *Psychol Med* 23:591–604, 1993.

Hathout GM, Kirlew KAT, So GJK, et al. MR imaging signal response to sustained stimulation in human visual cortex. *J Magn Reson Imaging* 4:537–543, 1994.

Hoffman EJ, Phelps ME. Positron emission tomography: principles and quantitation. In: Phelps ME, Mazziotta JC, Shelbert, HR, eds. *Positron Emission Tomography and Autoradiography: Principles and Applications for the Brain and Heart.* New York: Raven Press, 1986, pp. 237–286.

Holcomb HH, Links J, Smith C, Wong D. Positron emission tomography: Measuring the metabolic and neurochemical characteristics of the living human nervous system. In: Andreasen NC, ed. *Brain Imaging: Applications in Psychiatry.* Washington, DC: American Psychiatric Press, Inc., 1989, pp. 235–370.

Honer WG, Bassett AS, Smith GN, Lapointe JS, Falkai P. Temporal lobe abnormalities in multigenerational families with schizophrenia. *Biol Psychiat* 36:737–743, 1994.

Hoyer S. The abnormally aged brain: Its blood flow and oxidative metabolism. A review—part II. *Arch Gerontol Geriatr* 1:195–207, 1982.

Hoyer S, Oesterreich K. Blood flow and oxidative metabolism of the brain in the course of acute schizophrenia. In: Ingvar DH, Lassen NA, eds. *Cerebral Function, Metabolism and Circulation.* Copenhagen, Munksgaard, 1977.

Huang S-C, Phelps ME. Principles of tracer kinetic modeling in positron emission tomography and autoradiography. In: Phelps ME, Mazziotta JC, Shelbert HR, eds. *Positron Emission Tomography and Autoradiography: Principles and Applications for the Brain and Heart.* New York: Raven Press, 1986, pp. 287–346.

Ingvar D.H. Abnormal distribution of cerebral activity in chronic schizophrenia: A neurophysiological interpretation. Baxter C, Melnechuk T, eds. *Perspectives in Schizophrenia Research.* New York: Raven Press, 1980.

Ingvar DH, Franzen G. Abnormalities of cerebral blood flow distribution in patients with chronic schizophrenia. *Acta Psychiatr Scan* 50:452–462, 1974.

Innis RB. Neuroreceptor imaging with SPECT. *J Clin Psychiatr* 53:11, 1992 (suppl).

Jernigan TL, Sargent T, Pfefferbaum A, et al. 18-Fluorodeoxyglucose PET in schizophrenia. *Psychiat Res* 16:317–329, 1985.

Jernigan TL, Zisook S, Heaton RK, Moranville JT, Hesselink JR, Braff DL. Magnetic resonance imaging abnormalities in lenticular nuclei and cerebral cortex in schizophrenia. *Arch Gen Psychiat* 48:881, 1991.

Johnstone EC, Crow TJ, Frith CD, Husband J, Kreel L. Cerebral ventricular size and cognitive impairment in chronic schizophrenics. *Lancet* 2:924–926, 1976.

Jones PB, Owen MJ, Lewis SW, Murray RM. A case-control study of family history and cerebral cortical abnormalities in schizophrenia. *Acta Psychiatr Scan* 87:6–12, 1993.

Kawasaki Y, Maeda Y, Suzuki M, Urata K, Higashima M, Kiba K, Yamaguchi N, Matsuda H, Hisada K. SPECT analysis of regional cerebral blood flow changes in patients with schizophrenia during the Wisconsin Card Sorting Test. *Schizophr Res* 10:109–116, 1993.

Kemali D, Maj M, Galderisi S, Milici N, Salvati A. Ventricle-to-brain ratio in schizophrenia: A controlled follow-up study. *Biol Psychiat* 28:756–759, 1989.

Kessler RM, Ansari MS, de Paulis T, et al. High affinity dopamine D2 receptor radioligands. Regional rat brain distribution of iodinated benzamides. *J Nucl Med* 32:1593–1600, 1991.

Kety SS, Schmidt CF. The nitrous oxide method for quantitative determination of cerebral blood flow in man: Theory, procedure, and normal values. *J Clin Invest* 27:475–483, 1948.

Kling AS, Metter EJ, Riege WH, et al. Comparison of PET measurement of local brain glucose metabolism and CAT measurement of brain atrophy in chronic schizophrenia and depression. *Am J Psychiat* 143:175–180, 1986.

Komoroski RA, Newton JEO, Karson C, et al. Detection of psychoactive drugs in vivo in humans using 19F NMR spectroscopy. *Biol Psychiat* 29:711–714, 1991.

Kraepelin E. (1919). Dementia Praecox and Paraphrenia. Chapter VIII. *Morbid Anatomy*. Reprinted facsimile, Huntington, NY: Robert E. Krieger Publishing Co. Inc, 1971, pp. 213–223.

Kung HF, Tramposh K, Blau M. A new brain imaging agent: (I123) HIPDM(N-N-N-trimethyl-N'-(2-hydroxy-3-methyl-5-iodobenzyl)-1,3-propanediamine 2 HCl. *J Nucl Med* 24:66–72, 1983.

Kwong KK, Belliveau JW, Chesler DA, et al. Dynamic magnetic resonance imaging of human brain activity during primary sensory stimulation. *Proc Natl Acad Sci USA* 89:5675–5679, 1992.

Leonard J-P, Nowotnik DP, Neirinckx RD. Technetium-99m-d,1-HM-PAO: A new radiopharmaceutical for imaging regional brain perfusion using SPECT—a comparison with ^{123}I-HIPDM. *J Nucl Med* 27:1819–1823, 1986.

Levy DL, Bogerts B, Degreef G, Dorogusker B, Waternaux C, Ashtari M, Jody D, Geisler S, Lieberman JA. Normal eye tracking is associated with abnormal morphology of medial temporal lobe structures in schizophrenia. *Schizophr Res* 8:1–10, 1992.

Lewine RR, Risch SC, Risby E, Stipetic M, Jewart RD, Eccard M, Caudle J, Pollard W. Lateral ventricle-brain ratio and balance between CSF HVA and 5-HIAA in schizophrenia. *Am J Psychiat* 148:1189–1194, 1991.

Lewis SW. Computerized tomography in schizophrenia 15 years on. *Brit J Psychiatr* 157:16–24, 1990.

Liddle PF, Friston KJ, Frith CD, et al. Patterns of cerebral blood flow in schizophrenia. *Br J Psychiat* 160:179–186, 1992.

Mason GF, Pan JW, Ponder SL, et al. Detection of brain glutamate and glutamine in spectroscopic images at 4.1 T. *Mag Res Med* 32:142–145, 1994.

Matthew RJ, Meyer JS, Francis DJ, et al. Regional cerebral blood flow in schizophrenia: a preliminary report. *Am J Psychiat* 138:112–113, 1981.

McCarley RW, Shenton ME, O'Donnell BF, Faux SF, Kikinis R, Nestor PG, Jolesz FA. Auditory P300 abnormalities and left posterior superior temporal gyrus volume reduction in schizophrenia. *Arch Gen Psychiat* 50:190–197, 1993.

McCarthy G, Blamire AM, Rothman DL, et al. Echo-planar magnetic resonance imaging studies of frontal cortex activation during word generation in humans. *Proc Natl Acad Sci USA*, 90:4952–4956, 1993.

McGuire PK, Shah GM, Murray RM. Increased blood flow in Brocca's area during auditory hallucinations in schizophrenia. *Lancet* 342(8873):703–706, 1993.

Mozley PD, Gur RE, Resnick SM, Shtasel DL, Richards J, Kohn M, Grossman R, Herman G, Gur RC. Magnetic resonance imaging in schizophrenia: Relationship with clinical measures. *Schiz Res* 12:195–203, 1994.

Musalek M, Podreka I, Walter H, Suess E, Passweg V, Nutzinger D, Strobl R, Lesch OM. Regional brain function in hallucinations: A study of regional cerebral blood flow with 99m-Tc-HMPAO-SPECT in patients with auditory hallucinations, tactile hallucinations, and normal controls. *Comp Psychiat* 30:99–108, 1989.

Nasrallah HA, Pettegrew JW, eds. *NMR Spectroscopy in Psychiatric Brain Disorders.* Washington, DC: American Psychiatric Press, Inc., 1995.

Nasrallah HA, Olson SC, McCalley-Whitters M, et al. Cerebral ventricular enlargement in schizophrenia: A preliminary follow-up study. *Arch Gen Psychiat* 43:157–159, 1986.

Nasrallah HA, Kuperman SJ, Jacoby CG, et al. Clinical correlates of sulcal widening in schizophrenia. *Psychiat Res* 19:237–242, 1983.

Nasrallah HA, Skinner TE, Schmalbrock P, et al Proton magnetic resonance spectroscopy (^{1}H MRS) of the hippocampal formation in schizophrenia: a pilot study. *Brit J Psychiat* 165:481–485, 1994.

Ogawa S, Lee TM, Kay AR, et al. Brain magnetic resonance imaging with contrast dependent on blood oxygenation. *Proc Natl Acad Sci USA*, 87:9868–9872, 1990.

Owens DGC, Johnstone EC, Crow TJ, et al. Lateral ventricular size in schizophrenia: Relationship to the disease process and its clinical manifestations. *Psychol Med* 14:27–41, 1985.

Pearlson GD, Marsh L. Magnetic resonance imaging in psychiatry. *Rev Psychiat* 12:347, 1993.

Pedro BM, Pilowsky LS, Costa DC, Hemsley DR, et al. Stereotypy, schizophrenia and dopamine D2 receptor binding in the basal ganglia. *Psychol Med* 24:423–429, 1994.

Petersen SE, Fox PT, Posner MI, et al. Positron emission tomographic studies of the cortical anatomy of single-word processing. *Nature* 331:385–389, 1988.

Pettegrew JW, Keshavan MS, Panchalingam K, et al. Alterations in brain high-energy phosphate and membrane phospholipid metabolism in first-episode, drug-naive schizophrenics. *Arch Gen Psychiat* 48:563–568, 1991.

Pfefferbaum A, Lim KO, Rosenbloom M, et al. Brain magnetic resonance imaging: Approaches for investigating schizophrenia. *Schiz Bull* 16:453–476, 1990.

Pfefferbaum A, Zipursky RB, Lim KO, Zatz LM, Stahl SM, Jernigan TL. Computed tomographic evidence for generalized sulcal and ventricular enlargement in schizophrenia. *Arch Gen Psychiat* 45:633–640, 1988.

Pilowsky LS, Costa DC, Ell PJ, Murray RM, et al. Clozapine, single photon emission tomography, and the D2 dopamine receptor blockade hypothesis of schizophrenia. *Lancet* 340(8814):380, 1992.

Pilowsky LS, Costa DC, Ell PJ, Verhoeff NP, et al. Dopamine receptor binding in the basal ganglia of antipsychotic-free schizophrenic patients. A ^{123}I-IBZM single photom emission computerized tomography study. *Br J Psychiatry*, 164(1):16–26, 1994.

Raichle ME. Circulatory and metabolic correlates of brain function in normal humans. In: Montcastle VB, Plum F, eds. *Handbook of Physiology: Section I. The Nervous System*

V. *Higher Functions of the Nervous System, Part 2*. Washington, DC: American Psychological Society, 1987, pp. 643–674.

Rauch SL, Renshaw PF. Clinical neuroimaging in psychiatry. *Harvard Rev Psychiat* 2:297–312, 1995.

Raz N, Raz S, Bigler ED. Ventriculomegaly in schizophrenia: The role of control groups and the perils of dichotomous thinking. *Psychiat Res* 26:245–248, 1988.

Renshaw PF, Yurgelun-Todd DA, Tohen M, et al. Temporal lobe proton magnetic resonance spectroscopy of patients with first-episode psychosis. *Am J Psychiat* 152:444–446, 1995.

Renshaw PF, Yurgelun-Todd DA, Cohen BM. Greater hemodynamic response to photic stimulation in schizophrenic patients: An echo planar MRI study. *Am J Psychiat* 151:1493–1495, 1994.

Renshaw PF, Guimaraes AR, Fava M, et al. Accumulation of fluoxetine and norfluoxetine in human brain during therapeutic administration. *Am J Psychiat* 149:1592–1594, 1992.

Renshaw PF, Wicklund S. In vivo measurement of lithium in humans by nuclear resonance spectroscopy. *Biol Psychiat* 23:465–475, 1988.

Rothman DL, Howseman AM, Graham GD, et al. Localized proton NMR observation of [$3-^{13}$C]lactate in stroke after [$1-^{13}$C]glucose infusion. *Magn Reson Med* 21:302–307, 1991.

Rothman DL, Novotny EJ, Shulman GI, et al. 1H-[^{13}C] NMR measurements of [$4-^{13}$C] glutamate turnover in human brain. *Proc Natl Acad Sci USA* 89:9603–9606, 1992.

Rubin P, Hemmingsen R, Holm S, Moller-Madsen S, Hertel C, Povlsen UJ, Karle A. Relationship between brain structure and function in disorders of the schizophrenic spectrum: single positron emission computerized tomography, computerized tomography and psychopathology of first episodes. *Acta Psychiatr Scand* 90(4):281–289, 1994.

Rubin P, Holm S, Friberg L, Videbech P, Andersen HS, Bendsen BB, Stromso N, Larsen JK, Lassen NA, Hemmingsen R. Altered modulation of prefrontal and subcortical brain activity in newly diagnosed schizophrenia and schizophreniform disorder: A regional cerebral blood flow study. *Arch Gen Psychiat* 48:987–995, 1991.

Sanders JA. Magnetic resonance imaging. In: Orrison WW, Lewine JG, Sanders JA, Hartshorne MF, eds. *Functional Brain Imaging*. New York: C.V. Mosby Co, 1995, p. 145.

Scherer J, Tatsch K, Schwarz J, Oertel WH, et al. D2-dopamine receptor occupancy differs between patients with and without extrapyramidal side effects. *Acta Psychiatr Scan* 90:266–268, 1994.

Seibyl JP, Woods SW, Zoghbi SS, et al. Dynamic SPECT imaging of dopamine D2 receptors in human subjects with ^{123}I-IBZM. *J Nucl Med* 33:1964–1971, 1992.

Seidman LJ, Yurgelun-Todd D, Kremen WS, Woods BT, Goldstein JM, Faraone SV, Tsuang MT. Relationship of prefrontal and temporal lobe MRI measures to neuropsychological performance in chronic schizophrenia. *Biol Psychiat* 35:235–246, 1994.

Shelton R, Weinberger DR. X-ray computed tomographic studies in schizophrenia: A review and synthesis. In: Nasrallah HA, Weinberger DR, eds. *The Neurology of Schizophrenia*. Amsterdam, The Netherlands: Elsevier Publishing, 1986, pp. 157–174.

Shenton ME, Kikinis R, Jolesz FA, Pollak SD, LeMay M, Wible C, Hikama H, Martin J, Metcalf D, Coleman M, McCarley RW. Abnormalities of the left temporal lobe and thought disorder in schizophrenia: A quantitative MRI study. *N Engl J Med* 327:604–612, 1992.

Sheppard G, Gruyzelier J, Manchanda R, et al. 15-O Positron emission tomographic scanning in predominantly never-treated acute schizophrenic patients. *Lancet* 24/31:1448–1452, 1983.

Shulman RG, Blamire AM, Rothman DL, et al. Nuclear magnetic resonance imaging and spectroscopy of human brain function. *Proc Natl Acad Sci USA* 90:3127–3133, 1993.

Shungu DC, Bhujwalla ZM, Li S-J, et al. Determination of absolute phosphate metabolite concentrations in RIF-1 tumors in vivo by ^{31}P-^{1}H-^{2}H NMR spectroscopy using water as an internal intensity reference. *Mag Res Med* 28:105–121, 1992.

Singh M, Kim H, Huang H, et al: Effect of stimulus rate on lactate in the human auditory cortex. *Soc Magn Reson Med Abstr* 11:2146, 1992.

Sokoloff L, Reivich M, Kennedy C, et al. The [^{14}C]deoxyglucose method for the measurement of local cerebral glucose utilization: Theory, procedure, and normal values in the conscious and anesthetized albino rat. *J Neurochem* 28:897–916, 1977.

Stanley JA, Williamson PC, Drost DJ, et al. An in vivo study of the prefrontal cortex of schizophrenic patients at different stages of illness via phosphorus magnetic resonance spectroscopy. *Arch Gen Psychiat* 52:399–406, 1995.

Stanley JA, Drost DJ, Williamson PC, et al. In vivo proton MRS study of glutamate and schizophrenia. In: Nasrallah HA, Pettegrew JW, eds. *NMR Spectroscopy in Psychiatric Brain Disorders*. Washington, DC: American Psychiatric Press, Inc., 1995, pp. 21–44.

Stern C, Jennings P, Sugiura R, et al. Functional MRI studies of memory activation. 31st Annual Meeting of the American Society of Neuroradiology, Vancouver, BC, 1993.

Suddath RL, Christison GW, Torrey EF, Casanova MF, Weinberger DR. Anatomical abnormalities in the brains of monozygotic twins discordant for schizophrenia. *New Engl J Med* 322:789–794, 1990.

Suzuki M, Yuasa S, Minabe Y, Murata M, Kurachi M. Left superior temporal blood flow increases in schizophrenic and schizophreniform patients with auditory hallucination: A longitudinal case study using ^{123}I-IMP SPECT. *Eur Arch Psychiat Clin Neurosci* 242:257–261, 1993.

Szechtman H, Nahmias C, Garnett S, et al. Effect of neuroleptics on altered cerebral glucose metabolism in schizophrenia. *Arch Gen Psychiat* 45:523–532, 1988.

Tamminga CA, Dannals RF, Frost JJ, Wong DF, Wagner HN. Neuroreceptor and neurochemistry studies with positron-emission tomography in psychiatric illness: Promise and progress. In: *Review of Psychiatry* Vol 12. Washington, DC: American Psychiatric Press, 1993, pp 487–510.

Tofts PS, Wray S. A critical assessment of methods of measuring metabolite concentrations by NMR spectroscopy *NMR in Biomed* 1:1–8, 1988.

Tsunoda M, Kurachi M, Yuasa S, Kadono Y, et al. Scanning eye movements in schizophrenic patients. Relationship to clinical symptoms and regional cerebral blood flow using ^{123}I-IMP SPECT. *Schizophr Res* 7:159–168, 1992.

Van Heertum RL, Tikofsky RS. *Cerebral SPECT Imaging*, 2nd Edition, 1995.

Weibel CG, Shenton ME, Hokama H, Kikinis R, Jolesz FA, Metcalf D, McCarley RW. Prefrontal Cortex and Schizophrenia: A Quantitative Magnetic Resonance Imaging Study. *Arch Gen Psychiat* 52:279, 1995.

Weinberger DR, Gibson R, Coppola R, et al. The distribution of cerebral muscarinic acetylcholine receptors in vivo in patients with dementia. *Arch Neurol* 48:169–176, 1991.

Weinberger DR, Berman KF, Suddath R, et al. Evidence of dysfunction of a prefrontal-limbic network in schizophrenia: a magnetic resonance imaging and regional cerebral blood flow study of discordant monozygotic twins. *Am J Psychiat* 149:890–897, 1992.

Weinberger DR, Torrey EF, Neophytides AN, et al. Structural abnormalities in the cerebral cortex of chronic schizophrenic patients. *Arch Gen Psychiat* 36:935–939, 1979.

Wenz F, Schad LR, Baudendistel K, et al. Effects of neuroleptic drugs on signal intensity during motor cortex stimulation: functional MR-imaging performed with a standard 1.5 T clinical imager. *Proc Soc Magn Res Med* 12:1419, 1993.

Wiesel FA, Blomqvist G, Halldin C, Sjogren I, Bjerkenstedt L, Venizelos N, Hagenfeldt L. The transport of tyrosine into the human brain as determined with L-[1-^{11}C]tyrosine and PET. *J Nucl Med* 32:2043–2049, 1991.

Wiesel FA, Wik G, Sjogren I, Blomqvist G, Greitz T, Stone-Elander S. Regional brain glucose metabolism in drug free schizophrenic patients and clinical correlates. *Acta Psychiatr Scand* 76:628–641, 1987.

Wiesel FA, Wik G, Sjogren I, et al. Altered relationships between metabolic rates of glucose in brain regions of schizophrenic patients. *Acta Psychiatr Scand* 76:642–647, 1987.

Wiesel FA, Blomqvist G, Halldin C, et al. The transport of tyrosine into the human brain as determined with L-[1-^{11}C]tyrosine and PET. *J Nucl Med* 32:2043–2049, 1991.

Winchell HS, Baldwin RM, Lin TH. Development of ^{123}I-labeled amines for brain studies: Localization of 123-iodophenylalkylamines in rat brain. *J Nucl Med* 21:940–946, 1980.

Wolkin A, Angrist B, Wolf A, et al. Low frontal glucose utilization in chronic schizophrenia: A replication study. *Am J Psychiat* 145:251–253, 1988.

Wong DF, Wagner HN, Tobe LE, et al. Positron emission tomography reveals elevated D2 dopamine receptors in drug-naive schizophrenics. *Science* 234:1558–1563, 1986.

Woodruff PW, Pearlson GD, Geer MJ, Barta PE, Chilcoat HD. A computerized magnetic resonance imaging study of corpus callosum morphology in schizophrenia. *Psychol Med* 23:45–56, 1993.

Woods BT, Yurgelun-Todd D, Benes FM, Frankenburg FR, Pope HG, McSparren J. Progressive ventricular enlargement in schizophrenia: comparison to bipolar affective disorder and correlation with clinical course. *Biol Psychiat* 27:341–352, 1990.

Yurgelun-Todd DA, Renshaw PF, Gruber SA, et al. Echo planar MRI of schizophrenics and normal controls during word production. *Proc Soc Mag Res* 2:686, 1994.

Yurgelun-Todd DA, Renshaw PF, Waternaux CM, et al. ^{H}MRS of n-acetyl aspartate (NAA) in the temporal lobes in schizophrenia. *Biol Psychiat* 33:45A, 1993.

Zipursky RB, Lim KO, Sullivan EV, Brown BW, Pfefferbaum A. Widespread cerebral gray mattter volume deficits in schizophrenia. *Arch Gen Psychiat* 49:195–205, 1992.

Zipursky RB, Marsh L, Lim KO, DeMent S, Shear PK, Sullivan EV, Murphey GM, Csernansky JG, Pfefferbaum A. Volumetric assessment of temporal lobe structures in schizophrenia. *Biol Psychiat* 35:501–516, 1994.

Recent Progress and Future Directions for Neuropathologic Studies of Schizophrenia

ANDREW J. DWORK, M.D.

While the neuropathologic features of a disease may not directly demonstrate its etiology, they do provide important clues. For example, the senile plaques and neurofibrillary tangles of Alzheimer's disease (AD) have dictated the direction of much productive research into its etiology, which nonetheless remains unknown. Neuropathology also contributes invaluably to nosology, e.g., the multiple illnesses that give rise to dementia are distinguished primarily by their anatomic features. There is thus great reason to hope that elucidation of the neuropathologic features of schizophrenia (or perhaps, schizophrenias) will prove a tremendous advance in our understanding of this disorder. So far, however, despite enthusiastic claims otherwise (e.g., Bloom 1993) the neuropathology of schizophrenia is virtually unknown. Most of the reported findings are unconfirmed, and even if correct, are of such a nonspecific nature that their implications for the etiology of schizophrenia are far from certain.

METHODOLOGIC CONSIDERATIONS

In this chapter, we will review some of the reported neuropathologic abnormalities in schizophrenia and discuss their possible implications for etiologic hypotheses. First, however, we will consider some methodologic factors that apply to postmortem studies in general.

Postmortem examination of a human brain generally involves gross examination and dissection, followed by microscopic examination of selected regions. Histologic sections are routinely stained with hematoxylin and eosin (H&E), which demonstrates cytologic and nuclear morphology, while other staining procedures are applied selectively. Senile plaques and neurofibrillary tangles, for example, are difficult to visualize with H&E but are demonstrated dramatically with silver impregnation techniques (e.g., Bielschowsky stain) or the fluorescent dye, thioflavine S. The specificity and range of staining possibilities have been greatly expanded by the use of immunohistochemistry, which allows the detection of individual antigenic substances, and in situ hybridization, which allows the detection of specific species of messenger RNA.

Most reported neuropathologic abnormalities in schizophrenia are relatively mild, and consist of subtle changes such as shrinkage of individual structures, loss of neurons, gliosis, or cytoarchitectural abnormalities. Quantitative evaluation of such changes is helpful to eliminate subjective differences between observers. Furthermore, these changes are neither sensitive nor specific indicators; they are simply associated statistically with schizophrenia. Often, they cannot be evaluated as present or absent by subjective evaluation of a brain or slide, and thus must be evaluated quantitatively.

Such quantitative measurements are generally of three types: volume, cell density, and total cell number. They are related to a specific anatomic structure, such as the cerebral cortex or the anterior nucleus of the thalamus. Cell density is the number of cells of a given type (usually neurons) per unit volume. Total cell number, equal to cell density multiplied by volume, is the number of such cells in an entire anatomic structure.

Usually, these three-dimensional quantities are estimated from two-dimensional measurements. Volume of a neuroanatomic structure is estimated by measuring its cross-sectional area in several parallel planes. The cross-sectional areas are multiplied by the distance between cross-sections, and the results are summed. Clearly, these measurements must be made throughout the length of a structure, since the relationship between volume and cross-section depends upon the length of the structure and the orientation of the cross-section.

Estimates of neuronal density depend on: 1) accurate distinction of neurons from glia, and 2) a method of counting all neurons with equal probability, regardless of size or shape. Sophisticated yet simple methods are now available for achieving the second condition. These involve examining two adjacent sections and counting a neuron only when it first appears, i.e., when it is present in the second section but not in the first (e.g., see West and Gundersen 1990). Earlier work achieved this condition reasonably well by counting neurons only if the nucleolus was present in the section, since nucleoli vary in size and shape much less than do neuronal cell bodies. The distinction of neurons (especially small neurons) from glia is more problematic. There is no stain that selectively labels all neurons or all glia. The distinction is always somewhat subjective and depends upon cell shape, nuclear morphology, and the presence of Nissl substance. Since large neurons are more easily recognized than small ones, there is always a danger that neuronal shrinkage will be interpreted as neuronal loss.

Artifactual shrinkage or swelling of tissue during fixation or processing will affect measurements of volume and cell density. However, since these effects are inversely proportional, total cell number is not affected.

OVERVIEW OF ANATOMIC ABNORMALITIES

The major postmortem findings that have been reported in schizophrenia are: 1) cytoarchitectural abnormalities, mainly in the entorhinal cortex; 2) abnormal orientation of pyramidal neurons, mainly in the hippocampus; 3) morphometric abnormalities; 4) gliosis, mainly around the cerebral ventricles and aqueduct; and 5) increased frequency of senile degeneration of the type occurring in Alzheimer's disease. In the following sections, we explore the evidence for and against each of these types of abnormality, paying particular attention to the hippocampus and adjacent structures. We also discuss some recent evidence for abnormalities in expression of specific neuronal proteins.

Cytoarchitectural abnormalities

A frequently cited finding in schizophrenia is that of distorted cytoarchitecture in the entorhinal cortex. This was described by Jacob and Beckman (1986), who studied the brains of 64 schizophrenics with an average age of 63 years. Forty-two of these contained equivocal histologic changes in limbic allocortex, not further described. The remaining 20 contained "well-defined" changes, which consisted of pre-α neurons in the pre-β layer, pre-α neurons in bands, rather than clusters, and "poorly developed" pre-β and pri-α layers. The findings described are subtle, and are in fact similar or identical to normal variations in entorhinocortical architecture: in the medial portion of the entorhinal cortex, the pre-α neurons are arranged in a band, rather than in clusters; in transentorhinal cortex, immediately lateral to entorhinal cortex, pre-α neurons are found at the same depth as the pre-β and pre-Γ layers. The widths of the pre-β and pri-α layers vary enormously over small changes in medial or lateral position (Braak 1980). Braak divides the entorhinal cortex into nine cytoarchitectonic regions; superficial clusters of pre-α neurons are seen only in the three most lateral regions, which are adjacent to transentorhinal cortex.

Jacob and Beckman (1986) included ten brains from nonschizophrenic subjects. The findings in these control brains are not clearly stated, although it is noted that these, too, contained pre-α neurons in the pre-β and pre-Γ layers. Thus, it is not clear precisely how the brains of schizophrenics differed from those of controls. Since there is no statement that the neuropathologic evaluations were performed without knowledge of clinical diagnosis, the possibility of a subjective bias is strong.

A possible confound in this study is that all cases with neuropathologic findings of organic brain disease, inflammation, degenerative processes, senile atrophy, or presenile atrophy were excluded. The number of brains so excluded was not stated, nor was there any statement regarding the relative frequency of such cases among schizophrenics and controls. Theoretically, if a neuropathologic change were more common in schizophrenia than in controls, but occurred only in cytoarchitecturally normal entorhinal cortices, exclusion of cases with the change would bias the results towards finding cytoarchitectural abnormalities in the brains of schizophrenics. Furthermore, the study was designed *not* to find organic brain disease in the brains of schizophrenics, while the presence of such disease might be a significant aspect of schizophrenia.

An expansion of this study, apparently including the original cases plus additional ones, was published later by the same authors (Jacob and Beckman 1989). The methodology and findings were similar to those in the original report, but it is unclear why the number of grossly normal cases in the schizophrenia group and the number of histologically equivocal cases in this group are lower than previously. These investigators later described similar alterations in the brains of 4 patients with manic-depressive illness (Beckman and Jacob 1991).

Arnold et al. (1991a) described similar findings in the brains of six leukotomized schizophrenic patients, mean age 47 yr, from the Yakovlev collection, while these abnormalities were not seen in five neurosurgical control brains, including two with frontal leukotomy or lobotomy, nor in 11 other control brains. This study, too, was performed essentially unblinded. Although photomicrographs were examined by two investigators without knowledge of the clinical diagnoses, the photographs were taken by an investigator who was aware of the diagnoses and hence subject to bias in the areas chosen for photography. A recent study by this researcher (Arnold et al. 1995b), described further below, found normal neuronal densities in entorhinal cortex and made no mention of cytoarchitectural abnormality.

The reports of cytoarchitectural abnormality were interpreted by their authors and others as evidence for fetal abnormalities in neuronal migration. This idea was further championed by Akbarian et al. (1993a,b) who found a decrease of ~50% in *numerical densi-*

ties of NADPH-diaphorase positive neurons in frontal and temporal neocortex and in hippocampal grey matter, and increased densities of these neurons in deep white matter underlying neocortex, in a small series of schizophrenic patients. They argued that these neurons, which are relatively resistant to hypoxic or degenerative death, remain as markers of an arrested migration of neurons from germinal matrix to cortex.

While parsimony may favor this explanation, the findings could also be explained by abnormal expression of NADPH-diaphorase activity, which is associated with the expression of nitric oxide synthase, by cortical and subcortical neurons. If neuronal migration were drastically altered, one would expect to find decreased numerical densities of neurons in neocortical grey matter and hippocampus. Although the question of loss of grey matter *volume* and *absolute neuronal number* in various brain regions is quite controversial, there is only one report of decreased *numerical density* of hippocampal neurons in schizophrenia, and the loss is considerably less than 50% (Jeste and Lohr 1989). A loss of 50% of neuronal density would be readily apparent on routine histologic examination, and this has not been reported.

If the migration of neurons were arrested in white matter, as proposed, one might also expect an increased incidence of grey matter heterotopias in the white matter, and this has not been described in schizophrenia. Furthermore, there was no loss of NADPH-diaphorase-positive neurons in entorhinal cortex, the area in which cytoarchitectural abnormalities had been reported (Jacob and Beckman 1986, 1989, Arnold et al. 1991a). Finally, there appears to be a statistical error in the reports of the NADPH-diaphorase studies (Akbarian et al. 1993 a,b), since repeated measures of each variable for individual patients were combined across the cohort and treated as independent measurements. However, at least for the frontal cortex, since variance within individuals is greater than that among individuals, the findings remain statistically significant.

Bruton et al. (1990) examined the brains of 48 schizophrenics (mean age 68 yr) and 56 controls collected from a prospective study (described below). Eight brains of schizophrenics had been eliminated because of leukotomy, epilepsy, multiple sclerosis, and acute infarction. The neuropathologists were blind to the clinical diagnosis and found no evidence of histologic abnormality in entorhinal cortex and no differences between groups with regard to abnormalities of gyration. Compared to the studies cited above, this study had the advantages of prospective design, larger and more appropriate control group, fewer conditions requiring elimination of brains from the original sample, and blindness to clinical diagnosis. While these advantages lend considerable credibility to the negative result, one cannot rule out the possibility that these investigators failed to recognize certain subtle abnormalities that were appreciated by Arnold et al. (1991a) and Jacob and Beckman (1986, 1989). However, if this is the case, the burden is on the latter investigators to define more precisely the criteria for cytoarchitectural abnormality.

In summary, there is little solid evidence for altered neuronal migration in schizophrenia. While an abnormality in cortical cytoarchitecture would strongly support this hypothesis, the studies reporting such an abnormality (Arnold et al. 1991a, Jacob and Beckman 1986, 1989) were vulnerable to unintentional bias, and the findings are contradicted by the study of Bruton et al. (1990), which conversely, could have been subject to a negative bias. We also note that, with one exception (Arnold et al. 1991b), such abnormalities were not mentioned in any of the numerous other studies of the temporal lobe in schizophrenia cited elsewhere in this review.

Disorganization of hippocampal neurons

Another commonly cited finding in the brains of schizophrenics is the disorganization of hippocampal neurons. The technical issues involved in the measurement of neuronal orientation and the statistical analysis of variation in these measurements are complex. For a detailed comparison of the techniques employed in different studies, the reader is referred elsewhere (Dwork, in press; Heckers, in press). The major positive findings are those of Kovelman and Scheibel (1984), who studied the left hippocampi of ten chronic paranoid schizophrenics, average age 50 yr, and eight controls, and of Conrad et al. (1991) who performed a similar study on the right hippocampi of eleven schizophrenics and seven controls, including some of the subjects from the earlier study (Kovelman and Scheibel 1984). In the left hippocampi, the schizophrenics demonstrated a greater variation of neuronal orientation at a middle rostrocaudal level of the interface of CA1 and prosubiculum. Smaller but statistically significant differences were also seen at the CA1/2 and CA2/3 interfaces. In contrast, no differences were seen in posterior hippocampus. However, it appears that blocks at the middle rostrocaudal level were available from only four schizophrenics and five controls, and we do not know how these subgroups compared with regard to age, cause of death, or concurrent neurologic disease. Posterior blocks were present in greater number and presumably represented a greater number of subjects. In the study of right hippocampi, all were sampled at three rostrocaudal levels, and the data from the three levels were pooled for each interface. At all three interfaces, there was greater disorganization in the samples from schizophrenics, but this reached statistical significance only at CA1/2 and CA2/3, where the schizophrenic disorganization numbers were nearly double those at the prosubiculum/CA1 interface.

Several studies produced negative findings. A study of left hippocampi from the Yakovlev collection revealed no difference between schizophrenics treated with lobotomy or leukotomy and neurosurgical controls (Altschuler et al. 1987). This negative finding may be explained by missing sections of anterior hippocampus. Christison et al. (1989), using a more extensive sample from the Yakovlev material and statistics specifically developed for the analysis of spatial orientation, also failed to detect any difference between leukotomized schizophrenics, leukotomized controls, and nonleukotomized controls. Benes et al. (1991) found no difference between schizophrenics and controls in orientation of pyramidal cells at the CA1/prosubiculum interface, but since the examination was limited to a posterior level of hippocampus, this result does not contradict that of Kovelman and Scheibel (1984). Arnold et al. (1995a, b) compared the brains of 14 prospectively examined patients with schizophrenia (mean age at death 71) to those of 10 subjects without neuropsychiatric disorder (mean age 76). No differences were found between the two groups in the variance of pyramidal cell orientation in the central regions (not the interfaces, as in earlier studies) of 4 hippocampal subfields (CA1-4), subiculum, or 3 layers of entorhinal cortex.

In aggregate, the results are unconvincing, but methodological differences preclude direct comparisons among the studies. When considering the positive results, it should be remembered that hippocampal anatomy, especially at the rostral end of the hippocampus, is exquisitely sensitive to rostrocaudal position. When the number of cases in each group is small, the possibility exists that a few brains from one group, but not from the other, were randomly sampled at a level with a normally higher variance of orientation. Such a result would be consistent with the observation in one positive study (Conrad et al. 1991) that most of the dissociation measures from the brains of schizophrenics were similar to those from controls, but a small portion were considerably higher.

Even if abnormal orientation of hippocampal pyramidal cells were confirmed, its significance would be obscure. While this could represent a form of cortical dysplasia, there are other possibilities. For example, an acquired abnormality in dendritic morphology, either due to a primary abnormality of hippocampal neurons or secondary to altered afferent influences, could also affect neuronal orientation. Neuronal orientation could also be altered by changes in the neural or glial processes that form the adjacent neuropil. Thus, while confirmation of abnormal neuronal orientation would provide important evidence for a localized abnormality in schizophrenia, it would be difficult to determine when this abnormality developed, and much additional work would be required to determine whether the abnormality represented a cause or a result of schizophrenia.

Alterations of volume, neuronal number, and neuronal size

These studies have generally concentrated on the whole brain, the lateral ventricles, the frontal lobe, or the various components of the temporal lobe with particular attention to the hippocampal formation. We note at the outset that these studies have yielded widely differing results. Some of these differences are probably the result of different populations or different inclusion criteria, while others may be the result of methodologic differences. These factors are reviewed in detail elsewhere (Dwork, in press; Heckers, in press).

Total brain weight in schizophrenia was found in two studies (Brown et al. 1986, Pakkenberg 1987) to be reduced by up to 8%, while other studies (Arnold et al. 1995a, Jeste and Lohr 1989, Bogerts et al. 1990) showed no difference from controls. Another study (Crowe et al. 1989, Bruton et al. 1990) found a reduction of 4.5% in the weight of fixed brains, but no differences from controls in the weight of fresh brains. In the study by Pakkenberg (1987), reductions were also found in hemispheric volume and cerebral cortical volume. The measurements were flawlessly performed by a renowned pioneer in the field of stereology, but the medical exclusion criteria for controls were considerably more rigorous than for schizophrenics: CNS infection, dementia, coma for more than 24 hours before death, or death from cancer would exclude an individual from the control group, but not from the schizophrenia group. Heckers et al. (1990a) applied modern stereologic techniques, with individualized adjustments for shrinkage, to the brains of 20 schizophrenics, average age 64, and 20 controls matched for age and sex. Eight brains of schizophrenics and seven of controls had been eliminated because of histopathologic changes; two brains with "incipient senile changes" were not excluded. Hemispheric volume did not differ between the two groups.

Diminished volume of hippocampus or one or more of its subfields was reported by Falkai and Bogerts (1986), Jeste and Lohr (1989), and Bogerts et al. (1990) but denied by Heckers et al. (1990a, 1991) and by Benes et al. (1991b). Pyramidal cell density in one or more hippocampal subfields was reported by Jeste and Lohr (1989) to be reduced but by Falkai and Bogerts (1986), Heckers et al. (1991) and Arnold et al. (1995b) to be normal, while a reduction total pyramidal cell number in one or more hippocampal subfields was reported by Falkai and Bogerts (1986) but not by Heckers et al. (1991) or Benes et al. (1991b). A reduction in the size of hippocampal pyramidal cells was described by Benes et al. (1991b) and Arnold et al. (1995b) but not by Christison et al. (1989). Measurements of these parameters in entorhinal cortex or parahippocampal gyrus (Brown et al. 1986, Colter et al. 1987; Falkai et al. 1988; Heckers et al. 1990b; Arnold et al. 1995b) and in prefrontal cortex (Benes et al. 1991a; Colon et al. 1972; Akbarian et al. 1995) are similarly contradictory.

The results for lateral ventricular size are more consistent. Brown et al. (1986) compared 41 brains of schizophrenics, mean age 67 yr, to 35 from patients with affective disorders, mean age 68 yr. Cross-sectional area of the temporal horn of the lateral ventricle, at the level of the foramen of Monro, was approximately twice as large in the brains of the schizophrenics as in the brains of the patients with affective disorders. Another large study was reported by Crow et al. (1989) and Bruton et al. (1990). The subjects were 56 schizophrenics, mean age 72 yr, and 56 age- and sex-matched controls. The schizophrenics apparently represent all autopsies of schizophrenics meeting certain clinical diagnostic criteria over an 8-year period at two large British psychiatric hospitals.

One hemisphere, randomly chosen, was examined from each brain. All morphologic evaluations were performed blind to clinical diagnosis. Qualitative, naked-eye assessment of lateral ventricular size (excluding eight schizophrenic patients with psychosurgery or severe neurologic disease subsequent to the diagnosis of schizophrenia) revealed a trend toward larger lateral ventricles in the brains of schizophrenics (Bruton et al. 1990). Ventricular size was also examined by filling the lateral ventricle with radio-opaque material and measuring area on a lateral view X-ray (Crow et al. 1989). The projected area of the left temporal horn was twice as large in the schizophrenics as in the controls; there was no difference between groups on the right side. These differences persisted when applied to a "purified" sample of schizophrenics and controls whose brains showed no evidence of significant Alzheimer-type change, cerebrovascular disease, or focal pathology.

Heckers et al. (1990a) found a nonsignificant trend towards larger lateral ventricles in the brains of schizophrenics (24% larger on left, 17% on right), with similar results for the anterior and posterior horns bilaterally and the left temporal horn, but not the right. When the sample was restricted to paranoid schizophrenics (11 patients) and their age- and sex-matched controls, the lateral ventricles of the brains of schizophrenics were significantly larger on the left side, but not on the right. In the Pakkenberg (1987) study cited above, ventricular volume was 33% larger in schizophrenia. While this difference could be the result of selection criteria (see above), two findings of this study suggest a true abnormality in ventricular size in schizophrenia: 1) Among controls, ventricles were significantly larger in the subgroup above age 65, while this was not the case for the schizophrenics; 2) ventricles of Type II schizophrenics were significantly larger than those of Type I schizophrenics. No difference was found between paranoid and nonparanoid schizophrenics.

Ventricular enlargement, at least of the left temporal horn, appears to be a confirmed finding in schizophrenia. The finding of Pakkenberg (1987) strongly suggests that this enlargement occurs early in the course of the disease and then remains static. Ventricular enlargement can be caused by cerebral atrophy or hypoplasia, obstruction to the flow of cerebrospinal fluid, or increased production of cerebrospinal fluid. The question of periaqueductal gliosis in schizophrenia is controversial (see below); if present, this could be interpreted as evidence for a prior infection with transient aqueductal stenosis. An interesting line of investigation, that could be pursued with existing data, would be to look for correlations between ventricular size and periaqueductal gliosis. An argument against aqueductal stenosis as the cause of ventricular enlargement in schizophrenia is the absence of reports of persistent aqueductal stenosis and hydrocephalus in schizophrenia, but it is conceivable that the neurologic complications of congenital or early hydrocephalus mask the signs and symptoms of schizo-phrenia, prevent their expression, or result in death at a young age, before schizophrenia would become manifest. While it seems most likely that ventricular enlargement in schizo-phrenia reflects a loss of brain volume, rather than hydrocephalus, there is clearly no agree-ment regarding the location or cause of such a loss of tissue.

Gliosis

Nieto and Escobar (1972) employed Hortega's lithium-silver carbonate impregnation for the demonstration of glia in 10 brains of chronically hospitalized schizophrenics, aged 29–52, and three nonpsychiatric controls, aged 31–43. In "all of the cases of schizophrenia that can be considered as uncomplicated by other diseases," there was a diffuse gliosis that involved the mesencephalic reticular formation, hypothalamus, medial and anterior nuclei of the thal-amus, and periaqueductal grey matter. In four cases, there was a marked gliosis of the hip-pocampal formation. Nissl and myelin stains revealed no abnormalities. The report does not include many details crucial to its interpretation, such as method of selection of cases and the method of comparison to controls. The authors conclude, "The gliosis observed in these diencephalic structures either may or may not have a pathologic significance."

From a collection of about 60 patients with a clinical diagnosis of schizophrenia who died and were autopsied at St. Elizabeths Hospital, Washington, DC, between 1956 and 1963, Stevens (1982) reviewed the brains of all patients who were under age 50, fulfilled ICD criteria for schizophrenia, were free of vascular or infectious diseases that might pro-duce diffuse cerebral gliosis, and on whom adequate pathologic material was available. This group consisted of 28 patients with a mean age of 44 yr. Controls consisted of a group of 28 patients, from the same hospital, with nonschizophrenic neuropsychiatric disorders (mostly neurologic diseases with well-established neuropathologic findings), and a third group of cases free of neurologic or psychiatric disease, three from the Yakovlev collec-tion and eighteen from another hospital. The mean ages of these control groups were 46 and 37, respectively; the nonpsychiatric controls included two children, aged 10 and 12 years. Except for the three cases from the Yakovlev collection, Holzer stain was performed on all sections. This stain demonstrates very clearly the cytoplasm and processes of reac-tive astrocytes. Slides were examined blind to clinical diagnosis. Gliosis was observed in 18 cases. Midbrain tegmentum was involved in 12 cases. Subependymal region, bed nu-cleus of stria terminalis, hypothalamus, amygdala, substantia innominata, and hippocam-pus were each involved in 9–16 cases.

In the neuropsychiatric controls, gliosis was felt to be more specifically related to the ex-pected lesions, and with the exception of one case, the nonpsychiatric controls "did not show the degree or distribution of gliosis observed in the schizophrenic or psychiatric control ma-terial." One difficulty in interpreting this study is that the results for the two control groups are given only in descriptive terms. For example, the authors do not specify how many of the neuropsychiatric controls showed periaqueductal gliosis, nor what the differences in de-gree of gliosis were between the nonpsychiatric controls and the schizophrenics. It is also not clear how many of the brains of schizophrenics had focal lesions in the basal ganglia; there are a total of 14 instances of neuronal loss or infarction, but these could have occurred in as few brains as 4 or as many as 14. As pointed out by Bruton et al. (1990), some of the gliosis observed in the brains of schizophrenics could have been secondary to these lesions.

Furthermore, although cases were examined blind to clinical diagnosis, it is not clear whether all sections from a single case were given the same code number, in which case evaluation of one section could be subjectively influenced by focal pathology in another from the same brain. Finally, although the presence of gliosis in the brains of schizophrenics did not appear to correlate with age, the lack of gliosis in the nonpsychiatric control group could nonetheless be related to the younger age of the subjects.

Bruton et al. (1990) found increased gliosis in the cerebral cortex, white matter, and periventricular structures of unselected schizophrenics compared to controls. However, focal lesions were present in 44% of the brains of schizophrenics and 21% of the controls; when these cases were eliminated, there was no evidence of increased gliosis in the brains of schizophrenics. Jellinger (1985) found brain stem gliosis as the *major* neuropathologic finding in the brains of 6 of 100 psychotic patients; 47 were normal, but the remainder had other neuropathologic diagnoses, and some of these presumably had brain stem gliosis as well.

Roberts et al. (1986) evaluated gliosis by densitometric measurements of immunoreactivity for glial fibrillary acidic protein, an intermediate filament protein of astrocytes. No difference was found between controls and schizophrenics. It is possible that the measurement employed in this study, while capable of detecting gliosis in the striatum of Huntington's chorea, which can be striking, was not sufficiently sensitive to detect a lesser degree of gliosis that might occur in schizophrenia. Also, while both Holzer and GFAP stains are sensitive for active gliosis, the Holzer stain is probably better for evaluating long-standing, static gliosis. There was no comment regarding focal lesions in these brains.

These studies suggest that if there is increased gliosis in the brains of schizophrenics, it is secondary to more frequent presence of focal lesions. This points to the importance of studying the frequency of conventional neuropathologic lesions in the brains of schizophrenics, rather than eliminating such cases from studies in order to find a "pure" neuropathologic lesion of schizophrenia. Jellinger (1985) remarked on the frequent presence of a variety of neuropathologic lesions in the brains of schizophrenics, and several studies report increased senile degeneration (see below).

Of interest in this regard are four individuals in the report of Stevens (1982), who were originally diagnosed with schizophrenia but switched to the mentally ill nonschizophrenic group after neuropathologic examination. These were a 48–year-old with cerebral sarcoidosis, a 47-year-old with a colloid cyst of the third ventricle and consequent hydrocephalus, a 30-year-old with a diffusely infiltrating malignant astrocytoma, and a patient with AD, whom we cannot identify in the list of control subjects. One possibility is that this is a remarkably high incidence of florid neuropathologic conditions in the brains of young schizophrenics (i.e., excluding the patient with Alzheimer's disease, of 31 young individuals with schizophrenia, at least four had infarcts in the basal ganglia and three had other major neuropathologic conditions).

The other possibility, of equal interest and evidently favored by Stevens, is that colloid cyst, glioma, sarcoidosis, and Alzheimer's disease may all mimic schizophrenia. Perhaps coincidentally, each of these conditions can be associated with enlarged cerebral ventricles.

Senile degeneration

The coexistence of AD with schizophrenia is controversial. This is in part because of changing neuropathologic criteria for AD. AD is characterized by senile plaques and neurofibrillary tangles, but these occur in normal aging as well (see, for example, Dickson et al. 1992). Although standards for the neuropathologic diagnosis of AD have been recommended (Khachaturian 1985, Mirra et al. 1991), these contain ambiguities and depend in part on clinical criteria. Normal levels of senile degeneration in the general population are not well established. Thus, the pathologist attempting to study senile degeneration in schizophrenia must decide whether the observed changes differ from those that would be found in the general population, which includes some individuals with AD.

Prohovnik et al. (1993) reviewed the reports from all 1,046 neuropathologic examinations performed at New York State Psychiatric Institute from 1978 through 1987. After exclusion of 6 cases for missing data and 45 of patients who died before age 50, there remained 544 with a clinical diagnosis of schizophrenia (mean age, 78 yr), 258 with a clinical diagnosis (as reported to the neuropathologist—usually the chart diagnosis) of dementia (mean age, 77 yr) and 47 with a diagnosis of affective disorder (mean age, 75 yr). The primary analysis was based on the original neuropathologic diagnoses, which were not blind to clinical diagnosis. A pathologic diagnosis of AD had been made in 51% of the brains of dements, 28% of the brains of schizophrenics, and 15% of the brains of patients with affective disorder. When the data were stratified by age, the frequency of AD diagnoses was constant at ~50% for dements, but increased steadily among schizophrenics from ~3% in the sixth decade to ~50% in the ninth decade.

The original neuropathologic diagnoses had been based largely on H&E-stained sections, without reference to standardized research criteria, such as those of Khachaturian (1985) and the Consortium to Establish a Registry for AD (Mirra et al. 1991), which at the time of the original neuropathologic examinations did not exist. The investigators then reevaluated a small sample of the original cases, blind to clinical diagnosis, applying stringent diagnostic criteria to sections stained with Bielschowsky silver stain, thioflavine S stain, and immunohistochemistry with Alz 50. Eighty-two percent of the original AD diagnoses were confirmed for dementia patients, but only 33% were confirmed as definite AD (50% definite or possible) for schizophrenia patients. All cases originally thought free of AD were confirmed as such. If one obtains a conservative estimate of AD in schizophrenia by multiplying the number of original neuropathologic AD diagnoses in schizophrenics by 0.33, the rates obtained are greater than population estimates based on living people until the ninth decade, when the difference disappears. Similar results are obtained by comparing the total number of original neuropathologic diagnoses of AD, many of which were based primarily on senile degeneration in the hippocampal formation, to the rates of "many" neurofibrillary tangles and senile plaques in the temporal lobes of an unselected autopsy series (Miller et al. 1984). Thus, it appears that chronically institutionalized schizophrenics dying in the sixth through eighth decades probably have a greater than normal frequency of significant neurofibrillary pathology in the hippocampal formation, and possibly also an elevated frequency of neocortical findings consistent with AD.

The strength of this study is in the unusually large number of schizophrenic subjects. Weaknesses include minimal and possibly unreliable clinical information, unblinded and loosely defined original pathological diagnoses of which only a small subsample was tested more rigorously, and a possible bias in the selection of patients for autopsy. The possibility has also been suggested that hospitalized schizophrenics may have AD because AD plus schizophrenia could prevent discharge. This explanation seems unlikely, however, since most of the patients had remained in the hospital continuously or nearly so since the fourth or fifth decade of life. If AD were causing these patients to remain hospitalized, the rate should already be quite high in patients dying in the fifth decade, and the dramatic age-associated increase would probably not be seen. It is not unlikely, however, that these patients represent an unusually pernicious form of schizophrenia. This is one possible explanation for the finding by Wisniewski et al. (1994) of increased neurofibrillary pathology in the brains of elderly schizophrenic patients treated with neuroleptics but not in those of elderly schizophrenics who died before the introduction of these drugs. While the pathologic changes may be a result of the drugs, it is also possible that the discharge of patients who responded well to neuroleptics caused the inpatient population to become enriched in patients whose underlying condition was less responsive to neuroleptics.

Buhl and Bojsen-Møller (1988) reviewed the brains from 100 consecutive deaths in a psychiatric department. Neuropathologic criteria for AD were appropriately stringent, requiring neurofibrillary tangles in neocortex and hippocampus and large numbers of neuritic senile plaques in frontal and temporal neocortex. The group included 23 schizophrenics, mean age 80, of whom 8 (35%) fulfilled neuropathologic criteria for AD. None of 10 age-matched controls without clinical evidence of neurologic or psychiatric disease showed any senile plaques or significant numbers of hippocampal neurofibrillary tangles. Jellinger (1985) reviewed two autopsy series of 101 and 100 psychotic patients. AD or senile dementia of the Alzheimer type (SDAT) was present in 38 from the former series and 19 from the latter. The three largest groups in the latter series were paranoid schizophrenics, n = 22, median age 62, AD/SDAT frequency 14%; schizophrenia defect state, n = 38, median age 67, 21% AD/SDAT; and paranoid psychosis, n = 16, median age 76, 38% AD/SDAT.

Bruton et al. (1990) found senile plaques in 40% of the brains of schizophrenics and neurofibrillary tangles in 33%; the results in the control group were virtually identical. In a study of ten intellectually impaired and seven intellectually intact schizophrenics (mean ages 84 and 62, respectively) and seven control subjects, El-Mallakh et al. (1991), found no difference between either schizophrenic group and the controls in terms of cell density in the nucleus basalis of Meynert, frontal plaque density, or hippocampal plaque density. There was a statistically significant increase in hippocampal plaques in the brains of intellectually impaired schizophrenics compared to intellectually intact schizophrenics, but this could be explained by the 22 year age difference between the groups. Casanova et al. (1993) found very few senile plaques or neurofibrillary tangles in the brains of 10 cognitively impaired schizophrenics, mean age 66. Purohit et al. (1993) examined the brains of 13 cognitively impaired schizophrenics, mean age 79. No brain had sufficient evidence of senile degeneration to warrant a diagnosis of AD. There were no neocortical neurofibrillary tangles, and neocortical senile plaque densities were similar to those in a group of 12 nondemented, nonschizophrenic controls. Moderate numbers of hippocampal neurofibrillary tangles were present in 4 schizophrenics (30%); comparison to controls is not given. There was no correlation between senile degenerative changes and degree of cognitive impairment. Arnold et al. (1994) found AD in one brain from a group of ten elderly patients with dementia and schizophrenia. In the remaining brains and in those of five nondemented schizophrenics, plaque and tangle counts did not differ from those in a group of five elderly, nondemented, nonschizophrenic controls. In eight of the ten brains from patients with dementia and schizophrenia, no neuropathologic basis for dementia was identified.

Until large studies with quantitation of senile degeneration are completed, it will remain unclear whether the true prevalence of AD is elevated among schizophrenics (or among chronically institutionalized patients with schizophrenia). For example, an observed rate of 5% among controls and 10% among schizophrenics would require over 200 subjects in each group to be statistically significant ($\chi^2 = 3.841$, df = 1, $p < 0.05$). It is nonetheless clear from all of the studies that many elderly patients with schizophrenia are demented but lack AD. Finding the substrate of this dementia is another challenge for neuropathology.

Neuronal proteins

Arnold et al. (1991b), in a series of six schizophrenics, mean age 78, found a pronounced loss of neuronal immunoreactivity for the microtubule-associated proteins MAP2 and MAP5 in the subiculum of five subjects and the entorhinal cortex of four, compared to six normal control subjects. No changes were found in tau, high or middle molecular wight neurofilament protein, or α- or β-tubulin. We initially reported a partial replication of this finding (Rosoklija et al. 1995) in a sample consisting of 15 unselected schizophrenics, mean age 73, 14 unselected psychiatric controls, mean age 78, and 6 brains from nonpsychiatric patients without neuropathologic abnormalities, mean age 51. Psychiatric diagnoses were determined by review of clinical records (Keilp et al. in press).

Recently, we have enlarged this study to include 51 cases of schizophrenia, 11 of mood disorder, 18 of dementia, 15 of other psychiatric conditions, and 14 nonpsychiatric controls. In each group, except for the nonpsychiatric controls, approximately one-third of subjects showed dramatic loss of MAP2 immunoreactivity in subiculum and CA1, as compared to CA4, but there were also a substantial number of psychiatric cases with relatively high levels of subicular MAP2. By contrast, there were no dramatic differences between subicular and CA4 MAP2 in any of the nonpsychiatric control cases (Rosoklija et al., in press). It thus appears that abnormal levels of subicular MAP2 are common in schizophrenia but also in other psychiatric abnormalities. Both antemortem (reviewed in Johnson and Jope 1992) and postmortem (Schwab et al. 1994) factors have been reported to affect MAP2 immunoreactivity, but we have detected no effect of these factors on our results.

Akbarian et al. (1995) detected, by in situ hybridization for glutamic acid decarboxylase (GAD), a dramatic decrease in the density of GABA-ergic neurons in the prefrontal cortices of a group of 10 schizophrenics, with no change in the numerical density of cortical neurons. The difference was statistically significant. However, the sensitivity and specificity of this deficit are not indicated.

Both the MAP2 results and the GAD results are intriguing, but both may represent secondary abnormalities. For example, it has recently been demonstrated that in the rat, depletion of serotonin by systemic administration of a tryptophan hydroxylase inhibitor results in a loss of MAP2 immunoreactivity throughout the brain, but most markedly in the subiculum and the CA1 region of the hippocampus (Whitaker-Azmatia et al. 1995). It is easy to believe that the loss of subicular MAP2 in the brains of some individuals with schizophrenia is the result of a diffuse or localized alteration in neurotransmitters. However, whether the alteration is primary or secondary, it may represent an alteration in structure and function of subicular dendrites. Since the subicular neurons give rise to the major outflow tracts of the hippocampus, functional abnormalities in their dendrites could well contribute to cognitive impairment as well as other features of schizophrenia. The loss of prefrontal GAD mRNA is likely to be a result, rather than a cause, of diminished prefrontal activity in schizophrenia. Both of these studies need to be expanded in two ways: other re-

74

gions of the brain must be studied, and additional brains must be added to the studies. Of particular importance in expanded studies, the clinical and neuropathologic features of the subjects must be well characterized in order to permit the detection of subgroups in which the abnormalities may be more consistently present or absent.

FUTURE STUDIES

It appears likely that postmortem studies of schizophrenia will go in the direction of examining specific neuronal proteins. The possibilities for such studies are unlimited, and careful consideration must be given to the choices of antibodies and probes. The examination of specific markers may also indicate promising avenues for the use of conventional stains; for example, the abnormalities of subicular MAP2 suggest that Golgi staining might be of interest.

Undoubtedly, morphometric studies will continue. To ensure comparability of different morphometric studies, these should employ stereologic techniques for the unbiased estimate of total neuronal number in structures of interest.

Regardless of the specific direction of a study of schizophrenia, certain general considerations apply. Elimination of cases because of classical neuropathologic findings seems unwise. These findings are very common. Jellinger (1985) found structural abnormalities in 45% of the brains of schizophrenics. Brown et al. (1986), from 70 schizophrenics who met appropriate diagnostic criteria and had not had leukotomy, eliminated 23 (33%) from their study because of pathologic findings of senile or vascular disease. The only way to determine whether a neuropathologic abnormality is related to schizophrenia is to include all cases, rather than to let the results dictate the definition of the experimental group. Of course, when examining other abnormalities (such as alterations in specific proteins), it is important to identify potentially confounding variables, and conventional neuropathologic abnormalities should be treated as such.

Large studies are therefore desirable, but many studies are of necessity small, and their number is likely to increase. To compare different studies or to combine data across studies, it would be helpful to have standardized clinical and pathological evaluations that were included in published reports. Until a consensus on such evaluations is reached, it would be helpful to include as much such information as possible. This approach may lead not only to the determination of biologic factors important in schizophrenia, but also to an improved nosology of this condition.

REFERENCES

Akbarian S, Bunney WE Jr, Potkin SG, Wigal SB, Hagman JO, Sandman CA, Jones EG. Altered distribution of nicotinamide-adenine dinucleotide phosphate-diaphorase cells in frontal lobe of schizophrenics implies disturbances of cortical development. *Arch Gen Psychiat* 50:169–177, 1993a.

Akbarian S, Viñuela A, Kim JJ, Potkin SG, Bunney WE Jr, Jones EC. Distorted distribution of nicotinamide-adenine dinucleotide phosphate-diaphorase neurons in temporal lobe of schizophrenics implies anomalous cortical development. *Arch Gen Psychiat* 50:178–187, 1993b.

Akbarian S, Kim JJ, Potkin SG, Hagman JO, Tafazzoli A, Bunney WE Jr, Jones EG. Gene expression for glutamic acid decarboxylase is reduced without loss of neurons in prefrontal cortex of schizophrenics. *Arch Gen Psychiat* 52:258–266, 1995.

Altshuler LL, Conrad A, Kovelman JA, Scheibel A. Hippocampal pyramidal cell orientation in schizophrenia. A controlled neurohistologic study of the Yakovlev collection. *Arch Gen Psychiat* 44:1094–1098, 1987.

Arnold SE, Franz BR, Gur RC, Gur RE, Shapiro RM, Moberg PJ, Trojanowski JQ. Smaller neuron size in schizophrenia in hippocampal subfields that mediate cortical-hippocampal interactions. *Am J Psychiat* 152:738–748, 1995b.

Arnold SE, Franz BR, Trojanowski JQ. Elderly patients with schizophrenia exhibit infrequent neurodegenerative lesions. *Neurobiol Aging* 15:299–303, 1994.

Arnold SE, Gur RE, Shapiro RM, Fisher KR, Moberg PJ, Gibney MR, Gur RC, Blackwell P, Trojanowski JQ. Prospective clinicopathologic studies of schizophrenia: Accrual and assessment of patients. *Am J Psychiat* 152:731–737, 1995a.

Arnold SE, Hyman BT, Van Hoesen GW, Damaslo AR. Some cytoarchitectural abnormalities of the entorhinal cortex in schizophrenia. *Arch Gen Psychiat* 48:625–632, 1991a.

Arnold SE, Lee VA-Y, Gur RE, Trojanowski JQ. Abnormal expression of two microtubule-associated proteins (MAP2 and MAP5) in specific subfields of the hippocampal formation in schizophrenia. *Proc Natl Acad Sci USA* 88:10850–10854, 1991b.

Beckmann H, Jakob H. Prenatal disturbances of nerve cell migration in the entorhinal region: a common vulnerability factor in functional psychoses? *J Neural Trans* 84:155–164, 1991.

Benes FM, McSparren J, SanGiovanni JP, Vincent SL. Deficits in small interneurons in cingulate cortex of schizophrenic and schizoaffective patients. *Arch Gen Psychiat* 48:996–1001, 1991a.

Benes FM, Sorensen I, Bird ED. Reduced neuronal size in posterior hippocampus of schizophrenic patients. *Schizoph Bull* 17:597–608, 1991b.

Bloom FE. Advancing a neurodevelopmental origin for schizophrenia. *Arch Gen Psychiat* 50:224–227, 1993.

Bogerts B, Falkai P, Haupts M, Greve B, Ernst S, Tapernon-Franz U, Heinzmann U. Postmortem volume measurements of limbic system and basal ganglia structures in chronic schizophrenics. Initial results from a new brain collection. *Schiz Res* 3:295–301, 1990.

Braak H. *Architectonics of the Human Telencephalic Cortex*. New York: Springer-Verlag, 1980.

Brown R, Colter N, Corsellis JAN, Crow TJ, Frith CD, Jagoe R, Johnstone EC, Marsh L. Postmortem evidence of structural brain changes in schizophrenia. Differences in brain weight, temporal horn area, and parahippocampal gyrus compared with affective disorder. *Arch Gen Psychiat* 43:36–42, 1986.

Bruton CJ, Crow TJ, Frith CD, Johnstone EC, Owens DGC, Roberts GW. Schizophrenia and the brain: A prospective clinico-neuropathological study. *Psychol Med* 20:285–304, 1990.

Buhl L, Bojsen-Møller M. Frequency of Alzheimer's disease in a postmortem study of psychiatric patients. *Dan Med Bull* 35:288–290, 1988.

Casanova MF, Carosella NW, Gold JM, Kleinman JE, Weinberger DR, Powers RE. A topographical study of senile plaques and neurofibrillary tangles in the hippocampi of patients with Alzheimer's disease and cognitively impaired patients with schizophrenia. *Psychiat Res* 49:41–62, 1993.

Christison GW, Casanova MF, Weinberger DR, Rawlings R, Kleinman JE. Quantitative investigation of hippocampal pyramidal cell size, shape, and variability of orientation in schizophrenia. *Arch Gen Psychiat* 46:1027–1032, 1989.

Colon EJ. Quantitative cytoarchitectonics of the human cerebral cortex in schizophrenic dementia. *Acta Neuropathologica* (Berlin), 20:1–10, 1972.

Colter N, Battal S, Crow TJ, Johnstone EC, Brown R, Bruton C. White matter reduction in the parahippocampal gyrus of patients with schizophrenia. *Arch Gen Psychiat* 44:1023, 1987.

Conrad AJ, Abebe T, Austin R, Forsythe S, Scheibel AB. Hippocampal pyramidal cell disarray in schizophrenia as a bilateral phenomenon. *Arch Gen Psychiat* 48:413–417, 1991.

Crow TJ, Ball J, Bloom SR, Brown R, Bruton CJ, Colter N, Frith CD, Johnstone EC, Owens DGC, Roberts GW. Schizophrenia as an anomaly of development of cerebral asymmetry. *Arch Gen Psychiat* 46:1145–1150, 1989.

Dickson DW, Crystal HA, Mattiace LA, Masur DM, Blau AD, Davies P, Yen SH, Aronson MK. Identification of normal and pathological aging in prospectively studied nondemented elderly humans. *Neurobiol Aging*, 13:179–89, 1992.

Dwork AJ. Post mortem studies of the hippocampal formation in schizophrenia. *Schiz Bull* (in press).

El-Mallakh RS, Kirch DG, Shelton R, Fan K-J, Pezeshkpour G, Kanhouwa S, Wyatt RJ, Kleinman JE. The nucleus basalis of meynert, senile plaques, and intellectual impairment in schizophrenia. *J Neuropsych* 3:383–386, 1991.

Falkai P, Bogerts B. Cell loss in the hippocampus of schizophrenics. *Euro Arch Psychiat Neurol Sci*, 236:154–161, 1986.

Falkai P, Bogerts B, Rozumek M. Limbic pathology in schizophrenia: The entorhinal region—a morphometric study. *Biol Psychiat* 24:515–521, 1988.

Heckers S, Heinsen H, Heinsen YC, Beckmann H. Limbic structures and lateral ventricle in schizophrenia. *Arch Gen Psychiat* 47:1016–1022, 1990a.

Heckers S, Heinsen H, Heinsen Y, Beckmann H. Morphometry of the parahippocampal gyrus in schizophrenics and controls. Some anatomical considerations. *J Neural Trans* 80:151–155, 1990b.

Heckers S, Heinsen H, Geiger B, Beckmann H. Hippocampal neuron number in schizophrenia. A stereological study. *Arch Gen Psychiat* 48:1002–1008, 1991.

Heckers S. Neuropathology of schizophrenia: Cortex, thalamus, basal ganglia, neurotransmitter-specific projection systems. *Schizo Bull* (in press).

Jakob H, Beckmann H. Prenatal developmental disturbances in the limbic allocortex in schizophrenics. *J Neural Trans* 65:303–326, 1986.

Jakob H, Beckmann H. Gross and histological criteria for developmental disorders in brains of schizophrenics. *J Royal Soc Med* 82:466–469, 1989.

Jellinger K. Neuromorphological background of pathochemical studied in major psychoses. In: Beckmann H, Riederer P, eds. *Pathochemical Markers in Major Psychoses*. Berlin, Germany: Springer/Verlag, 1985, pp. 1–23.

Jeste DV, Lohr JB. Hippocampal pathologic findings in schizophrenia. A morphometric study. *Arch Gen Psychiat* 46:1019–1024, 1989.

Johnson GVW, Jope RS. The role of microtubule-associated protein 2 (MAP2) in neuronal growth, plasticity, and degeneration. *J Neurosci Res* 33:502–512, 1992.

Keilp JG, Waniek C, Goldman RG, Zemishlany Z, Alexander GE, Gibbon M, Wu A, Susser E, Prohovnik I. Reliability of post-mortem chart diagnoses of schizophrenia and dementia. *Schizo Res* 17:221–228, 1995.

Khachaturian ZS. Diagnosis of Alzheimer's disease. *Arch Neurol* 42:1097–1105, 1985.

Kovelman JA, Scheibel AB. A neurohistological correlate of schizophrenia. *Biol Psychiat* 19:1601–1621, 1984.

Miller FD, Hicks SP, D'Amato CL, Landis JR. A descriptive study of neuritic plaques and neurofibrillary tangles in an autopsy population. *Am J Epidemiol* 120:331–341, 1984.

Mirra SS, Heyman A, McKeel D, Sumi SM, Crain BJ, Brownlee LM, Vogel FS, Hughes JP, van Belle G, Berg L. The Consortium to Establish a Registry for Alzheimer's Disease (CERAD). Part II. Standardization of the neuropathologic assessment of Alzheimer's disease. *Neurology* 41:479–486, 1991.

Nieto D, Escobar A. Major Psychoses. In: Minkler J, ed. *Pathology of the Nervous System.* Vol 3. New York: McGraw-Hill Book Company, 1972, pp. 2654–2665.

Pakkenberg B. Post-mortem study of chronic schizophrenic brains. *Brit J Psychiat* 151:744–752, 1987.

Prohovnik I, Dwork AJ, Kaufman MA, Willson N. Alzheimer-type neuropathology in elderly schizophrenia patients. *Schizo Bull* 19:805–816, 1993.

Purohit DP, Davidson M, Perl DP, Powchik P, Haroutunian VH, Bierer LM, McCrystal J, Losonczy M, Davis KL. Severe cognitive impairment in elderly schizophrenic patients: A clinicopathological study. *Biol Psychiat* 33:255–260, 1993.

Roberts GW, Colter N, Lofthouse R, Bogerts B, Zech M, Crow TJ. Gliosis in schizophrenia: A survey. *Biol Psychiat* 21:1043–1050, 1986.

Rosoklija G, Hays AP, Latov N, Sadiq SA, Kaufman MA, Waniek C, Keilp J, Prohovnik I, Dwork AJ. Subicular MAP-2 immunoreactivity is diminished in a variety of psychiatric disorders. *J Neuropathol Exp Neurol* (in press).

Rosoklija G, Kaufman MA, Liu D, Hays AP, Latov N, Waniek C, Keilp JG, Sadiq SA, Gorman J, Prohovnik I, Dwork AJ. Subicular MAP2 immunoreactivity is altered in schizophrenia. *Soc Neurosci Abstr* 21:2126, 1995.

Schwab C, Bondada V, Sparks DL, Cahan LD, Geddes JW. Postmortem changes in the levels and localization of microtubule-associated proteins (tau, MAP2 and MAP1B) in the rat and human hippocampus. *Hippocampus* 4:212–225, 1994.

Stevens JR. Neuropathology of schizophrenia. *Arch Gen Psychiat* 39:1131–1139, 1982.

West MJ, Gundersen HJG. Unbiased stereological estimation of the number of neurons in the human hippocampus. *J Compar Neurol* 296:1–22, 1990.

Whitaker-Azmatia PM, Borella A, Raio N. Serotonin depletion in the adult rat causes loss of the dendritic marker MAP-2: A new animal model of schizophrenia? *Neuropsychopharmacology* 12:269–272, 1995.

Wisniewski HM, Constantinidis J, Wegiel J, Bobinski M, Tarnawski M. Neurofibrillary pathology in brains of elderly schizophrenics treated with neuroleptics. *Alzheimer Dis Assoc Disord* 4:211–227, 1994.

Neurochemistry of Schizophrenia

ZAFAR SHARIF, M.D.

Schizophrenia is a chronic mental disorder with a lifetime morbid risk of about 0.8%. The onset of illness is usually in adolescence or early adulthood and diverse areas of functioning, including perception, cognition, inferential and goal directed thinking, emotional state, and organized and adaptive behavior, are affected. It was suggested by Kraeplin in 1896 that an underlying abnormality in brain structure and/or function was responsible for the symptoms of schizophrenia but this abnormality has been difficult to demonstrate. Only in the past 10–15 years have data begun to converge from the disciplines of neuropathology, brain imaging, neuroscience, and genetics, about some of the abnormalities of brain structure and function that accompany this disorder.

This chapter is a review of neurochemical abnormalities in schizophrenia. It will begin with an outline of the approaches to examining neurochemical abnormalities and their limitations, followed by a review of the neurochemical abnormalities that have been demonstrated thus far in this disease. The final section will attempt to project future directions for the field.

CONCEPTS

The dopamine hypothesis will be used as an illustration of the conceptual framework that has evolved to investigate the neurochemical abnormalities in schizophrenia. This hypothesis postulates that an abnormal increase in dopaminergic transmission underlies at least the positive symptoms of schizophrenia, and is based on the following observations: neuroleptics which are primarily dopamine antagonists are efficacious in the treatment of positive symptoms; amphetamine, an indirect dopamine agonist, when administered chronically to normals results in an organic psychosis with delusions and hallucinations (Ellinwood 1967); in schizophrenic patients, amphetamine causes a worsening of psychosis—these effects of amphetamine are reversed by neuroleptics (Angrist 1974). Perhaps the strongest evidence in support of the dopamine hypothesis is that affinities of various neuroleptic drugs for the D_2 receptor in the brain are directly proportional to their clinical potency (Creese 1976; Seeman 1976). The dopamine hypothesis spawned a multitude of studies in attempts to identify evidence of increased dopamine transmission in schizophrenia.

Theoretically, transmission at the dopamine synapse could be increased either because of increased release of dopamine by the presynaptic neuron (which could be due to increased production, more efficient release, reduced reuptake, or reduced breakdown by monoamine oxidase), or by an increase in the number and/or affinity of post synaptic dopamine receptors. Increased dopaminergic transmission could also occur secondary to reduced activity of a neurotransmitter that would normally inhibit the action of dopamine, or increased activity of one that would enhance dopamine transmission. Based on this conceptualization various strategies have been employed to search for evidence of abnormalities in neurotransmitters and receptors in schizophrenia. These have included measurements of levels of neurotransmitter and their metabolites in the cerebrospinal fluid (CSF) and plasma, and examination of postmortem tissue from brains of schizophrenic patients for alterations in levels of neurotransmitters, their reuptake sites, and receptors in specific brain regions. More recently, in vivo functional brain imaging has enabled us to measure regional metabolic activity and receptor densities in living patients and controls, and advances in the field of molecular biology have led to the identification of multiple receptor subtypes that have unique amino acid sequences but for which specific pharmacological ligands may not yet be available.

Brain regions that have been examined in postmortem neurochemical studies of schizophrenia have included the basal ganglia, nucleus accumbens, hippocampus, amygdala, parahippocampal gyrus, temporal lobe, frontal (including dorsolateral prefrontal) cortex, cingulate gyrus, thalamus and brain stem. Selection of these brain regions for study was guided by several factors including: knowledge about neuroanatomic substrates of various human functions; regions that are projection areas for dopaminergic tracts; neuropathologic literature that has demonstrated reduced size of the amygdala/hippocampal complex (Bogerts 1985, Brown 1986, Jakob and Beckmann 1986), reduced neuronal numbers in the prefrontal cortex and cingulate gyrus (Benes and Bird 1987), and cytoarchitectural abnormalities in the cortex (Jakob and Beckmann 1986, Falkai 1988, Arnold 1991). Results of high resolution morphologic brain imaging studies with magnetic resonance imaging that have revealed reduction in size of the hippocampal/amygdala complex (Bogerts 1990), and in temporal lobe gray matter volume (Sudath 1989, Shenton 1992); and functional brain imaging demonstrating reduced frontal cortical metabolism and blood flow in schizophrenic patients (Buchsbaum 1984, Weinberger 1986).

As will be detailed later, the neurochemistry literature is replete with nonreplications and inconsistencies. Several factors may account for this, some generic (such as patient and control selection), and some specific to the investigative modality. These factors will be briefly reviewed.

METHODOLOGIC LIMITATIONS

Probably the most important factor affecting results is patient and control selection. Numerous characteristics of patients may potentially impact on observed results. First, current diagnostic schemes in psychiatry rely on nosology and are, therefore, dependent to some degree on accuracy and interpretation of data collected. Structured interviews and rigorous syndromal diagnostic criteria have significantly lessened diagnostic confusion. However, even in careful evaluation of patients it is sometimes difficult to distinguish between clinical syndromes, e.g., between schizophrenia and schizoaffective disorder. Family studies reveal that genetic vulnerability to schizophrenia may result in various phenotypic expressions. These observations underscore the probable biologic heterogeneity of the construct of 'schizophrenia' and suggest that even in an ideal situation in which every patient was perfectly diagnosed according to current diagnostic criteria, we would probably be dealing with a biologically heterogeneous group of disorders.

Second, specific features of the illness are likely to have varying neurochemical substrates, e.g., acute exacerbation of symptoms versus remission; onset of illness versus chronic disease state; positive, negative or disorganized symptoms; treatment responsive versus treatment refractory; and presence of marked cognitive impairment or tardive dyskinesia. These two factors, biologic heterogeneity and state variability, would result in significant variation within the 'test group' of schizophrenia even in ideal circumstances.

The third factor is related to selection of comparison control groups. It is likely that neurochemical abnormalities are not specific to the schizophrenia but are related to symptom clusters, such as psychosis, that cut across diagnostic categories. This is supported by the observation that neuroleptics are effective not only in the control of psychotic symptoms in schizophrenia but also in psychosis associated with organic states, dementia and other 'functional' psychiatric illnesses. A similar situation exists for other symptom clusters such as depression, mania, and severe anxiety. Selection of appropriate controls is therefore of paramount importance, and studies in which other psychiatric patients (e.g., those with psychotic depression or bipolar disorder) have been used as the control group might suffer from a type II error.

Another generic factor that affects all investigative modalities is the effects of neuroleptic treatment. Acute neuroleptic blockade affects the release of dopamine from the presynaptic neurons, initially causing an increase in dopamine turnover followed after about 2 weeks by a state of relative inactivity resulting presumably from 'depolarization block' (Bunney and Grace 1978). Postmortem studies that measure regional levels of neurotransmitter metabolites and in which the medication status at the time of death is not known, might suffer from this confound. It is also well known that chronic neuroleptic treatment can result in elevation of brain D_2 receptors in rats which may persist for up to 6 months after withdrawal of the neuroleptic (Clow et al. 1979; Muller and Seeman 1978). D_1 receptor elevations may persist for up to 1 year after neuroleptic withdrawal (Marsden and Jenner 1980). If an increase in dopamine receptors is also causally associated with schizophrenia it becomes quite problematic to tease out the contributions of the disease process from iatrogenic effects of neuroleptic treatment given the almost universal use of these agents in the clinical management of patients with schizophrenia. In vivo positron emission tomography (PET) imaging may allow us to circumvent this problem by measuring receptor densities in neuroleptic naive patients.

Other than the above mentioned 'generic' factors there are methodologic issues related to each investigative modality that increase confounding variables and decrease sensitivity. In postmortem studies the patient may not have had rigorous antemortem diagnosis and assessment of symptoms. Reliable history may not be available on illicit substance use and medication status prior to death. Agonal events and post mortem interval also affect the integrity of neurotransmitters and receptors. Comparison across studies is further complicated by use of different brain regions, at times from only one side of the brain, and different methods to quantify the binding site (homogenate binding with or without determination of K_d and B_{max}, and autoradiography). Lastly, the cause of death may have independent associated neurochemical abnormalities (e.g., suicide with increased $5HT_2$ receptors in the frontal cortex).

In CSF neurochemical studies one is attempting to draw conclusions about the aberrant functional state of a neurotransmitter system, or even more ambitiously, one of its specific neuroanatomic tracts, based on the CSF concentration of the neurotransmitter or its metabolites. CSF is extracted from the lumbar spine far from the site of production of the neurotransmitter or its metabolite. CSF concentrations of neurotransmitter/metabolite represent the net effect of contributions from all brain regions and active transport out of the CSF. Other factors that influence neurotransmitter/ metabolite levels include rostral-caudal concentration gradients, diet, exercise and gender of the patient. Many of these factors have not been controlled for in individual studies. Peripheral measures like plasma and urine homovanillic acid (HVA-metabolite of dopamine) suffer from the additional contribution from systemic sources.

Given all these confounding variables, what is surprising is not that frequent inconsistencies and nonreplications are reported, but that it is possible to draw some, albeit tentative, conclusions from the neurochemistry literature. This literature will be reviewed next.

SPECIFIC NEUROTRANSMITTER SYSTEM ABNORMALITIES

Dopamine

Ultimately, any pathophysiologic hypothesis for schizophrenia must include a role for dysregulated dopamine transmission because of the undeniable fact of neuroleptic efficacy in the treatment of this disorder. Dopamine is synthesized from the amino acid tyrosine which is converted to DOPA by tyrosine hydroxylase. This is the rate-limiting step in dopamine synthesis. DOPA is converted by aromatic amino acid decarboxylase to dopamine. Dopamine projections in the brain include the nigrostriatal, mesolimbic, mesocortical, and the tuberoinfundibular tracts. Synaptic action of dopamine is terminated primarily by active reuptake into the presynaptic neuron where it may be catabolized by monoamine oxidase, or actively transported into synaptic vesicles for storage and later release. Extracellular dopamine is inactivated by catechol-O-methyl-transferase. Five dopamine receptor subtypes have been identified using techniques of molecular biology, D_1-D_5. The D_1 and D_5 receptors are only present on post synaptic sites and are linked to adenyl cyclase. The D_2, D_3 and D_4 are similar and are also located on post synaptic sites. In addition, D_2 and D_3 receptors may be located on the presynaptic neuron and act as autoreceptors. All dopamine receptors are linked to G proteins and have seven transmembrane domains. The third cytoplasmic loop is important for binding of G protein.

Many investigators have attempted to find evidence of increased dopamine activity in schizophrenic patients. These have included post mortem studies of brain tissue to measure levels of dopamine or its primary metabolite homovanillic acid (HVA) and densities of dopamine receptors. Antemortem studies have measured the level of dopamine and its metabolites in CSF, plasma and urine. Recently, functional brain imaging studies with PET have been employed to visualize and quantify dopamine receptors in the brains of schizophrenic patients and controls.

Postmortem studies of regional brain concentration of dopamine or HVA. These studies have attempted to measure the levels of dopamine and its metabolites in brain regions thought to be involved in the pathophysiology of schizophrenia. Overall, the results have been inconclusive with some investigators finding elevation in HVA levels in the nucleus accumbens (Bird et al. 1979), caudate (Crow 1979), and amygdala, especially on the left (Reynolds 1983), while others have reported no change (Farley 1980, Winblad 1979, Kleinman 1982).

Postmortem studies of dopamine receptors. Earlier studies demonstrated the existence of two types of dopamine receptors, those that stimulate adenyl cyclase (D_1) and those that were not linked to adenyl cyclase (D_2). However, further work revealed that in the striatum stimulation of the D_2 receptor inhibits adenyl cyclase (Stoof and Kebabian 1981) while in the nucleus accumbens the D_2 receptor was not linked to adenyl cyclase. Most of the dopamine receptor studies in schizophrenia have examined the D_2 receptor as this is thought to be the site of neuroleptic action. Only a few studies have examined D_1 receptor levels in the caudate/putamen from schizophrenic postmortem brains. Two studies (Cross 1981; Seeman 1987) found normal levels of D_1 receptors while one study (Hess 1987) found decreased levels of D_1 receptors.

The study of D_2 receptor densities has been much more fruitful. Increase in the level of D_2 receptors in the striatum is one of the best replicated findings in neurochemical studies of schizophrenia. A 50–75% increase in D_2 receptors was first reported by Lee and Seeman (1977). Independent replication was provided by Owen (1978), Crow (1979), Cross (1981), Joyce (1988). Some reports finding no increase in D_2 receptors (Mackay 1980 and Reynolds 1980) have been criticized on methodologic grounds (Seeman 1981). As mentioned earlier, the confound of neuroleptic treatment is especially important in the quantification of D_2 receptors. D_2 receptor elevations have, however, been demonstrated in postmortem caudate/putamen and nucleus accumbens of patients who had never received neuroleptics, or those who had been neuroleptic-free for at least 1 year prior to death (Lee and Seeman 1980; Owen 1978). Seeman (1984) examined a new cohort of 59 DSM III-diagnosed schizophrenic patients and showed a bimodal elevation of D_2 receptors in the caudate, putamen and nucleus accumbens. The lower elevation was in the order of 13%–37% while the higher mode elevation was 130% above control values. They suggested that the lower elevations might be due to neuroleptic effects while the higher mode represented the combined effects of neuroleptic treatment and disease process. On balance, the evidence is quite robust for an increase in D_2 receptors in the basal ganglia and limbic regions in at least a subgroup of schizophrenic patients. The problem of medication effects, however, continues to plague the field.

Recently, more dopamine receptor subtypes have been identified and we now know of the existence of dopamine receptors D_3, D_4, and D_5. Our knowledge of the distributions of these receptors in the brain is based on the distribution of mRNA coding for these receptors as determined by in situ hybridization. These studies have been conducted primarily on rats. The D_5 receptor is similar to the D_1 although its affinity for dopamine is ten times that of the D_1 receptor. The D_3 and D_4 receptors are similar to the D_2 receptor but have distinct regional distributions. The D_4 receptor is especially interesting in view of the high selective affinity of clozapine for this receptor. The D_4 receptor is found in the hippocampus, islands of Calleja, and cortex, and is expressed at lower levels than the D_2 and D_3 receptors. No specific ligand for the D_4 receptor is currently available. The two studies attempting to quantify this receptor in the striatum of post mortem schizophrenic striatum have relied on a subtraction technique. Various results have been obtained, with Seeman (1993) finding an increase, while Reynolds and Mason (1995) using the same methodology found no increase.

The D_3 receptor is also of interest because it is localized predominantly in the nucleus accumbens, ventral caudate-putamen, and Islands of Calleja in the limbic striatum which is thought to subserve emotion. A specific ligand is available for the D_3 receptor (7-OH-DPAT). Joyce (1995) found a 45–56% increase in [^{125}I]trans-7-OH-DPAT binding in the basal ganglia and ventral forebrain of schizophrenic patients.

These studies of D_3 and D_4 receptor densities are preliminary reports and they await replication. Discovery of specific ligands for the D_4 and D_5 receptors for autoradiography, and specific antibodies to D_3, D_4, and D_5 for use in immunohistochemical studies, will dramatically increase our knowledge about the distribution and functional role of these receptors.

Measurement of dopamine receptors by positron emission tomography. Positron emission tomography has provided a powerful tool to explore the question of elevated D_2 receptors in living schizophrenic patients. This mode of investigation potentially allows investigators to control for drug status, stage of illness, and other 'state' factors of the illness. Unfortunately, even here the results are inconsistent, with the two foremost groups reporting divergent results. Wong (1986) found about a two fold increase in D_2 receptor density in the striatum in neuroleptic-naive schizophrenic patients and in psychotic patients with bipolar disorder (Wong 1990). This group used a kinetic compartmental model with $[^{11}C]$3-N-methylspiperone as ligand. Farde (1990), using $[^{11}C]$-raclopride in an equilibrium model found no difference in D_2 receptor densities in the caudate between schizophrenics and matched controls. Similarly, Martinot (1990) using $[^{76}Br]$-bromospiperone and striatal/cerebellum ratios of D_2 binding, found no differences between patients and controls. Hietala (1994) using the $[^{11}C]$-raclopride equilibrium model also did not find an elevation in D_2 receptors in the caudate/putamen of 13 neuroleptic-naive patients (schizophrenia and schizoaffective) compared with 10 controls.

Other than the differences in theoretical models, the patient populations in the studies were different, the Wong et al. patients being older and having significantly longer duration of illness. Interestingly, in both the Martinot and Hietala studies, the subgroup of patients with the longest duration of illness had the highest levels of D_2 receptors. Differences in ligand may also contribute to the observed discrepancies as it has been shown that raclopride may be susceptible to competition from endogenous dopamine, thereby resulting in a artificially lower observed value for D_2 receptor density (Seeman).

To my knowledge, only one PET study of D_1 receptor density in striatum has been published. D_1 receptor density normalized to cerebellum was measured in 10 neuroleptic naive patients and 16 healthy controls by PET using the $[^{11}C]$-labeled D_1 antagonist SCH 23390 (Karlsson 1995). They found a 20% reduction in D_1 receptors in the striatum (compared with the 43% reduction reported by Hess in postmortem samples).

Studies of CSF and plasma HVA. Earlier CSF studies of levels of dopamine and its metabolite HVA in schizophrenic patients were wrought with methodologic confounds and yielded conflicting results. More recent studies have generally found a lower level of HVA in CSF of patients as compared to controls (Lindstrom 1985; Alfredsson and Wiesel 1990; Karoum 1987). These levels have been inversely correlated with the severity of negative symptoms (Lindstrom 1985), and degree of cortical atrophy and ventricular enlargement. Because of the difficulties involved in studies of CSF, investigators have examined the level of HVA in plasma with the hope that this would provide a peripheral noninvasive indicator of brain dopamine turnover. Plasma HVA levels are influenced by many factors including diet, gender, level of physical activity, neuroleptic treatment, diurnal variation, and changes in renal clearance over short periods of time (Amin 1991). Only about 17% of plasma HVA is contributed by the brain, the remainder coming from the peripheral nervous system. Despite these limitations (Lieberman and Koreen 1993), fairly consistent results have emerged about the state of plasma HVA in schizophrenic patients, and especially its relationship to treatment response.

Most investigators have found an increase in plasma HVA with acute treatment (Davidson 1987a, 1987b; Chang 1988; Davila 1988; Koreen 1994), and a reduction with chronic treatment. Higher baseline plasma HVA (Chang 1988, Van Putten 1989, Chang 1990, Davidson 1991, Koreen 1994), and a greater initial rise in plasma HVA in response to neuroleptic treatment (Chang 1988, Davila 1988, Koreen 1994), were both associated with an increased likelihood of response. The magnitude of the initial increase in plasma HVA after neuroleptic treatment was found to be greater in first episode schizophrenic patients (Koreen 1994) as compared to chronically treated patients (Davidson 1987b; Pickar 1986). Additionally, plasma HVA levels never went below baseline values with chronic treatment in this first episode group (Koreen 1994). These observations suggest that the dopaminergic system appears less able to react to a neuroleptic 'challenge' with increasing age and duration of illness. This change in plasticity of the dopaminergic system may represent a primary effect of progression of the illness or secondary effects of long term neuroleptic treatment (Koreen 1994).

Serotonin

Serotonin is an indoleamine that is synthesized from the amino acid tryptophan which must be taken up by the brain by an active transport mechanism. Tryptophan is converted to 5-hydroxytryptophan by tryptophan hydroxylase and this is the rate-limiting step for serotonin biosynthesis. Tryptophan hydroxylase is not fully saturated under normal conditions and it is possible to alter brain serotonin concentrations by severe dietary restriction of tryptophan. Serotonin is catabolized to 5-hydroxyindoleacetic acid (5-HIAA).

Numerous serotonin receptors have been identified from pharmacologic studies and more recently from molecular cloning. These include the $5\text{-}HT_1$ class (A-F), $5\text{-}HT_2$ class (A,B,C), $5\text{-}HT_3$, $5\text{-}HT_4$, $5\text{-}HT_5$, $5\text{-}HT_6$ and the $5\text{-}HT_7$ receptors. Many of these receptor subtypes have only recently been discovered and specific ligands are not available for all. The $5\text{-}HT_{1A}$ receptor is a somatic autoreceptor which is negatively coupled to adenyl cyclase and is found in the superficial layers of cortex, hippocampus and raphe nucleus. It is the site of action of the atypical anxiolitic, buspirone. The $5\text{-}HT_2$ receptor is G-protein linked and coupled to the phosphotidylinositol system. Specifically, the $5\text{-}HT_{2a}$ receptor is the predominant subtype in the brain and is the site of action of hallucinogens such as LSD and atypical neuroleptics such as clozapine and risperidone. These receptors are found in the frontal cortex, nucleus accumbens, olfactory tubercle and striatum. $5\text{-}HT_{2b}$ receptors are found in the stomach fundus while the $5\text{-}HT_{2c}$ receptor is located in the choroid plexus and in some limbic regions such as hippocampus, cingulate cortex, amygdala and nucleus accumbens.

A role for serotonin dysregulation in the pathophysiology of schizophrenia was suggested in 1954 by Wooley and Shaw. Evidence for serotonergic dysfunction in schizophrenia includes the psychotomimetic effects of the serotonin agonist lysergic acid diethylamide (LSD) in normal subjects, the efficacy of atypical antipsychotics such as clozapine (a weak D_2 antagonist but a potent $5HT_2$ antagonist) in treatment refractory patients, and the observation that low pretreatment CSF HVA/5-HIAA ratio predicted likelihood of response

(Kahn 1993, Hsiao 1993) to clozapine. Also, m-CPP, a selective serotonin receptor agonist, has been reported to worsen psychotic symptoms in schizophrenic patients (Iqbal 1991; Krystal 1991, 1993). This effect could be antagonized by clozapine (Krystal 1991), and ritansirin, a selective $5HT_2$ antagonist (Seibyl 1991).

Concentrations of serotonin and its metabolite 5-hydroxyindoleacetic acid in postmortem brain and in antemortem CSF from schizophrenic patients have been measured and compared with controls. There have also been several studies examining the serotonin levels and uptake of serotonin by platelets from blood of schizophrenic patients and controls; these studies, because they are so inconclusive, will not be reviewed. Postmortem receptor studies in schizophrenia have looked primarily at the $5HT_{1A}$ (using $[^3H]$8-OH-DPAT and $[^3H]$-serotonin), and $5HT_2$ (using $[^3H]$-LSD, $[^{125}I]$-LSD, and $[^3H]$-ketansirin), groups of receptors. Densities of serotonin reuptake sites (using $[^3H]$-paroxitine, $[^3H]$-cyanoimipramine or $[^3H]$-serotonin) in schizophrenic postmortem brains have also been measured. The serotonin reuptake site is important as this is the site of action of selective serotonin reuptake inhibitor and most tricyclic antidepressants. These studies will be reviewed.

Postmortem studies of regional brain concentration of serotonin. Postmortem studies of serotonin concentration have suffered the same limitations of postmortem studies of dopamine and replicated results are infrequent. The only replicated results are an increase in 5HT in the putamen (Farley 1980, Korpi 1986, Toru 1988), and an increase of 5HT in the globus pallidus (Winblad 1979, Korpi 1986).

Postmortem studies of serotonin receptors. The densities of $5-HT_1$ and the $5-HT_2$ receptors and the presynaptic serotonin reuptake site in different brain regions have been examined in schizophrenia. In the frontal cortex different groups have reported a decrease (Mita 1986), no change (Owen 1981), or increase (Whitaker 1981) of levels of serotonin receptors. These studies are difficult to interpret because different regions of the cortex were sampled and the receptor ligands were not specific in their binding to the various subtypes of serotonin receptors, and in some cases, even bound to other classes of receptors. More recent studies have attempted to utilize more specific ligands and to study multiple but discrete brain regions.

Hashimoto (1990) demonstrated an increase in $5-HT_{1A}$ densities in the frontal and temporal cortices of schizophrenic patients. These findings were replicated and extended by Joyce (1993) who found significantly increased $[^3H]$8-OH-DPAT binding in the prefrontal and motor cortex, temporal cortex, parietal cortex, dentate gyrus of hippocampus, and markedly increased binding in the anterior cingulate gyrus of schizophrenic patients compared with controls. No increase was seen in $5-HT_{1A}$ receptors in the nucleus accumbens, entorhinal cortex, caudate or putamen in this study.

Some studies of $5-HT_2$ receptor densities in postmortem samples from schizophrenic patients have reported reduced levels in the prefrontal cortex (Mita 1986, Arora and Meltzer 1991, Laruelle 1993). However, Joyce (1993) using autoradiography found no increase in $[^{125}I]$-LSD binding in the prefrontal, parietal, anterior cingulate, entorhinal cortex and caudate nucleus. In this sample, $5-HT_2$ density was increased in the temporal cortex, posterior cingulate, hippocampus, and the nucleus accumbens and putamen.

Recent studies have also examined densities of the serotonin reuptake site in postmortem tissue. Reduced binding was demonstrated in dorsolateral prefrontal cortex, frontal pole and cingulate cortex, but not in occipital cortex by Laruelle (1993). This finding was replicated by Joyce 1993 using [^{3}H]-cyanoimipramine and autoradiography. He demonstrated significantly reduced binding in laminae 1-IV in prefrontal cortex and in laminae 1–III in the cingulate gyrus, but no change in the motor cortex. Hippocampal densities of the serotonin reuptake site did not differ from control while the nucleus accumbens, caudate and putamen all showed increased binding.

In summary, replicated findings in serotonergic receptors in schizophrenia include increased density of 5-HT$_{1A}$ in regions of the frontal and temporal cortices, decreased density of 5-HT$_2$ in the prefrontal cortex, and decreased density of the serotonin reuptake site in the prefrontal and cingulate cortices. The pathophysiologic significance of these findings is unclear but they provide further evidence of deviant serotonergic function in schizophrenia. We await further advances as more stringent standards that are now used in postmortem studies (e.g., antemortem diagnosis and assessments, short postmortem intervals, etc.) result in higher quality of postmortem material that can then be evaluated by the rapidly evolving techniques of neuroscience.

Studies of CSF serotonin and 5-HIAA. Numerous studies have been conducted in an effort to identify possible differences in concentrations of serotonin or its metabolite 5-HIAA in the CSF of schizophrenic patients and controls. Data from these studies have been inconclusive with some studies finding reduced levels of 5-HIAA (Ashcroft 1966, Bowers 1969, Gattaz 1982) and others finding no difference from normals (Bowers 1974, Post 1975, Potkin 1983, Nyback 1983). In the studies of Nyback and Potkin, patients with enlarged sulci and ventricles demonstrated lower CSF 5-HIAA levels as compared to controls. Low levels of 5-HIAA have also been associated with suicide attempts in schizophrenic patients (Banki 1984, Ninan 1984). From this literature it appears that low CSF 5-HIAA levels in schizophrenia may be limited to those patients with evidence of cortical atrophy/ventricular enlargement and/or those with a history of suicide attempts.

Glutamate

Glutamate is an amino acid and is the main excitatory neurotransmitter in the brain. Other than its role as a neurotransmitter glutamate is also involved in metabolic processes such as protein synthesis in the brain. This duality of function makes it difficult to identify that portion of glutamate which functions as a neurotransmitter. It is now known that cortico-cortical neurons in cortical association areas, corticostriatal and corticothalamic projections use glutamate as the major neurotransmitter. The main afferent glutamatergic projection to the frontal cortex is from the dorsomedial nucleus of the thalamus via the nucleus accumbens. Glutamate is also extensively used as a neurotransmitter in the hippocampus and the entorhinal cortex. As expected, these regions (cortex, hippocampus, parahippocampal gyrus) have high concentrations of glutamate receptors.

The classification of glutamate receptors is pharmacologically defined and is based on the binding of specific agonists. Broadly, two categories are recognized; the ionotropic receptors which contain cation-specific ion channels, and the metabotropic receptors which are linked to G-proteins and modulate intracellular messengers. The functions of the metabotropic receptors are poorly understood. The ionotropic receptors are further subdivided into NMDA (N-methyl, D-aspartate), AMPA (alpha-amino-3-hydroxy-5-methyl-4-

isoxazole propionic acid), kainate, and L-AP4 (L-amino-4-phosphobutanoate). The NMDA receptor controls the influx of Na^+ and Ca^{2+}, while AMPA and kainate receptors allow influx of Ca^{2+}. In conditions of anoxia or hypoglycemia, glutamate activation of these receptors leads to a large influx of Ca^{2+} resulting in uncontrolled activation of various intracellular enzyme systems including proteases, and eventual cell death. For this reason glutamate has been termed an 'excitotoxic amino acid'.

An etiologic role for aberrant glutamatergic neurotransmission in schizophrenia was hypothesized based on observations of the behavioral effects of phencyclidine in humans. Phencyclidine is an antagonist of the NMDA glutamate receptor and its behavioral effects mimic both the positive and negative symptoms of schizophrenia. The first report of altered glutamate levels in the CSF of schizophrenic patients was by Kim (1980) who found a 50% reduction in the level of glutamate in CSF of patients compared to controls. He proposed that schizophrenia was associated with reduced function of the glutamatergic system. The results of this study were not supported by Perry (1982) and Korpi (1987) who found no changes in glutamate concentrations in post mortem schizophrenic brains. However, Toru (1992) did find lower glutamate levels in superior temporal and angular cortex of schizophrenic subjects. As mentioned earlier, identifying that portion of total glutamate that functions as a neurotransmitter is difficult, if not impossible. Recent focus has, therefore, shifted to the measurement of glutamate receptors.

The densities of the NMDA, AMPA, and kainate receptor subtypes of glutamate receptors have been examined in schizophrenia. The first study of glutamate receptors in post mortem schizophrenic brains examined kainate receptors and was conducted by Nishikawa (1983). Using tissue homogenates he found *increased* [^{3}H]-kainate binding in two prefrontal areas in patients who were off neuroleptics at time of death. B_{max} was increased without a change in K_d. No change in kainate receptors was seen in the orbitofrontal, parietal and occipital cortices, or in the putamen. Deakin (1989), using homogenates found bilateral *increase* in [^{3}H]-kainate binding in the orbital frontal cortex with no change in the prefrontal cortex, hippocampus and amygdala. Kerwin (1988), using tissue homogenates found a *decrease* in [^{3}H]-kainate binding in the left hippocampus with no change in receptor density in the right hippocampus.

A paired analysis revealed significant L < R asymmetry. In a new cohort of patients, and using autoradiography, Kerwin and co-workers replicated and further expanded previous results (Kerwin et al. 1990). They demonstrated a significant bilateral reduction in [^{3}H]-kainate binding in the dentate gyrus, the CA4 and CA3 regions of the hippocampus, and in the parahippocampal gyrus. Unilateral reductions were seen in the left CA2 and CA1 regions of the hippocampus in schizophrenic patients. Consistent with these findings, Harrison et al. (1991) showed a reduction of messenger-RNA that codes for non-NMDA receptors in the CA3 region of the hippocampi from six schizophrenic patients compared to eight controls.

These findings suggest increased kainate-mediated glutamatergic transmission in portions of the frontal cortex and reduced transmission in the medial temporal lobe. This is intriguing in light of information from neuropathology and in vivo structural/functional imaging that have shown fairly consistent abnormalities in these regions.

The AMPA class of glutamatergic receptors have also been examined in schizophrenia although results have varied. AMPA receptors were found to be decreased bilaterally in the CA4 region of the hippocampus with significantly greater reduction on the left (Kerwin et al. 1990). No change was seen in other hippocampal regions or the parahippocampal gyrus.

Kurumaji et al. (1992) and Freed et al. (1993) did not find alterations of AMPA receptor densities in several cortical and subcortical brain regions examined. It has been suggested that significant alterations in AMPA receptors are not involved in the pathophysiology of schizophrenia (Toru et al. 1994).

The last subtype of glutamate receptor that has been studied is the NMDA receptor. The NMDA receptor has numerous pharmacologically distinct binding sites. These include a binding site for glutamate and possibly aspartate, a site within the ion channel that binds PCP, ketamine and dizocilpine (MK801), and several regulatory binding sites for glycine (strychnine insensitive), Zn^{2+}, Mg^{2+} and polyamines. The strychnine-insensitive glycine binding site facilitates binding of glutamate to its binding site on the NMDA receptor. Binding sites on the NMDA receptor that have been investigated in schizophrenia include the glutamate binding site, the ion channel, and the strychnine insensitive glycine site. Kerwin et al. (1990) found no difference in [^{3}H]-glutamate binding in the dentate gyrus, CA4, CA3, CA2, CA1, or the parahippocampal gyrus between schizophrenics and normal controls using autoradiography. Significant increase in the density of the ion channel has been demonstrated in the putamen (Kornhuber et al. 1989), and in the superior temporal, superior parietal, supramarginal cortices (Suga et al. 1990), and the orbital frontal cortex, bilaterally (Simpson et al. 1992a). The strychnine-insensitive glycine binding site was shown to be increased in the premotor cortex, somesthetic cortex, supramarginal cortex, angular cortex and visual cortex. No change was seen in the prefrontal cortex, motor cortex, temporal cortex and superior parietal cortex (Ishimaru et al. 1994).

The significance of these findings in the pathophysiology of schizophrenia is unknown. However, reciprocal interactions between dopamine and glutamate are well documented. For example, glutamate receptors on terminals of dopaminergic neurons in the striatum stimulate the release of dopamine (Carter et al. 1988). On the other hand, presynaptic NMDA receptors on mesocortical dopamine neurons projecting to the cingulate cortex inhibit the release of dopamine (Deutch et al. 1989). Dopamine receptors are located on the terminals of glutamatergic corticostriate neurons and their stimulation inhibits glutamate release (Roberts et al. 1982). Thus, reduced glutamatergic transmission (from reduced levels of glutamate receptors) in the medial temporal lobe could conceivably result in increased dopaminergic transmission resulting in psychosis, while increased glutamatergic transmission in frontal cortical regions (from increased numbers of glutamate receptors) may result in decreased dopaminergic transmission in the frontal cortex and negative symptoms. This is of course, highly speculative. The exact nature of glutamatergic system abnormality in schizophrenia is as yet unclear and it is unknown if these changes are related to neuroleptic effects, changes in other neurotransmitter systems, alterations in gene expression, or abnormal neuronal development. Future studies will help provide answers to these important questions.

Gamma aminobutyric acid (GABA).   GABA is the main inhibitory neurotransmitter in the brain and is synthesized from glutamic acid by the action of glutamic acid decarboxylase (GAD) in an activity dependent manner. GABA is degraded by the enzyme GABA transaminase and is actively taken up by GABAergic nerve terminals. This reuptake site can be labeled with the radioactive ligand [^{3}H]-nipocotic acid. Neurons that use GABA as a neurotransmitter include interneurons in the cerebral cortex, and larger neurons in the caudate, thalamus and cerebellum. Two major types of GABA receptors have been identified, $GABA_A$ and $GABA_B$ receptors. The $GABA_A$ receptor is an ion channel and is involved in fast inhibitory synaptic transmission in the brain. It is selective for the chloride ion and activation of the receptor leads to hyperpolarization of the cell membrane. The $GABA_A$ receptor is composed of multiple subunits and has at least three distinct binding sites; the GABA binding site is located on the β subunit and muscimol is an agonist and bicuculline an antagonist at this site; a binding site located in proximity to the ion channel at which picrotoxin (a proconvulsant) is an antagonist and barbiturates are agonists; and a benzodiazepine site located on the alpha subunit that increases affinity of GABA for the β subunit thereby facilitating GABAergic transmission. The $GABA_B$ receptor on the other hand, is G-protein-linked and inhibits adenyl cyclase and activates a specific type of K^+channel. Baclofen is an agonist and phaclofen is an antagonist at this receptor.

A role for disordered GABAergic transmission in schizophrenia was proposed by Roberts in 1972. Pharmacologic evidence for GABAergic involvement in schizophrenia includes the observation that $GABA_A$ agonist muscimol and the $GABA_B$ agonist baclofen both have psychotogenic effects. Benzodiazepines which are $GABA_A$ agonists, have been reported to improve psychotic symptoms when used in conjunction with neuroleptics (Wolkowitz et al. 1988; Douyon et al. 1989; Pato et al. 1989), as well as worsen psychotic symptoms in schizophrenic patients (Holden et al. 1968; Hanlon et al. 1970).

CSF studies of GABA levels in schizophrenic patients and controls have yielded conflicting results. Thus, higher (Gattaz et al. 1985), and lower (Gold et al. 1989) levels have been reported in schizophrenic patients compared to controls.

A more productive line of investigation has involved measuring $GABA_A$ receptors, the GABA reuptake site, and very recently, a quantitative study of alterations in messenger RNA (mRNA) coding for glutamic acid decarboxylase in the prefrontal cortex of schizophrenic patients. Cross et al. (1985), using tissue homogenates, found no elevation of GABA receptors in the caudate, nucleus accumbens or globus pallidus in schizophrenic patients with or without abnormal involuntary movements. However, Hanada et al. (1987), using [^{3}H]-muscimol, found an increase in $GABA_A$ receptors in tissue homogenates from the left prefrontal cortex and the head of left caudate of schizophrenic patients. The caudate findings were significant only for those patients who died suddenly. Neuroleptic medication status in the 2 months prior to death had no effect on receptor density in this study. Benes et al. (1992) found increased binding of [^{3}H]-muscimol in layers I, II and III of the anterior cingulate gyrus. This finding was quite provocative as the same group had earlier demonstrated a loss of small neurons (which represent the majority of GABAergic neurons) in the prefrontal and cingulate cortices of schizophrenic patients. These findings together with reports of reduced GABA reuptake sites in the hippocampus (Simpson et al. 1989; Reynolds et al. 1990), amygdala (Simpson et al. 1989, though not replicated by Reynolds et al. 1990), and putamen (Simpson et al. 1992b), suggested a state of reduced GABAergic transmission in schizophrenia.

To directly address the question of reduced GABA transmission being secondary to neuronal cell loss, Akbarian et al. (1995), conducted an elegant study using in situ hybridization, cell counting methods and computerized densitometry to measure the level of GAD mRNA and numbers of neurons expressing GAD mRNA in six layers of the dorsolateral prefrontal cortex from post mortem brains of schizophrenic patients and matched controls. These data were compared with total number of neurons, and small, round or ovoid neurons (which represent the majority of GABAergic neurons). Reduced GAD mRNA expression (30%–48%) was found in cortical layers I–IV in schizophrenic patients compared to controls. There was no difference in the total number of neurons, or in the number of small, round or ovoid neurons between patients and controls. Akbarian et al. concluded that the reduced expression of GAD in the prefrontal cortex of schizophrenic patients in the absence of neuronal cell loss is consistent with an activity dependent down-regulation, which may be associated with functional hypoactivity of the prefrontal cortex that has been demonstrated in schizophrenia (Weinberger et al. 1986, Buchsbaum et al. 1984).

Norepinephrine, acetyl choline, peptides, and other neurotransmitters

A role for disordered norepinephrine (NE) transmission in the pathophysiology of schizophrenia was first suggested by Stein and Wise in 1971. Numerous modulatory interactions between the noradrenergic and dopaminergic systems have been reported (Tassin 1992). Breier et al. (1990) found no difference in plasma NE between schizophrenics and controls although plasma NE levels were correlated with positive and negative symptoms within the schizophrenic group. Kemali et al. (1990) found increased CSF NE in patients compared with controls, and increased NE levels were correlated with positive symptoms and paranoid symptoms. Van Kammen et al. (1990) found low levels of CSF NE were inversely correlated with negative symptoms in patients that did not relapse during a drug-free period. These observations suggest that NE changes in schizophrenia may be state-dependent (Van Kammen et al. 1990). In postmortem samples, increased norepinephrine levels have been demonstrated in limbic areas (Farley et al. 1978; Kleinman et al. 1982), but others have not replicated this finding (Crow et al. 1979).

Similarly, postmortem studies of adrenergic receptors have not been very fruitful. No alterations in levels of alpha 1 and alpha 2 receptors were found in multiple brain regions sampled (Toru et al. 1988; Meana et al. 1992). Joyce et al. (1992) in an extensive study of $\beta1$ and $\beta2$ receptors in multiple brain regions of schizophrenic patients found increased density of $\beta1$ receptors in the ventral striatum and a loss of normal asymmetry of $\beta2$ receptors in the hippocampus. The implications of these findings for the pathophysiology and treatment of schizophrenia are unclear. However, Pickar and colleagues (1992) have proposed a role for NE in the unique action of clozapine. They found that clozapine produces marked increases in CSF and plasma NE, whereas typical neuroleptics have little or no effect on NE. The increase in plasma NE in clozapine-treated patients was significantly related to clinical improvement suggesting a possible role for NE in the superior clinical efficacy of clozapine (Breier et al. 1994).

The only replicated findings involving neuropeptides in schizophrenia are those of neurotensin (NT) and cholecystokinin (CCK). NT is a 13-amino-acid peptide that is colocalized with dopamine. Because its behavioral effects in animals are similar to those of neuroleptics, NT has been termed an "endogenous neuroleptic" (Nemeroff 1980). Postmortem studies of NT levels in schizophrenic patients have yielded equivocal results with Nemeroff et al. (1983) showing a significant increase in NT in the medial prefrontal cortex, while Kleinman et al. (1985) found no difference in NT concentrations in the nucleus accumbens, globus pallidus, and hypothalamus between schizophrenic patients and controls. A series of studies of NT levels in CSF conducted by Nemeroff and colleagues (Widerlov et al. 1982, Lindstrom et al. 1988, Nemeroff et al. 1989, Garver et al. 1991), revealed that a subset of patients with schizophrenia had decreased CSF NT levels that increased after treatment with standard neuroleptics. However, there has been difficulty correlating these changes in NT levels with clinical improvement. Butler et al. (personal communication) in our group, are currently examining CSF NT levels in schizophrenic patients when they are medication-free, and again after treatment with either a standard neuroleptic, or with the atypical antipsychotic, clozapine. The relationships between changes in NT levels after treatment with standard and atypical neuroleptics and treatment response will be examined. A positive association would support a role for NT as an endogenous neuroleptic and may lead to development of a new class of antipsychotic agents that were lipophilic NT agonists and could cross the blood brain barrier.

CCK is a 33-amino-acid peptide that is colocalized with mesolimbic dopaminergic neurons and is thought to act as a neurotransmitter or neuromodulator. Decreased levels of CCK have been found in the hippocampus and frontal cortex (Farmery et al. 1985) using homogenate binding. Kerwin et al. (1992), using autoradiography, found decreased CCK binding in the CA1 region of the hippocampus, the parahippocampal gyrus and the subiculum in schizophrenic patients.

Abnormalities in other neurotransmitters/neuromodulators such as acetyl choline, endogenous opiates, somatostatin, substance P, and neurotensin have been reported but these have not been consistently replicated.

CONCLUSION FOR REVIEW SECTION

Despite methodologic and technical limitations, neurochemical studies in schizophrenia have made substantial contributions to our understanding of the pathophysiology of this disease. What is clear is that schizophrenia is not characterized by localized and specific neurochemical abnormalities. Rather, significant deviations are present in widespread cortical and subcortical regions in multiple neurotransmitter systems, involving neurotransmitter release and reuptake, and receptor density and symmetry of distribution. Neurotransmitter systems interact and influence one another at several hierarchical levels, and it is to be expected that derangement in one would lead to perturbations in others. One goal of neurochemical research in schizophrenia is to identify which neurotransmitter system is primarily affected and which changes are secondary compensatory responses. Conversely, multiple neurotransmitter systems may be simultaneously disrupted in neurodevelopment.

Amino acid neurotransmitters such as glutamate and GABA have widespread distribution in the central nervous system comprising 80%–90% of all neurons and they are integrally involved in primary sensory and motor pathways and other metabolic processes. Monoaminergic systems (dopamine, norepinephrine and serotonin) on the other hand, constitute less than 1% of the neurons in the brain and are not involved in the primary pathways subserving sensory stimuli and motor outputs. The cell bodies of these systems are located in the mesencephalon and they send projections to large cortical and subcortical brain areas. The rate of neuronal firing and conduction velocity in monoaminergic neurons is slow, and the neurotransmitter action on the postsynaptic receptor may last for several seconds. Also, at least in the cortex, a single monoaminergic axon may innervate several functionally distinct regions suggesting an integrative role for these systems. It has also been shown that rather than altering the firing rate of the postsynaptic neuron, these neurotransmitters may potentiate the usual response of that neuron to a particular afferent input (Chiodo and Berger 1986, Sawaguchi and Matsumura 1985). All these characteristics of monoaminergic systems suggest that they serve a modulatory role in neural transmission.

Within the monoaminergic systems, the noradrenergic and serotonergic systems have a wider distribution of innervation compared to dopaminergic neurons. Destruction of the noradrenergic system in rats impairs attention and learning but no gross behavioral effects are noticeable, while serotonergic ablation results in increased aggressivity and impulsivity (Soubrie 1986). On the other hand, destruction of the ascending dopamine neurons results in impairment of learning and memory, cognitive functions, and reinforcement processes, and these animals have "total behavioral disorganization with inability to initiate and adapt" (Simon and Le Moal 1991). The identification of the exact nature of the neurochemical dysregulation(s) in schizophrenia will depend to a large degree on acquiring an understanding of the distribution and function of these systems in normal individuals. Only then will we be able to interpret the etiological and pathophysiological significance of the subtle neurochemical abnormalities that have been demonstrated thus far in this illness.

FUTURE DIRECTIONS

Past approaches to investigate the neurochemical abnormalities in schizophrenia have employed rather basic approaches such as measurement of neurotransmitter or metabolite levels and measurement of receptor densities. At least in part, this was due to conceptual and technological limitations of the period. Advances in neuroscience and molecular biology in the past decade have begun to decipher the complexity of neuronal organization and transmission and have highlighted not only the limitations of prior approaches but also the difficulties that lie ahead. The dynamic nature of gene/environment interactions which alter brain function on a continual basis at the molecular, and ultimately, organismal level, is just being realized. These gene/environment interactions are not limited to neurodevelopment but continue in the mature brain. Investigation of the molecular mechanisms that underlie this concept of 'neural plasticity' are currently an area of intense study, and will impact on our understanding of such diverse entities as state variables, mechanisms of drug action, and role of stress in mental illness. These two broad and somewhat overlapping areas, i.e., the complexity of neural transmission and neural plasticity, will be briefly reviewed as they provide a window into the future of neurochemical research in schizophrenia.

Complexity of neuronal organization and transmission

The complexity of brain organization is matched by no other organ. There are approximately 100 billion neurons in the brain arranged in specific neuronal circuits with specific regional topographies. Each individual neuron may form more than a thousand synapses with other neurons, and most neurons colocalize two or even three neurotransmitters. Multiple receptor subtypes exist for each neurotransmitter and these may have specific regional distributions in the brain, may be pre- or postsynaptic with opposing actions, may exist in different affinity states, and may be physiologically linked to each other. Just based on these facts, the level of complexity is staggering. However, another whole level of complexity exists in signal transduction mechanisms that are initiated when a neurotransmitter binds to its specific receptor. Five superfamilies of receptors have been identified but only two, ligand-gated ion channels and G-protein-linked receptors, will be described. Receptors that are ligand-gated ion channels such as glutamate receptors, $GABA_A$, and nicotinic receptors have rapid off-on action; binding of the transmitter to the receptor results in a change in ion permeability in the ion pore that lies within the receptor and sudden influx of an ion results in either depolarization or hyperpolarization. Ion channels can also be G-protein-linked as described below.

The second superfamily of receptors are called guanosine nucleotide binding, or G-protein-linked and include dopaminergic, noradrenergic, serotonergic, muscarinic, $GABA_B$, and metabotropic subtype of glutamate receptors. G proteins are membrane linked proteins that are the transduction mechanism between receptors and intracellular second messenger systems or ion channels. Several forms of G proteins have been recognized and linkage to specific second messengers may involve stimulation or inhibition. G proteins provide one step in signal transduction at which various neurotransmitters may interact, and also provide an amplification in the transduced signal. G proteins can be linked to various second messengers including cyclic AMP, cyclic GMP, phosphatidylinositol, and arachidonic acid, as well as to ion channels such as Ca^{2+}. The end result of activation of each of these second messenger systems is to activate protein kinase which is the major enzyme involved in protein phosphorylation.

Phosphorylation is the addition of a phosphate group to a protein and is the primary method of posttranslational modification of protein activity. It is integral to all aspects of cellular function. Proteins can undergo phosphorylation at multiple sites by various forms of protein kinase resulting in similar or even opposite actions. Addition of a phosphate group changes the charge of the protein and, therefore, its conformation. A change in conformation translates into a change in functional activity. For example, various receptors such as serotonergic, adrenergic, dopaminergic, and ion channels undergo phosphorylation and are thought to be desensitized by phosphorylation. Phosphorylation of ion channels and pumps results in an alteration in their level of activity, e.g., phosphorylation Na^+-K^+ATPase and the Ca^{2+}-Mg^{2+} ATPase pumps may change intraneuronal ionic distributions and, therefore, excitability of the neuron. Many of the intermediary pathways in second messenger system activation involve proteins that are phosphorylated by protein kinases. These interactions allow a very complex and dynamic control on the final output of a neuron from the initial activation of various signal transduction mechanisms.

Phosphorylation is also involved in the regulation of synthesis and release of neurotransmitters. Phosphorylation of tyrosine hydroxylase and tryptophan hydroxylase increases their activity thereby increasing the rate of synthesis of dopamine/noradrenaline and serotonin, respectively. Phosphorylation of synaptic vesicle-associated phosphoproteins such as synapsins increases their rate of release of neurotransmitter. Finally, phosphorylation may also be involved in 'forward regulation' of gene expression by activation of transcription factors such as cAMP response element binding (CREB) protein which may result in increased expression of early immediate gene products such as *c-fos* (see below).

The complexity of intracellular signal transduction and the intricate mechanisms for maintaining homeostasis can be appreciated from the above description which has been greatly simplified for the sake of clarity. How these intracellular metabolic pathways are influenced by genes and environment will be reviewed next.

Neural plasticity

Neural plasticity refers to the dynamic capacity of the brain to change, as for example in learning. The two main mechanisms underlying neural plasticity are protein phosphorylation and alteration in gene expression. These two processes are intricately linked but differ on the time scale of their action with phosphorylation occurring on a fairly rapid basis while changes in gene expression operate in the relative long term. Protein phosphorylation has been discussed previously. This section will provide a brief overview of mechanisms influencing gene expression.

The basic process of protein synthesis involves transcription of DNA to mRNA which is translated to protein in the cytoplasm. Proteins are involved in all aspects of cellular function from serving as cytoskeletal structures of cells to enzymes, receptors, and membrane transporters that regulate the flow of ions and small molecules across cell membranes. Therefore, regulation of protein synthesis from DNA essentially controls all aspects of cellular function. The major point of this regulation is the initiation of transcription of RNA from DNA. Initiation of transcription is catalyzed by RNA polymerase II which must form a complex with regulatory proteins called transcription factors. Specific coding sites exist near the transcription initiation site for binding of transcription factors. These specific coding sites on the DNA are called cis-regulatory elements. Each gene therefore has a combination of cis-regulatory elements which determine the unique expression of that gene. Many genes share cis-regulatory elements that bind transcription factors that confer a basal level of activity to the gene.

Differential gene expression at different stages of neuronal development or in response to physiologic changes within the neuron is accomplished by several factors: specific cis-regulatory elements that bind transcriptional factors found only in specific cell types; repressor proteins in specific cell types that prevent initiation of gene expression; and specific cis-regulatory elements, called response elements, that can only initiate transcription after they have first bound to proteins in response to a specific physiologic signal. Examples of response elements include the cAMP response element that binds CREB (cAMP response element binding protein) and can activate transcription when phosphorylated by cyclic-AMP-dependent protein kinase. This may be one mechanism by which drugs that affect cAMP influence gene expression. In general, activation of protein kinases results in phosphorylation of many transcription factors and their subsequent binding to the response element sites exerts control over gene expression. Another example of a response element is the activator protein-1 (AP-1) response element which is linked to the protein kinase C signal transduction pathway. The AP-1 response element binds transcription factors *c-fos* and *c-jun*. (also called proto-oncogenes or immediate early genes). These proto-oncogenes respond rapidly to neuronal stimulation. Stimulation of NMDA receptor and electroconvulsive therapy stimulate production of *c-fos*, *c-jun*, jun-B, and zif/268 proto-oncogenes (Cole et al. 1989; Saffen et al. 1988).

As can be seen from this brief overview, external factors such as stimulation or antagonism of receptors, through second and third messenger systems and eventual protein phosphorylation, can clearly alter the rate of gene expression in neurons and other cells. An individual neuron is therefore, in a constant state of flux with extremely complex mechanisms continually operative to maintain not only a constant intracellular milieu, but also to respond to changes in its environment by alteration of gene expression.

In conclusion, disordered neural function resulting in psychopathology could result from subtle perturbations at many levels: reduction in the actual numbers of neurons; disordered connections between neurons where normal topography is not maintained; abnormalities in neurotransmitter synthesis, release and degradation; abnormalities in numbers, distributions, or functional state of receptor subtypes; abnormal linkage between receptors and transduction mechanisms such as G proteins; abnormalities in second messenger systems; abnormalities of protein phosphorylation; and abnormalities in transcription factors or their binding sites, the cis-regulatory element. Any or all of these factors could operate in isolation or collectively to result in a disordered psychological state. As the operative factors in neuronal function are better understood, the refinement with which we approach investigation of neurochemical abnormalities in schizophrenia will surely improve.

ACKNOWLEDGMENT

Supported in part by NARSAD Young Investigator Award to the author.

REFERENCES

Akbarian S, Kim JJ, Potkin SG, Hagman JO, Tafazzoli A, Bunney WE Jr, Jones EG. Gene expression for glutamate acid decarboxylase is reduced without loss of neurons in prefrontal cortex of schizophrenics. *Arch Gen Psychiat* 52:258–266, 1995.

Alfredsson G, Wiesel F. Relationships between clinical effects and monoamine metabolites and amino acids in sulpiride-treated schizophrenic patients. *Psychopharmacology* 101:324–331, 1990.

Amin F, Davidson M, Davis KL. Homovanillic acid measurement in clinical research: A review of methodology. *Schiz Bull* 18:123–148, 1991.

Angrist B, Lee HK, Gershon S. The antagonism of amphetamine-induced symptomatology by a neuroleptic. *Am J Psychiat* 131:817, 1974.

Arnold SE, Hyman BT, Van Hoesen GW, Damasio AR. Some cytoarchitectural abnormalities of the entorhinal cortex in schizophrenia. *Arch Gen Psychiat* 48:625–632, 1991.

Arora RC, Meltzer HY. Serotonin-2 (5-HT2) receptor binding in the frontal cortex of schizophrenic patients. *J Neur Transm* 85:19–29, 1991.

Ashcroft GW, Crawford TBB, Eccleston K, Sharman DF, MacDougal EG, Stanton JB, Binns JK. 5-Hydroxyindole compounds in the cerebrospinal fluid of patients with psychiatric or neurologic disease. *Lancet* 2:1049–1052, 1966.

Banki CM, Arato M, Papp Z, Kurkz M. Cerebrospinal fluid amine metabolites and neuroendocrine changes in psychoses and suicide. In: Usdin E, Carlsson A, Dahlstrom A, eds. *Catecholamines: Neuropharmacology and CNS. Therapeutic Aspects.* New York: Alan R. Liss, 1984, pp. 153–159.

Benes FM, Bird ED. An analysis of the arrangement of neurons in the cingulate cortex of schizophrenic patients. *Arch Gen Psychiat* 44:608–616, 1987.

Benes FM, Vincent SL, Alsterberg G, Bird ED, SanGiovanni JP. Increased GABAa receptor binding in superficial layers of cingulate cortex in schizophrenics. *J Neurosci* 12:924–929, 1992.

Bird ED, Spokes EG, Iverson LL. Increased dopamine concentration in limbic areas of brain from patients dying with schizophrenia. *Brain* 102:347–360, 1979.

Bogerts B, Meertze E, Schonfeldt-Bausch R. Basal ganglia and limbic system pathology in schizophrenia: A study of brain volume and shrinkage. *Arch Gen Psychiat* 42:784–791, 1985.

Bogerts B, Ashtari M, Degreef G, et al. Reduced temporal limbic structure volumes on magnetic resonance images in first episode schizophrenia. *Psychiat Res* 35:1–13, 1990.

Bowers MB, Henninger GR, Gerbode FA. Cerebrospinal fluid 5-hydroxyindoleacetic acid and homovanillic acid in psychiatric patients. *Int J Neuropharmacol* 8:255–262, 1969.

Bowers MB Jr. Central dopamine turnover in schizophrenic syndrome. *Arch Gen Psychiat* 31:50–57, 1974.

Breier A, Buchanan RW, Waltrip RWII, et al. The effects of clozapine on plasma norepinephrine: Relationship to clinical efficacy. *Neuropsychopharmacology* 10:1–7, 1994.

Breier A, Wolkowitz OM, Roy A, Potter WZ, Pickar D. Plasma norepinephrine in chronic schizophrenia. *Am J Psychiat* 147:1467–1470, 1990.

Brown R, Colter N, Corsellis JAN, et al. Postmortem evidence of structural brain changes in schizophrenia. *Arch Gen Psychiat* 43:36–42, 1986.

Buchsbaum MS, DeLisi LE, Holcomb HH, Cappelletti J, King AC, Johnson J, Hazlett E, Dowling-Zimmerman S, Post RM, Morihisa J, Carpenter W, Cohen R, Pickar D, Weinberger DR, Margolin R, Kessler RM. Anteroposterior gradients in cerebral glucose use in schizophrenia and affective disorders. *Arch Gen Psychiat* 41:1159, 1984.

Bunney BS, Grace AA. Acute and chronic haloperidol treatment: Comparison of effects on nigral dopaminergic cell activity. *Life Sci* 23:1715–1728, 1978.

Carter CJ, Heureux RL, Scatton B. Differential control by NMDA and kainate of striatal dopamine release in vivo: A trans-striatal dialysis study. *J Neurochem* 51:462–468, 1988.

Chang W, Chen T, Lee C, Hung J, Hu W, Yeh E. Plasma homovanillic acid levels and subtyping of schizophrenia. *Psychiat Res* 23:239–244, 1988.

Chang W, Chen T, Lin S, Lung F, Lin W, Hu W, Yeh E. Plasma catecholamine metabolites in schizophrenics: Evidence for the two-subtype concept. *Biol Psychiat* 27:510–518, 1990.

Chiodo LA, Berger TW. Interactions between dopamine and amino acid-induced excitation and inhibition in the Striatum. *Brain Res* 375:198–203, 1986.

Clow A, Theodorou A, Jenner P, et al. Cerebral dopamine function in rats following withdrawal from one year of continuous neuroleptic administration. *Eur J Pharmacol* 63:145–147, 1979.

Cole AJ, Saffen DW, Baraban JM, et al. Rapid increase of an immediate early gene messenger RNA in hippocampal neurons by synaptic NMDA receptor activation. *Nature* 340:474–476, 1989.

Creese I, Burt DR, Snyder SH. Dopamine receptor binding predicts clinical and pharmacological potencies of antischizophrenic drugs. *Science* 192:481–483, 1976.

Cross AJ, Crow TJ, Ferrier IN, Johnson JA, Johnstone EC, Owen F, Owens DGC, Poulter M. Chemical and structural changes in the brain in patients with movement disorder. *Psychopharmacology* 2(Suppl):104–110, 1985.

Cross AJ, Crow TJ, Owen F. ^{3}H-flupenthixol binding in post-mortem brains of schizophrenics: evidence for a selective increase in dopamine D2 receptors. *Psychopharmacology* 74:122–124, 1981.

Crow TJ, Baker HF, Cross AJ, et al. Monoamine mechanisms in chronic schizophrenia: Post-mortem neurochemical findings. *Brit J Psychiat* 134:249–256, 1979.

Davidson M, Giordani A, Mohs R, Horvath T, Davis B, Powchik P, Davis K. Short-term haloperidol administration acutely elevates human plasma homovanillic acid concentration. *Arch Gen Psychiat* 44:189–190, 1987a.

Davidson M, Losonczy M, Mohs R, Lester J, Powchik P, Fried L, Davis B, Mykytyn M, Davis K. Effects of debrisoquin and haloperidol on plasma homovanillic acid concentrations in schizophrenic patients. *Neuropsychopharmacology* 1:17–23, 1987b.

Davidson M, Kahn R, Knott P, Kaminsky R, Cooper M, DuMont K, Aptu S, Davis K. Effects of neuroleptic treatment on symptoms of schizophrenia and plasma homovanillic acid concentrations. *Arch Gen Psychiat* 48:910–913, 1991.

Davila R, Manero E, Zumarraga M, Andia I, Schweitzer J, Friedhoff A. Plasma homovanillic acid as a predictor of response to neuroleptics. *Arch Gen Psychiat* 5:564–567, 1988.

Deakin JFW, Slater P, Simpson MDC, Gilchrist AC, Skan WJ, Royston MC, Reynolds GP, Cross AJ. Frontal cortical and left temporal glutamatergic dysfunction in schizophrenia. *J Neurochem* 52:1781–1786, 1989.

Deutsch SJ, Mastropaolo J, Schwartz BL, Rosse RB, Morishisa JM. A "glutamatergic hypothesis" of schizophrenia: Rationale for pharmacotherapy with glycine. *Clin Neuropharmacol* 12:1–13, 1989.

Douyon R, Angrist B, Peselow E, Cooper T, Rotrosen J. Neuroleptic augmentation with alprazolam: Clinical effects and pharmacokinetic correlates. *Am J Psychiat* 146:231–234, 1989.

Ellinwood EH. Amphetamine psychosis, I: Description of the individuals and the process. *J Nerv Mental Disord* 144:274–283, 1967.

Falkai P, Bogerts B, Rozumek M. Limbic pathology in schizophrenia: The entorhinal region: a morphometric study. *Biol Psychiat* 24:515–521, 1988.

Farde L, Wiesel F-A, Stone-Elander S, Halldin C, Nordstrom A-L, Hall H, Sedvall G. D2 dopamine receptors in neuroleptic-naive schizophrenic patients: A positron emission tomography study with [^{11}C]raclopride. *Arch Gen Psychiat* 47:213–219, 1990.

Farley IJ, Price KS, McCullough E, et al. Norepinephrine in chronic paranoid schizophrenia: Above-normal levels in limbic forebrain. *Science* 200:456–457, 1978.

Farley IJ, Shannak KS, Hornydiewicz O. Brain monoamine changes in chronic paranoid schizophrenia and their possible relation to increased dopamine receptor sensitivity. In: Pepeu G, Kuhar MJ, Enna SJ, eds. *Receptors for Neurotransmitters and Peptide Hormones*. New York: Raven Press, 1980. pp. 427–433.

Farmery SM, Owen F, Poulter M, Crow TJ. Reduced high affinity cholecystokinin binding in hippocampus and frontal cortex of schizophrenic patients. *Life Sci* 36:473–477, 1985.

Freed WJ, Dillon-Carter O, Kleinman JE. *Exp Neurol* 121:48–56, 1993.

Garver DL, Bissette G, Yao JK, Nemeroff CB. Relation of CSF neurotensin concentrations to symptoms and drug response of psychotic patients. *Am J Psychiat* 148:484–488, 1991.

Gattaz WF, Waldmeier P, Bechman H. CSF monoamine metabolism in schizophrenic patients. *Acta Psychiatr Scand* 66:350–360, 1982.

Gattaz WF, Gasser T, Beckmann H. Multidimensional analysis of the concentration of 17 substances in the CSF of schizophrenics and controls. *Biol Psychiat* 20:360–366, 1985.

Gold B, Bowers MB, Roth R, Sweeney P. GABA levels in CSF of patients with psychiatric disorders. *Am J Psychiat* 137:362–364, 1989.

Hanada S, Mita T, Nishino N, Tanaka C. [^{3}H]Muscimol binding sites increased in autopsied brains of chronic schizophrenics. *Life Sci* 40:259–266, 1987.

Hanlon TE, Ota KY, Kurland AA. Comparative effects of fluphenazine, fluphenazine-chlordiazepoxide and fluphenazine-imipramine. *Dis Nerv Syst* 31:171–177, 1970.

Harrison PJ, McLaughlin D, Kerwin RW. Decreased hippocampal expression of a glutamate receptor gene in schizophrenia. *Lancet* 337:450–452, 1991.

Hashimoto T, Nishino N, Nakai H, Tanaka C. Increased 5-HT-1a receptors in prefrontal and temporal cortices of brains from patients with chronic schizophrenia. *Life Sci* 48:355–363, 1990.

Hess EJ, Brancha HS, Kleinman JE, et al. Dopamine receptor subtype imbalance in schizophrenia. *Life Sci* 40:1487–1497, 1987.

Hietala J, Syvalahti E, Vuorio K, Nagren K, Lehikoinen P, Ruotsalainen U, Rakkolainen V, Lehtinen V, Wegelius U. Striatal D2 dopamine receptor characteristics in neuroleptic-naive schizophrenic patients studied with positron emission tomography. *Arch Gen Psychiat* 51:116–123, 1994.

Holden JMC, Itil TM, Keskiner A, Fink M. Thioridazine and chlordiazepoxide, alone and combined, in the treatment of chronic schizophrenia. *Comp Psychiat* 9:633–642, 1968.

Hsiao JK, Colison J, Bartko JJ, et al. Monoamine neurotransmitter interactions in drug-free and neuroleptic-treated schizophrenics. *Arch Gen Psychiat* 50:606–614, 1993.

Iqbal N, Asnis GM, Wetzler S, Kay SR, van Praag HM. The role of serotonin in schizophrenia: New findings. *Schiz Res* 5:181–182, 1991.

Ishimaru M, Kurumaji A, Toru M. Increases in strychrine-insensitive glycine binding sites in cerebral cortex of chronic schizophrenics: evidence for glutamate hypothesis. *Biol Psychiat* 35:84–95, 1994.

Jakob H, Beckmann H. Prenatal developmental disturbances in the limbic allocortex in schizophrenics. *J Neural Transm* 65:303–326, 1986.

Joyce JN, Lexow N, Bird E, et al. Organization of dopamine D1 and D2 receptors in human striatum: receptor autoradiographic studies in Huntington's disease and schizophrenia. *Synapse* 2:546–557, 1988.

Joyce JN, Lexow N, Kim SJ, Artymyshyn R, Senzon S, Lawerence D, Casanova MF, Kleinman JE, Bird ED, Winokur A. Distribution of beta-adrenergic receptor subtypes in human post-mortem brain: Alterations in limbic regions of schizophrenics. *Synapse* 10:228–246, 1992.

Joyce JN, Shane A, Lexow N, Winokur A, Casanova MF, Kleinman JE. Serotonin uptake sites and serotonin receptors are altered in the limbic system of schizophrenics. *Neuropsychopharmacology* 8:315–336, 1993.

Joyce JN, Gurevich EV, Kung HF, Kung M-P, Bordelon Y, Shapiro R, Arnold SE, Gur RE. Dopamine D3 receptors are elevated in schizophrenic brain and decreased by neuroleptic treatment. *Schiz Res* 15:61, 1995.

Kahn RS, Davidson M, Knott P, et al. Effect of neuroleptic medication on cerebrospinal fluid monoamine metabolite concentrations in schizophrenia: Serotonin-dopamine interactions as a target for treatment. *Arch Gen Psychiat* 50:599–605, 1993.

Karlsson P, Farde L, Halldin C, Sedvall G. Decreased D1-dopamine receptor binding in drug naive schizophrenic patients examined by PET. *Schiz Res* 15:86, 1995.

Karoum F, Karson CN, Bigelow LB, Lawson WB, Wyatt RJ. Preliminary evidence of reduced combined output of dopamine and its metabolites in chronic schizophrenia. *Arch Gen Psychiat* 44:604–607, 1987.

Kemali D, Maj M, Galderisi S, Ariano MG, Starace F. Factors associated with increased noradrenaline levels in schizophrenic patients. *Prog Neuropsychopharmacol Biol Psychiat* 14:49–59, 1990.

Kerwin RW, Patel S, Meldrum BS, Czudek C, Reynolds GP. Asymmetrical loss of a glutamate receptor subtype in left hippocampus in schizophrenia. *Lancet* 1:583–584, 1988.

Kerwin RW, Patel S, Meldrum BS. Quantitative audioradiographic analysis of glutamate binding sites in the hippocampal formation in normal and schizophrenic brain post-mortem. *Neuroscience* 39:25–32, 1990.

Kerwin R, Robinson P, Stephenson J. Distribution of CCK binding sites in the human hippocampal formation and their alteration in schizophrenia: A postmortem autoradiographic study. *Psychol Med* 22:37–43, 1992.

Kim JS, Kornhuber HH, Schmid-Burgk W, Holzmuller B. Low cerebrospinal fluid glutamate in schizophrenic patients and a new hypothesis on schizophrenia. *Neurosci Lett* 20:379–382, 1980.

Kleinman JE, Karoum F, Rosenblatt JE, et al. Postmortem neurochemical studies in chronic schizophrenia. In: Hanin I, Usdin E. eds. *Biological Markers in Psychiatry and Neurology*. New York: Pergamon Press, 1982, pp. 67–76.

Kleinman JE, Hong J, Iadorola M, Govoni S, Gillin JC. Neuropeptides in human brain—postmortem studies. *Prog Neuropsychopharmacol Biol Psychiat* 9:91–95, 1985.

Koreen AR, Lieberman J, Alvir J, Mayerhoff D, Loebel A, Chakos M, Amin F, Cooper T. Plasma homovanillic acid levels in first-episode schizophrenia: Psychopathology and treatment response. *Arch Gen Psychiat* 51:132–138, 1994.

Kornhuber J, Mack-Burkhardt F, Riederer P, Hebenstreit GF, Reynolds GP, Andrews HB, Beckmann H. [^{3}H]MK-801 binding sites in postmortem brain regions of schizophrenic patients. *J Neural Trans* 77:231–236, 1989.

Korpi ER, Kleinman JE, Goodman, SI, et al. Serotonin and 5-hydroxyindoleacetic acid concentrations in different brain regions of suicide victims: Comparison in chronic schizophrenic patients with suicide as cause of death. *Arch Gen Psychiat* 43:594–600, 1986.

Korpi ER, Kaufman CA, Marneal K-M, Weinberger DR. Cerebrospinal fluid amino acid concentrations in chronic schizophrenia. *Psychiat Res* 20:337–345, 1987.

Krystal JH, Seibyl JP, Price LP, Woods SW, Heninger GR, Charney DS. MCPP effects in schizophrenia patients before and after typical and atypical neuroleptic treatment. [Letter] *Schiz Res* 4:350, 1991.

Krystal JH, Seibyl JP, Price LH, Woods SW, Heninger GR, Aghajanian GK, Charney DS. m-Chlorophenylpiperazine (MCPP) effects in neuroleptic-free schizophrenic patients. *Arch Gen Psychiat* 50:624–635, 1993.

Kurumaji A, Ishimaru M, Toru M. a-[3H]Amino-3-hydroxy-5-methylisoxazole-4-propionic acid binding to human cerebral cortical membranes: Minimal changes in postmortem brains of chronic schizophrenics. *J Neurochem* 59:829–837, 1992.

Laruelle M, Abi-Dargham A, Casanova MF, Toti R, Weinberger DR, Kleinman JE. Selective abnormalities of prefrontal serotonergic receptors in schizophrenia. *Arch Gen Psychiat* 50:810–818, 1993.

Lee T, Seeman P. Dopamine receptors in normal and schizophrenic human brains. *Soc Neurosci Abstr* 3:443, 1977.

Lee T, Seeman P. Elevation of brain neuroleptic/dopamine receptors in schizophrenia. *Am J Psychiat* 137:191–197, 1980.

Lieberman JA, Koreen AR. Neurochemistry and neuroendocrinology of schizophrenia: A selective review. *Schiz Bull* 19:371–429, 1993.

Lindstrom LH. Low HVA and normal 5-HIAA CSF levels in drug-free schizophrenic patients compared to healthy volunteers: Correlations to symptomatology and family history. *Psychiat Res* 14:265–273, 1985.

Lindstrom L, Widerlov E, Bissette G, Nemeroff CB. Reduced CSF neurotensin concentration in drug free schizophrenic patients. *Schiz Res* 1:55–59, 1988.

Mackay AVP, Bird EO, Spokes EG, et al. Dopamine receptors and schizophrenia: Drug effect or illness? *Lancet* 2:915–916, 1980.

Marsden CD, Jenner P. The pathophysiology of extrapyramidal side-effects of neuroleptic drugs. *Psychol Med* 10:55–72, 1980.

Martinot J-L, Peron-Magnan P, Huret J-D, Mazoyer B, Baron J-C, Boulenger J-P, Loc'h C, Maziere B, Caillard V, Loo H, Syrota A. Striatal D2 dopaminergic receptors assessed with positron emission tomography and 76-Br-bromospiperone in untreated patients. *Am J Psychiat* 147:44–50, 1990.

Meana JJ, Barturen F, Garcia-Sevilla JA. alpha-2-Adrenoceptors in the brain of suicide victims: Increased receptor density associated with major depression. *Biol Psychiat* 31:471–490, 1992.

Mita T, Hanada S, Nishino N, et al. Decreased serotonin S2 and increased dopamine D2 receptors in chronic schizophrenics. *Biol Psychiat* 21:1407–1414, 1986.

Muller P, Seeman P. Dopaminergic supersensitivity after neuroleptics: time course and specificity. *Psychopharmocology* 60:1–11, 1978.

Nemeroff CB. Neurotensin: Perchance an endogenous neuroleptic? *Biol Psychiat* 15:283–302, 1980.

Nemeroff CB, Youngblood WW, Manberg PJ, Prange AJ, Kizer JS. Regional brain concentrations of neuropeptides in Huntington's chorea and schizophrenia. *Science* 221:972–975, 1983.

Nemeroff CB, Bissette G, Widerlov E, Beckmann H, Gerner R, Manberg PJ, Lindstrom L, Prange AJ, Gattaz WF. Neurotensin-like immunoreactivity in cerebrospinal fluid of patients with schizophrenia, depression, anorexia nervosa-bulimia, and premenstrual syndrome. *J Neuropsychiat* 1:16–20, 1989.

Ninan PT, Van Kammen DP, Schenin M, Linnoila M, Burney WE Jr, Goodwin FK. CSF 5-hydroxyindoleacetic acid levels in suicidal schizophrenic patients. *Am J Psychiat* 141:566–569, 1984.

Nishikawa T, Takashima M, Toru M. Increased [^{3}H]kainic acid binding in the prefrontal cortex in schizophrenia. *Neurosci Lett* 40:245–250, 1983.

Nyback H, Berggren BM, Hindmarsh T, Sedvall G, Wiesel FA. Cerebroventricular size and cerebrospinal fluid monoamine metabolites in schizophrenic patients and healthy volunteers. *Psychiat Res* 9:301–308, 1983.

Owen F, Crow TJ, Poulter M, et al. Increased dopamine receptor sensitivity in schizophrenia. *Lancet* 2:223–226, 1978.

Owen F, Cross AJ, Crow TJ, Lofthouse R, Poulter M. Neurotransmitter receptors in brain in schizophrenia. *Acta Psychiatr Scand* 63:20–27, 1981.

Pato CN, Wolkowitz OM, Rapaport M, Schultz SC, Pickar D. Benzodiazepine augmentation of neuroleptic treatment in patients with schizophrenia. *Psychopharmocol Bull* 25:263–266, 1989.

Perry TL. Normal cerebrospinal fluid and brain glutamate levels in schizophrenia do not support the hypothesis of glutamatergic neuronal dysfunction. *Neurosci Lett* 28:81–85, 1982.

Pickar D, Labarca R, Linnoila M, Roy A, Hommer D, Everett D, Paul S. Neuroleptic-induced decrease in plasma homovanillic acid and antipsychotic activity in schizophrenic patients. *Science* 25:954–957, 1984.

Pickar D, Owen RR, Litman RE, et al. Clinical and biologic response to clozapine in patients with schizophrenia: Crossover comparison with fluphenazine. *Arch Gen Psychiat* 49:345–353, 1992.

Post RM, Fink E, Carpenter WT, Goodwin F.K. Cerebrospinal fluid amine metabolites in acute schizophrenia. *Arch Gen Psychiat* 32:1063–1069, 1975.

Potkin SG, Weinberger DR, Linnoila M, Wyatt RJ. Low CSF 5-hydroxyindoleacetic acid in schizophrenic patients with enlarged ventricles. *Am J Psychiat* 140:21–25, 1983.

Reynolds GP, Reynolds LM, Riederer P, et al. Dopamine receptors and schizophrenia: Drug effect or illness? *Lancet* 2:1251, 1980.

Reynolds GP. Increased concentrations and lateral asymmetry of amygdala dopamine in schizophrenia. *Nature* 305:527–529, 1983.

Reynolds GP, Czudek C, Andrews HB. Deficit and hemispheric asymmetry of GABA uptake sites in the hippocampus in schizophrenia. *Biol Psychiat* 27:1038–1044, 1990.

Reynolds GP, Mason SL. Are there detectable D4 receptors in the brain in schizophrenia? *Schiz Res* 15:69, 1995.

Roberts E. An hypothesis suggesting that there is a defect in the GABA system in schizophrenia. *Neurosci Res Prog Bull* 10:468–481, 1972.

Roberts PJ, McBean GJ, Sharif NA, Thomas EM. Striatal glutamatergic function: Modifications following specific lesions. *Brain Res* 325:83–91, 1982.

Saffen DW, Cole AJ, Worley PF, et al. Convulsant-induced increase in transcription factor messenger RNAs in rat brain. *Proc Natl Acad Sci USA* 85:7795–7799, 1988.

Sawaguchi T, Matsumura M. Laminar distributions of neurons sensitive to acetyl choline, noradrenaline, and dopamine in the dorsolateral prefrontal cortex of the monkey. *Neurosci Res* 2:255–273, 1985.

Seeman P, Lee T, Chau-Wong M, et al. Antipsychotic drug doses and neuroleptic/dopamine receptors. *Nature* 261:717–719, 1976.

Seeman P. Dopamine receptors in post-mortem schizophrenic brains. *Lancet* 1:1103, 1981.

Seeman P, Ulpian C, Bergeron C, et al. Bimodal distribution of dopamine receptor densities in brains of schizophrenics. *Science* 225:728–731, 1984.

Seeman P, Ulpian C, Bergeron C, et al. Human brain D1 and D2 dopamine receptors in schizophrenia, Alzheimer's, Parkinson's, and Huntington's disease. *Neuropsychopharmacology* 1:5–15, 1987.

Seibyl JP, Krystal JH, Price LH, Woods SW, D'Amico CD, Heninger GR, Charney DS. Effects of ritanserin on the behavioral, neuroendocrine, and cardiovascular responses to metachlorophenylpiperazine in healthy subjects. *Psychiat Res* 38:227–236, 1991.

Shenton ME, Kikinis R, Jolesz FA, et al. Abnormalities of the left temporal lobe and thought disorder in schizophrenia: a quantitative magnetic resonance imaging study. *N Engl J Med* 327:604–12, 1992.

Simon H, LeMoal M. Mesocorticolimbic dopaminergic network: Functional and regulatory roles. *Physiol Rev*, 155–233, 1991.

Simpson MDC, Royston MC, Slater P, Deakin JFW, Skan WJ. Reduced GABA uptake sites in the temporal lobe in schizophrenia. *Neurosci Lett* 107:211–215, 1989.

Simpson MDC, Slater P, Royston MC, Deakin JFW. Alterations in phencyclidine and sigma binding sites in schizophrenic brains: Effects of disease process and neuroleptic medication. *Schiz Res* 6:41–48, 1992a.

Simpson MDC, Slater P, Royston MC, Deakin JFW. Regionally selective deficits in uptake sites for glutamate and gamma-aminobutyric acid in the basal ganglia in schizophrenia. *Psychiat Res* 42:273–282, 1992b.

Soubrie P. Reconciling the role of central 5-HT neurons in human and animal behaviour. *Brain Behav Sci* 9:319–335, 1986.

Stein L, Wise CD. Possible etiology of schizophrenia: Progressive damage to the noradrenergic reward system by 5-hydroxydopamine. *Science* 171:1032–1036, 1971.

Stoof J, Kebabian J. Opposing roles for D-1 and D-2 dopamine receptors in efflux of cAMP from rat neostriatum. *Nature* 294:366–368, 1981.

Suddath RL, Casanova MF, Goldberg TE, Daniel DG, Kelsoe J, Weinberger DR. Temporal lobe pathology in schizophrenia: A quantitative magnetic resonance imaging study. *Am J Psychiat* 146:464–472, 1989.

Suga I, Kobayashi T, Ogata H, Toru M. Satellite Symp. 17th CINP, Abst, p.28, 1990.

Tassin JP. NE/DA interactions in prefrontal cortex and their possible roles as neuromodulators in schizophrenia. *J Neural Trans* 36(suppl):135–136, 1992.

Toru M, Watanabe S, Shibuya H, Nishikawa T, Noda K, Mitsushio H, Ichikawa H, Kurumaji A, Takashima M, Mataga N, Ogawa A. Neurotransmitters, receptors and neuropeptides in post-mortem brains of chronic schizophrenic patients. *Acta Psychiatr Scand* 78:121–137, 1988.

Toru M, Kurumaji A, Kumashiro S, Suga I, Takashima M, Nishikawa T. *Mol Neuropharmacol* 2:241–243, 1992.

Toru M, Kurumaji A, Ishimaru M. Excitatory amino acids: implications for psychiatric disorders research. *Life Sci* 55:1683–1699, 1994.

Van Kammen DP, Peters J, Yao J, van Kammen WB, Neylan T, Shaw D, Linnoila M. Norepinephrine in acute exacerbations of chronic schizophrenia. *Arch Gen Psychiat* 47:161–168, 1990.

Van Putten T, Marder SR, Aravagiri M, Chabert N, Mintz J. Plasma homovanillic acid as a predictor of response to fluphenazine treatment. *Psychopharmacol Bull* 1:89–91, 1989.

Weinberger DR, Berman KF, Zec RF. Physiological dysfunction of dorsolateral prefrontal cortex in schizophrenia: I. Regional cerebral blood flow (rCBF) evidence. *Arch Gen Psychiat* 43:114, 1986.

Whitaker PM, Crow TJ, Ferrier IN. Tritiated LSD binding in frontal cortex in schizophrenia. *Arch Gen Psychiat* 38:278–280, 1981.

Widerlov E, Lindstrom L, Besev G, Manberg PJ, Nemeroff CB, Breese GR, Kiser JS, Prange AJ. Subnormal CSF levels of neurotensin in a subgroup of schizophrenic patients: normalization after neuroleptic treatment. *Am J Psychiat* 139:1122–1126, 1982.

Winblad B, Bucht G, Gottfries CG, et al. Monoamines and monoamine metabolites in brains from demented schizophrenics. *Acta Psychiatr Scand* 60:17–28, 1979.

Wolkowitz OM, Breier A, Doran A, Kelsoe J, Lucas P, Paul SM, Pickar D. Alprazolam augmentation of the antipsychotic effects of fluphenazine in schizophrenic patients. *Arch Gen Psychiat* 45:664–671, 1988.

Wong DF, Wagner HN, Tune LE, Dannals RF, Pearlson GD, Links JM, Tamminga CA, Broussolle EP, Ravert HT, Wilson AA, Thomas-Toung JK, Malat J, Williams JA, O'Tuama LA, Snyder SH, Kuhar MJ, Gjedde A. Positron emission tomography reveals elevated D2 dopamine receptors in drug-naive schizophrenics. *Science* 234:1558–1563, 1986.

Wong DF, Tune L, Pearlson G, et al. Dopamine receptor elevations in drug-naive schizophrenia and bipolar affective illness measured by [¹¹C]NMSP PET studies: Update and methodological considerations. *Clin Neuropharmacol* 13(suppl):85–86, 1990.

Wooley DW, Shaw E. A biochemical and pharmacological suggestion about certain mental disorders. *Proc Natl Acad Sci USA* 40:228–231, 1954.

Epidemiology of Schizophrenia: Findings Implicate Neurodevelopmental Insults in Early Life

ALAN S. BROWN, M.D., and EZRA S. SUSSER, M.D., Dr.P.H.

INTRODUCTION

During the past ten years, we have witnessed dramatic developments in research on the etiology of schizophrenia. Among these advances, a "neurodevelopmental" hypothesis of schizophrenia has emerged, as a result of converging evidence from several diverse fields of study. This hypothesis posits that adverse events during early brain development, especially the prenatal and perinatal periods, play an important role in the origin of at least some schizophrenia cases. Thus, an exploration of the array of potential factors that could influence maldevelopment of the brain is likely to prove fruitful in the identification of particular causes of this illness.

In this chapter, we seek first to review evidence obtained during the past ten years in support of the neurodevelopmental hypothesis of schizophrenia. We shall then address specific prenatal and perinatal factors that may contribute to the etiology of this illness, including exposure to viral agents, nutritional deficiencies, and obstetric complications. Following this discussion, we present research strategies planned for the next ten years aimed at delineating these prenatal factors in designs that use birth cohorts and genetic pedigrees.

THE PAST 10 YEARS: FINDINGS IN SUPPORT OF THE NEURODEVELOPMENTAL HYPOTHESIS OF SCHIZOPHRENIA

Within the past 10 years, converging lines of evidence have emerged in support of the neurodevelopmental hypothesis of schizophrenia. The strongest support has come from three areas of schizophrenia research: brain imaging/neuropathology, premorbid abnormalities, and minor physical anomalies.

Startling advances in brain imaging techniques have permitted increasingly precise in vivo measurements of specific brain regions in studies of schizophrenia. The findings from these studies include increased ventricular size and reduced volumes of medial temporal lobe structures, including the hippocampus, parahippocampal gyrus, and the thalamus

(Waddington 1993a,b, Andreasen et al. 1986, Suddath et al. 1990, Bogerts et al. 1990, Breier et al. 1992, Andreasen et al. 1994). These anomalies are present in "first episode" patients, indicating that they are likely present before the onset of illness (Waddington 1993). A related field which has advanced substantially during the past ten years is the study of brain cytoarchitecture, which likewise has produced findings suggestive of early brain insult (Kovelman and Scheibel 1986, Jakob and Beckmann 1986, Benes and Bird 1987, Akbarian et al. 1993a,b, Waddington 1993a, Waddington 1993b).

The presence of these gross and ultrastructural brain abnormalities at this early stage of development appears inconsistent with the fact that the onset of psychosis rarely occurs before late adolescence. However, a second line of evidence suggests that children destined to develop schizophrenia have several early indicators of brain dysfunction prior to the onset of psychosis (Done et al. 1994, Walker et al. 1994, Jones et al. 1994). As early as the first two years of life, neuromotor abnormalities have been demonstrated in these individuals. The psychosocial anomalies consist of difficulties in social adjustment, manifested by withdrawal, disruptive behavior, and emotional lability. These particular developmental abnormalities appear to be specific to pre-schizophrenic patients, as they have not been observed in infants and children who later develop affective or neurotic disorders.

Another clinical indicator of an early developmental disruption are represented by minor physical anomalies (MPAs). MPAs are minor malformations of the head, eyes, ears, hands, mouth, or feet, that are ectodermal in origin, and that are believed to be secondary to first or second trimester prenatal or genetic insults (Green et al. 1989). Investigations of MPAs in schizophrenia are of value in our understanding of its etiology for two main reasons: ectodermal development closely parallels maturation of the fetal brain, and patients with schizophrenia, as compared to controls, have an increased occurrence of MPAs (Cox and Ludwig 1979; Green et al. 1989). Indeed, a recent study has demonstrated that MPAs in schizophrenia are associated with poor premorbid intellectual function and qualitative developmental anomalies of the cerebral ventricles (O'Callaghan et al., in press). Therefore, MPAs might provide important clues to the nature and timing of neurodevelopmental etiologic factors in schizophrenia.

Genetic versus environmental contributions

Both genetic and environmental factors have been implicated in the etiology of known neurodevelopmental disorders. In the case of schizophrenia, however, the relative contribution of genes and environment to adverse neurodevelopmental events has yet to be elucidated. Recently, a unique method for teasing apart these two etiologies has emerged: studies of discordant monozygotic twins. Since it is presumed that identical twins share 100% of their genes, any differences observed are likely to be environmental in origin. In a landmark study of discordant monozygotic twins using magnetic resonance imaging (MRI), Suddath et al. (1990) demonstrated that almost every affected twin had increased ventricular size and diminished volumes of temporolimbic structures, including the hippocampus, compared to their respective unaffected co-twins. Using positron emission tomography (PET), Berman et al. (1992) found lower frontal blood flow in each schizophrenic twin of discordant twin pairs, than in their corresponding co-twins without the illness.

Finally, Bracha et al. (1992) reported greater intrapair differences in finger ridge counts (thought to be determined during early fetal development and related embryologically to the brain) in discordant monozygotic twins with schizophrenia versus normal control twins. Since both structural (and perhaps functional) brain abnormalities and finger ridge counts are believed to be largely neurodevelopmental in origin, these studies indicate that prenatal environmental factors play a role in the neuropathology observed in schizophrenia. However, other evidence also indicates a strong genetic component to neurodevelopmental disorders (Little and Nevin 1992; Hughes and Newton 1992).

THE PAST 10 YEARS: A REVIEW OF FINDINGS ON HYPOTHESIZED NEURODEVELOPMENTAL ETIOLOGIES

Prenatal and perinatal exposures that have been shown to disrupt fetal brain development fall into six main groups (Hobel 1985, Kline et al. 1989, Paneth 1994), namely, infectious, nutritional, toxic, hormonal, immunologic, and obstetric. We select three of these areas for review: prenatal infection, prenatal nutritional deficiency, and obstetric complications.

Prenatal infection

Neurobiologic plausibility. A substantive literature has established that many infectious agents have detrimental effects on fetal brain development. The possibility that prenatal viral exposures are etiologic factors in schizophrenia is supported by work proving that several viral agents adversely affect CNS development. These teratogens include rubella, cytomegalovirus (CMV), and herpes simplex virus (HSV) (Whitley and Stagno 1991; Klein and Remington 1990). Each is associated with CNS malformations and with neurologic and cognitive dysfunction, such as mental retardation, learning disabilities, and behavioral disturbances. These congenital syndromes result from prenatal or perinatal exposure to these viruses. Some studies also suggest that prenatal exposure to the influenza virus can affect brain development, but the results for influenza remain controversial (Coffey and Jessop 1955, Hakosalo and Saxen 1971, Lynberg et al. 1994, Leck 1963, Leck 1971, Rogers et al. 1972, Walker and McKee 1959, Hardy et al. 1961).

Let us consider how the teratogenic effects of viruses on CNS development relate to the neuropathology and pathogenesis of schizophrenia. The pathogenesis of prenatal viral infection with respect to adverse effects on the developing fetus has yet to be firmly established, and varies with the type of infecting virus. Viral infection of the placenta may result in fetal damage by direct fetal invasion, with or without placental infection (Mims 1968, Catalano and Sever 1971); or indirectly, by inducing hyperthermia (Edwards, 1986; Milunsky et al, 1992) or by a maternal immune response (Laing et al. 1989). It is of interest that several infectious agents are neurotropic, that is, have a predilection for the CNS. In particular, ventriculomegaly and temporolimbic abnormalities are commonly observed after prenatal infection with several of the viral agents reviewed above (although not in the case of influenza) (Whitley and Stagno 1991).

While prenatal viral infection is usually associated with neuropathologic lesions of much greater severity than those found in schizophrenia, it is nonetheless possible that a more subtle effect of a neurovirus, such as that which gives rise to schizophrenia, is likely to escape detection in neonates and infants. Moreover, the presence of a congenital viral syndrome at birth markedly diminishes the chances of survival to the age of risk for schizophrenia. Additional parallel findings between congenital viral syndromes and schizophrenia include an increased occurrence of dermatoglyphic anomalies in rubella and CMV (Achs et al. 1966, Purvis-Smith and Menser 1973, Wright 1973), and in schizophrenia (Green et al. 1989). In addition, investigators have reported delayed psychomotor and neuromotor development and childhood behavioral disturbances after viral exposures (Chess et al. 1971, Ho 1991, Whitley and Stagno 1991) and in children destined to develop schizophrenia (Walker et al. 1994, Fish et al. 1992, Jones et al. 1994).

Epidemiologic studies of prenatal viral exposures

Converging evidence from epidemiologic studies supports the plausibility of a role for prenatal viral insults in schizophrenia. Studies conducted throughout the world have consistently demonstrated a 5%–15% excess of births in the winter and early spring among individuals destined to develop schizophrenia (Bradbury and Miller 1985, Torrey and Kaufmann 1986). A parsimonious interpretation of this season-of-birth effect is that it is related to seasonal viral epidemics. An increased incidence of schizophrenia has been reported among cohorts raised in urban areas (as compared to rural births) (Lewis et al. 1992), in which more crowded living conditions contribute to a higher rate of contagious illnesses. Moreover, the rate of schizophrenia is increased in individuals who had siblings of a young age while in utero, suggesting that these individuals had an increased likelihood of prenatal exposure to respiratory infections (Sham et al. 1993).

Prenatal influenza. Several recent investigations have provided evidence for prenatal influenza exposure as a risk factor for schizophrenia. The 1957 type A2 influenza epidemic, the second most severe pandemic of this century, has provided investigators with the opportunity to examine the relationship between a brief, time-limited exposure affecting up to 30% of the population, and schizophrenia among those in utero during the epidemic. In 1988, the first such investigation, conducted in Finland, suggested a higher incidence of schizophrenia among cohorts in the second trimester of gestation than in unexposed cohorts (Mednick et al. 1988). Subsequent investigations of cohorts exposed to the 1957 epidemic in Great Britain (O'Callaghan et al. 1991, Adams et al. 1993, Takei et al. 1994), Ireland (Cannon et al. 1994), Japan (Kunugi et al. 1995), and Australia (Welham et al. 1993) replicated the initial finding, and all but one showed second trimester specificity for the association.

Other studies have attempted to relate the occurrence of influenza epidemics over extended time periods to the risk of schizophrenia. Significant associations between exposure to second trimester prenatal influenza and schizophrenia were reported for birth cohorts in Denmark (Barr et al. 1990), England and Wales (Sham et al. 1992, Adams et al. 1993), and Australia (McGrath et al. 1993).

There have also been negative studies. In a notable study using individual rather than group data on a cohort born in March, 1958 (in which one would expect a high rate of second trimester exposure to the 1957 influenza epidemic), Crow et al. (1991) found no increased risk of schizophrenia; however, exposure was based on maternal reports of influenza after giving birth, which are subject to underreporting due to both the inability to recall the event and to asymptomatic infection (O'Callaghan et al. 1991). Other negative studies, each of which were based on the 1957 epidemic, include those by Torrey et al. (1991) in ten states of the USA, Susser et al. (1994) in Holland, and Erlenmeyer-Kimling (1994) in Croatia.

In evaluating studies that examine associations between prenatal influenza and neurodevelopmental disorders, one must consider the potential effects of intervening or confounding factors. The use of over-the-counter or prescribed flu remedies, which are commonly taken during pregnancy, may have teratogenic potential. Lynberg et al. (1994) demonstrated that the risk of neural tube defects was significantly increased in offspring of women who medicated the flu and fever during pregnancy, while those taking no medications had no increased risk.

A second possible intervening factor is poor maternal nutrition. An association between prenatal nutritional deficiency with both schizophrenia (Susser et al. 1992, Susser et al. submitted) and the anorexia that accompanies influenza infection could explain the observed relationship between prenatal influenza infection and schizophrenia. Finally, a secondary infection in influenza-exposed mothers, rather than influenza itself, may increase risk for schizophrenia in the offspring.

Therefore, the role of prenatal influenza as a risk factor for schizophrenia is still unresolved. Possibly, the inherent limitations of the research designs used in these studies lie at the root of the uncertainty. First, with only one exception, these studies used data that applied to groups rather than to individuals (i.e., it was known whether a woman was in the second trimester of pregnancy during a month in a peak period of an influenza epidemic, but not whether the woman had influenza). Second, none of these studies serologically documented influenza exposure during pregnancy. In the absence of serologically confirmed infection, these studies rely on imprecise definitions of the timing and severity of exposure. Third, because all of these studies used hospital registry data, misclassification of outcomes is likely to have occurred. This controversy is unlikely to be resolved until advancements are made to more precise methods.

Prenatal exposure to other viruses. Relationships between prenatal exposure to several other infectious agents and schizophrenia have also been demonstrated, although to date, few studies have been conducted. Watson et al. (1984) tested relationships between the season of birth effect and yearly variations in the incidence of eight seasonal diseases and climatologic temperature extremes in a large sample of patients with schizophrenia who had been hospitalized at a Minnesota Veterans Administration Hospital. The authors found significant positive correlations between winter schizophrenic births and prenatal exposure to diphtheria and pneumonia (causes unspecified). Torrey et al. (1988), in a study attempting to correlate the birth month and year of schizophrenia admissions with the occurrence of several reportable viral diseases in Connecticut and Massachusetts, found statistically significant associations between schizophrenia and prenatal exposure to measles in both states, and polio and varicella-zoster virus (VZV) in Connecticut only. More recently O'Callaghan et al. (1994), in an examination of 16 infections and schizophrenia birth dates in the United Kingdom, reported that schizophrenia was associated with prenatal exposure to bronchopneumonia (causes unspecified) and VZV. Thus, despite the lack of studies, there is some reason to suspect that prenatal exposure to other viral agents, particularly VZV and measles, may also merit further testing as risk factors for schizophrenia.

Prenatal nutritional deprivation

Of the causes of neurodevelopmental disorders in humans, one of the best-documented exposures with adverse effects on the developing brain is prenatal nutritional deficiency (Brown et al. in press). Neurodevelopmental disorders that result from deficiencies of micronutrients occur in both the developed and developing world (Little and Elwood 1992), as does schizophrenia (Jablensky et al. 1992). Neural tube defects (NTDs) represent the best known example of a neurodevelopmental disorder from nutrient deficiency. These malformations of the central nervous system are secondary to failure of neural tube closure, and are proven to be related to prenatal folate deficiency (MRC Vitamin Research Study Group 1991, Czeizel and Dudas 1992). The prevalence of NTDs follows no simple gradient across rich and poor countries, and there appears to be a strong contribution of environmental factors to their etiology (Leck 1984). Thus, gestational nutritional deprivation must be considered as a potential causal candidate for neurodevelopmental schizophrenia.

Neurobiologic plausibility. The preclinical literature is also replete with studies indicating adverse brain and behavioral outcomes after prenatal malnutrition. Prenatally malnourished animals tested as adults have morphologic, electrophysiologic, behavioral, and neurochemical abnormalities, consistent with hippocampal dysgenesis and disruption of neurotransmitter function (Butler et al. 1994). These anomalies parallel findings from neuropathologic, neuroimaging, and electrophysiologic studies of patients with schizophrenia (Lieberman et al. 1994).

Furthermore, there is evidence that minor prenatal micronutrient deficiencies—such as are common in even the wealthiest societies—can interact with genetic predisposition to produce brain disorders. A recent study by Mills et al. (1995) provides compelling evidence that a *minor* deficiency of B_{12} or folate, combined with an inherited enzyme defect, may be sufficient to cause NTDs. This may represent a useful model of a gene-environment interaction that could be further explored in investigations of schizophrenia.

The Dutch famine study. A series of investigations by our group on the effects of the Dutch Hunger Winter of 1944–45 has demonstrated an association between severe prenatal nutritional deprivation and schizophrenia (Susser et al. 1992, Susser et al. submitted, Brown et al. 1995). Toward the end of World War II, the Nazi blockade of occupied western Holland created a unique, although tragic, natural experiment. Since the famine was both sudden and time-limited, and relatively complete data on health outcomes in the population were available, it was possible to relate the degree and timing of nutritional deprivation to a variety of reproductive indices and CNS anomalies (such as NTDs) (Stein et al. 1975), and, a generation later, to the occurrence of schizophrenia.

Using dates of birth of cohort members and information on monthly caloric rations in the population, the gestational timing of exposure to the famine was determined in exposed birth cohorts. Using psychiatric registry data, schizophrenia outcomes were compared between cohorts exposed or unexposed to famine. Our group found a significant—greater than twofold—effect of severe famine exposure in early gestation on the risk of hospitalized schizophrenia in the offspring (Susser et al. 1992). In this initial study, the finding was significant only for females; in a subsequent study using an expanded data set on hospitalized

110

schizophrenia, we found that the association was significant in men as well as in women (Susser et al. submitted). Moreover, the additional number of cases in this follow-up study enabled us to define the timing of exposure more precisely. A remarkable concordance was demonstrated between the occurrence of schizophrenia and congenital neural defects (including spina bifida and anencephaly) following severe famine in early gestation.

Perinatal trauma

Neurobiologic plausibility. Various types of perinatal traumatic events, sometimes referred to as obstetric complications (OCs), induce brain damage in newborns, and have frequently been cited as causes of neurodevelopmental disorders, including at least some cases of mental retardation (Broman 1979), epilepsy (Hauser and Nelson 1989), and cerebral palsy (CP) (Nelson and Ellenberg 1986). Although the types of OCs are numerous and varied, their effects on the developing brain are mediated by one or more of the following factors: hemorrhage, increased intraventricular pressure, hypoxia, infection, circulatory disturbances, or toxins. Certain brain regions are especially sensitive to hemorrhages, internal pressure changes, and hypoxia, including the lateral and third ventricular walls, the area below the rostral corpus callosum, and the CA2 hippocampal region (Gilles et al. 1983, Lyon et al. 1989). Indeed, severe delivery complications have been associated with enlargement of the lateral and third ventricles (Cannon et al. 1989). These particular abnormalities are believed to be secondary, in part, to periventricular and intraventricular hemorrhage, resulting in cell necrosis and consequent dilatation of the ventricular system (Gilles et al. 1983).

Specific types of perinatal trauma have been studied in relation to neurodevelopmental disorders in infancy and childhood. Perinatal anoxia, primarily due to respiratory difficulty at birth, has been associated with lower cognitive scores in infancy and at age 7 (Broman 1979). Some studies have related toxemia and assisted delivery with the development of seizure disorders in children, although the large, prospective Collaborative Perinatal Project (CPP) found no relationship between obstetric complications and seizure disorders (Hauser and Nelson 1989). Finally, perinatal antecedents of cerebral palsy, including premature delivery, birth asphyxia, and breech presentation were each significantly associated with cerebral palsy, although these complications did not identify a substantially larger number of cases than when consideration was limited to events occurring prior to the onset of labor (Nelson and Ellenberg 1986).

Findings in schizophrenia. Several studies have reported an association between the number and/or severity of OCs variously defined and the risk of schizophrenia in the offspring (McNeil and Kaij 1978, Lewis and Murray 1987, Parnas et al. 1982, Cannon et al. 1989, Schwarzkopf et al. 1989, Eagles et al. 1990). In addition, several indicators at the time of birth that may be reflective of prenatal insults, including decreased head circumference (McNeil et al. 1993), low birthweight (Lane and Albee 1966, Pollin and Stabenau 1968) or respiratory difficulty (Pollin and Stabenau 1968, McNeil and Kaij 1978), appear to occur more frequently in infants who developed schizophrenia in adulthood compared to controls. Each of these studies utilized retrospective case-control methodology, with the exposure variables determined either by recall of the mother or obstetric record reviews. These methods are subject to inaccurate reporting of events, and the possibility of recall bias is high when information is obtained from mothers who are aware that their child has schizophrenia.

On the other hand, a notable study by Done et al. (1991), that obtained cases and controls from defined birth cohorts in which obstetric histories were prospectively and systematically collected, did not replicate the association between OCs and schizophrenia (Done et al. 1991). The study population consisted of the 16,980 individuals assessed in the British perinatal mortality survey, which represented virtually all births in England, Scotland and Wales from March 3–9, 1958. Their well documented birth histories were examined in relation to the later development of schizophrenia using psychiatric admission records from 1974–1986, abstracted from the Mental Health Enquiry. In both the main and exploratory analyses, patients with schizophrenia, broadly or narrowly defined, had no increase in perinatal factors predictive of stillbirth or neonatal death.

Recent evidence also suggests that obstetric complications may interact with genetic factors in producing ventriculomegaly. In a cohort prospectively ascertained for obstetric complications, Cannon et al. (1993) found an increased effect of birth complications on ventricular enlargement as genetic risk for schizophrenia increased.

It should also be noted that an observed association between schizophrenia and a perinatal/neonatal condition may be due to confounding if an antecedent prenatal insult causes both the perinatal/neonatal condition and schizophrenia (Goodman 1988). For example, Nelson and Ellenberg (1986) found that 58% of the sample with cerebral palsy had at least one prenatally determined abnormality, most often a congenital malformation. Their evidence supports the assertion that fetal maldevelopment influences the likelihood of labor complications and conditions associated with the presence of asphyxia. Thus, the potential role of OCs and their pathogenic mechanisms in schizophrenia remain to be determined.

THE NEXT 10 YEARS: FUTURE DIRECTIONS IN EPIDEMIOLOGIC RESEARCH OF NEURODEVELOPMENTAL ETIOLOGIES OF SCHIZOPHRENIA

While significant advances have been made in the past 10 years, much research work remains as we strive toward a better understanding of neurodevelopmental etiologies of schizophrenia. There is little question that progress in uncovering these etiologies is restricted by the limitations inherent in the research design of prior studies. These limitations include: 1) crude prenatal exposure data; 2) clinical, rather than research diagnoses; 3) inadequate control of bias due to loss to follow-up; 4) lack of control for confounding; and 5) inadequate statistical power. Thus, analogous to the new horizons that advances in imaging technologies have opened on our knowledge of brain structure and function, achieving a definitive understanding of the role of prenatal factors in schizophrenia will also require sophisticated new methods. We are presently embarking on a birth cohort study utilizing these new methods, which will provide us with an unparallelled level of precision.

Birth cohort studies

In the 1950s and 1960s, investigators throughout the world initiated several large birth cohort studies originally intended to test hypotheses on prenatal and perinatal risk factors on childhood developmental disorders. In a select number of these studies, the investigators had the foresight to obtain blood samples from women during pregnancy, and to store them for future research. The use of these samples represents an extraordinary opportunity for researchers to relate precisely documented prenatal exposures to the later occurrence of schizophrenia and other developmental disorders. At present, our group is forging a multisite international consortium of birth cohort studies consisting of over 100,000 individuals, aimed at pooling serologic data on specific prenatal exposures and schizophrenia outcomes. To illustrate their potential, we shall describe the most advanced of these studies, the Prenatal Determinants of Schizophrenia (PDS) study, proposed by our group.

The Prenatal Determinants of Schizophrenia (PDS) study will build upon the unique California Child Health and Development Study (CHDS), which included 19,044 live births during 1959–1966 in Oakland, California. The PDS aims, first, to test whether specific prenatal exposures are associated with an increased incidence of schizophrenia among cohort members. The second aim is to elucidate the pathways that may connect these prenatal exposures with schizophrenia; these pathways will be examined using comprehensive data on parental characteristics, perinatal events, and neonatal indicators.

Compared to prior studies in schizophrenia, the PDS vastly extends the range of prenatal exposures that can be directly examined, allows for more precise assessments of exposure and of diagnosis, is less subject to bias, and yields greater statistical power. The CHDS cohort is the only sizable birth cohort in which serum samples and previously collected exposure data are available for the *early* prenatal period. Using the stored prenatal maternal serum samples, we shall test for: maternal infection with influenza in mid-gestation by quantitating serial antibody titers; maternal folate deficiency in early gestation by measurement of serum homocysteine; and maternal thyroid deficiency by determination of thyroid stimulating hormone and thyroxine. Each of these prenatal exposures will be compared between individuals with schizophrenia and non-schizophrenia controls. In addition, we will examine previously collected data on early prenatal exposures, including prescribed amphetamines, smoking, and alcohol, for a relationship with schizophrenia. Other prenatal factors can be explored as new hypotheses emerge.

Linking birth cohort and genetic studies

Related initiatives have been undertaken to examine the interplay between prenatal and genetic determinants of neurodevelopmental schizophrenia. These initiatives are well illustrated by two projects developed by our research group in collaboration with others.

One of these projects seeks first to clarify suspected genetic etiologies of schizophrenia, utilizing large pedigrees from the NIMH Genetics Initiative described in the chapter by Johnson et al. The next phase will entail an unprecedented opportunity: to explore prenatal-gene interactions in the etiology of schizophrenia. This will be accomplished by combining precise data on prenatal exposures from the PDS study with identified genes or genetic markers from the genetic pedigree studies. Birth cohort and family members of the CHDS cohort, in whom prenatal exposure status has been determined, will be assessed for presence of the gene(s). We will then analyze the relationship between prenatal exposures, genes, and the risk of schizophrenia. It is hoped that this study will set a precedent for studies of schizophrenia using birth cohorts and genetic pedigrees, preferably from multisite international partnerships.

The second project involves the follow-up of a cohort of one thousand infants of very low birthweight (<2,000 grams) who are therefore at risk for brain damage. Brain structure and function have been documented precisely from the time of birth and the cohort has been comprehensively assessed at several time-points in childhood (Paneth 1994). In these infants, the prenatal and perinatal experience is already documented, and we are now initiating the collection of family/genetic data so that the relative contribution and potential interaction of genes and environment can be examined.

CONCLUSION

After a long period of relatively slow advance, in the past decade we have witnessed unprecedented growth in our understanding of the role of prenatal risk factors for schizophrenia. These developments opened a new vista for epidemiologic research in schizophrenia, and in particular, for investigations of potential neurodevelopmental etiologies. The coming decade presents the opportunity to implement research designs that will use this new knowledge to discover the causes of schizophrenia.

REFERENCES

Achs R, Harper RG, Siegel M. Unusual dermatoglyphic findings associated with rubella embryopathy. *New Engl J Med* 274:148–150, 1966.

Adams W, Kendell, RE, Hare EK, Munk-Jorgensen P. Epidemiological evidence that maternal influenza contributes to the aetiology of schizophrenia. *Brit J Psychiat* 163:522–534, 1993.

Akbarian S, Bunney WF, Potkin SG, Wigal SB, Hagman JO, Sandman CA, Jones EG. Altered distribution of nicotinamide-adenine dinucleotide phosphate-diaphorase cells in frontal lobe of schizophrenics implies disturbances of cortical development. *Arch Gen Psychiat* 50:169–177, 1993a.

Akbarian S, Vinuela A, Kim JJ, Potkin SG, Bunney WE, Jones EG. Distorted distribution of nicotanamide-adenine dinucleotide phosphate-diaphorase neurons in temporal lobe of schizophrenics implies anomalous cortical development. *Arch Gen Psychiat* 50:178–187, 1993b.

Andreasen NC, Nasrallah HA, Dunn V, Olson SC, Grove WM, Ehrhardt JC, Coffman JA, Crossett JHW. Structural abnormalities in the frontal system in schizophrenia: A magnetic resonance imaging study. *Arch Gen Psychiat* 43:136–144, 1986.

Andreasen NC, Arndt S, Swayze V, Cizadlo T, Flaum M, O'Leary D, Ehrhardt JC, Yuh WT. Thalamic abnormalities in schizophrenia visualized through magnetic resonance image averaging. *Science* 266:294–298, 1994.

Barr CE, Mednick SA, Munk-Jorgensen P. Exposure to influenza epidemics during gestation and adult schizophrenia. *Arch Gen Psychiat* 47:869–874, 1990.

Benes FFM, Bird ED. An analysis of the arrangement of neurons in the cingulate cortex of schizophrenic patients. *Arch Gen Psychiat* 44:608–616, 1987.

Berman KF, Torrey EF, Daniel DG, et al. Regional cerebral blood flow in monozygotic twins discordant and concordant for schizophrenia. *Arch Gen Psychiat* 49:927–934, 1992.

Bogerts B, Ashtari M, Degreef G, Alvir JMJ, Bilder RM, Lieberman JA. Reduced temporal limbic structures on magnetic resonance images in first episode schizophrenia. *Psychiat Res* 35:1–13, 1990.

Bracha HS, Torrey EF, Gottesman II, Bigelow LB, Cunniff C. Second trimester markers of fetal size in schizophrenia: A study of monozygotic twins. *Am J Psychiat* 149:1355–1361, 1992.

Bradbury TN, Miller GA. Season of birth in schizophrenia: A review of evidence, methodology, and etiology. *Psychol Bull* 3:569–594, 1985.

Breier A, Buchanan RW, Elkashef A, Munson RC, Kirkpatrick B, Gellad F. Brain morphology and schizophrenia: A magnetic resonance imaging study of limbic, prefrontal cortex, and caudate structures. *Arch Gen Psychiat* 49:921–926, 1992.

Broman SH. Perinatal anoxia and cognitive development in early childhood. In: Field TM, ed. *Infants Born at Risk*. New York: Spectrum Publications, 1979.

Brown AS, Susser ES, Lin SP, Neugebauer R, Gorman JM. Increased risk of affective disorders in males after second trimester prenatal exposure to the Dutch Hunger Winter of 1944–45. *Brit J Psychiat* 166:601–606, 1995.

Butler PD, Susser ES, Brown AS, Kaufmann CA, Gorman JM. Prenatal nutritional deprivation as a risk factor in schizophrenia: Preclinical evidence. *Neuropsychopharmacology* 11:227–235, 1994.

Cannon TD, Mednick SA, Parnas J. Genetic and perinatal determinants of structural brain deficits in schizophrenia. *Arch of Gen Psychiat* 46:883–889, 1989.

Cannon TD, Mednick SA, Parnas J, Schulsinger F, Praestholm J, Vestergaard A. Developmental brain abnormalities in the offspring of schizophrenia mothers. I. Contributions of genetic and perinatal factors. *Arch Gen Psychiat* 50:551–564, 1993.

Catalano LW, Sever JL. The role of viruses as causes of congenital defects. *Ann Rev Microbiol* 25:255–282, 1971.

Chess S, Korn SJ, Fernandez PB. *Psychiatric Disorders of Children with Congenital Rubella* New York: Brunner/Mazel, 1971.

Coffey VP, Jessop WJE. Congenital abnormalities. *Irish Med Sci* 349:30–46, 1955.

Cox SM, Ludwig AM. Neurological soft signs and psychopathology. I. Findings in schizophrenia. *J Nerv Mental Dis* 167:161–165, 1979.

Crow TJ, Done DJ, Johnstone EC. Schizophrenia and influenza. *Lancet* 338:116–117, 1991.

Czeizel A, Dudas I. Prevention of the first occurrence of neural tube defects by periconceptional vitamin supplementation. *New Engl J Med* 327:1832–1835, 1992.

Done DJ, Johnstone EC, Frith CD, Golding J, Shepherd PM, Crow TJ. Complications of pregnancy and delivery in relation to psychosis in adult life: Data from the British perinatal mortality survey sample. *Brit Med J* 302:1576–1580, 1991.

Done DJ, Crow TJ, Johnstone EC, Sacker A. Childhood antecedents of schizophrenia and affective illness: Social adjustment at ages 7 and 11. *Brit Med J* 309:699–703, 1994.

Cannon M, Cotter D, Coffey VP, et al: Prenatal exposure to the 1957 influenza epidemic and adult schizophrenia. *Schiz Res* 1994.

Catalano LW, Sever JL. The role of viruses as causes of congenital defects. *Ann Rev Microbiol* 25:255–282, 1971.

Crow TJ. Prenatal exposure to influenza as a cause of schizophrenia. *Brit J Psychiat* 164:588–592, 1994.

Eagles JM, Gibson I, Bremner MH, Clinie F, Ebmeier KP, Smith NC. Obstetric complications in DSM-III schizophrenics and their siblings. *Lancet* 335:1139–1141, 1990.

Edwards MJ. Hyperthermia as a teratogen: A review of experimental studies and their clinical significance. *Teratogen Carcinogen Mutagen* 6:563–582, 1986.

Erlenmeyer-Kimling L, Folnegovic Z, Hrabak-Zerjavic Boracic B, Folnegovic-Smalc V,

Susser E. Schizophrenia and prenatal exposure to the 1957 A2 influenza epidemic in Croatia. *Am J Psychiat* 151:1496–1498, 1994.

Fish B, Marcus J, Hans SL, Auerbach JG, Perdue S. Infants at risk for schizophrenia: sequelae of a genetic neurointegrative defect. *Arch Gen Psychiat* 49:221–235, 1992.

Gilles FH. Introduction. In: Gilles FH, Leviton A, Dooling EC, eds. *The Developing Human Brain: Growth and Epidemiologic Neuropathology*. Boston: John Wright, PSG Inc., 1983.

Goodman R. Are complications of pregnancy and birth causes of schizophrenia? *Devel Med Child Neurol* 30:391–395, 1988.

Green MF, Satz P, Gaier DJ, Gancell S, Kharabi F. Minor physical anomalies in schizophrenia. *Schiz Bull* 15:91–99, 1989.

Hakosalo J, Saxen L. Influenza epidemic and congenital defects. *Lancet* 2:1346–1347, 1971.

Hardy JMB, Azarowicz EN, Mannini A, et al. The effect of Asian influenza on the outcome of pregnancy, Baltimore, 1957–58. *Am J Pub Health* 51:1182–1188, 1961.

Hauser WA, Nelson KB. Epidemiology of epilepsy in children. *Cleve Clin J Med* 56:S185–194, 1989.

Ho M. *Cytomegalovirus: biology and infection*. New York: Plenum Medical Book Co., 1991, p. 207.

Hobel CJ. Factors during pregnancy that influence brain development. In: Freeman JM, ed. *Prenatal and Perinatal Factors Associated with Brain Disorders*. Bethesda, MD: US Dept. of Health and Human Services, 1985.

Hughes I, Newton R. Genetic aspects of cerebral palsy. *Dev Med Child Neurol* 34:80–86, 1992.

Jablensky A, Sartorius N, Ernberg G, Anker M, Korten A, Cooper JE, Day R, Bertelsen A. Schizophrenia: Manifestations, incidence, and course in different cultures. A World Health Organization Study. *Psychol Med Monog Suppl* 20, 1992.

Jakob J, Beckmann H. Prenatal developmental disturbances in the limbic allocortex in schizophrenics. *J Neur Trans* 65:303–326, 1986.

Johnson KP, Klasnja R, Johnson RT. Neural tube defects of chick embryos: An indirect result of influenza A virus infection. *Neuropathol Exp Neurol* 30:68–74, 1971.

Johnson RT. Effects of viral infection on the developing nervous system. *New Engl J Med* 12:599–604, 1972.

Jones P, Rodgers B, Murray R, Marmot M. Child developmental risk factors for adult schizophrenia in the British 1946 birth cohort. *Lancet* 344:1398–1402, 1994.

Kirke PN, Molloy AM, Daly LE, Burke H, Weir DG, Scott JM. Maternal plasma folate and vitamin B12 are independent risk factors for neural tube defects. *Quart J Med* 86:703–708, 1993.

Kunugi H, Nanko S, Takei N, Saito K, Hayashi N, Kazamatsuri H. Schizophrenia following in utero exposure to the 1957 influenza epidemics in Japan. *Am J Psychiat* 152:450–452, 1995.

Klein RZ, Haddow JE, Saix JD, Brown S, Hermos RJ, Pulkkinen A, Mitchell MI. Prevalence of thyroid deficiency in pregnant women. *Clin Endocrin* 35:41–46, 1991.

Klein JO, Remington JS. Current concepts of infections of the fetus and newborn infant. In: Remington JS, Klein JO, eds. *Infectious Diseases of the Fetus and Newborn Infant*, 3rd edition. 1990, Philadelphia: W.B. Saunders Co., pp. 1–16.

Kline J, Stein Z, Susser M: Conception to Birth: Epidemiology of Prenatal Development. Monographs in Epidemiology and Biostatistics, Vol. 1. New York: Oxford University Press, 1989.

Kovelman JA, Scheibel AB. A neurohistologic correlate of schizophrenia. *Biol Psychiat* 19:1601–1621, 1986.

Laing P, Knight JG, Hill JM, et al. Influenza viruses induce autoantibodies to a brain specific 37 kDa protein in rabbit. *Proc Natl Acad Sci USA*, 86:1998–2002, 1989.

Lane EA, Albee GW. Comparative birth weights of schizophrenics and their siblings. *J Psychol* 64:227–239, 1966.

Leck I. Incidence of malformation following influenza epidemics. *Brit J Prev Soc Med* 17:70–80, 1963.

Leck I. Further tests of the hypothesis that influenza in pregnancy causes malformations. *HSMHA Health Rep* 86:265–269, 1971.

Leck I. The geographical distribution of neural tube defects and oral clefts. *Brit Med Bull* 40:390–395, 1984.

Lewis SW, Murray RM. Obstetric complications, neurodevelopmental deviance and risk of schizophrenia. *J Psychiat Res* 21:413–421, 1987.

Lieberman JA, Brown AS, Gorman JM. In: Oldham JM, Riba MB, eds. *Biological Markers: Schizophrenia. American Psychiatric Press Review of Psychiatry, Volume 13.* Washington, DC: American Press, 1994.

Little J, Nevin N. Genetic models. In: Elwood JM, Little J, Elwood JH, eds. *Epidemiology and Control of Neural Tube Defects.* Oxford: Oxford University Press, 1992.

Little J, Elwood M. Geographical variation. In: Elwood JM, Little J, Elwood JH, eds. *Epidemiology and Control of Neural Tube Defects.* Oxford: Oxford University Press, 1992, pp. 195–246.

Lynberg MC, Khoury MJ, Lu X, Cocian T. Maternal flu, fever, and the risk of neural tube defects: A population-based case-control study. *Am J Epidemiol* 140:244–255, 1994.

Lyon M, Barr CE, Cannon TD, Mednick SA, Shore D. Fetal neural development and schizophrenia. *Schiz Bull* 15:149–161, 1989.

McNeil TF, Kaij L. Obstetric factors in the development of schizophrenia: Complications in the birth of preschizophrenics and in reproduction by schizophrenic parents. In: Wynne, LC, Cromwell RL, Matthysse S, eds. *The Nature of Schizophrenia.* New York, NY: John Wiley and Son, 1978, pp. 401–429.

McNeil TF, Cantor-Graae E, Nordstrom LG, Rosenlund T. Head circumferences in 'preschizophrenic' and control neonates. *Brit J Psychiat* 162:517–523, 1993.

Mednick SA, Machon RA, Huttenen MO, Bonett D. Adult schizophrenia following prenatal exposure to an influenza epidemic. *Arch Gen Psychiat* 49:63–72, 1992.

Mills JL, McPartlin JM, Kirke PN, Lee YJ, Conley MR, Weir DG, Scott JM. Homocysteine metabolism in pregnancies complicated by neural-tube defects. *Lancet* 345:149–151, 1995.

Milunsky A, Ulcickas M, Rothman KF, et al. Maternal heat exposure and neural tube defects. *JAMA* 268:882–885, 1992.

Mims CA. Pathogenesis of viral infections of the fetus. *Prog Med Virol* 10:194–237, 1968.

MRC Vitamin Research Study Group: Prevention of neural tube defects: Results of the Medical Research Council Vitamin Study. *Lancet* 338:131–137, 1991.

Nelson KB, Ellenberg JH. Antecedents of cerebral palsy: Multivariate analysis of risk. *New Engl J Med* 315:81–86, 1986.

O'Callaghan E, Sham P, Takei N, Glover G, Murray RM. Schizophrenia after prenatal exposure to 1957 A2 influenza epidemic. *Lancet* 337:1248–1250, 1991.

O'Callaghan EO, Sham PC, Takei N, Murray G, Glover G, Hare EH, Murray RM. The relationship of schizophrenic births to 16 infectious diseases. *Brit J Psychiat* 165:353–356, 1994.

O'Callaghan E, Buckley P, Madigan C, Redmond O, Stack JP, Kinsella A, Larkin C, Ennis JT, Waddington JL. The relationship of minor physical anomalies and other putative indices of neurodevelopmental disturbance in schizophrenia to abnormalities of cerebral structure on MRI. *Biol Psychiat* (in press).

Paneth N. The impressionable fetus? Fetal life and adult health. *Am J Pub Health* 84:1372–1374, 1994.

Parnas J, Schulsinger F, Teasdale TW, Schulsinger H, Feldman PM, Mednick SA. Perinatal complications and clinical outcome within the schizophrenia spectrum. *Brit J Psychiat* 140:416–420, 1982.

Pollin W, Stabenau JR. Biological, psychological and historical differences in a series of monozygotic twins discordant for schizophrenia. In: Rosenthal D, Kety SS, eds. *The Transmission of Schizophrenia*. London: Pergamon Press, 1968.

Purvis-Smith SG, Menser MA. Genetic and environmental influences on digital dermatoglyphics in congenital rubella. *Ped Res* 7:215–219, 1973.

Rogers SC. Influenza and congenital abnormalities. *Lancet* 1972; 1:261.

Schwarzkopf SB, Nasrallah HA, Olson SC, Coffman JA, McLaughlin JA. Perinatal complications and genetic loading in schizophrenia: Preliminary findings. *Psychiat Res* 27: 233–239, 1989.

Sham PC, O'Callaghan E, Takei N, Murray GK, Hare EH, Murray RM. Schizophrenia following prenatal exposure to influenza epidemics between 1939 and 1960. *Brit J Psychiat* 160:461–466, 1992.

Sham PC, MacLean CJ, Kendler KS. Risk of schizophrenia and age difference with older siblings. Evidence for a maternal viral infection hypothesis? *Brit J Psychiat* 163:627–633, 1993.

Stein Z, Susser M, Saenger G, Marolla F. *Famine and Human Development: The Dutch Hunger Winter of 1944–45*. New York: Oxford University Press, 1975, pp. 119–148.

Suddath RL, Christison GW, Torrey EF, Casanova MF, Weinberger DR. Anatomical abnormalities in the brains of monozygotic twins discordant for schizophrenia. *New Engl J Med* 322:789–794, 1990.

Susser ES, Lin SP. Schizophrenia after prenatal exposure to the Dutch Hunger Winter of 1944–45. *Arch Gen Psychiat* 49:983–988, 1992.

Susser ES, Neugebauer R, Hoek HW, Brown AS, Lin SP, Labovitz D, Gorman JM. Schizophrenia after prenatal exposure to famine: Further evidence (submitted).

Susser ES, Lin SP, Brown AS, Lumey LH, Erlenmeyer-Kimling L. No relation between risk of schizophrenia and prenatal exposure to influenza in Holland. *Am J Psychiat* 151:922–924, 1994.

Takei N, Sham PC, O'Callaghan E, Murray GK, Glover G, Murray RM. Prenatal exposure to influenza and the development of schizophrenia: Is the effect confined to females? *Am J Psychiat* 151:117–119, 1994.

Torrey EF, Kaufmann CA. Schizophrenia and Neuroviruses. In: Nasrallah HA, Weinberger DR, eds. *Handbook of Schizophrenia, vol 1: The Neurology of Schizophrenia*. Amsterdam: Elsevier Science Publishers, 1986.

Torrey EF, Bowler AE, Rawlings R. *An influenza epidemic and the seasonality of schizophrenic births*. In: Kurstak E ed. *Second World Congress on Viruses and Mental Health*. New York: Plenum, 1991.

Torrey EF, Rawlings R, Waldman IN. Schizophrenic births and viral diseases in two states. *Schiz Res* 1:73–77, 1988.

Waddington JL. Schizophrenia: developmental neuroscience and pathobiology. *Lancet* 341:531–536, 1993.

Waddington JL. Neurodynamics of abnormalities in cerebral metabolism and structure in schizophrenia. *Schiz Bull* 19:55–69, 1993

Walker EF, Savoie T, Davis D. Neuromotor precursors of schizophrenia. *Schiz Bull* 20:441–451, 1994.

Walker WM, McKee AP. Asian influenza in pregnancy. Relationship to fetal anomalies. *Obstet Gynecol* 13:394–398, 1959.

Watson CG, Kucala T, Tilleskjor C, Jacobs L. Schizophrenic birth seasonality in relation to the incidence of infectious diseases and temperature extremes. *Arch Gen Psychiat* 41:85–90, 1984.

Welham JL, McGrath JJ, Pemberton MR. Schizophrenia, birthrates, and three Australian epidemics. *Abstracts of the IVth International Congress on Schizophrenia Research*, 1993.

Whitley RJ, Stagno S. Perinatal viral infections. In: Scheld WM, Whitley RJ, Durack DT, eds. *Infections of the Central Nervous System*, New York, Raven Press, Ltd., 1991.

Wright HT. *Cytomegaloviruses.* In Kaplan AS, ed. *The Herpesviruses.* New York: Academic Press, 1973.

Genetics of Schizophrenia

JANET E. JOHNSON, M.D., JILL HARKAVY FRIEDMAN, Ph.D.,
DOLORES MALASPINA, M.D., and CHARLES A. KAUFMANN, M.D.

INTRODUCTION

Schizophrenia is a devastating, common and costly disease, affecting men and women equally. An estimated four million Americans are at risk of developing the disorder and the prevalence is approximately 150 in every 100,000 persons (APA 1988) The costs, both direct and indirect, are staggering, an estimated $30 billion to $48 billion per year. Revolutionary advances in human genetics are having profound effects on the theory and practice of psychiatry, and clinical, molecular and statistical genetic strategies promise to reveal much about the etiology, pathogenesis and treatment of mental illness. Of the estimated 50,000 to 100,000 genes in the human body, a significant proportion, approximately 25%, affect the brain and mental functioning (McKusick 1983). Much effort has been directed toward unraveling the etiology of schizophrenia and there is good evidence, which is increasing continually, that genetic factors play an important role in the etiology of this illness.

HISTORICAL OVERVIEW

Historical overview of schizophrenia/psychosis

The recognition of psychotic symptoms dates back to the earliest recorded records and references to insanity or madness can be found in numerous classical works. In the Greek tragedy *Ajax* by Sophocles, the hero is driven mad by the goddess Athena so that he slaughters animals he believes to be his human rivals. In this case, his insanity is believed to be the result of an avenging deity. This idea of causation is seen again in Euripide's *The Madness of Heracles* where the hero Heracles is seen to undergo a delusional reenactment of some of his famous labors (Simon 1992). The Greek doctors attributed mental illness to an imbalance or disharmony between the various bodily humors, in particular an excess of black bile.

In medieval times, Christianity dominated most views of the Western world and calamities of all kinds, social and individual, were considered as an expression of God's inscrutable plans (Mora 1978, 1980). Thus, behavioral abnormalities were seen as part of the divine plan for mankind and the mentally ill in general were accepted with a great deal of tolerance (Mora 1992). In the early 15th century the first institution exclusively for the insane was opened in Valencia and staffed by religious orders. The Reformation emphasized the role of individual conscience and guilt and tended to group mental illness with drunkenness, delinquency and other forms of aberrant behavior (Mora 1992). The well documented case histories of King Charles VI of France and George III, the last king of America, reveal clear indications of psychotic illness, as well as demonstrating the stigma associated with mental illness.

In the late 18th and early 19th centuries there was a growing acceptance among both physicians and laymen that the mind is a function of the brain and that mental physiology exists and is somehow related to the mind and therefore to behavior (Brizendine 1992). It was during this time that asylums were developed and the new subspecialty of Psychiatry emerged.

Emil Kraeplin (1828–1899) is generally credited with the delineation of schizophrenia, based on course and outcome. Kraeplin named the illness *dementia praecox* and distinguished it both from Alzheimer's disease and manic-depressive illness. Eugen Bleuler (1857–1939) felt that the illness was better characterized by symptoms than course and outcome and renamed the illness schizophrenia. He believed that a lack of cohesion in mental capacities was the essential and pathognomonic symptom and thus named the illness after this symptom; schizophrenia, or a splitting in mental capacities (Black et al. 1988). Bleuler also delineated the four As of schizophrenia: disturbance of *a*ssociations, *a*ffective blunting, *a*utism, and *a*mbivalence, enabling an increasingly broad definition of schizophrenia to emerge. In the 1960s much attention and research was devoted to diagnostic systems and brought about the development of structured examinations and more defined criteria. This process continues to date, with the most recent revision of the Diagnostic and Statistical Manual of Mental Disorders (DSM IV) published in 1994.

Historical overview of genetics

References to genetics and the transmission of familial traits can also be found as far back as the earliest recorded history of man. Ancient civilizations utilized basic genetic principles in breeding animals and plants in an effort to improve their physical characteristics. The Greeks proposed the theory of *pangenesis*, which stated that traits are inherited through the blood, a principle that endured for nearly 2,000 years and has found modern expression in Galtonian notions of quantitative, polygenic inheritance. An example of an early genetic understanding can be found in the Talmud, the ancient Jewish compendium of civil and criminal law. A Talmudic provision exists that exempts a Jewish boy from circumcision if a maternal uncle (but not a paternal one) is a hemophiliac, thus illustrating an understanding of sex-linked traits (Jaroff 1991).

In 1865, Gregor Mendel applied scientific methodology to the questions of heredity and proposed his now famous laws of heredity. His work went largely unnoticed and unappreciated until the early 1900s, when it was rediscovered by European biologists. Thomas Hunt Morgan and his colleagues at Columbia University produced the first genetic map in the first decade of the 20th century using the fruit fly. In 1911, the first human gene, that for color-blindness, was correctly assigned to a particular chromosome. In 1953, Watson and Crick made one of the most important discoveries of our time, elucidating the double helical structure of DNA. Hybrid and chemical staining techniques were discovered in the 1960s, thus facilitating genetic mapping. By the mid-1970s, several genes had been assigned to the X chromosome as well as some of the autosomes, through functional cloning, the technique of isolating a gene through its associated protein.

Restriction fragment length polymorphisms (RFLPs) were widely used beginning in the late 1970s and enabled the successful localization of the gene for Huntington's Disease in 1983. Since then, molecular genetic techniques have expanded at a remarkable pace, and have included many new and innovative methods, for example statistical methods (i.e., linkage and segregation analysis), and molecular starategies (i.e., representational difference analysis [RDA] and genomic mismatch scanning [GMS]). These advances have made the prospect of mapping the entire human genome a realistic goal and one that is underway through the Human Genome Project (HGP). The HGP is an international collaborative research initiative to produce detailed genetic and physical maps of each of the 24 human chromosomes and to determine the sequence of the three billion nucleotides that make up human DNA. The estimated cost of this project is three billion dollars and is expected to be completed by the year 2000. A 1–cM genetic map now exists (Cooperative Human Linkage Center (CHLC)/Centre D'Etude Polymorphisme Humain (CEPH), 1994).

APPROACHES TO PSYCHIATRIC GENETICS

Many different research strategies are necessary to clarify the role of genes in psychiatric disorders including schizophrenia. Family, twin and adoption studies have provided important genetic clues in the search for an etiology. In addition, many new innovative techniques in multiple areas have been discovered and are currently being used.

Family studies

Family studies often provide the first evidence that an illness involves genetic factors. The morbid risk (adjusted prevalence) of the illness is determined within families, and the rate for patient's relatives is compared with that for relatives of control groups or for the general population. During the past 70 years, approximately 20 family-risk studies have been conducted, and have examined the risk of schizophrenia in relatives of over 5,000 individuals. These studies have consistently demonstrated an elevated risk for schizophrenia in the first-degree relatives of schizophrenic patients (parents, mean 5.6%; siblings, 10.1%; and children, 12.8%), compared with that in the general population (0.9%), thus suggesting that schizophrenia is familial (Kaufmann and Malaspina 1993). Recent studies have corroborated these earlier findings. In and of themselves, family studies cannot establish that an illness is hereditary as familial aggregation may also reflect a shared environment, for example common exposure to a virus or culture.

Twin studies

Twin studies compare the concordance rate for illness in pairs of monozygotic twins with the rate in dizygotic twins. The underlying assumptions in these types of studies are that: 1) monozygotic twins share 100% of genes, while dizygotic twins, on average, share only 50% of genes; and 2) both types of twins are exposed to the same prenatal and postnatal environment. This latter premise is one that is still debated, as prenatal environments can differ, as in the case of shunt syndromes. Likewise, postnatal and home environments are unlikely to be exactly identical for two individuals. Even given these caveats, one would expect monozygotic twins to show greater concordance for hereditary illnesses than dizygotic twins. Twin studies in schizophrenia have consistently shown this to be true, with concordance rates for monozygotic twins ranging from 35%–58% and for dizygotic twins from 13%–27% (Gottesman and Shields 1982). Discordant identical twins can provide valuable information regarding environmental contributions to the full-blown illness as well as provide information on endophenotypes, formes hurste of the disorder that may display more classical (Mendelian) modes of inheritance. Gottesman and Bertelsen (1989) found that the offspring of nonschizophrenic MZ twins and the offspring of their ill co-twins had an equal morbid risk for the illness, suggesting that the well twin is a genetic carrier of liability for the illness but did not experience precipitating or contributing environmental insults.

Adoption studies

Adoption studies attempt to separate the contribution of nature and nurture by studying children raised away from their biologic parents. Adoption studies were important in leading researchers to consider genetic factors as well as environmental. Support for involvement of a genetic factor in schizophrenia would include findings that: 1) adopted-away children develop the disorder of the biologic parent, and 2) biologic relatives (but not adoptive relatives) develop the disorder of ill adoptees.

There are four different adoptive study models or strategies which have been usd by researchers. The first model is that of the adoptees' study method in which the prevalence rates of the disorder among adoptees born to schizophrenic and non-schizophrenic parents respectively are compared. This method was used in one of the first adoption studies in schizophrenia by Heston in 1966. In this classic study, Heston examined the offspring of schizophrenic mothers who had been adopted at birth and compared their rate of schizophrenia to a control group of adopted offspring. He found a significantly greater risk for schizophrenia among the offspring of schizophrenic mothers than in the offspring of control mothers. This finding was replicated in a Danish sample by Rosenthal et al. (1971). The same strategy was recently employed by Tienari et al. (1987) who have not only replicated these findings but have also conducted a detailed examination of family interactions, thus permitting an analysis of genotype-environmental interactions.

Another research design that has been used is the adoptee's relatives study in which the biological relatives of schizophrenic adoptees and non-schizophrenic control adoptees are compared. Kety et al. (1975, 1978) conducted a study of 34 adoptees in Copenhagen with a diagnosis of chronic, borderline or acute schizophrenia. He was able to interview personally nearly all of the available relatives of these cases and found a concentration of schizophrenia spectrum disorders in the biological relatives of schizophrenic adoptees. These data have been reanalyzed using DSM III-R criteria (Kendler 1984, 1994) with similar results.

A third design for adoption studies is that of the cross-fostering method, in which adoptees born to schizophrenic parents are compared with adoptees born to healthy parents, but reared by schizophrenic adoptive parents. This method was employed by Wender et al. (1974) who collected a sample from the national registers in Denmark, generating 38 subjects. These were divided into index cases (adults who had been adopted in infancy and whose biologic parents were diagnosed with a schizophrenia spectrum disorder), cross-fostered cases (individuals whose adoptive parents were diagnosed with a schizophrenia spectrum disorder) and control cases. He found that the control and cross-fostered cases were almost identical , suggesting that deviant rearing does not increase the risk of psychopathology in individuals without a genetic endowment. Wender et al. (1968) used the adoptive parents method, in which adoptive parents of affected adoptees are compared with the biologic parents of their schizophrenic offspring and with adoptive parents of healthy control adoptees.

Wender compared three groups: 1) ten adoptive parent pairs of adopted schizophrenics, 2) ten biologic parent pairs of schizophrenics and 3) ten adoptive parent pairs of adoptees with serious psychiatric illness. He found that the biologic parents of schizophrenics were appreciably more disturbed than the adopting parents of schizophrenics. This is consistent with the hypothesis that if the disorder is biologically transmitted versus socially or psychologically, one would expect a low frequency of psychopathology in the adoptive parents. Thus, through the different strategies of adoption studies, much has been learned regarding both the genetics of schizophrenia, as well as its environmental contributions.

Complex traits and disorders

Genetic research throughout the medical disciplines has shown that more than 3,000 human diseases are monogenic, or caused by defects in a single gene. These diseases follow the classical (Mendelian) patterns of recessive, dominant, or sex-linked. Approximately 25% of these illnesses affect mental functioning in some way. However, the appearance of any one of these monogenic illnesses (e.g., the Lesch-Nyhan syndrome or phenylketonuria) is fairly rare. In contrast, more common illnesses such as diabetes, coronary heart disease, and most psychiatric disorders, including schizophrenia, do not follow simple Mendelian patterns. These diseases are classified as "complex" genetic disorders.

Complex patterns can arise from multiple genetic phenomena. Genetic heterogeneity is one such phenomenon and refers to the fact that the disorder can be caused by an abnormal gene at two (or more) genetic loci and can present in different ways (i.e., recessive in one case and dominant in another), thus supporting neither model in segregation analysis. Another cause of complex inheritance patterns is termed multifactorial or polygenic transmission. Such findings occur if multiple genes interact with each other to cause the illness, but no single gene by itself is sufficient to cause the disease. In addition, various environmental factors all contribute to disease expression.

In polygenic disorders, relatives of affected probands are at greater risk of being affected, with increasing severity of illness in the proband and with greater number of affected relatives (Rieder et al. 1994). Monogenic disorders are known to have a low population prevalence; thus common diseases are thought to be polygenic, as are many traits that have been studied such as intelligence and height.

The recent identification of genes underlying three Mendelian inherited diseases—cystic fibrosis (an autosomal recessive disease), neurofibromatosis type I (an autosomal dominant disease), and Duchenne muscular dystrophy (an X-linked disease) illustrates the profound capabilities of modern genetics to elucidate the etiology of human disease (Rieder et al. 1994). Even more recently, advances in understanding the genetic basis for such complex diseases as diabetes (Davies et al. 1994) and breast cancer (Futreal et al. 1994) have occurred.

Unfortunately, success in the application of positional cloning strategies to the psychiatric disorders has been less predictable, but not due to lack of effort. Potential clues to disease pathogenesis have been exploited; the identification of a balanced trisomy of chromosome 5q11.2–13.3 in a Chinese-Canadian pedigree segregating schizophrenia (Bassett et al. 1988) rapidly led to reports for (Sherrington et al. 1988) and against (Kennedy et al. 1988) linkage to this region. Several authors have argued for genetic anticipation, the phenomenological counterpart of trinucleotide expansion on both bipolar disorder (McInnis et al. 1993) and schizophrenia (Bassett and Honer 1994), and other authors have directly sought such expansions (O'Donovan 1995, Morris et al. 1995), yet reports of anticipation are potentially confounded by inescapable ascertainment biases (Hodge, *personal communication*). There have been several candidate gene studies in schizophrenia, notably of the dopamine (D2, D3) receptor genes (Crocq et al. 1992) but they have not withstood replication.

Attendant with these endeavors there has been a greater appreciation of the complexities that accompany the application of positional cloning to complex disorders. These complexities include: 1) unknown mode of inheritance; 2) etiologic heterogeneity; 3) variable expression; 4) incomplete penetrance; 5) allele interaction (epistasis); 6) diagnostic instability; 7) assortative mating; and 8) loci of small phenotypic effect.

The concept of gene-environment interaction has likewise gained a greater appreciation with the endeavors to characterize complex disorders. Kendler and Eaves (1986) propose three major models for the joint effect of genes and environment on liability to psychiatric illness. The first model, additive genetic and environmental effects, hypothesizes that liability to illness results from the simple addition of the genetic and environmental contributions. The second model, genetic control of sensitivity to the environment, proposes that genes control the degree to which an individual is sensitive to either risk-increasing or risk-reducing aspects of the environment. The third model, genetic control of exposure to the environment, postulates that a genotype's influence on the liability to illness is to alter the probability of exposure to a predisposing environment. Kendler and Eves conclude that a complete understanding of the etiology of most psychiatric disorders will require an understanding of the relevant genetic risk factors, the relevant environmental risk factors, and the ways in which these two risk factors interact.

STRATEGIES—THE PAST TEN YEARS

Clinical

Advances in clinical genetics that may facilitate the study of psychiatric disorders such as schizophrenia include refinements in clinical populations and phenotypes for study along with increasing reliance on animal models of disease. Many of the intricacies of complex diseases such as etiologic heterogeneity and epistasis can be resolved by sheer numbers, and there has been an increasing reliance on large samples and clinical consortia to address this issue. Etiologic heterogeneity can also be resolved by studying populations in which a finite number of founders limit the number of disease genes entering a population, a phenomenon known as a genetic bottleneck. Geographically and/or ethnically isolated populations have been employed in the study of a number of disorders.

Another clinical approach involves searching for quantitative measures of disease or "endophenoptypes," disease-associated physiological abnormalities demonstrating Mendelian inheritance and/or more complete penetrance than the clinical phenotypes themselves. Subclinical phenotypes such as psychometric deviation (Moldin et al. 1990) and psychophysiological gating impairment (Waldo et al. 1991) have been described in schizophrenia. Likewise, smooth-pursuit eye tracking performance has been shown to display a bimodal distribution in schizophrenic patients and their relatives, perhaps reflecting major gene action, in addition to the finding that poor tracking runs in families (Iacono et al. 1992).

Molecular approaches

Complementing these clinical approaches have been several molecular genetic developments, including approaches to rapid genome scanning for candidate genes, as well as for anonymous genomic segments shared between affected individuals or differing between affected and suitably matched unaffected individuals. These approaches promise to identify many epistatic loci contributing to complex disorders, even if their contribution to overall phenotypic variation is modest. Over 80,000 partially sequenced complementary DNA (cDNA)s (clones that are complementary to endogenous mRNAs), also known as expressed sequence tags (ESTs), have been placed onto the physical map of the genome.

While the sequences that are currently available often only partially represent full-length mRNAs and are to some degree redundant with one another, a major step toward a transcriptional map, i.e., a physical map of all 100,000 genes that are thought to comprise the human genome, has been achieved. Moreover, the profound implications for psychiatric genetics are apparent if one considers that over half of these genes are exclusively expressed in the brain (Adams et al. 1992). Specific sets of these genes that are expressed in particular brain regions, or during particular neurodevelopmental stages, implicated in the pathoetiology of specific disorders (e.g., the hippocampus and second gestational trimester, respectively, in schizophrenia) may be directly cloned through the techniques of library normalization and subtractive hybridization (MB Soares, *personal communication*). Other potentially pathogenic sequences, such as expanded trinucleotide repeats, which to date, have been implicated in the development of nine neuropsychiatric disorders, may be directly isolated (Kennedy and Ross, *personal communication*). Once these complete sets or specific subsets of candidate genes are isolated, their roles in particular diseases may be rapidly evaluated through advances in linkage disequilibrium scanning (Pacek et al. 1993; Knowles, *personal communication*) and mutation detection.

These "candidate" gene approaches depend on first "nominating" the candidate (either through specific associations with neuroanatomic regions, neurodevelopmental stages, or neuropathic changes such as trinucleotide repeat expansion) and then having the candidate "run for office."

Genomic mismatch scanning (GMS) is a molecular technique to isolate all regions of identity (by descent) between two individuals, based on the ability of these regions to form extensive mismatch-free hybrid molecules (Nelson et al. 1993). GMS is most powerful when used to compare the DNA of distantly related affected individuals, especially in pedigrees from isolated populations having undergone genetic "bottlenecks." Application of this technique should permit the identification of regions as small as 10 kb (the approximate size of individual genes) which contribute to disease expression. The technique has been demonstrated to work in yeast and experiments to extend it to humans are in progress (Brown, *personal communication*).

Conversely, representational difference analysis (RDA), is a molecular technique for cloning the difference between two complex genomes (Lisitsyn et al. 1993). In this method, restriction endonuclease fragments which differ in length between two individuals (so-called polymorphic amplifiable restriction endonuclease fragments—PARFs) are selectively enriched by repetitive subtractive hybridization. PARFs, so generated, will be linked to the phenotypic trait which discriminates the two individuals. They are generated without knowledge of the chromosomal location(s) of the genes) controlling the trait; once generated they can direct the search for such locations. The RDA approach has been successfully used to directly isolate polymorphic markers linked to phenotypic traits in congenic experimental organisms, those that are genetically identical except for a relatively small region surrounding a gene of interest (Lisitsyn et al.1994). In extending this approach to human diseases, significantly inbred populations may be particularly informative.

Statistical approaches

Statistical genetics is another crucial component of contemporary human genetics and rapid advances have also been made in this field. Statistical developments promise to facilitate phenotype definition, make linkage analysis more efficient and sensitive, and enable more powerful linkage disequilibrium analysis, thereby surmounting obstacles to positional cloning presented by unknown mode of inheritance, incomplete penetrance, and etiologic heterogeneity.

Segregation analysis is a powerful statistical method which compares the observed frequency of an illness in a pedigree with the pattern that would occur if a hypothesized mode of inheritance (e.g., one of the monogenic patterns or polygenic transmission) were true (Pardes et al. 1989). This method has several limitations however, including the fact that it may be relatively insensitive to single-gene effects.

Linkage analysis is another statistical technique and may be more sensitive than segregation analysis. This approach begins by identifying the area of the genome within which the disease gene lies. Radioactively or fluorescently labeled probes (relatively short sections of DNA with known chromosomal locations) are used to seek out complementary nucleic acid sequences. If one of these is a sequence consistently transmitted with the disease (i.e., "linked" with the presumed aberrant gene), the approximate chromosomal location of the gene is revealed (Pardes et al. 1989). The statistical significance of linkage study results is reported as a maximum lod score, defined as the ratio of the likelihood of the observed pedigree data under the alternative hypothesis of linkage and non-linkage (free recombination). Linkage analysis also has inherent pitfalls including the fact that the calculation of statistical significance levels from maximum lod scores requires care, and that as for all statistical tests, statistical significance levels must be interpreted in the light of what is believed before the study is conducted, ascertainment problems, and choice of significance level and power issues (Elston 1994).

Multivariate approaches to phenotype definition (such as pedigree discriminant analysis) may allow aggregate Mendelian statistical phenotypes to be identified (Zlotnik et al. 1983). Conversely, other approaches, like phenometric analysis, may allow detection of differentiated phenotypic features resulting from individual genetic loci (George et al. 1987). Multitiered approaches to linkage analysis [initially screening with widely spaced markers and maximizing sensitivity at the expense of specificity (Elston 1994)] may permit more rapid genomic scanning, a boon for oligogenic disorders in which the serendipitous discovery of a single major locus may only be the beginning of the search for several susceptibility genes. Nonparametric approaches to linkage analysis (such as affected sib pair, Davies et al. 1994) and affected pedigree member strategies (Weeks and Lange 1993) may be robust in the face of model misspecification (again a plus for disorders in which genetic models are unknown), while other approaches (such as bivariate analyses combining categorical disease definitions with quantitative phenotype measure) (SO Moldin, *personal communication*) may increase the power to detect loci in the face of etiologic heterogeneity. The ability of nonallelic genetic heterogeneity to weaken linkage analyses can be offset by statistical approaches that allow for such heterogeneity (MacLean et al. 1992). Given the possibility of undetected heterogeneity, however, greater caution may need to be adopted in reporting that linkage has been excluded from particular chromosomal regions (Pakstis et al. 1991).

Despite these developments, the various intricacies of complex disorders conspire to hinder linkage replication (Suarez et al. 1994) and to render the exact genetic location of linked loci uncertain (Sandkujl, *personal communication*), even if these loci can be detected. Thus, linkage analysis for psychiatric disorders may localize a susceptibility locus to a region spanning 20–30 cM, far beyond the 1–2 cM capabilities of current physical mapping and gene isolation strategies. Even this obstacle, however, may be circumvented through developments in linkage disequilibrium or shared segment scanning, an alternative approach to linkage analysis, in which strings of alleles (haplotypes) surrounding disease loci will be shared among affected individuals in populations of known genetic structure.

THE NEXT TEN YEARS

The genetic elucidation of insulin-dependent diabetes mellitus (IDDM) can be used as a methaphor in the search for vulnerability genes for schizophrenia. The recent successes in determining genetic susceptibility in this complex disease are promising for other complex illnesses such as schizophrenia. The two illnesses share many common characteristics despite the fact that one is an endocrine/metabolic disease and the other a neuropsychiatric disease. Both are complex disorders with all the accompanying uncertainties inherent in such diseases. These complexities of the two diseases are summarized in Table 1.

Neither schizophrenia nor IDDM demonstrates a clear Mendelian mode of inheritance, and dominant, recessive, additive (i.e., intermediate gene dosage), and oligogenic (i.e., multilocus) forms have been proposed for both. The various transmitted forms may reflect various genetic, environmental, and interactive etiologies all resulting in a common phenotype (Hyde et al. 1992). As regards IDDM, genetic heterogeneity for glucose intolerance has been well documented in rodent models such as the NOD mouse and the BB rat, thus illustrating that there is no one-to-one correspondence between genotype and phenotype. This correspondence breaks down in other ways. In both disorders, presumably single genetic forms result in a panoply of phenotypic expression. Animal models of diabetes suggest that the genetic background of the individual (including its gender) may influence this expression (Leiter et al. 1981). Not all MZ twins are concordant for either IDDM or schizophrenia (i.e., both disorders demonstrate incomplete penetrance), suggesting that what is inherited in each disorder is not disease, but disease susceptibility, susceptibility which must interact with other factors to produce clinical symptoms. As noted previously, at least two loci of major effect (HLA, insulin) and four loci of minor effect have been implicated in human IDDM. While epistasis (gene interaction) has not been demonstrated for schizo-

TABLE 1. COMPARISON OF GENETIC CHARACTERISTICS OF INSULIN-DEPENDENT
DIABETES MELLITUS AND SCHIZOPHRENIA

Complexity	Diabetes (IDDM)	Schizophrenia
Unknown inheritance	Dominant, recessive, additive, oligogenic	Dominant, recessive, additive, oligogenic
Etiologic heterogeneity	Over 60 rare genetic disorders with glucose intolerance; heterogeneity in rodent models	A variety of neuro-psychiatric disorders (e.g., metachromatic leuko-dystrophy) with psychosis
Variable expression	Variations in age of onset, clinical presentation (ketosis vs. vascular complications), insulin autoantibodies, viral antibodies	Variations in age of onset, clinical presentation (psychosis, affective symptoms), neuronal autoantibodies, viral antibodies
Incomplete penetrance	MZ twin concordance 36%	MZ twin concordance 59%
Epistasis	IDDM-5,7: multiple susceptibility loci in the NOD mouse	Presumed, based on optimal model-fitting with 3-locus model
Loci of small effect	IDDM3 (15q), 4 (11)q, 5 (6q), 7 (2q)	Presumed
Multifactorial etiology	HLA, insulin, coxsackievirus	Possibly HLA, influenza virus
Diagnostic instability	Present	Present

phrenia, optimal model-fitting to empirical recurrence risk data suggests that at least 3 loci may contribute to the disorder (Risch 1990). Of course, the more loci that are implicated in the pathogenesis of a disorder, the smaller their individual effect on the disease phenotype. This has been demonstrated for the minor loci in both human and murine diabetes, and is presumed to pertain to schizophrenia. This is not surprising if one considers that many loci, significantly affecting a variety of quantitative traits in experimental organisms like maize, contribute less than 5% to the variance of the final phenotype.

Finally, as previously discussed, it would appear that a variety of genetically determined host factors (such as specific HLA alleles like DR4) interact with epigenetic environmental factors (like coxsackievirus) to produce IDDM. Conceivably, host genes and viruses could also interact to produce the schizophrenia phenotype. In this regard, it is interesting to note that: 1) recent, provisionally replicated evidence for a schizophrenia susceptibility locus at 6p21–22 implicates the HLA region contained therein; 2) prenatal influenzavirus has long been suggested as an environmental risk factor in the development of schizophrenia; and 3) patients with schizophrenia bear many of the stigmata of autoimmune injury, including elevated CD56 T lymphocytes and autoantibodies against the 60 kD heat shock protein.

The identification of major susceptibility genes for Alzheimer's disease, schizophrenia and other psychiatric disorders can be expected to result in significant changes in our concepts of psychiatric nosology, etiology, and therapeutics.

Although nosologists have been divided into "lumpers" and "splitters," advances in psychiatric genetics may provide insights to integrate both views. For example, symptomatic features such as psychosis may ultimately prove to reflect major gene effects that cut across current nosologic boundaries, such as the one which currently separates bipolar disorder and schizophrenia (Tsuang and Lyons 1989).

The identification of major genes may yield clearer specification of polygenic and epigenetic/environmental factors which influence disease penetrance and expression. Epigenetic influences may range from pre-, peri-, and postnatal biologic insults to shared intrafamilial conflict to nonshared, unique traumas (mediated by birth order, temperament, etc.) (Reiss et al. 1991). Clearly, environmental influences need not be exclusively permissive; to the extent that protective influences can be identified, nongenetic approaches to the prevention and treatment of ostensibly genetic disorders may be developed.

There are many stages in the development of multifactorial psychiatric disorders that may be amenable to therapeutic intervention: consequently, such intervention may be viewed as achieving primary, secondary, or tertiary prevention. Regarding primary prevention, genetic discoveries may permit more informed genetic counselling, which historically has had to rely on unsatisfactory empirical risk data. This may allow more realistic reproductive options to be exercised, especially in families heavily burdened by illness. Primary prevention may also involve gene therapy. This, in turn, may be direct (i.e., genetic engineering of somatic or germline cells), or indirect (as in efforts to pharmacologically compensate for mutations or deficiencies in various illnesses). Furthermore, while the anatomically complex and remote nervous system was once thought to be inaccessible to direct gene therapy, the development of novel neurotropic vectors and engrafted (ex vivo) genetically transformed mature cells or immature but pleuripotential neural progenitor cells (cells which assume the phenotypic characteristics of cell types common to the brain region to which they are grafted) all suggest that direct gene therapy for neuropsychiatric disorders could someday be a reality.

Secondary prevention may be achieved prenatally, in disorders like schizophrenia thought to develop in response to adverse in utero experiences. Pregnancies of fetuses at special genetic risk might be monitored more closely and shielded from identified epigenetic risk factors such as prenatal micronutrient deficiencies or viral exposure. Tertiary prevention might be achieved postnatally in schizophrenia, to the extent that high-risk presymptomatic individuals could be reliably identified and acute illness forestalled. Such interventions might be especially important, if as has been proposed, florid symptoms of schizophrenia are pathogenic in their own right (e.g., through kindling or free-radical induced neurotoxicity).

Clinical and public policy issues

The identification of major genes conferring vulnerability to psychiatric disorders such as schizophrenia may have important social implications, in such areas as ethics, the law, discrimination and genetic counseling. The HGP has established an Ethical, Legal, and Social Implications (ELSI) program in response to concerns over these implications.

Ethical implications of the new medical genetics relates to such issues as confidentiality and privacy, equity and extending the role of patient beyond the individual initially seeking treatment to other family members. Another concern is one that has already arisen with Huntington's disease, namely the additional risk that attends the notification of genetic risk status, especially for serious neuropsychiatric disorders for which a diagnosis can be made but no treatment provided. By the very nature of their illnesses, patients with psychiatric disorders often may have impaired judgment and limited insight, especially true in schizophrenia. These are deficits which often result in decreased autonomy, increased paternalism, and necessarily greater reliance on institutional ethical safeguards.

Psychiatric disorders present all the risks of genetic discrimination inherent in other medical disorders, along with additional risks. The risk of genetic discrimination, defined by Goston (1991) as "the denial of rights, privileges, or opportunities on the basis of information obtained from genetically based diagnostic and prognostic tests," is real and exists in several arenas, including insurance coverage, employment and social stigma. This is particularly true in the case of mental illnesses for which discrimination and stigma are already realities. For example, mental health benefits are invariably less than those for other medical conditions.

Stigma has oppressed the mentally ill for over 500 years (Foucault 1965). While we can hope that psychiatric disorders, as complex illnesses, will be recognized as worthy of the same concern, consideration, and compassion as other complex illnesses, such as diabetes, and while we can hope that revolutionary advances in genetic understanding will be accompanied by revolutionary changes in social attitudes, history suggests otherwise.

Psychiatrists are especially well equipped, by nature of their training, to help people with the feelings, concerns and issues that are raised by hereditary illness (Pardes et al. 1989). The emotional impact of genetic disease is great and is accompanied by serious concerns regarding whom to test, when to offer testing, and how to interpret results to patients. These concerns are laden with ethical as well as psychotherapeutic issues. The traditional role of genetic counseling has been to impart information concerning the nature of the illness, recurrence risks, anticipated burden of care, and reproductive options in a nondirective way. Counseling has generally been conducted by a team of genetic specialists including genetically trained clinicians and genetic counselors. As genetic knowledge continues to expand, the need for genetic counseling services will dramatically increase and the concern has been voiced that sufficient genetic counseling services may not be available to meet this increased demand. Whatever form psychiatric genetic counseling takes, it will be essential that it maintains its nondirective approach, as well as a regard for such important ethical principles as autonomy, confidentiality, informed consent and voluntariness.

CONCLUSION

Contemporary genetics has brought a remarkable transformation to all of medicine, including psychiatry. Technological advances, along with a fundamental change in the way we view disease, have elucidated the etiologies and pathophysiologies of a number of genetically simple, Mendelian disorders. Inspired by these successes, geneticists have now turned their attention to more common, costly, and complex conditions. Here too, positional cloning has revealed important genetic determinants of illnesses ranging from breast cancer to diabetes to hypertension. Psychiatric illnesses are likely to be no more complex, and we can anticipate that major genes contributing to schizophrenia, as well as other psychiatric disorders will soon be in hand. We can also anticipate that these genetic discoveries will provide important insights into the influence of epigenetic factors on psychiatric disease expression, into the basic pathophysiology of brain disruption, and into novel therapeutic interventions.

REFERENCES

Adams MD, Dubnick M, Kerlavage AR, et al. Sequence identification of 2,375 human brain genes. *Nature* 355:632–634, 1992.

American Psychiatric Association Joint Commission on Public Affairs and the Division of Public Affairs: *Let's Talk Facts About Schizophrenia.* Washington, DC: American Psychiatric Press, 1988.

Bassett AS. Chromosome 5 and schizophrenia: Implications for genetic linkage studies. *Schizo Bull* 15:393–402, 1989.

Bassett AS, Honer WG. Evidence for anticipation in schizophrenia. *Am J Hum Gene* 54:864–870, 1994.

Black DW, Yates WR, Andreason NC. Schizophrenia, schizophreniform disorder, and delusional (paranoid) disorders. In: Talbott JA, Hales RE, Yudofsky SC, eds, *Textbook of Psychiatry.* American Psychiatric Press, 1988, pp. 357–402.

Brizendine L. The Devon Asylum: A brief history of the changing concept of mental illness and asylum treatment. In: Fink PJ, Tasman A, eds, *Stigma and Mental Illness.* American Psychiatric Press, pp. 59–71, 1992.

Davies JL, Kawaguchi Y, Bennett ST, et al. A genome-wide search for human type I diabetes susceptibility genes. *Nature* 371: 130–136, 1994.

Elston RC, Hoch Award lecture: P values, power, and pitfalls in the linkage analysis of psychiatric disorders. In: Gershon ES, Cloninger CR, eds, *Genetic Approaches to Mental Disorders.* Washington, DC: American Psychiatric Press Inc., 1994, p. 3–23.

Foucault M. *Madness and Civilization: A History of Insanity in the Age of Reason.* New York: Random House, 1965.

Futreal PA et al. BRCA1 Mutations in primary breast and ovarian carcinomas. *Science* 266:120–122, 1994.

George VT, Elston RC, Amos CI, et al. Association between polymorphic blood markers and risk factors for cardiovascular disease in a large pedigree. *Genet Epidem* 4:267–275, 1987.

Goston L. Genetic Discrimination: The use of genetically based diagnosis and prognostic tests by employers and insurers. *Am J Law Med* 17:109–144, 1991.

Gottesman II, Bertelson A. Confirming unexpressed genotypes for schziophrenia: Risks in the offspring of Fischer's Danish identical and fraternal discordant twins. *Arch Gen Psychiat* 46:867–872, 1989.

Gottesman I, Shields J. *Schizophrenia: The Epigenetic Puzzle.* New York: Cambridge University Press, 1982.

Heston LL. Psychiatric disorders in foster-home-reared children of schizophrenic mothers. *Brit J Psychiat* 112:819–825, 1966.

Hodge S, Wickramaratne P. Statistical pitfalls in detecting age-of-onset anticipation: The role of correlation in studying anticipation and detecting ascertainment bias. *Psychiat Genet*, 1995 (in press).

Hyde TM, Ziegler JC, Weinberger DR. Psychiatric disturbances in metachromatic leukodystrophy: Insights into the neurobiology of psychosis. *Arch Neurol* 49:401–406, 1992.

Iacono WG, et al. Smooth-pursuit eye tracking in first-episode psychotic patients and their relatives. *J Abnor Psych* 101:104–116, 1992.

Jaroff L. *The New Genetics*. Whittle Direct Books, 1991.

Kaufmann CA, Malaspina D. Molecular genetics of schizophrenia. *Psychiatr Ann* 23:3:111–122, 1993.

Kendler KS, Eaves LJ. Models for joint effect of genotype and environment on liability to psychiatric illness. *Am J Psychiat* 143:279–289, 1986.

Kendler KS, Gruenberg AM. An independent analysis of the Copenhagen sample of the Danish adoption study of schizophrenia—The relationship between psychiatric disorders as defined by DSM-III in the relatives and adoptees. *Arch Gen Psych* 41:555–564, 1984.

Kendler KS, Gruenberg AM, Kinney DK. Independent diagnoses of adoptees and relatives as defined by DSM-III in the provincial and national samples of the Danish adoption study of schizophrenia. *Arch Gen Psychiatry* 51:456–468, 1994.

Kennedy JL, et al. Evidence against linkage of schizophrenia to markers on chromosome 5 in a Northern Swedish pedigree. *Nature* 336:167–170, 1988.

Kety SS, et al. Mental illness in the biologic and adoptive families of adoptive individuals who have become schizophrenic: A preliminary report based on psychiatric interviews In: Fieve RR, Rosenthal D, Brill H, eds, *Genetic Research in Psychiatry*. Baltimore: The Johns Hopkins University Press, 1975, pp. 147–165.

Kety SS, et al. The biologic and adoptive families of adopted individuals who become schizophrenic: Prevalence of mental illness and other characteristics. In: Wynne LC, Cromwell RL, Matthysee S, eds, *The Nature of Schizophrenia*. New York: John Wiley and Sons, 1978.

Leiter EH, Coleman DL, Hummel KP. The influence of genetic background on the expression of mutations at the diabetes locus in the mouse III. Effect of H-2 haplotype and sex. *Diabetes* 30:1029–1034, 1981.

Lisitsyn N, et al. Cloning the difference between two complex genomes. *Science* 259:946–951, 1993.

Lisitsyn NA, Serge JA, Kusumi K, et al. Direct isolation of polymorphic markers linked to a trait by genetically directed representational difference analysis. *Nature Genetics* 6:57–63, 1994.

MacLean CJ, Ploughman LM, Diehl S, et al. A new test for linkage in the presence of locus heterogeneity. *Am J Hum Genet* 50:1259–1266, 1992.

McInnis MG, et al. Anticipation in bipolar affective disorder. *Am J Hum Genet* 53:385–390, 1993.

McKusick VA. *Mendelian Inheritance in Man. Catalogs of autosomal dominant, autosomal recessive, and X-linked phenotypes*. Tenth ed. Baltimore: The Johns Hopkins University Press, 1992.

Moldin SO, Gottesman II, Erlenmeyer-Kimling L, et al. Psychometric deviance in offspring at risk for schizophrenia, I: Initial delineation of a distinct subgroup. *Psychiat Res* 32:297–310, 1990.

Mora G. Mind-body concepts in the middle ages, I. *J Hist Behav Sci* 14:344–361, 1978.

Mora G. Mind-body concepts in the middle ages, II. *J Hist Behav Sci* 16:58–72, 1980.

Mora G. Stigma during the medieval and renaissance periods. In: Fink PJ, Tasman A, eds, *Stigma and Mental Illness*. Washington, DC: American Psychiatric Press, Inc., 1992, pp 41–57.

Morris AG, Gaitonde E, McKenna PJ, Mollon JD, Hunt DM. Association study of CAG expansions with schizophrenia. *Schiz Res* 15:41, 1995.

Nelson SF, et al. Genomic mismatch scanning: A new approach to genetic linkage mapping. *Nat Genet* 4:11, 1993.

O'Donovan MC, Guy C, Craddock N, Murphy KC, Cardno AG, et al. Expanded CAG repeats in schizophrenia and bipolar disorder. *Nat Genet* 10:380–81, 1995.

Pacek P, Sajantila A, Syvanen AC. Determination of allele frequencies at loci with length polymorphism by quantitative analysis of DNA amplified from pooled samples. *PCR Meth Appl* 2:313–317, 1993.

Pakstis AJ, Heutink P, Pauls DL, et al. Progress in the search for genetic linkage with tourette syndrome: An exclusion map covering more than 50% of the autosomal genome. *Am J Hum Genet* 48:281–294, 1991.

Pardes H, Kaufmann CA, Pincus HA, et al. Genetics and psychiatry: Past discoveries, current dilemmas, and future directions. *Am J Psychiat* 146:435–443, 1989.

Reiss, Plomin R, Hetherington EM. Genetics and psychiatry: An unheralded window on the environment. *Am J Psychiat* 148:283–291, May 11, 1991.

Rieder R, Kaufmann CA, Knowles JA. Genetics. In: Talbott JA, Hales RE, Yudofsky SC, eds, *Textbook of Psychiatry*. Washington, DC: American Psychiatric Press, 1994, pp. 35–79.

Risch N. Linkage strategies for genetically complex traits, I: Multilocus models. *Am J Hum Genet* 46:22–228, 1990.

Rosenthal D, et al. The adopted-away offspring of schizophrenics. *Am J Psychiat* 128:307–311, 1971.

Sherrington R, Brynjolfsson J, Petursson H, et al. Localization of a susceptibility locus for schizophrenia on chromosome 5. *Nature* 336:164–167, 1988.

Simon B. Shame, Stigma, and Mental Illness in Ancient Greece. In: Fink PJ, Tasman A, eds, *Stigma and Mental Illness*. Washington, DC: American Psychiatric Press, Inc., 1992, p. 29–41.

Suarez BK, Hampe CL, van Eerdewegh P. Problems in replicating linkage claims in psychiatry. In: Gershon ES, Cloninger CR, eds, *Genetic Approaches to Mental Disorders*, Washington, DC: American Psychiatric Press, 1994, pp 23–46.

Tienari P, et al. Genetic and psychosocial factors in schizophrenia: The Finnish adoptive family study. *Schizo Bull* 13:447–484, 1987.

Tsuang MT, Lyons MJ. Drawing the boundary of the schizophrenia spectrum: Evidence from a family study. In: Scholz SC, Tamminga CA, eds, *Schizophrenia: Scientific Progress*. New York: Oxford University Press, 1989, pp 23–27.

Waldo MC, Carey G, Myles-Worsley M, et al. Codistribution of a sensory gating deficit and schizophrenia in multi-affected families. *Psychiat Res* 39:257–268, 1991.

Weeks DE, Lange K. The affected pedigree member method of linkage analysis. *Am J Hum Genet* 42:315–326, 1993.

Wender PH, et al. A psychiatric assessment of the adoptive parents of schizophrenics. In: Rosenthal D, Kety SS, eds, *The Transmission of Schizophrenia*. Oxford: Pergamon Press, 1968, pp 235–250.

Wender PH, et al. Crossfostering: A research strategy for clarifying the role of genetics and experimental factors in the etiology of schizophrenia. *Arch Gen Psych* 30:121–128, 1974.

Zlotnik LH, Elston RC, Namboodiri KK. Pedigree discriminant analysis: A method to identify monogenic segregation. *Am J Med Genet* 15:307–313, 1983.

Autoimmune Phenomena, Neuronal Stress, and Schizophrenia

DAVID H. STRAUSS, M.D., and DAVID J. PRINTZ, M.D.

It has long been suggested that schizophrenia shares clinical, epidemiological and genetic characteristics with the classical autoimmune diseases. More recently, technological advances have permitted the identification of an array of soluble factors and cell types whose hyperactivity has been associated with autoimmunity. Aberrant immune measures typical of diseases such as systemic lupus erythematosus (SLE), multiple sclerosis (MS), and rheumatoid arthritis (RA) have been reported in schizophrenia and provide another indirect link between schizophrenia and autoimmunity. Further interest in the concept of an immune-mediated pathogenesis in schizophrenia has been stimulated by the awareness that antibodies and cytokines can affect neuronal function in the absence of a classical inflammatory response. Still, the gap between individual observations of abnormal autoimmune phenomena and the description of specific autoimmune mechanisms, in schizophrenia as with other "putative" autoimmune diseases, is a difficult one to bridge. Whether observed autoimmune phenomena in schizophrenia represent evidence of autoimmune pathogenesis per se, arise secondary to nonimmune CNS damage, or suggest alternative pathologic processes is a critical question for the field. This chapter reviews evidence of autoimmunity in schizophrenia and data which might implicate the neuronal response to biologic stress and injury as a link between "autoimmune phenomena" and pathogenesis in schizophrenia.

CLINICAL CHARACTERISTICS OF CLASSICAL AUTOIMMUNE ILLNESS RELEVANT TO SCHIZOPHRENIA

Autoimmune disorders are common and affect 5–7% of the population (Sinha et al. 1990). MS, SLE, insulin-dependent diabetes mellitus (IDDM), and RA are familiar examples. Autoimmune mechanisms have been identified or are postulated for a range of diseases, including many which affect the nervous system (see Table 1). Theories of an immune etiology for schizophrenia are nearly 100 years old, and clinical similarities between schizophrenia and known immune disorders has often been cited. Like schizophrenia, many autoimmune illnesses have a peak onset shortly after puberty, a waxing and waning course, and a tendency for exacerbations which lead to progressive deterioration and impairment. Significant gender differences in disease type and clinical syndromes characterize both autoimmune disorders and schizophrenia.

TABLE 1. NEUROIMMUNE DISEASE

Amyotrophic lateral sclerosis?
Chronic relapsing polyneuropathy
Guillan-Barré syndrome
Lyme disease?
Multiple sclerosis
Myasthenia gravis
Paraneoplastic diseases
Post-infectious encephalomyelitis
Post-rabies vaccination polyneuritis
Post-rabies vaccination encephalomyelitis
Rasmussen's encephalitis
Schizophrenia?
Stiff-man syndrome
Sydenham's chorea
Systemic lupus erythematosus

Infection, autoimmune disease, and schizophrenia

Although genes are believed to exert a strong influence in the diathesis to all of the ill-nesses thought to be autoimmune, pathology is believed to be triggered by environmental factors in genetically susceptible individuals, an idea consistent with current etiologic models of schizophrenia (Wright and Murray 1993). Other evidence that etiology is likely to be multifactorial in both autoimmune disease and schizophrenia is suggested by the concordance rates of less than 100% for monozygotic (MZ) twins with schizophrenia (30%–50%), IDDM (30%) and MS (5%–30%).

The association of many autoimmune diseases with preceding infection raises the question of whether the critical environmental influence is a pathogenic organism (Figure 1). In schizophrenia, early interest in the notion of immune pathology arose in parallel with theories of an infectious etiology for the psychoses. Indirect evidence links schizophrenia to viral infection (Kaufmann and Ziegler 1988; Crow 1983) and epidemiologic data supports an association between *in utero* exposure to influenza and later development of schizophrenia (Mednick et al. 1988). Some have speculated that autoimmune mechanisms might explain these epidemiologic associations of schizophrenia with influenza infection (Wright and Murray 1993). Recent reports of a schizophrenia linkage to Chromosome 6, the site of the major histocompatibility locus, suggests another indirect association between genes and immunity in schizophrenia (Wang et al. 1995). The connection between infection, immune pathology and schizophrenia is also supported by data from our group on circulating autoantibodies to the 60-kD heat shock protein in patients with schizophrenia, which is reviewed later.

Exposure to infectious agents or other environmental trauma is believed to trigger the breakdown in self-tolerance which leads to autoimmunity. One putative mechanism of autoantibody production is termed "molecular mimicry." Antibodies against self-proteins arise as a result of significant structural homology between that self-protein and a foreign protein, against which the immune reaction was initiated (Cohen 1990). Antibodies raised against the foreign protein, perhaps a viral antigen, will recognize the self-protein on the body's own cells or tissues, causing disease or dysfunction. Alternatively, the development

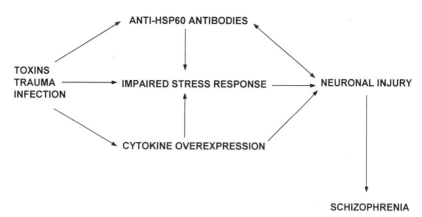

FIG. 1. Possible interactions between environmental stressors, the immune system, and neuronal injury in the pathophysiology of schizophrenia.

of autoantibodies could result from the physical association of cellular proteins with infectious proteins. This might occur through the incorporation of cellular proteins into virus particles (Zingernagel et al. 1990). When presented to the immune system in conjunction with the viral antigens, an immune response to the self-antigen can be triggered, with subsequent loss of tolerance to that antigen.

Immune activation in autoimmunity

The defect in immune regulation that leads to autoimmune disease is incompletely understood. Under normal circumstances, the immune system differentiates the body's own proteins and cells from foreign ones. When this process fails, as described above via infectious mechanisms, the immune system may target and attack the body's own tissues as if they were foreign, causing autoimmune disease. Other environmental factors, such as blood-brain-barrier (BBB) disruption, as may occur in inflammation, infection, head trauma, and in response to certain circulating immune mediators, with resultant exposure of previously sequestered antigenic determinants, are also thought to promote immune-mediated pathology. Advances in technology have permitted the identification and characterization of an array of soluble factors and cell types whose overexpression is associated with the many known or suspected autoimmune disease states. Similar findings have been reported in schizophrenia. The vast arsenal of cellular, antibody, and cytokine immune mediators mobilized by the immune system for surveillance, identification and elimination of foreign organisms may contribute in newly appreciated ways to the pathophysiology of many central nervous system (CNS) diseases, including schizophrenia.

Cytokines, autoimmunity, and schizophrenia. The cytokines provide a line of evidence linking autoimmunity, infection, neuronal response to injury, and schizophrenia. Cytokines are a functionally diverse group of soluble polypeptide hormones with homeostatic and regulatory functions in the immune system. Overexpression of cytokines such as interleukin 1 (IL-1), interleukin 2 (IL-2) and interleukin 6 (IL-6) is seen in human autoimmune diseases. (Halper 1991, Nakanishi et al. 1990, Capra et al. 1990, Greenberg et al. 1988, Wood et al. 1988, Linker-Israel et al. 1991).

IL-1 modulates the proliferation, maturation, and activity of T and B lymphocytes. Increased serum levels of IL-1 have been observed during infection and inflammatory disease, and IL-1 has direct pyrogen effects. IL-2 is produced and secreted by activated T lymphocytes in response to antigen presentation and secretion of IL-1 by macrophages. Interleukin 2 has wide-ranging effects on T-cell and natural-killer-cell activity and has been shown to induce both the proliferation and differentiation of B cells mediated by cell-surface receptors. Elevated serum levels of IL-2 have been reported in SLE and in MS.

The soluble IL-2 receptor (SIL2R) is a polypeptide shed from the surface of activated T cells. Elevated levels of the SIL-2R receptor have likewise been related to the immune activation of the autoimmune process in MS and RA. Kittur et al. (1990) found elevated CSF levels of sIL-2R in MS, meningitis, and lymphoid CNS tumors.

Findings of impaired in vitro mitogen-induced IL-2 production in IDDM (Zier et al. 1984), SLE (DeFaucal et al. 1984), and RA (Cathely et al. 1984) have been used in support of a theory of immune dysregulation in autoimmunity based on a "defective" IL-2 system. However, the relationship of this finding to observed elevated levels of IL-2 in the serum and CSF in patients with autoimmune disease noted above is unclear.

IL-6 is a cytokine with an important role in the final differentiation of B cells into immunoglobulin G (IgG)-secreting cells (Kishimoto 1989). Cardiac myxoma patients show autoimmune symptoms and autoantibody production and cells from these tumors produce large amounts of IL-6 (Hirano et al. 1987). Resection of such tumors is associated with return of serum IL-6 to undetectable levels and regression of the immunologic features (Sutton et al. 1980).

Elevation in plasma and cerebrospinal fluid (CSF) levels of IL-1, -2, and -6 and aberrant mitogen-induced production of IL-2 have been demonstrated in patients with schizophrenia and have been used to support autoimmune theories of the disorder (Rappaport et al. 1989, Licina et al. 1994, Ganguli et al. 1989, 1994, Villemain et al. 1987, 1989, Shintani et al. 1991, Xu et al. 1994, Maes et al. 1994, Wei et al. 1992, Katil et al. 1994).

The neurobiologic effects of cytokines.   Cytokines are produced in the periphery by a range of leukocytes and in the central nervous system by microglia, neurons, endothelial cells, and astroglia. Expression and activity of cytokines is heightened during infection, local tissue damage, and fever. Cytokine receptor sites in the CNS are seen in the highest concentrations in the hypothalamus and hippocampus.

Direct neuromodulatory roles have been identified for certain cytokines. For example, intra-ventricular injections of IL-1, IL-2 and IL-3 can induce slow wave sleep. Interleukins also produce sedation and electroencephalograph (EEG) synchronization, which are attributed to effects in the locus coeruleus.

Cytokines modify synaptic plasticity, influence ion channels, and support the survival of damaged neurons in culture (Hopkins and Rothwell 1995b). For example, IL-6 promotes neuronal survival and inhibits NMDA toxicity and ischemic damage. However, neurotoxic effects of IL-6 are known. Hariri et al. (1994) reported that traumatic injury induces production of IL-6 by human astrocytes in culture in relationship to the severity of the barotrauma, and further, that IL-6 may trigger secondary damage by inflammation after traumatic brain injury. Campbell et al. (1993) demonstrated that cerebral overexpression of IL-6 in transgenic mice induced "neurologic disease" characterized by runting, ataxia, tremor and seizure. He concluded that IL-6 can have a direct pathogenic role in inflammatory, infectious and neurodegenerative diseases. Steffenson et al. (1994) described distinctive hippocampal interneuron pathology and behavioral seizures in transgenic mice that overexpress the IL-6 gene. Furthermore, overproduction of IL-6 selectively disrupts cholinergic transmission by inducing changes in hippocampal neurons.

Likewise, IL-1 is protective in low concentrations, and appears to be produced in higher concentrations in response to stress. Neurotoxic concentrations of excitatory amino acids induce expression of IL-1. Infusions of IL-1 can lead to glial-cell activation and neuronal loss. Furthermore, injection of the IL-1 receptor antagonist inhibits neurodegeneration induced by focal cerebral ischemia and excitatory amino acids.

Cytokines in CNS disease. IL-1 expression is induced by the human immunodeficiency virus (HIV) and IL-1 has been implicated in the neurologic symptoms observed in acquired immunodeficiency syndrome (AIDS). Elevated brain IL-1 and IL-6 has been linked to the immune depression and neuropathologic changes observed in both Down's syndrome and Alzheimer's disease, and high concentrations of IL-1 immunoreactivity are observed in the microglia-like cells at the core of neuritic plaques. These cytokines may contribute to neuronal degeneration in these diseases (Griffin et al. 1989). Endogenous inhibitors of cytokines have been identified in normal brains. Other inhibitors of cytokine action diminish clinical symptoms in MS, and reduce neuronal damage caused by ischemia and toxins.

Although studies of cytokines in schizophrenia were undertaken in an effort to demonstrate the aberrant expression that occurs in classical autoimmune disease, the array of cytokine effects on neuronal activity suggest that overexpression of cytokines in schizophrenia may represent evidence of cell injury, may indicate ongoing immune or autoimmune activity or may itself be responsible for neuronal injury or dysfunction. Cytokines can induce disruption of the BBB, which thereby indirectly enhances CNS exposure to the action of circulating immune factors. Interestingly, Denicoff et al. (1991), in studies of the behavioral and psychological sequelae of treatment with IL-2 in cancer patients, demonstrated that IL-2 frequently induces psychosis and other significant neurobehavioral changes. It is noteworthy that the hippocampus, which is anatomically and functionally related to the clinical pathology of schizophrenia, is particularly vulnerable to the cytotoxic effects of cytokines.

AUTOANTIBODY-CNS INTERACTIONS IN NEUROLOGIC DISEASE

Autoantibodies can cause clinically significant disease by mimicking natural ligands, inducing allosteric changes in receptors and interacting with cell surface and intracytoplasmic components. A classical example is Graves' disease, where autoantibodies bind to the thyroid stimulating hormone (TSH) receptor, activate the thyroid and produce clinical hyperthyroidism (Smith et al. 1988). Several less common diseases of the CNS provide interesting examples of antibody action on specific neuronal functions. For example, stiff-man syndrome, a disorder characterized by muscular rigidity and painful muscular spasms, also results from the effects of a specific autoantibody. In this disease, impaired transmission at gamma amino-butyric acid (GABA) synapses has recently been linked to the presence of autoantibodies to glutamic acid decarboxylase (GAD), the enzyme that catalyzes the rate-limiting step in GABA synthesis. Antibodies to GAD are present in 60% of patients with stiff-man syndrome and in controls with other inflammatory or degenerative nervous system diseases (Solimena et al. 1990). In paraneoplastic degenerative syndrome, antiglutamate subunit antibodies have been found to increase receptor sensitivity to glutamate and hasten neuronal degeneration typical of the disease (Greenlee et al. 1995).

Sydenham's chorea (SC) provides an example of a neuropsychiatric disease putatively linked to a cross-reacting antibody triggered by an infectious agent. SC is a classical manifestation of rheumatic fever, a potential sequelae of Group A streptococcal infection. Patients with SC develop adventitious choreic movements, other motor disturbances and psychiatric symptoms. SC usually occurs in childhood or early adolescence and has a female predominance. It also occurs at an increased rate in family members of affected patients. Significant psychopathology has been described in patients with SC, many of whom manifest overt obsessive compulsive symptoms (Swedo et al. 1993). Chorea in SC has been linked to central presynaptic dopaminergic dysfunction and other dopaminergic changes (Naidu and Narasimhachari 1980, Nausieda et al. 1983). In addition, pathologic changes in the basal ganglia have been recognized in postmortem studies. Husby et al. (1976) demonstrated antibodies against a cytoplasmic structure in caudate and subthalamic neurons in 47% of patients with SC. Autoantibody titers correlated with disease severity.

Finally, Rasmussen's encephalitis (RE) is a syndrome with a recently identified autoimmune etiology. RE is a rare progressive neurologic disease of childhood onset which is characterized by intractable seizures, hemiparesis and dementia. Recent work by Rogers et al. (1994) has linked the pathology in RE to direct autoantibody stimulation of the glutamate receptor. Homology between this receptor and a microbial amino acid binding protein suggests that the autoimmune response in RE may result from cross-reactivity between these two antigens. Circulating autoantibodies are hypothesized to gain access to CNS glutamate receptors after focal disruption of the blood brain barrier after a seizure or head injury, events known to precede the onset of RE. Based on the presumed autoimmune nature of the illness, treatment using plasmapheresis to clear the autoantibody has been undertaken and has proven successful.

SC and RE are CNS autoimmune diseases in which autoimmunity following environmental insults produces complex and varied neurologic and neuropsychiatric syndromes via antibody effects on neurotransmission. In both, however, the actions of mediators of the inflammatory response which accompanies the disease may also contribute to pathology.

Autoantibodies, autoimmunity, and schizophrenia

The search for serum antibrain autoantibodies in schizophrenia has yielded intriguing but controversial results that have not been replicated; this has been extensively reviewed elsewhere (Strauss 1995, Knight et al. 1987), Reports of increased levels of autoantibodies to neuronal and non-neuronal tissues (Ehrnst et al. 1982, Lehmann-Facius 1967, Heath and Krupp 1967, Baron et al. 1977, Pandey et al. 1981, Delisi 1986, Shima et al. 1991) are cited as indicators of a putative autoimmune mechanisms or as evidence of nonspecific autoimmune activation in patients with schizophrenia. Much of this work has been disputed on methodologic grounds. Furthermore, no specific antigens have been identified.

Antibody studies at Columbia University and the NYS Psychiatric Institute

In the course of investigating the specificity of antibodies to neural cells in patients with schizophrenia, we found that 14 (44%) of 32 patients had serum IgG antibodies that bound to a human neuroblastoma cell protein of 60 kD molecular weight (Kilidireas et al. 1992). Partial sequence analysis of this antigen identified it as the 60–kD heat shock protein (hsp60). Of 100 normal or nonpsychiatric controls, antibodies to hsp60 were detected in only eight.

Autoantibodies to recombinant hsp60. To confirm the pilot data generated using neuroblastoma cell extracts, and to minimize the risk that serum antibodies were reacting to proteins which comigrated with hsp60, reactivity of patient and control serum to 5 μg of recombinant generated hsp60 was tested by Western blot analysis at dilutions of 1:1000, 1:4000 and 1:10000. Affinity-purified recombinant hsp60 (rhsp60) was generated in our laboratory and used in all subsequent studies. Interpretation of anti-hsp60 reactivity was appreciably easier and more accurate when using rhsp60 as antigen (see Figure 2).

Results of this study using patients with schizophrenia compared to medical, psychiatric and normal controls confirmed our previous results (Table 2). At serum dilutions of 1:10000, anti-hsp60 antibodies were present in 32.5% of the patients with schizophrenia but in none of 97 controls without illness or with other nonpsychotic psychiatric or neurologic illnesses. At this same dilution, 20% of patients with rheumatologic diseases and 20% of patients with tuberculosis, and had anti-hsp60 antibodies. Antibody at high titer was detected in patients with other psychotic disorders, raising questions about the specificity of this finding to schizophrenia, and possible confounding effects of neuroleptic medication.

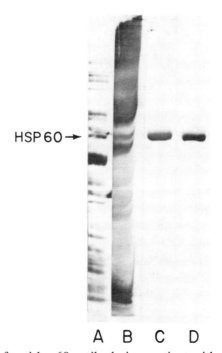

FIG. 2. Demonstration of anti-hsp60 antibody in a patient with schizophrenia.

TABLE 2. PERCENTAGE OF SUBJECTS IN VARIOUS DIAGNOSTIC CATEGORIES WITH
ANTIBODIES TO HSP60 IN SERIAL DILUTION

Diagnosis	Total N	Negative	1:1,000	1:4,000	1:10,000
Schizophrenia	40	42.5% (17)	57.5% (23)	42.5% (17)	32.5% (13)
Schizoaffective disorder	12	50% (6)	50% (6)	25% (3)	25% (3)
Other psychosis	6	66% (4)	33% (2)	17% (1)	17 (1)
Other psychiatric	48	46% (22)	44% (26)	10% (5)	0% (0)
Neurologic illness	33	88% (29)	12% (4)	3% (1)	0% (0)
Rheumatic disease	20	60% (12)	40% (8)	30% (6)	20% (4)
Tuberculosis	10	50% (5)	50% (5)	30% (5)	20% (2)
Healthy	16	87% (14)	13% (2)	0% (0)	0% (0)

CSF autoantibodies to hsp60 in schizophrenia. The ability to detect anti-hsp60 antibodies in the CSF of patients with schizophrenia would strongly link hsp60 antibodies to pathophysiology in these patients. The failure to detect CSF antibodies might suggest that the serum antibody merely crossreacts in a nonspecific manner with the neuronal antigen. Additional support would be provided by evidence of intrathecal antibody production or demonstration of CSF titers in seronegative patients. In pilot studies to determine CSF-hsp60 reactivity, we examined CSF from eight patients with schizophrenia and 50 controls with various CNS inflammatory disorders, neurodegenerative diseases and organic psychoses. CSF reactivity to rhsp60 was detected by Western blot analysis in only 1 of 50 (2%) controls but in 3 of 8 (37.5%) patients with schizophrenia. All of the patients with CSF reactivity also exhibited serum reactivity to hsp60. These preliminary results confirm the presence of anti-hsp60 antibodies in the CSF. The question of whether intrathecal antibody production occurs is currently being investigated.

Hsps and autoimmunity

Antibodies to hsps in high titer do not occur in healthy individuals, although they are found in a small number of patients with rheumatologic and infectious disease, such as tuberculosis (Jarjour et al. 1991). In our work, however, patients with schizophrenia without clinical or laboratory evidence of medical illness have the highest frequency of anti-hsp60 antibody reactivity. Other studies of autoimmune phenomena in schizophrenia have revealed nonspecific patterns of immune reactivity consistent with classical autoimmune disease. To our knowledge, the finding of reactivity to hsp60 represents the first identification of a putative autoantigen in schizophrenia. It is relevant, therefore, to consider the biologic role of this antigen and its relationship to infection, autoimmunity and the pathophysiology of schizophrenia.

Hsps evidence significant sequence homology among widely divergent species. The observed reactivity to hsp60 seen in some patients with tuberculosis or autoimmune illness may arise as a result of a structural feature (an epitope) recognized by the antibody on both human hsp60 and the bacterial analogue of hsp60. Antibodies raised against foreign hsps could give rise to autoimmune reactivity to native hsp, and result in disease or dysfunction. Hsp60 is approximately 50% homologous with the 65kD mycobacterial hsp (hsp65) (Jindal et al. 1989). Human antigens that are cross-reactive with hsp65 have been implicated in the pathogenesis of adjuvant-induced arthritis in rats and of autoimmune diabetes in humans and mice (Elias et al. 1990, Van Eden et al. 1987). In adjuvant-induced arthritis, a proteoglycan link protein is the presumed antigen for cross-reacting anti-hsp65 antibodies (Van Eden et al. 1985).

Antibodies to hsp60 could arise in schizophrenia as a result of infection with an organism which contains antigens homologous to hsp60, by molecular mimicry. Alternatively, viral infection could result in the incorporation of hsp60 into the budding virus, making it immunogenic. Finally, hsp60 could become immunogenic because of structural alterations or post-translational modifications secondary to mutation, metabolic changes, or infection (Shattner and Rager-Zisman 1990).

The biologic role of hsps. HSP are expressed at low levels in all cells and function in protein assembly and transport. HSP expression is increased in response to a range of insults including infection, toxins, trauma, cytokine activation, and ischemia. Under conditions of cellular stress, hsps function to maintain cellular integrity (Lindquist 1986, Morimoto et al. 1994). They may aid in the recovery from myocardial infarction, surgery and stroke (Mestrill and Dillmann 1995, Black and Lucchesi 1993). The experimental induction of hsps has been shown to protect organs and tissues exposed to environmental insults. For example, Tytell (1993) has examined the protective effects of hsp70 in the retinal cells of albino rats exposed to damage from bright lights. Injection of purified hsp70 reduces photoreceptor cell damage from prolonged light exposure. Similar protection results from mild heat stress, which induces hsp. After receiving the heat stress, maximal protection from light-damage occurs concurrent with the maximal induction of endogenous hsp70, suggesting that heat-induced expression of hsp70 is the mechanism by which treated rats endure bright light exposure.

DISCUSSION AND FUTURE DIRECTIONS

Recent work on cytokines and our group's finding of antibodies to hsp60 in patients with schizophrenia may suggest an interesting new link between observed autoimmune phenomena in schizophrenia and a specific pathophysiologic mechanism. Autoimmune phenomena may: 1) be evidence of active autoimmune disease, 2) be nonspecific markers of neuronal injury from other causes, or 3) may suggest mechanisms of disease in schizophrenia related to cellular responses to injury.

For example, hsp60 antibodies could directly relate to disease in schizophrenia if they interact with normal or aberrantly produced or modified hsp60 in neuronal cells. It is intriguing to speculate that antibodies against hsp60 or neuronal population-specific subtypes of hsp60 might directly interfere with the neuronal stress response (Figure 1). Certain neuronal populations would be left vulnerable to fever, infection, head injury or oxidative stress. Alternatively, aberrant production of hsp60 as a result of mutation or viral modification could impair the neuronal response to environmental stress and secondarily give rise to nonpathogenic autoantibodies. Cellular damage or dysfunction during development or later could give rise to the phenomenology of schizophrenia. The disease process could involve a physiologically important but as yet unidentified neuronal antigen which merely cross-reacts with hsp60. Finally, autoantibodies to hsp60 may represent markers of neuronal damage (rather than causes of it).

Overexpression of cytokines such as that observed in schizophrenia and a range of other neurologic disorders could relate to acute or persistent infection, autoimmune activation, or other CNS stressors, trauma or toxic metabolites. Cytokines may directly mediate neuronal injury during development or in persistent fashion, or elevated cytokine levels may instead result from a neuronal response to injury.

Epitope mapping studies may help elucidate and characterize the hsp60 antibody binding site recognized by antibodies from patients with schizophrenia as opposed to antibodies from control populations. Epitope mapping analysis will help identify other functionally important cross-reacting proteins that may be relevant to the disease process. The hypothesis that hsp60 may be aberrantly expressed, altered, or distributed in the brains of patients with schizophrenia can be tested using immunohistochemical techniques on post-mortem tissue.

Animal studies of the neurodevelopmental, neuropathologic and neurobehavioral effects of impaired neuronal stress responses in the setting of environmental insults may shed light on the physiologic role of HSPs in schizophrenia. Similarly, behavioral studies of cytokines and cytokine antagonists may provide clues to the action of these molecules in disease states.

Whether hsp60 antibodies and cytokine abnormalities are causally related to the pathology of schizophrenia, or are secondary responses to neuronal injury is the fundamental question requiring further investigation. The elucidation of a pathophysiology in schizophrenia and other diseases related to abnormal stress response would suggest new therapeutic strategies aimed at modifying the action of immune mediators or altering cellular vulnerability to biologic stress.

REFERENCES

Amital H, Shoenfeld Y. Autoimmunity and schizophrenia: An epiphenomenon or an etiology? *Isr J Med Sci* 29:593–597, 1993.

Baron M, Stern M, Anavi R, Witz J. Tissue binding factor in schizophrenic sera: A clinical and genetic study. *Biol Psychiat* 12:199, 1977.

Barinaga M. Antibodies linked to rare epilepsy. *Science* 268:362–363, 1995.

Bartalena L, Grassi L, Brogioni S, Aghini-Lombardi F, Braverman LE, Martino E. Serum interleukin-6 amiodarone-induced thyrotoxicosis. *J Clin Endocrin Metab* 78:423–427, 1993.

Bird G. Autoantibodies—A Perspective in B Lymphocytes in Human Disease. Bird G, Calvert JA, eds. London: Oxford University Press, 1978.

Black SC, Lucchesi BR. Heat shock, stress proteins, chaperones, and proteotoxicity. *Cell* 66:191, 1991.

Bohen SP, Kralli A, Yamamoto KR. Hold'em and fold'em: Chaperones and signal transduction. *Science* 268:1303–1304, 1995.

Bonfa E, Golombek SJ, Kaufman LD, Skelly S, Weissbach H, Brot N, Elkon KB. Association between lupus psychosis and anti-ribosomal P protein antibodies. *N Engl J Med* 317:265–271, 1987.

Bronze MS, Dale JB. Epitopes of streptococcal M proteins that evoke antibodies that cross-react with human brain. *J Immunol* 151:2820–2828, 1993.

Buchanan RW, Heinrichs DW. The Neurological Evaluation Scale (NES): A structured instrument for the assessment of neurological signs in schizophrenia. Psychiat Res
27:335–350, 1989.

Campbell IL, Abraham CR, Masliah E, Kemper P, Inglis JD, Oldstone MBA, Mucke L.
Neurologic disease induced in transgenic mice by cerebral overexpression of interleukin
6. *Proc Natl Acad Sci USA* 90:10061–10065, 1993.

Capra R, Mattioli F, Marciano N, Vignoli LA, Bettinzioli M, Airo P, and Cattaneo.
Significantly higher levels of soluble interleuken 2 in patients with relapsing-remitting
multiple sclerosis compared with healthy subjects. *Arch Neurol* 47:254, 1990.

Carpenter WT Jr, Buchanan RW. Domains of psychopathology relevant to the study of etiology and treatment in schizophrenia. In: Schulz SC, ed. *Schizophrenia: Scientific
Progress.* New York: Oxford University Press, 1989, pp. 13–22.

Castle DJ, Abel K, Takei N, Murray RM. Gender differences in schizophrenia: hormonal
effect or subtypes? *Schizo Bull* 21:1–12, 1995.

Chengappa KN, Roy, Carpenter AB, Keshavan MS, Yang ZW, Rabin BS, Ganguli R.
Elevated IGG and IGM anticardiolipin antibodies in a subgroup of medicated and unmedicated schizophrenia patients. *Biol Psychiat* 30:731–735, 1991.

Chengappa KN, Roy, Ganguli R, Yang ZW, Shurin G, Brar JS, Rabin BS. Impaired mito-
gen (PHA) responsiveness and increased autoantibodies in Caucasian schizophrenic patients with the HLA B8/DR3 phenotype. *Biol Psychiat* 37:546–549, 1995.

Chengappa KN, Roy, Carpenter AB, Yang ZW, Brar JS, Rabin BS, Ganguli R. Elevated
IGG anti-histone antibodies in a subgroup of medicated schizophrenia patients. *Schiz Res*
7:49–54, 1992.

Chengappa KN, Roy, Ganguli R, Ulrich R, Rabin BS, Cochran J, Brar JS, Yang ZW, Deleo
M. The prevalence of autoantibodies among right and left handed schizophrenia patients
and control subjects. *Biol Psychiat* 32:803–811, 1992.

Cohen IR. A heat shock protein, molecular mimicry and autoimmunity. *Isr J Med Sci*
26:673–676, 1990.

Crow TJ. Is schizophrenia an infectious disease? *Lancet* 173–175, 1983.

Daoud AS, Zaki M, Shakir R, Al-Saleh Q. Effectiveness of sodium valproate in the treatment of Sydenham's chorea. *Neurology* 1140–1141, 1990.

Davis JO, Phelps JA. Twins with schizophrenia: genes or germs? *Schiz Bull* 21:13–18, 1995.

Delisi LE. Neuroimmunology: Clinical Studies of Schizophrenia and other Psychiatric
Disorders. In: Nasrallah HA, Weinberger DR, eds, *Handbook of Schizophrenia*, Vol 1:
The Neurology of Schizophrenia. New York: Elsevier Science Publishers 1986.

Denicoff KD, Rubinow DR, Papa MA, Simpson C, Seipp CA, Lotze MT, Chang AE,
Rosenstein D, Tosenberg SA. The neuropsychiatric effects of treatment with interleukin-
3 and lymphokine-activated killer cells. *Ann Intern Med* 107:293–300, 1987.

de Pablo F, de la Rosa E. The developing CNS: a scenario for the action of proinsulin, insulin and insulin-like growth factors, A review. *Trend Neurosci* 18:143–150, 1995.

Dinarello CA. Inflammatory cytokines: interleukin-1 and tumor necrosis factor as effector
molecules in autoimmune diseases. *Immunology* 3:941–948, 1991.

Drachman DB. How to recognize antibody-mediated autoimmune disease criteria. In:
Waksman BH, ed, *Imunologic Mechanisms in Neurologic and Psychiatric Disease.* New
York: Raven Press, 1990.

Ehrnst A, Wiesel FK, Bjerkenstedt L, Tribukait B, Jonsson J. Failure to detect immunologic stigmata in schizophrenia. *Neuropsychobiology* 8:169–171, 1982.

Elias D, Markovits D, Reshef T, van der Zee R, Cohen IR. Induction and therapy of autoimmune diabetes in the non-obese diabetic (NOD/Lt) mouse by a k5kDa heat shock protein. *Proc Natl Acad Sci, USA* 87:1576–1580, 1990.

El-Mallakh RS, Suddath RL, Wyatt RJ. Interleukin-1a and interleukin-2 in cerebrospinal fluid of schizophrenic subjects. *Prog Neuro-Psychopharmacol & Biol Psychiat* 17:383–391, 1993.

Elkon KB. Origin and clinical relevance of autoantibodies. In: *Rheumatic Disorders in Clinical Practice*, 7–18.

Ezzell C. Hot stuff: Medical application of the heat-shock response. *J NIH Res* 7:42–45, 1995.

Ganguli R, Rabin BS. Increased serum interleukin-2 receptor concentration in schizophrenic and brain-damaged subjects. *Arch Gen Psychiatry* 46:292, 1989

Ganguli R, Rabin BS, Brar JS. Antinuclear and Gastric parietal cell autoantibodies in schizophrenia patients. *Biol Psychiat* 32:735–738, 1992.

Ganguli R, Yang A, Shurin G, Chengappa KNR, Brar JS, Gubbin AV, Rabin BS. Serum interleukin-6 concentration in schizophrenia: Elevation associated with duration of illness. *Psychiat Res* 51:1–10, 1994.

Ganguli R, Brar JS, Chengappa KNR, Yang ZW, Nimgaonkar FL, Rabin BS. Autoimmunity in schizophrenia: A review of recent findings. *Ann Med* 25:389–496, 1993.

Grave L, Baumann M, Heinrich PC. Interleukin-6 in autoimmune diseases. *Clin Invest* 71:664–671, 1993.

Greenberg SJ, Marcon L, Hurwitz BJ, Waldmann TA, Nelson DL. Elevated levels of soluble interleukin-2 receptors in multiple sclerosis. *N Engl J Med* 319:1019–1020,1988.

Griffin WST. Neuronal and immune dysfunction mediated by IL-1. *Clin Immunol Spect* 6–7, 1991.

Griffin WS, Stanley LC, Ling C. Brain interleukin 1 and S-100 immunoreactivity are elevated in Down's Syndrome and Alzheimer's disease. *Proc Ntl Acad Sci USA* 86:7611–7615, 1989.

Haregewoin A, Singh B, Gupta RS, Finberg RW. A mycobacterial heat-shock protein-responsive? T-cell clone also responds to the homologous human heat-shock protein: A possible link between infection and autoimmunity. *J Infect Dis* 163:156–160, 1991.

Halper J. Immunocyte receptors and second messengers in psychoneuroimmunology. In: Gorman JG, Kirstner RM, eds, *Psychoimmunology Update*. Washington, DC: APA Press, 1991.

Hariri RJ, Chang VA, Barie PS, Wang RS, Sharif SF. Traumatic injury induces interleukin-6 production by human astrocytes. *Brain Res* 636:139–142, 1993.

Hariri RJ, Chang VA, Barie PS, Wang RS, Sharif SF, Chajar JB. Traumatic injury induces interleukin-6 production by human astrocytes. Brain Res 636:139–142, 1994.

Heath RG, Krupp IM. Schizophrenia as an immunologic disorder I, II, I II. *Arch Gen Psychiatry* 16:1–33, 1967.

Hopkins SJ, Rothwell NJ. Cytokines and the nervous system 1: Expression and recognition. *Trend Neurosci* 18:83–88, 1995.

Hopkins SJ, Rothwell NJ. Cytokines and the nervous system 11: Actions and mechanisms of action. *Trend Neurosci* 18:130–136, 1995.

Husby G, van de Rijn I, Zabriskie JB, Abdin ZH, Williams Jr, RC. Antibodies reacting with cytoplasm of subthalamic and caudate nuclei neurons in chorea and acute rheumatic fever. *J Exp Med* 144:1094–1110, 1976.

Jarjour WN, Jeffried BD, Davies JS, Welch WJ, Mimura T, and Winfield. Autoantibodies to human stress proteins. *Arth Rheum* 34:1133–1138, 1991.

Jindal S, Dudani AK, Singh B, Harley CB, Gupta RS. Primary structure of a human mitochondrial protein homologous to the bacterial and plant chaperonins and to the 65kD mycobacterial antigen. *Mol Cell Biol* 9:2279–2283, 1989.

Katila H, Appelberg B, Hurme M, Rimon R. Plasma levels of interleukin-1 and interleukin-6 in schizophrenia, other psychoses, and affective disorders. *Schiz Res* 12:29–34, 1994.

Katila H, Hurme M, Wahlbeck K, Appelberg B, Rimon R. Plasma and cerebrospinal fluid interleukin-1 and interleukin-6 in hospitalized schizophrenic patients. *Neuropsychobiology* 30:20–23, 1994.

Kaufmann and Ziegler. The viral hypothesis of schizophrenia. In: Sen AK, Lee T, eds, *Receptors and Ligands in Psychiatry*. New York: Cambridge University Press, 1988, pp. 187–201.

Kemminger KA. The schizophrenic syndrome as a product of acute infectious disease. *Arch Neurol Psychiat* 464–481, 1928.

Kiessling LS, Marcotte AC, Culpepper L. Antineuronal antibodies in movement disorders. *Pediatrics* 92:39–43, 1993.

Kilidireas K, Latov N, Strauss DH, Gorig AD, Hasim GA, Gorman JM, Sadiq SA. Antibodies to the human 60 kDa heat-shock protein in patients with schizophrenia. *Lancet* 340:569–572, 1992.

Knight JG. Possible autoimmune mechanisms in schizophrenia. *Integr Psychiatry* 3:134–143, 1985.

Knight JG, Knight A, Pert CB. Is schizophrenia really a virally triggered antireceptor autoimmune disease? In: Helmchen HJ, Henn FA, eds. *Biological Perspectives on Schizophrenia*. New York: John Wiley and Sons, 1987.

Lehmann-Facius H. Uber die liquordiagnose der schizophrenien. *Klin Wochenschr* 16:164, 1937.

Licina J, Krystal JH, Seibyl JP, Altemus M, Charney DS. Elevated central levels of interleukin-2 in drug-free schizophrenia patients. *Schiz Res* 4:372, 1991.

Lindquist S. The heat shock proteins. *Ann Rev Biochem* 55:1151–1191, 1986.

Linker-Israeli M, Deans RJ, Wallace DJ, Prehn J, Ozeri-Chen T, Klinenberg JR. Elevated levels of endogenous IL6 in systemic lupus erythematosus. *J Immunol* 147:117–123, 1991.

Maes M, Meltzer HY, Bosmans E. Immune-inflammatory markers in schizophrenia: comparison to normal controls and effects of clozapine. *Acta Psychiatr Scand* 89:346–351, 1994.

Mayer J, Brown IR. *Heat Shock Proteins in the Nervous System*. London: Academic Press, 1994.

Mednick SA, Machon RA, Huttunen MO, Boknett D. Adult schizophrenia following prenatal exposure to an influenza epidemic. *Arch Gen Psychiat* 45:189–192, 1988.

Mestrill R, Dillmann WH. Heat shock proteins and protein against myocardial ischemia. *J Mol Cell Cardiol* 27:45, 1995.

Morimoto RI, Tissieres A, Georgopoulos C. *The Biology of Heat Shock Proteins and Molecular Chaperones*. Cold Spring Harbor, NY: Cold Spring Harbor Laboratory Press, 1994.

Muller N, Ackenheil M. The immune system and schizophrenia. In: Leonard B, Miller K, eds. *Stress, the Immune System and Psychiatry*. New York, NY: John Wiley & Sons, 1995, pp. 137–157.

Murray RM, Reveley AM. Schizophrenia as an infection. *Lancet* 583, 1983.

Nakanishi K, Malek TR, Smith KA, Hamaoka T, Shevach E, Paul WE. Both interleukin 2 and a second T cell derived factor in EL4 supernatants have activity as differentiation factors in IgM synthesis. *J Exp Med* 160:1605–1621, 1990.

Naidu S, Narasimhachari N. Sydenham's chorea: A possible presynaptic dopaminergic dysfunction initially. *Ann Neurol* 8:445–446, 1980.

Nausieda PA, Bieliauskas LA, Bacon LD, Hagerty M, Koller WC, Glantz RN. Chronic dopaminergic sensitivity after Sydenham's chorea. *Neurology* 33:750–754, 1983.

Nausieda PA, Grossman BJ, Koller WC, Weiner WJ, Klawans HL. Sydenham chorea: An update. *Neurology* 30:331–334, 1980.

Newsome-Davis J. Lambert Eaton myasthenic syndrome. *Monogr Allergy* 25:116–124, 1988.

Nurnberger JI Jr, Blehar MC, Kaufmann CA, York-Cooler C, Simpson GS, Harkavy-Friedman J, Severe JA, Malaspina D, Reich T. Diagnostic interview for genetic studies: Rationale, unique features and training. *Arch Gen Psychiatry* 51:849–859, 1994.

Pandey RS, Gutpa AK, Chaturvedi VC. Autoimmune model of schizophrenia with special reference to antibrain antibodies. *Biol Psychiatry* 16:1123, 1981, 1985.

Prasher VP, Barrett K. Neuropsychiatric aspects of Sydenham's chorea: A case report. *J Psychosom Obst Gynaecol* 14:159–162, 1993.

Rappaport MH, McAllister CG, Pickar D, Nelson DL, Paul SM. Elevated levels of interleukin 2 receptors in schizophrenia. *Arch Gen Psychiatry* 46:291–292, 1989.

Reichelt KL, Landmark J. Specific IgA antibody increases in schizophrenia. *Biol Psychiat* 37:410–413, 1995.

Richamn DP, Fairclough RH, Xu Q, Aius MA. Noninflammatory immune mechanisms in disease of the nervous system. In: Waksman BH, ed. *Immunologic Mechanisms in Neurologic and Psychiatric Disease.* New York: Raven Press, 1990.

Ritossa F. A new puffing pattern induced by temperature shock and DNP in drosophila. *J NIH Res* 4:65–66, 1992.

Rogers SW, Andrews PI, Gahring LC, Whisenand T, Cauley K, Crain B, Hughes TE, Heinemann SF, McNamara JO. Autoantibodies to glutamate receptor GluR3 in Rasmussen's encephalitis. *Science* 265:648–651, 1994.

Sasaki T, Nanko S, Fukuda R, Kawate T, Kunugi H, Kazamatsuri H. Changes of immunological functions after acute exacerbation in schizophrenia. *Biol Psychiat* 35:173–178, 1994.

Schatner A, Rager-Zisman B. Virus-induced autoimmunity. *Rev Infect Dis* 12:204–222, 1990.

Shannon KM, Fenichel GM. Pimozide treatment of Sydenham's chorea. *Neurology* 40:186–187, 1990.

Shinitzky M, Deckmann M, Kessler A, Sirota P, Rabbs A, Elizur A. Platelet autoantibodies in dementia and schizophrenia. *Ann NY Acad Sci* 205–217, 1991.

Shima S, Yano K, Sugiura M, Tokunaga Y. Anticerebral antibodies in functional psychoses. *Biol Psychiat* 29:322–328, 1991.

Shintani F, Kanba S, Maruo N, Nakaki T, Nibuya N, Suzuki E, Kinoshita N, Yagi G. Serum interleukin-6 in schizophrenic patients. *Life Sci* 49:661–664, 1991.

Sinha AA, Lopez MR, McDevitt HO. Autoimmune diseases: The failure of self tolerance. *Science* 248:1380–1388, 1990.

Sirota P, Firer MA, Schild K, Tanay A, Elizur A, Meytes D, Slor H. Autoantibodies to DNA in multicase families with schizophrenia. *Biol Psychiat* 33:450–455, 1993.

Smith BR, McLachlin SM, Furmaniak J. Autoantibodies to the thyrotropin receptor. *Endocr Rev* 9:106–121, 1988.

Solimena M, Folli F, Aparisi R, Possa G, De Camilli P. Autoantibodies to GABA-ergic neurons and pancreatic beta cells in stiff-man syndrome. *N Engl J Med* 322:1555–1560, 1990.

Sommers AA. Negative symptoms: Conceptual and methodological problems. *Schiz Bull* 11:364–379, 1985.

Steffensen SC, Campbell IL, Henriksen SJ. Site-specific hippocampal pathophysiology due to cerebral overexpression of interleukin-6 in transgenic mice. *Brain Res* 652:149–153, 1994.

Swedo SE, Leonard HL, Schapiro MB, Casey BJ, Mannheim GB, Lenane MG, Rettew DC. Sydenham's chorea: Physical and psychological symptoms of St. Vitus dance. *Pediatrics* 91(4):706–713, 1993.

Tsai C-Y, Wu T-H, Chen K-H, Lin W-M, Yu H-S, Yu C-L. Cerebrospinal fluid interleukin-6, prostaglandin E2 and autoantibodies in patients with neuropsychiatric systemic lupus erythematosus and central nervous system infections. *Scand J Rheumatol* 23:57–63, 1994.

Tytell M, Barbe MF, Brown IR. Stress (heat shock) protein accumulation in the central nervous system. Its relationship to cell stress and damage. *Adv Neurol* 59:293–303, 1993.

Van Eden W, Holoshitz J, Cohen IR. Antigen mimicry between mycobacterial and cartilage proteoglycans: The model of adjuvant arthritis. *Concepts Immunol Pathol* 4:144–170, 1987.

Van Eden W, Holoshitz J, Nevo Z, Frenkel A, Klajman A, Cohen IR. Arthritis induced by a T lymphocyte clone that responds to mycobacteria tuberculosis and to cartilage proteoglycan. *Proc Natl Acad Sci, USA* 82:5117–5120, 1985.

Villemain F, Chatenoud L, Guillibert. Decreased production of IL2 in schizophrenia. *Ann NY Acad Sci* 496:669–675,1987.

Villemain F, Chatenoud L, Galinowsky A, Homo-Delarche, Gineset D, Loo H, Zarifian E, Bach J-F. Aberrant Ti cell-mediated immunity in untreated schizophrenic patients: Deficient interleukin-2 production. *Am J Psychiatry* 146(5):609–616, 1989.

Waltrip II RW, Carrigan DR, Carpenter Jr, WT. Immunopathology and reactivation. *J Nerv Ment Dis* 178(12):729–738, 1990.

Wagman AMI, Heinrichs DW, Carpenter WT. The deficit and non-deficit forms of schizophrenia: Neuropsychological evaluation. *Psychiatry Res* 22(4)319–330, 1985.

Wang S, Sun C, Walczak CA, Ziegle JS, Kipps BR, Goldin LR, Diehl SR. Evidence for a susceptibility locus for schizophrenia on chromosme 6pter-p22. *Nature Genet* 10:41–46, 1995.

Wei J, Xu H, Davies JL, Hemmings CP. Increase of plasma IL-6 concentration with age in health subjects. *Life Sci* 51:1953–1956, 1992.

Weiner HL, Hauser SL. Neuroimmunology 1: Immunoregulation in neurological disease. *Ann Neurol* 11:437–449, 1982.

Weiner HL, Hauser SL. Neuroimmunology 11: Antigenic specificity of the nervous system. *Ann Neurol* 12:499–509, 1982.

Weissberg MP, Friedrich EV. Sydenham's chorea: Case report of a diagnostic dilemma. *Am J Psychiat* 135:607–609, 1978.

Wilcox JA, Nasrallah HA. Sydenham's chorea and psychopathology. *Neuropsychobiology* 19:6–8, 1988.

Wilcox JA, Nasrallah HA. Sydenham's chorea and psychosis. *Neuropsychobiology* 15:13–14, 1986.

Wittingham S, Mackay IR, Jones IH, Davies B. Absence of brain antibodies in patients with schizophrenia. *Br Med J* 1:347, 1968.

Wood NC, Symons JA, Duff GW. Serum interleukin-2 receptor in rheumatoid arthritis: A prognostic indicator of disease activity. *J Autoimmunol* 1:353, 1988.

Wright P, Murray RM. Schizophrenia: Prenatal influenza and autoimmunity. *Ann Med* 25:497–502, 1993.

Xu H-M, Wei J, Hemmings GP. Changes of plasma concentrations of interleukin-1a and interleukin-6 with neuroleptic treatment for schizophrenia. *Brit J Psychiat* 164:251–253, 1994.

Zinkemagel RM, Cooper S, Chambers J, Lazzarini RA, Hengartner H, Amheiter H, Virus-induced autoantibody response to a transgenic viral antigen. *Nature* 345:68–71, 1990.

SCHIZOPHRENIA
AND THE SELF

Ten Years of Psychiatry Involving Schizophrenia: A Patient's View

LUANNE HOLSINGER

The past decade has seen phenomenal growth in activism by families, professionals, and patients. I am part of that growth: I am a consumer activist who is ill with the disease of schizophrenia.

The story of my illness spans the years from 1983 to the present. It is a sad story, not as terrible as some, but still painful to recall. The death in 1983 of an aunt who was only 48 years old, from stomach cancer, triggered the problems. Anyone who has lost a close relative at a young age realizes the level of stress and grief involved. Obviously, the emotions were too much for my delicate mental condition, and within nine months I was hospitalized at a psychiatric facility.

Before that hospitalization I had chronic sinus problems, a brief total paralysis, tunnel vision, and finally, paranoid delusions about my family. These symptoms gradually advanced until I demanded that my internist have me hospitalized and sedated. I was desperately trying to understand what was going on and trying to get help. However, as many of us found in the 1980s, no one knew what was happening. The internist I originally saw wanted me to just go to a hotel room so that I could get away from my family—how I wish the answer had been so simple.

Seven private hospitalizations of 3–6 weeks each followed in the next 6 years. All of these were brought on by the stress of working, romantic relationships, and attempts to stop taking my medication (which my psychiatrist okayed). As this odyssey continued, I realized I was chronically and seriously ill, and no one seemed to know how to treat me effectively. When I asked if my symptoms could be schizophrenia, my first two psychiatrists told me no, that I just 'wanted' to have schizophrenia. When I had a major psychotic breakdown that lasted from May 1989 to February 1990, they changed their minds.

Haloperidol saved me at that time and, later, trifluoperazine. Finally my psychiatrist decided it was time for me to go on disability. After reading my application and speaking with me on the phone, the Social Security Administration awarded me disability; obviously they realized I was much too ill to work.

By March of 1990 I had regained many of the analytical skills that I had lost in the previous years. My current psychiatrist, Dr. Eloise Haun, and I feel that possibly my right brain began to compensate for some of the problems with my left brain. She had seen this type of recovery with stroke victims. I was speaking more fluently and the tone of my voice had changed. It was during this year—1990—that I began my advocacy work.

During the 1980s the family and patients' movement truly matured. Without the support of these groups, I firmly believe that psychiatry could not have advanced to the level it has today. As a patient, I have been part of the family movement since the fall of 1990. My official roles were in Virginia as the Second Vice-president of the Central Virginia chapter of the National Alliance for the Mentally Ill (NAMI), Secretary of the Harrisonburg chapter, and currently a State Board Member. These years have been the most fulfilling of my life, as I have joined families across the nation who have united to confront the devastating problems of mental illness.

Early on, I felt that my word would be more effective with the families than with the patients groups alone. The patients groups have at times been somewhat radical in their concept of what schizophrenia is and how best to treat it—I feel more at home with the philosophy of the family movement. I do NOT agree that my illness is an alternative lifestyle that I have chosen, and that to take medication is wrong.

The pain I feel about the years of 1983 to 1990 will never go away. However, that pain motivates me to act. No one should EVER have to go through what we with schizophrenia have had to deal with. My paternal grandfather and father have been politically active during the years in Virginia, and I guess at heart I am also a political activist.

There is a misconception among many that schizophrenia is an illness that strikes only the poor and those with low IQs. I was a member of the National Honor Society in high school, and graduated cum laude from college. My third cousin is married to General Norman Schwarzkopf. My family has owned the same farm in Virginia for over 200 years. The maternal great-grandmother from whom I inherited this illness was a distant cousin of President Grover Cleveland, through the Sewell family. My vocational rehabilitation counselor, Norman Kropp, told me I have superior nonverbal skills. As you can see, we come from very successful families, also.

The problem with research into mental illnesses has been that families have often not talked about schizophrenia to the press, or even to their closest friends. Many families have put the patient into a treatment facility, and that is the extent of their dealing with the situation. To talk to the press takes some courage. I know because a story appeared in the *Richmond Times-Dispatch* about my struggle with schizophrenia. If families and consumers are open about the illness, better treatment will result and future generations will be helped. Even at the risk that some people will not "understand," and may even ridicule, the issue is too important to be silent about. I know that some psychiatrists advise their patients not to become mental health advocates. I think this is a tremendous tragedy. It only increases the patient's feeling of being stigmatized.

The current level of activism by families can largely be attributed to the efforts of Dr. E. Fuller Torrey. He became a role-model for us all with his public relations campaign for awareness of schizophrenia as a medical disease. To date, no one else has dealt with the problem as aggressively as he has. He has provided essential leadership for the growth of the NAMI movement. My favorite book after the Bible, is Dr. Torrey's *Surviving Schizophrenia*. It gave me courage when I had been figuratively knocked down and gave me hope when I was very depressed. Most of all, the book gave me a sense of direction when I was looking for a way to deal with the terrible burden of schizophrenia. Dr. Torrey would not have been able to write *Surviving Schizophrenia* if his sister had not been ill with the disease. The book is a tribute to her.

NEW MEDICINES FOR SCHIZOPHRENIA BRING NEW HOPE

The most crucial treatment breakthrough in the past 10 years has been the development of new medication. With the introduction of Clozaril™ (manufactured by Sandoz) and Risperidone™ (Janssen) into the United States market, those of us with schizophrenia have an increased arsenal to combat our disease. While some like myself have responded to older neuroleptics (I take trifluoperazine), others have not been so fortunate. Even those of us on the earlier generation of medicine may one day find that it is not as effective as it once was.

Perhaps we feel about our medication in much the same way that a person with diabetes feels about insulin. The medicine gives us the ability to live as close to a normal life as possible. While it can, at times, cause us the greatest frustration, it is also our dearest friend. New developments in drug therapies will reduce the number of treatment-resistant patients as the drugs more effectively work with the various manifestations of schizophrenia. Persons who have not responded to any medication are in a hell that only those of us who have experienced a psychosis can really understand. The work of the drug companies must be commended because, as they are well aware, the seriously mentally ill as a whole do not number among their most wealthy customers. Financially disadvantaged patients need to have access to medication, and the pharmaceutical industry needs to work on ways to make this possible.

The new medications of Seroquel™ (Zeneca Pharm.), Lanzac™ (Eli Lilly), Sertindole™ (Abbott Labs), and Ziprasidone™ (Pfizer) are in clinical trials. The seriously mentally ill need the pharmaceutical companies to continue to develop new medications to help stabilize their conditions. I am a living example of the power of trifluoperazine, and the companies can be proud of the other testimonies to the effectiveness of their products. My great-grandmother spent many years of her life in a state hospital after a breakdown at age thirty-three because no medicine was available in the early 1900s. Owing to the work of the often disparaged pharmaceutical industry, I am able to think, reason, feel, and even write this chapter.

NARSAD Artworks taps the creativity of the mentally ill

NARSAD Artworks, affiliated with the National Alliance for Research on Schizophrenia and Depression (NARSAD), continues to grow each year. Out of their modest office on the outskirts of Los Angeles has come over 2 million imprints with messages about mental illness. The company has used artwork designed by mentally ill persons to produce notecards, holiday cards, T-shirts, posters, postcards, and bookmarks. Napa State Hospital Center for Youth even supplies the organization with calendars, designed with children's art, for nationwide sales.

Hal and Patsy Hollister founded this nonprofit company in 1989, in an effort to tap the creativity of the mentally ill and use that talent to their benefit. They were aware of their daughter's artistic ability that existed despite her illness of schizophrenia. In fact, some of her finest work was created during acutely psychotic periods. The Hollisters became aware that other mentally ill persons also had distinct nonverbal talents. With this knowledge they began NARSAD Artworks. The company raises funds each year for the artists, NARSAD research and local or state affiliates of NAMI, National Mental Health Association (NMHA), and National Depressive and Manic Depressive Association (DMDA).

My relationship with the Hollisters has been very rewarding. I have designed two holiday cards for them, and run a statewide mail-order business for their products in Virginia. They continue to foster ideas of creating national markets for the artistic work of the mentally ill, including original works. The Hollisters' remarkable insight into what the seriously mentally ill can do, and their work in helping with the marketing, has made a great deal of difference in the lives of consumers involved. As Sandra Somers stated in the *Psychiatric Times*, "When mental illness strikes a child, the way the family responds to this vast new challenge can dramatically affect the outcome for all its members. Sometimes, the influence is felt far beyond the family circle, even across the nation." That has been the case with the family of Hal and Patsy Hollister.

NIMH, NARSAD, STANLEY FOUNDATION, AND THE SCOTTISH RITE

Foundations strike out for answers

During the past decade, biomedical psychiatry took over the reins of federal and private research money; this was one of the actions to have the most positive consequence. To the advantage of those of us with schizophrenia, the medical profession was starting to address the real problems that we were facing, and no longer guessing what was wrong. The Freudian and family system theories of schizophrenia were FINALLY buried.

Drs. Samuel Keith and Herbert Pardes are two of the many psychiatrists who took a role in making this happen. The *NARSAD Research Newsletter* in the summer of 1994 profiled Dr. Keith's career in schizophrenia research at NIMH. One can get a general idea of the influence that he has had in literally tackling the disease. Under his leadership came the National Plan for Schizophrenia Research, which covered many of the areas needing to be investigated. By the time he had left NIMH in 1993, he had set schizophrenia research going in the right direction by really listening to patients and family concerns. Those of us ill with this disorder owe him our deepest gratitude.

Dr. Herbert Pardes has a real sense of where the field of psychiatry is going, and he has the leadership skills to make sure it stays on the right track. His career has included being Director of NIMH, President of the American Psychiatric Association, and President of the Scientific Council of NARSAD. It is very moving for me to see someone devote so much of their life to a disorder that I suffer with. Dr. Pardes' career was outlined in the Spring of 1989 *NARSAD Research Newsletter*. He has helped bring about a revolution in psychiatry.

Both of these physicians were involved in the formation of NARSAD, also. In 1981, a national private nonprofit foundation was founded to fund schizophrenia research in Kentucky. By 1985 this foundation had evolved into NARSAD under the leadership of Philip Ardery and later, Gwill Newman. With a small office of full-time staff, and the collective support of NAMI, NMHA, and DMDA, NARSAD persists in growing each year. It has been under the able leadership of Constance Lieber since 1989, and continues to fund many young researchers, along with grants for innovative projects of established investigators. Stephen and Constance Lieber have done a great service to mankind with their financial support of NARSAD. They recognize that this is a critical time because new technology is in place to find the answers for the mentally ill.

I picked up a brochure about NARSAD at the first NAMI meeting I went to. Gradually during the next 4 years I have become more and more involved in what they have been trying to do. I have sold cards to publicize their existence, mailed brochures to every psychiatrist in Richmond, spoken for them many times, encouraged coverage on their behalf in newsletters of the Virginia AMI and MHA, and worked to have material about their existence in state hospitals around Virginia.

Other research funds have been supplied by the Stanley Foundation. Theodore Stanley is a businessman who, along with his wife, Vada, wanted to help the mentally ill. They formed the Stanley Foundation to work with NAMI. Under the direction of Dr. Torrey, the foundation appropriates approximately half of their funds to schizophrenia research. The Stanleys' willingness to share their wealth to help the less fortunate deserves commendation.

As early as the 1930s the Scottish Rite Foundation began to support studies in schizophrenia. Numerous individuals in the United States are involved with the Masonry, including my uncle. The foundation recognized very early the severe cost of schizophrenia to society, and decided to act when very little private money was available for schizophrenia research.

All research donors should be commended whether they are able to give large or small gifts. Most are families of the mentally ill—families that have suffered along with their loved ones, and have made the decision not just to sit and watch.

Two major bodies of research must be continually addressed: 1) treatment of existing schizophrenia and 2) preventing future illnesses. Neither area should be neglected. Most of us with chronic disease realize that there may be a limit to what can be done for us, but we are not all silent sufferers. We can choose to advocate for research just like persons with cancer, AIDS, and heart disease. My research advocacy work has given great meaning to my life and has psychologically removed much of my earlier depression. As I told one psychiatrist, I want something GOOD to come out of something very bad.

CRITICAL DEVELOPMENTS AT PRESENT

Possible causes of schizophrenia begin to be exposed

1994 was a watershed year for schizophrenia research. Evidence was unearthed about deformities of the thalamus, chromosomes, immunologic incompatibility, and other tantalizing clues. For the past decade, financial support had been set in place to allow such results to be achieved. Breakthroughs have come about, even though some of us have been worrying that schizophrenia would remain a dark mystery forever.

The team under Dr. Nancy Andreasen's direction at the University of Iowa used the latest technology of three-dimensional magnetic resonance imaging to pinpoint the deformities of the thalamus and surrounding tissue in patients ill with schizophrenia. Her team's findings appear to explain many of the clinical symptoms of the disease. The October 14, 1994 *Science* article describing their results may well prove to be a classic article in the history of mental illness research.

Another outstanding researcher is Dr. Kenneth Kendler at the Medical College of Virginia with whom I have worked as a volunteer since 1991. His team of 'gene-hunters,' including Drs. Charles MacLean and Richard Straub, is hard at work with the largest sample of

DNA in the world from families in which schizophrenia is prevalent. This team includes many researchers in Ireland who helped to collect the data; we can hope for some positive results from their efforts.

The work of mental health leaders in the research field continues to bear fruit. Those of us with the illness will benefit, but the children of the future are the ones who stand to gain the most by these discoveries. Sometimes I ask why has it has taken so long, but I realize that the mental health field has dealt with a great number of hurdles in the last century— the largest being the stigma toward mental illness research that even the psychiatric researchers feel. The brain is truly science's last frontier.

Research studies involving mentally ill closely scrutinized

In August 1993, *Time* magazine published an article that raised ethical questions about the use of the seriously mentally ill in research studies that involve removing medication from patients. This story noted that irreparable brain damage might occur when one suffers a psychotic breakdown while off medication.

A follow-up story in November 1994 reported that stricter guidelines were being put in place by NIMH which sent a warning to 100 researchers of schizophrenia. Dr. Nancy Andreasen, who edits the *American Journal of Psychiatry*, started requesting information about how authors of research articles had received consent from patients.

Reporter James Willwerth, who has become a crusading journalist for those of us with schizophrenia, represented the mentally ill in these *Time* articles. Upon receiving a NAMI award in 1992 for the *Time* lead story 'Awakenings' (done with Claudia Wallis), Mr. Willwerth shared with those attending the NAMI convention that his brother was ill with the disease.

The subject of giving informed consent before a patient enters a research program is a controversial one for patients, families and professionals. While there is a limited risk involved in giving blood, taking psychological tests, and having one's brain scanned, there are several potential problems in giving and removing psychiatric medication. If a patient has not responded to medication previously, he really has little to lose in trying a new drug being developed. However, if a medication is working, the wisest thing to do is not experiment with risky procedures. Giving L-dopa and amphetamines to patients to see if their symptoms recur is another problem procedure.

I have experienced medication-related breakdowns: once after I asked if I could try not taking medication, and once when medication was removed. The struggle that I had in regaining my previous level of functioning was tremendous, and my concentration has been affected ever since. Researchers need to remember that when someone is acutely psychotic, it is very difficult to give informed consent. A knowledgeable third party needs to be included in the decision-making process if a potentially negative outcome could result.

A person ill with schizophrenia wins a Nobel prize

On October 11, 1994, a Nobel Prize was awarded to John Forbes Nash, Jr. for his work in economics. Before he became ill with paranoid schizophrenia at age thirty, he had a brilliant academic and teaching career. He was awarded the Nobel Prize for his doctoral thesis on game theory, which he had completed by the age of twenty-one. His illness was a devastatingly cruel one, but with the support of his family he survived those years and has been doing better for about a decade. However, Dr. Nash lost many potentially productive years; he is now in his late sixties. A touching story of his life appeared in *The New York Times* after the Nobel Prize winners were announced, and showed the fortitude he, his family, and friends have had in dealing with his illness.

The recognition that Dr. Nash received is a step forward by SOCIETY in accepting the disease. Those of us with schizophrenia are often forgotten or written off after we have become tragically ill. In many cases this may not be because of any malevolence, but because other persons cannot face what has happened to us. The illness is often terrible to live with and is also hard for others to behold. Dr. Nash's friend, Professor Harold W. Kuhn, played a critical role in making sure the Nobel Prize committee did not overlook Dr. Nash and his early work because he was currently ill with schizophrenia. Society was ready for a person with this disorder to win an international prize based on intellectual achievement. As fellow game theorist Ariel Rubenstein told *The New York Times*, 'The main message to the world is that the academy says mental illness is just like cancer, nothing special.'

March of Dimes supports schizophrenia research

In March of 1995, I received word that the March of Dimes Birth Defects Foundation had funded a researcher at the University of Pennsylvania studying schizophrenia and neurodevelopment. Whatever made the board of the March of Dimes decide to support schizophrenia research may never be known, but I do know that we in Virginia worked very hard to try and persuade them that some of the serious mental illnesses may have genetic or prenatal developmental issues involved. A letter-writing campaign was announced to 2000 persons on the mailing list of the Virginia AMI. We asked each person to write a note of encouragement to the March of Dimes to support this research. I had previously asked various top researchers to write also. Constance Lieber, President of NARSAD, informed the March of Dimes about NARSAD's research funding of mental illness. All of these efforts were very heartening to me as a person suffering with this horrible affliction. The dedication that these researchers feel toward finding answers, along with the sorrow of the families, must have been understood by the March of Dimes Board and they have responded.

The position that the March of Dimes has taken is crucial, not so much for my generation, but the generations of the future. Their general mission statement is "to improve the health of babies by preventing birth defects and infant mortality." This is a noble mission—one the mental illness movement needs to claim in part, along with its other goals. We must not only think of those currently ill with schizophrenia but also work to prevent the illness. I would love for the March of Dimes to attack schizophrenia in the same way it tackled polio. We desperately need it on our side.

ROOM FOR FUTURE ADVANCEMENTS

What patients need mental health professionals to do

1. Educate general practitioners about the early signs of mental illness.
2. Take care to refer patients only to up-to-date and competant professionals.
3. Accurately diagnose the condition as early as possible in the illness.

4. Communicate with patients and their families about the potential prognosis in an honest and complete fashion.

5. Be realistic about your expectations of a patient's level of functioning.

6. Give the patient time to grieve over the loss of health in cases of severe schizophrenia.

7. Help the patient deal with the troublesome chronic symptoms such as lack of concentration, fatigue, disassociation, anxiety, depression, etc.

8. Take a leadership role in making sure the patient has appropriate resources to live comfortably.

9. Treat persons ill with schizophrenia with the same respect you would give to anyone with a neurologic disorder such as Parkinson's or Alzheimer's disease.

10. Care for your patients in the way you would like to be cared for if the positions were reversed and you had developed schizophrenia.

AREAS IN SCHIZOPHRENIA RESEARCH THAT NEED TO BE ADDRESSED

There are five areas of research that continue to need attention, not just independently, but also how they relate to each other. These are 1) viral, 2) immune system, 3) central nervous system, 4) genetic theories, and 5) research into services and treatment.

1) Theories about viral associations have been around for many years, but I would like to see more research done on the year of 1961. I have met several consumers born in May or June of 1961, including myself. I asked Dr. Rosemary Farmer at the Medical College of Virginia to check birthdates of participants in a study she was conducting of schizophrenia and social skills. When she checked the birthdates, her sample of 42 showed that 17% of participants were born in 1961. Was there a particular virus that year that affected the development of the fetal brain? Some of us with schizophrenia who were born that year have a slight dysgenesis of our faces, particularly the right side—could that be a clue?

Another aspect of theories about viruses that needs to be investigated is the risk that health care professionals such as female nurses and doctors take during pregnancy, as they work daily with viral diseases. My mother was a nurse working in a large hospital in Richmond while she was carrying me. A kindred occupation that includes exposure to viruses is teaching school, particularly elementary school. Are psychiatrists being lax in not aggressively encouraging research into this area, so that these possibly high-risk professionals can be informed about the potential dangers of exposure to viruses during pregnancy? I have met mothers through AMI meetings who had measles exposure, flu, and the mumps during pregnancy. Would they have made a decision to take a leave of absence during their pregnancy if they had known that this exposure could have resulted in brain damage to their fetus? I am sure that many mothers would say yes.

2) The immune system is a critical part of our bodies and may be strongly implicated in schizophrenia. The sensitivity the ill have to stress would be one area to be studied by an immunologist doing research on schizophrenia. The autoimmune hypothesis is a strong one and research should continue, including the possible relationship between multiple sclerosis (MS) and schizophrenia. I know of two persons who had been diagnosed with schizophrenia in their teens and later developed MS, and of a mother with a daughter with schizo-

phrenia who has a brother and sister with MS. I am also curious about the relationship between extremely fair skin and the immune system, and if these constitute a subset of persons who are vulnerable to schizophrenia.

3) Studies of the central nervous system and its structure in the brain also need to be investigated. I know of several prominent families in Virginia who have an ill family member—could there be a relationship between intelligence, the structure of the cranial nerves, and a subset of schizophrenia? Do larger cranial nerves expose the brain to more toxic substances? When I first became ill with this disease, before I ever laid eyes on a psychiatrist, I once became paralyzed in class for about 30 seconds and later briefly lost my peripheral vision (developing tunnel vision). My doctor indicates that these are symptoms of a problem with the central nervous system. We need to know what is going on in the brain that results in these symptoms that were precursors of my own descent into a paranoid state. Could the trigeminal nerve play a role?

In his book, *Creating Minds*, Dr. Howard Gardner who is a internationally known psychologist, has written: "We know neither whether creative individuals have distinctive genetic constitutions, nor whether there is anything remarkable about the structure of their nervous systems. Yet, any scientific study of creativity will ultimately need to address these biologically oriented questions, and I expect that such a study will soon be undertaken. The study of the mental illnesses that manifest themselves in these individuals and their families is also critical."

4) Those of us with schizophrenia in our families know that, in at least some cases, the disease has a genetic basis. My great-grandmother, great-great-aunt, great-uncle, and now family members of more recent generations have had a serious mental illness. The question is, why? I feel the genetic researchers need to work with various ill family members to see the ways their illness is similar, because I know for a fact that in my family common symptoms exist. If they look at pictures of patients around the time of their breakdowns and compare them to their ill relative's pictures, they will see the similarities in facial expressions. The genetic researchers also need to expand their view of what schizophrenia is—it may be just one type of manifestation of a constellation of illnesses resulting from a flawed gene. These various illnesses may have a 'physical' result, like cancer and MS, and not be typical psychiatric disorders. As science joins the mind with the body, so must our researchers in psychiatric genetics.

5) Service and treatment research requires further scientific scrutiny. The study of intensive case management (24-hour care, or more in-depth care than just a visit) is critical as states and professionals recognize that one cannot simply place some of the seriously mentally ill in an apartment and expect them to take care of themselves. Also the study should include how treatment should differ for men and women with schizophrenia, because their symptoms reflect the variance in their brain functioning. I would like to see more investigations of why persons tend to regress at certain stages of the disease and how they can be helped at that point. Early and effective intervention appears to play a critical role in the long-term prognoses of schizophrenia—can we document why? Lastly, studies need to be done to find areas where persons with schizophrenia function well so we can learn to channel our energy in those directions. The value of volunteer work would be a good study, because many of the seriously mentally ill have a difficult time concentrating in even a part-time job. Most people want to be productive members of society; mentally ill persons are no different in that respect.

Managing schizophrenia today and tomorrow

With the collective efforts of patients, families, professionals, and the rest of society, persons now ill with schizophrenia can be helped effectively if we aggressively tackle the problems involved. Professionals need to be armed with common sense and good scientific research. If they listen to how some families have managed their ill loved ones, they can learn how to handle those that do not have family support. We cannot continue the removal of patients from state hospitals who are not well enough to take their medicine regularly or take care of themselves unless we also provide a strong support system. The past policies of deinstitutionalization were a dream that state politicians and professionals had which was not based on reality. Persons ill with schizophrenia have a neurologic disorder that in the majority of cases will have to be dealt with the rest of their lives. Some will need long-term care just as some of those with Parkinson's or Alzheimer's disease now receive. The tragedy is that the illness strikes so young, making the long-term treatment so expensive. I personally feel that some professionals today expect too much from patients. Some seem to base their own feelings of self-worth on getting persons ill with schizophrenia as highly functional as possible. This places terrible guilt on patients when they cannot perform as well as their doctors or counselors expect.

What is the long-term answer to the problem of schizophrenia? I feel the answer lies with the United States President, Congress, National Institutes of Health, March of Dimes, NARSAD, and other foundations to support an all-out war against this disease. We need to inspire researchers, young and old, to achieve new heights in their research findings. We need to judiciously provide these researchers with increased financial support.

We must NEVER forget that schizophrenia affects 1 in every 100 people, no matter how painful the disease is for society to think about or how difficult it is for them to understand. In 1948, Dr. Karl Menninger wrote: "In a world of so much suffering, it is impossible to extend the gamut of our sympathies to all of the tragedies, the injustices, the miseries and suffering of our fellow men. But for that reason it is all the more necessary to the peace of our social consciences to insure as far as possible that these are miseries are kept at a minimum. There is not a man or woman in our country who, unless he himself be mentally ill, would find satisfaction in knowing that preventable agony was being experienced by a fellow citizen. The average citizen of this country rests in oblivious peace on this score, because he knows that most broken legs will be taken care of in short order through established channels—and not only broken legs, but broken heads and broken feet and sicknesses of all kinds—all except one. And about that one he knows so little that he can shut it out of his mind. And he does."

Many today—almost 50 years later—are still trying to shut schizophrenia and those of us ill with the disease out of their minds. Families, patients, and professionals have a sacred obligation not to let this happen. Too many people have suffered. As you read this chapter, more children are being born who will also have to suffer. We are already too late.

ACKNOWLEDGMENTS

I thank Mary Louise Trusdell, M.Ed. and Asha H. Solanky, M.S., R.N., for editorial assistance.

162

REFERENCES

Andreasen NC, Arndt S, Swayze II V, Cizadlo T, Flaum M, O'Leary D, Ehrhardt JC, Yuh WTC. Thalamic abnormalities in schizophrenia visualized through magnetic resonance image averaging. *Science* 266:294–298, 1994.

Challenging Schizophrenia: A Profile of Samuel J. Keith, M.D. *NARSAD Research Newsletter* Summer 1994:1–4.

Deutsch A. *The Shame of the States*. Introduction by Karl A. Menninger. New York: Harcourt, Brace, and Company, 1948.

Farmer R. Virginia Commonwealth University, Richmond, Virginia. Interview, 21 April 1995.

Gardner H. *Creating Minds*. New York: BasicBooks, 1993.

Hollister H, Hollister P. NARSAD Artworks. *J Calif Alliance Ment Ill* 4:51–4, 1993.

Holsinger L. Serious mental illness may be included in March of Dimes research funding. *Virg Allian Ment Ill: the Network*, 10:10, 1994.

Holsinger PG. *Descendants of David Holsinger of Virginia*. Ann Arbor, MI: Edwards Brothers, Inc., 1969.

March of Dimes Birth Defects Foundation Annual Report, 1993.

Nasar S. The Lost Years of a Nobel Laureate. *NY Times* 13:sec. 3, p.1+, November 1994.

Newman G. National Alliance for Research on Schizophrenia and Depression, Chicago, Illinois. Interview, 10 April 1995.

Our History. *National Alliance for Research on Schizophrenia and Depression Annual Report*, 2:1987.

Promising Medications on the Horizon. *NARSAD Res Newslett* Summer 1994:5–11.

Romney E. Breaking Through. *NARSAD Res Newslett* 1 Spring 1989:1–4.

Sewell WL. History of Some Sewell Families in America. Palm Beach, FL: By The Author, 1955.

Somers SL. Art of Involvement Raising Hopes, Funds for Mental Illness Research. *Psychiatr Times* 11:3+ , May 1994

Torrey EF. National Institute of Mental Health,Washington, D.C. Interview, 7 April 1995.

Torrey EF. *Surviving Schizophrenia: A Family Manual Revised Edition*. New York: Harper & Row, 1988.

Wallis C, Willwerth J. Awakenings. *Time* 140:52+, 6 July 1992.

Walsh M. *Schizophrenia: Straight Talk for Family and Friends*. New York: Warner Books, 1985.

Wells WJ. *History of Cumberland County*. Louisville, KY: Standard Print Co., 1947.

Willwerth J. Madness in Fine Print. *Time* 144: 62–63, 7 November 1994.

Willwerth J. Tinkering With Madness. *Time* 142:40–41, 30 August 1993.

Worthington JF. Seeking to Understand—and Change The Course of Schizophrenia: A Profile of Richard Jed Wyatt, M.D. *NARSAD Res Newslett* Winter 1994/1995.

Pharmacologic Treatment of Schizophrenia: Where Have We Been, Where Are We Now, and Where Are We Going?

LEWIS A. OPLER, M.D., Ph.D.

WHERE HAVE WE BEEN?

Medications have been used to treat mental disorders for thousands of years (Kramer and Merlin 1983). Until recently, however, psychopharmacologic agents, or "psychotropics," were used in a *nonspecific* manner for their sedating effects (Caldwell 1970). Psychiatrists today prescribe medications to treat specific psychiatric symptoms, syndromes, or disorders, e.g., antipsychotics, antidepressants, antianxiety medication (anxiolytics), mood stabilizers, and other agents with *specific* indications. Until the latter half of the 20th century, however, advances in psychopharmacology were few and far between, involving the development of safer and more effective sedating compounds. For example, advances in the pharmacologic treatment of schizophrenia during the past 150 years have included the introduction of chloroform and ether inhalation in 1847, of chloral hydrate in 1870, of sodium amytal in 1929, and of phenbenzamine in 1943.

The introduction of phenbenzamine into psychiatry marked the first use of an antihistamine in sedating agitated psychotic patients. In 1950, Guiraud used another sedating antihistamine, promethazine, to treat schizophrenia. Promethazine was from a class of chemicals called phenothiazines. While Guiraud noted that these new antihistamines appeared to be more effective in schizophrenia than other sedatives, it was not until 1952 with the introduction of another phenothiazine, chlorpromazine, that the antipsychotic efficacy of the phenothiazines was realized (Caldwell 1970): "For Guiraud, promethazine was but another, perhaps a better, sedative and this first use of an aminophenothiazine in psychosis remained without consequence."

WHERE ARE WE NOW?

Chlorpromazine: From sedatives to neuroleptic antipsychotics

Also in 1950, Charpentier, a chemist working at the Rhône Poulenc laboratories, synthesized a new phenothiazine called chlorpromazine. Chlorpromazine was first used clinically by Dr. Henri Laborit, a surgeon, to treat preoperative anxiety while significantly decreasing postsurgical shock (Laborit et al. 1952).

Delay and Deniker were the first psychiatrists to prescribe chlorpromazine to treat agitation in psychotic patients. To their surprise, chlorpromazine not only was a safe and effective sedative, but remarkably led to improvements in hallucinations and delusions. Impressed that chlorpromazine also induced parkinsonism at doses required to treat psychosis, Delay and Deniker named the new class of agents they had discovered "neuroleptics" to indicate these wide-ranging effects on the nervous system, which they believed were a necessary part of chlorpromazine's mechanism of action (Deniker 1983):

> ". . . therapy-induced Parkinsonism . . . gave us a new insight . . . we could then propose the term 'neuroleptic' (Greek, that takes hold of the nerves). . . . The term was introduced in a communication to the Académie Nationale de Médecine. . ."

Delay and Deniker's assumption that antipsychotic drugs must have neuroleptic properties, that is, have a broad range of effects on the nervous system including the induction of parkinsonism, limited the ways in which scientists searched for new antipsychotic agents until recently. The pharmacological profile of chlorpromazine guided the development of other neuroleptic antipsychotics, which fall into the following six major chemical classes:

1. *Phenothiazines:* There are three chemical subfamilies of phenothiazines named for the kind of side chain that is attached to the three-ring phenothiazine nucleus. Chlorpromazine (Thorazine™) is an aliphatic phenothiazine; thioridazine (Mellaril) is a piperidine phenothiazine; and trifluoperazine (Stelazine™), fluphenazine (Prolixin™), and perphenazine (Trilafon™) are piperazine phenothiazines.
2. *Butyrophenones:* Haloperidol (Haldol™), the most widely used antipsychotic worldwide, is a butyrophenone.
3. *Thioxanthenes:* The thioxanthenes are chemically related to the phenothiazines. Thiothixene (Navane™) is a thioxanthene.
4. *Dihydroindolone:* Molindone (Moban™) is the only member of this class of neuroleptic antipsychotics.
5. *Dibenzoxazepine:* Loxapine (Loxitane™) is a dibenzoxazepine.
6. *Diphenylbutylpiperidine:* While approved by the Food and Drug Administration (FDA) only as a backup treatment for Gilles de la Tourette's syndrome in this country, pimozide (Orap™) is approved in other countries as an antipsychotic.

While certainly effective, all of the neuroleptic antipsychotics share the following limitations:

• Neuroleptics treat active or "positive" schizophrenic symptoms such as hallucinations and delusions, but have little or no effect on deficit or "negative" schizophrenic symptoms such as blunted affect and emotional withdrawal.
• Neuroleptics cause both early and late motor side effects. Specifically, neuroleptics may cause dystonias, akathisia, and neuroleptic-induced parkinsonism (referred to as extrapyramidal side effects or EPS), as well as possibly inducing a late and at times irreversible movement disorder called tardive dyskinesia (TD).
• Neuroleptics raise the serum level of a hormone called prolactin. This is called hyperprolactinemia and may lead to increased weight, breast tenderness and/or swelling, lactation, and amenorrhea (neuroendocrine side effects).
• Neuroleptics are ineffective in as many as 30% of patients with chronic schizophrenia.

Compelling evidence exists suggesting that both the beneficial antipsychotic effects (i.e., decreasing positive symptoms) as well as the extrapyramidal and neuroendocrine side effects of the neuroleptic antipsychotics are due to blockade the D_2-dopamine receptor (Creese et al. 1976, Kebabian and Calne 1979).

Clozapine: The prototypical atypical antipsychotic

Like most major discoveries in clinical psychopharmacology, the major discoveries leading to the development and characterization of clozapine were serendipitous. A few years after Delay and Deniker's finding that chlorpromazine was an antipsychotic, several compounds structurally related to the phenothiazines were tested by Kuhn and others as potental antipsychotic agents in patients with various psychiatric disorders, including endogenous depression (Sulser and Mishra 1983). One of the three-ringed or tricyclic compounds, imipramine, was unexpectedly found to have antidepressant properties. Subsequently, Sandoz-Wander in Bern, Switzerland, launched a program of drug development based on heterotricyclic compounds containing seven-membered imipramine-like central rings in the hopes of developing other and better antidepressants. Clozapine, developed by Hünziker and colleagues as part of this program and patented in 1960, was subsequently found to have antipsychotic properties (Baldessarini and Frankenburg 1991). Clozapine was found to treat psychotic symptoms without inducing either EPS or TD, in direct contradiction to the prevailing "neuroleptic hypothesis," i.e., the supposition that inducing motor side effects was inextricably linked to antipsychotic efficacy. In fact, some reports suggested that pre-existing TD improves with clozapine treatment (Gerbino et al. 1980, Lieberman et al. 1991). Additionally, clozapine causes only a transient rise in serum prolactin, with prolactin levels returning to normal within days.

Clozapine was released in Europe in the early 1970s. Tragically, in 1975 clozapine was found to be associated with a agranulocytosis, an extremely serious and life-threatening loss of granulocytes, one type of white blood cell needed to combat infections (Idänpään-Heikkilä et al. 1977). Because of the risk of inducing agranulocytosis, between 1975 and 1982, only patients who began taking clozapine before 1975 and who were showing significant benefit were allowed to continue taking the drug, but no new patients could begin taking this medication during that time. By 1982, however, it had been established that close monitoring of white blood cell counts provided a means for rapid identification of those patients developing agranulocytosis so that clozapine could be withdrawn, and, if necessary, the patients treated for infection. With an effective screen for agranulocytosis established, the Food and Drug Administration (FDA) and Sandoz agreed on a research design in which clozapine was compared to chlorpromazine in the treatment of a group of schizophrenic inpatients who had failed to respond adequately to three or more standard neuroleptic medications. In this study, Kane et al. (1988) demonstrated clozapine's ability to cause significant improvement in 30% of patients with neuroleptic-refractory schizophrenia. In longer trials, even higher percentages of neuroleptic-refractory schizophrenics have been shown to benefit from clozapine treatment (Lindström 1988; Meltzer 1989).

Meltzer (1990) suggests that clozapine be called an "atypical antipsychotic" because it has been shown to possess the following four attributes as compared with standard neuroleptics: 1) has greater effects on both positive and negative symptoms, 2) causes fewer extrapyramidal side effects, 3) has never been reported to cause tardive dyskinesia, and 4) does not cause prolonged elevation of prolactin.

WHERE ARE WE GOING?

The discovery of clozapine's unique atypical properties offers new hope to patients with neuroleptic-refractory schizophrenia, i.e, both to those who have not responded to standard neuroleptics as well as to those unable to tolerate the motor side effects of the standard neuroleptics. Even more important, the demonstration that a *non-neuroleptic* antipsychotic is superior to standard neuroleptics has fundamentally changed the nature of new drug development in the ongoing search for medications with greater efficacy and less toxicity.

The search for "clozapine-like" antipsychotics

The major strategy at present in the search for more effective antipsychotics revolves around attempts to develop safe clozapine-like drugs, i.e., drugs that, like clozapine, treat neuroleptic-refractory schizophrenia, ameliorate negative as well as positive schizophrenic symptoms, and are devoid of both early and late extrapyramidal motor side effects, but which, unlike clozapine, do not have a high risk of causing agranulocytosis.

This is by no means a straightforward task. Clozapine has several biochemical properties which differentiate it from standard neuroleptics and no one knows which of these pharmacologic attributes is the basis for clozapine's atypical profile. Since clinical trials are necessarily slow and time-consuming, it will take time for this phase to unfold, as scientists based on heuristic models, synthesize compounds that have one or more clozapine-like biochemical features in the laboratory or behavioral pharmacologic features in animals. Only when these medications are brought to large-scale clinical trials, however, can we see whether these preclinical indications of an atypical profile are reflected in better outcome for patients. A few promising searches for safe clozapine-like medications are summarized below.

Selective D_2 receptor antagonists. One of the earliest, and to this day best-documented, findings regarding clozapine is that it is able to treat psychosis with minimal induction of motor side effects. Since there is compelling evidence that dopamine blockade in the mesolimbic region leads to improvements in positive symptoms whereas dopamine receptor blockade in the nigrostriatal region leads to motor side effects, one important strategy involves utilizing "site selective" dopamine receptor antagonists which are more effective in blocking mesolimbic than in blocking nigrostriatal dopamine receptors. Sulpiride, a substituted benzamide, has been shown in animals to block limbic dopamine receptors at doses well below those needed to antagonize nigrostriatal dopamine receptors. In clinical trials, sulpiride caused fewer and less intense motor side effects, while being as effective as, but not more effective than, haloperidol (Gerlach et al. 1985) and chlorpromazine (Bratfos and Haug 1979).

Combined serotonin-dopamine antagonists (SDAs). Clozapine blocks the S_2-serotonin receptor more potently than the D_2-dopamine receptor, and this has inspired a series of SDAs. Janssen et al. (1988) specifically synthesized a series of SDAs that antagonized both systems and subsequently, based upon its promising pharmacological profile, proposed that clinical testing of risperidone, a benzisoxazole derivative, be undertaken. In an open trial, Bersani et al. (1990) studied a sample of 31 schizophrenic outpatients with unsatisfactory response to conventional neuroleptic treatment, predominance of negative symptoms, and troublesome extrapyramidal side effects. On being switched to risperidone, patients showed a significant improvement on the anergia factor of the Brief Psychiatric Rating Scale (BPRS) and on the Scale for the Assessment of Negative Symptoms (SANS). The Janssen Research Foundation subsequently undertook a randomized, double-blind trial involving 20 sites in the United States (Marder and Meibach 1994) and 6 sites in Canada (Chouinard et al. 1993) to assess the efficacy and safety of risperidone in the treatment of positive and negative symptoms, enrolling a total of 523 subjects with chronic schizophrenia. Subjects were randomly assigned to one of six groups, receiving either placebo, 2 mg/day of risperidone, 6 mg/day of risperidone, 10 mg/day of risperidone, 16 mg/day of risperidone, or 20 mg/day of haloperidol for up to 8 weeks. All subjects were rated on the Positive and Negative Syndrome Scale (PANSS), and results were as follows:

1. Compared to placebo, all five treatment groups showed significantly greater overall clinical improvement, with the group receiving 6 mg/day of risperidone showing the greatest overall improvement, including achieving significantly greater clinical improvement than the group receiving 20 mg/day of haloperidol.
2. When the placebo, 6 mg/day of risperidone, and 20 mg/day of haloperidol groups were compared in terms of the improvement in positive symptoms, while both medications were significantly better than placebo, the risperidone group showed significantly greater improvement than the haloperidol group as well.
3. In terms of improvement in negative symptoms, the haloperidol group failed to demonstrate statistically superior performance than placebo, whereas the group receiving 6 mg/day of risperidone group showed significantly greater improvement than either the placebo or haloperidol groups.
4. On the general psychopathology subscale score, improvement was seen in both the risperidone and haloperidol treatment groups, but the greatest improvement ($p < 0.001$) was seen in the group receiving 6 mg/day of risperidone.
5. The PANSS depression cluster score (derived by summing the scores on four items: Somatic concern, Anxiety, Guilt feelings, and Depression) showed statistically significant improvement in the group receiving 6 mg/day of risperidone, compared with placebo and haloperidol.
6. The optimal dose of risperidone, 6 mg/day, caused significantly fewer and less severe motor side effects than did haloperidol.

Focusing on the Negative Scale, across all six groups the score at baseline was in the mid-twenties. In the group treated with haloperidol, there was less than a 1 point decrement in the mean Negative Scale score after 8 weeks (from 25.0 to 24.2) which failed to achieve statistical significance as compared with placebo, whereas in the group receiving 6 mg/day of risperidone, the Negative Scale rating dropped by 3.9, representing a statistically significant 15% drop in this rating (from 25.5 to 2 1.5) as compared with both placebo and haloperidol.

On the other hand, risperidone does increase serum prolactin; studies of the efficacy of risperidone in "neuroleptic refractory" schizophrenia are still in progress; and similarly it is too early to say whether or not risperidone has a role in patients with tardive dyskinesia. In summary, while risperidone has emerged as a promising first-line antipsychotic with a low EPS profile and an ability to treat negative as well as positive symptoms, it is too early to say whether or not it possesses other clozapine-like features.

ICI 204,636 (Seroquel™), a dibenzothiazepine derivative, also combines serotonin with dopamine antagonism (Hirsch 1994). In placebo-controlled clinical trials, Seroquel has been found to cause significant decreases in the BPRS scores in the treatment of hospitalized subjects with acute exacerbation of chronic and subchronic schizophrenia, while both EPS ratings and prolactin levels were no greater than in placebo-treated subjects. Based on this promising "clozapine-like profile," a study comparing Seroquel™ with chlorpromazine in the treatment of neuroleptic-refractory schizophrenia is underway.

Another promising SDA is ziprasidone. When ziprasidone was administered to patients with schizophrenia, improvements in BPRS scores were similar to those achieved with haloperidol, but the patients receiving ziprasidone required significantly less concomitant benztropine (an antiparkinsonian agent), leading Ko et al. (1995) to conclude that "ziprasidone may confer less risk for extrapyramidal side effects than traditional antipsychotic medications at efficacious dose levels." Data on the effects of ziprasidone in treatment-refractory schizophrenia is not yet available.

Olanzapine. Olanzapine, in addition to blocking the S_2-serotonin receptor and the D_2-dopamine receptor, possesses other biochemical features that suggest that it is clozapine-like:

- A member of the thienobenzodiazapine class, olanzapine is structurally similar to clozapine.
- Similar to clozapine, olanzapine exhibits high to moderate affinity for receptors of serotonin (5-HT_{1C}, 5-HT_2, and 5-HT_3), dopamine (D_1, D_2, and D_4), muscarinic acetylcholine (M_1, M_2, M_3, and M_4), and histamine (H_1) subtypes.
- Olanzapine substitutes for clozapine in animals trained to discriminate clozapine from test vehicle, suggesting similarities in the pharmacologic profile of clozapine and olanzapine.

A series of phase II clinical studies similarly suggest that olanzapine is an atypical antipsychotic agent affording unique benefit to patients with schizophrenia (Tran et al. 1994a, Tran et al. 1994b, Beasley et al. 1994). Compared to either haloperidol or placebo, patients placed on olanzapine showed significant reductions in both positive and negative symptoms, with minimal extrapyramidal symptoms as well as only moderate prolactin elevation. The results of phase III clinical trials are being analyzed.

Sertindole. Sertindole also has a promising biochemical profile with certain clozapine-like features, e.g., it antagonizes D_2-dopamine, S_2-serotonin, and alpha$_1$-adrenergic receptors, with preferential blockade of mesolimbic over nigrostriatal dopamine circuitry (Skarsfeldt and Perregaard 1990, Skarsfeldt 1992). Phase II clinical trials have demonstrated that sertindole is an effective antipsychotic with minimal motor side effects (Grebb et al. 1994). Phase III trials are in progress.

Other strategies in the search for new antipsychotics

While most of the ongoing searches for new and better antipsychotics can be traced to attempts to synthesize safe clozapine-like atypical antipsychotics, other intriguing strategies are also being used, including testing the efficacy of medications that potentiate neurotransmission mediated via N-methyl-D-aspartic acid (NMDA) receptors, augmenting GABA-benzodiazepine-mediated neural inhibition, and using serotonin agonist and antagonists.

Facilitation of NMDA-mediated neurotransmission. Luby et al. (1962) first reported that phencyclidine (PCP), popularly known as "angel dust," induced a schizophrenia-like condition. Zukin, Javitt, and colleagues (Zukin and Javitt 1992, Javitt et al. 1994) have further suggested PCP-induced psychosis is more similar to schizophrenia than other drug-induced psychoses (e.g., amphetamine-induced psychosis) because in addition to positive symptoms one also sees negative symptoms and cognitive features characteristic of schizophrenia. Javitt and Zukin (1990) review evidence suggesting the following:

- PCP acts as a psychotomimetic agent by binding to an inhibitory site located within the ion channel formed by the NMDA receptor complex.
- Both glutamate and glycine increase NMDA-receptor-mediated neurotransmission.

Based on this evidence, Javitt and Zukin hypothesize that agents which increase NMDA-receptor-mediated neurotransmission, either via stimulation of glutamate or glycine receptors, will improve positive, negative, and cognitive features of schizophrenia.

Thus far, clinical trials testing this hypothesis have been both limited and contradictory. Waziri (1988) and Javitt et al. (1994) report that glycine added to stable neuroleptic medication led to improvements in symptom ratings in schizophrenic patients. In contrast, when milacemide, a drug that increases brain levels of glycine, was given to five chronic schizophrenic patients who had been withdrawn from neuroleptics, a clinical worsening probably related to the withdrawal of neuroleptics was noted, with no apparent benefit (Rosse et al. 1990). Despite these contradictory results, the role of NMDA-receptor agonists remains a promising strategy meriting further study.

Augmentation of GABA-benzodiazepine-mediated neural inhibition. GABA is the major inhibitory transmitter in the brain, acting at two distinct types of receptors (GABA-A and GABA-B). Benzodiazepine receptors coexist on GABA-A receptor subunits, and benzodiazepines facilitate GABAergic synaptic transmission. Benzodiazepines are indirect agonists, however, in that they can only potentiate ongoing GABAergic activity, lacking direct GABA-receptor stimulating activity (Stephenson and Dolphin 1989).

Gerlach (1991) writes, "It has been proposed that the main function of the inhibitory GABA-mediated neuronal network in the mammalian brain is to preserve organized cognitive, affective, and behavioral activies . . . augmenting GABA-benzodiazepine-mediated neural inhibition should theoretically improve schizophrenia."

Direct-acting GABA-mimetic drugs, unfortunately, have thus far not been been found to improve schizophrenic symptoms (Tamminga and Gerlach 1987). On the other hand, some

171

studies using traditional benzodiazepines (indirect GABAergic agonists) have demonstrated improvements, including on core symptoms such as hallucinations, delusions, and thought disorder (Lingjaerde 1983, Nestoros et al. 1983, Arana et al. 1986, and Dixon et al. 1989). Gerlach concludes, "the therapeutic possibilities of a manipulation of the GABA-benzodiazepine complex are far from clarified. GABA-mimetics have not to date produced useful psychotropic effects, but possibly more selective GABA-A agonists, when available, will have some potential for antipsychotic treatment."

Serotonin agonists and antagonists. The "serotonin or 5-hydroxytryptamine (5-HT) theory" of schizophrenia preceded "the dopamine theory" of schizophrenia by several years. Specifically, the observation that the psychotomimetic drug lysergic acid diethylamide (LSD) was a 5-HT antagonist lead both Gaddum (1954) and Woolley and Shaw (1954) to propose that schizophrenia might result in part from a deficiency of 5-HT. Despite this early interest, the serotonin theory was eclipsed by the dopamine theory based on the success of the neuroleptic antipsychotics. An active interest in developing serotoninergic agents has only been reintroduced recently, in large part because clozapine's superior antipsychotic profile is believe to be due in part to its being a combined S_2-serotonin receptor and D_2-dopamine receptor antagonist. As summarized above, while this has primarily lead to great interest in developing other combined serotonin-dopamine antagonists, some research has focussed on the effects of agents with more selective effects on the serotonin system, including $5\text{-}HT_1$ agonists (e.g., eltoprazine), $5\text{-}HT_2$ antagonists (e.g., ritanserin), and $5\text{-}HT_3$ antagonists (e.g., ondansetron). At this time, while there is no consistent evidence suggesting a role for $5\text{-}HT_1$ agonists, some studies suggest that the $5\text{-}HT_2$ antagonist ritanserin may have a role alone in the treatment of negative symptoms (De Bleeker and Verslegers 1990) or in combination with standard neuroleptics in treating positive and negative symptoms (Reyntjens et al. 1986). Studies using the $5HT_3$ antagonist ondansetron have demonstrated up to a 50% decrease in symptom rating scores (Glaxo 1990, Williams 1990). More studies are needed, however, to clarify the role of selective serotonin agents in the treatment of schizophrenia.

Prophylaxis. As the multifactorial etiology of schizophrenia is elucidated, it will become important to use medications not only to treat active symptoms, but additionally as part of strategies aimed at preventing the development or worsening of schizophrenia in vulnerable individuals. Prophylactic approaches in schizophrenia are suggested by work indicating that antioxidants may have a role in preventing the development of symptoms such as depression and apathy (Lohr et al. 1988), that anticonvulsants may prevent increased dopamine sensitivity or "kindling" in the mesolimbic area of the brain (Csernansky et al. 1991), and that central nervous system infections and/or autoimmune reactions may trigger schizo-phrenia in vulnerable individuals (Kirch 1993).

From serendipity toward rationality. This chapter has discussed the major strategies being used in ongoing research aimed at developing better antipsychotic agents. While it is important to articulate the rationale behind the existing game plan for new drug development, in fact most major breakthroughs have occurred when new agents have fortuitously been found to have unexpected clinical properties. Examples would include the observation that the sedating antihistamine chlorpromazine is an antipsychotic, that imipramine is an antidepressant, and that the imipramine-like compound clozapine is an antipsychotic devoid of extrapyramidal side effects. Thus, while at least some of the strategies outlined above will undoubtedly lead to breakthroughs in new drug development, it is just as important to realize that other major discoveries are likely to occur due to chance, serendipitous observation, which will in turn provide the basis for new strategies in the search for better antipsychotic agents.

CONCLUSION

For the past 40 years, most antipsychotic medications have appeared to come from the same "standard neuroleptic" or "me-too D-2" mold. Now, however, we have entered an exciting and accelerating period in which new strategies are leading to the development of highly effective agents targeting a broader range of symptoms while inducing minimal extrapyramidal side effects. More effective antipsychotics, along with new forms of psychosocial treatment (e.g., assertive community treatment and recipient empowerment) and a climate of destigmatization, offer new hope to all—recipients, advocates, clinicians, and researchers.

REFERENCES

Arana GW, Ornstein ML, Kanter F, Friedman HL, Greenblatt DJ, Shader RI. The use of benzodiazepines for psychotic disorders: a literature review and preliminary clinical findings. *Psychopharmacol Bull* 22:77–86, 1986.

Baldessarini RJ, Frankenburg FR. Clozapine: a novel antipsychotic agent. *N Engl J Med* 324:746–754, 1991.

Beasley C, Satterlee W, Sanger T, Paul S, Tollefson G. Additional clinical experience with olanzapine, an "atypical" antipsychotic. *American College of Neuropsychopharmacology, 33rd Annual Meeting*, San Juan, Puerto Rico, 1994.

Bersani G, Bressa GM, Meco G, Marini S, Pozzi F. Combined serotonin-5-HT$_2$ and dopamine-D$_2$ antagonism in schizophrenia: clinical, extrapyramidal and neuroendocrine response in a preliminary study with risperidone (R 64 766). *Hum Psychopharmacol* 5:225–231, 1991.

Bratfos O, Haug JO. Comparison of sulpiride and chlorpromazine in psychoses. *Acta Psychiatrica Scand* 135:164–173, 1979.

Caldwell AE. History of psychopharmacology. In: Clark WG, del Giudice J, eds, *Principles of Psychopharmacology*. New York: Academic Press, 1970.

Chouinard G, Jones B, Remington G, Bloom D, Addington D, MacEwan GW, Labelle A, Beauclair L, Arnott W. A Canadian multicenter placebo-controlled study of fixed doses of risperidone and haloperidol in the treatment of chronic schizophrenic patients. *J Clin Psychopharmacol* 13:25–40, 1993.

Creese I, Burt DR, Snyder SH. Dopamine receptor binding predicts clinical and pharmacological potencies of antischizophrenic drugs. *Science* 192:481–483, 1976.

Csernansky JG, Murphy GM, Faustman WO. Limbic/mesolimbic connections and the pathogenesis of schizophrenia. *Biol Psychiatry* 30:383–400, 1991.

De Bleeker E, Verslegers W. Ritanserin in the treatment of negative symptoms in chronic schizophrenic patients. *Abstracts of the 17th Congress of CINP*. Vol. II. Kyoto, Japan, p. 221, 1991.

Deniker P. Introduction of neuroleptic chemotherapy into psychiatry. In: Parnham MJ, Bruinvel J, eds, *Discoveries in Pharmacology. Volume 1: Psycho- and Neuro-pharmacology*. New York: Elsevier Science Publishers, 1983.

Dixon L, Weiden PJ, Frances AJ, Sweeney J. Alprazolam intolerance in stable schizophrenic outpatients. *Psychopharmacol Bull* 25:213–218, 1989.

Gaddum JH. Drugs antagonistic to 5-hydroxytryptamine. In: Wolstenholm GW, ed *Ciba Foundation Symposium on Hypertension*. Boston: Little Brown and Company, 1954.

Gerbino L, Shopsin B, Collora M. Clozapine in the treatment of tardive dyskinesia: An interim report. In: Fann WE, Smith RC, Davis JM, Domino EF, eds. *Tardive Dyskinesia: Research and Treatment*. Jamaica, NY: Spectrum Publications, Inc, 1980.

Gerlach J. New antipsychotics: classification, efficacy, and adverse effects. *Schiz Bull* 17:289–309, 1991.

Gerlach J, Behnke K, Heltberg J, Munk-Andersen E, Nielsen H. Sulpiride and haloperidol in schizophrenia: A double-blind cross-over study of therapeutic effect, side effects and plasma concentrations. *Brit J Psychiatry* 147:283–288, 1985.

Glaxo, Ondansetron (GR38032F). *Clinical Investigators Manual (OND/CNS 0139)*. Greenford, Middlesex, United Kingdom: Glaxo, Medical Division, 1990.

Grebb JA, Sebree T, Kashkin KB. Sertindole: preclinical and clinical overview. *Continuing Medical Education Syllabus and Proceedings Summary of the 147th Annual Meeting of the American Psychiatric Association*, p. 99, 1994.

Hirsch SR. Seroquel™: An example of an atypical antipsychotic drug. *Neuropsychopharmacology* 10 (Suppl 1):371S, 1994.

Idänpään-Heikkilä J, Alhava E, Olkinuora M, Palva IP. Agranulocytosis during treatment with clozapine. *Eur J Clin Pharmacol* 11:193–198, 1977.

Janssen PAJ, Niemegeers CJE, Awouters F, Schellekens KHL, Megens AAHP, Meert TF. Pharmacology of risperidone (R 64 766), a new antipsychotic with serotonin-S_2 and dopamine-D_2 antagonistic properties. *J Pharmacol Exp Ther* 244:685–693, 1988.

Javitt DC, Zukin SR. Role of excitatory amino acids in neuropsychiatric illness. *J Neuropsychiatry and Clin Neurosci* 2:44–52, 1990.

Javitt DC, Zylberman I, Zukin S, Heresco-Levy U, Lindenmayer J-P. Amelioration of negative symptoms in schizophrenia by glycine. *Am J Psychiatry* 151:1234–1236, 1994.

Kane J, Honigfeld G, Singer J, Meltzer H, Clozaril Collaborative Study Group. Clozapine for the treatment-resistant schizophrenia: A double-blind comparison versus chlorpromazine/benztropine. *Arch Gen Psychiatry* 45:789–796, 1988.

Kebabian JW, Calne DB. Multiple receptors for dopamine. *Nature* 277:93–96, 1979.

Kirch DG. Infection and autoimmunity as etiologic factors in schizophrenia: A review and reappraisal. *Schiz Bull* 19:355–370, 1993.

Ko G, Goff D, Herz L, Wilner K, Posever T, Howard H, Heyn J, Wong D, Etienne P. Status report: Ziprasidone. *Schiz Res* 15:154, 1995.

Kramer JC, Merlin MD. The use of psychoactive drugs in the ancient old world. In: Parnham MJ, Bruinvel J, eds. *Discoveries in Pharmacology. Volume 1: Psycho- and Neuropharmacology*. New York: Elsevier Science Publishers, 1983.

Laborit H, Huguenard P, Alluaume R. Un nouveau stabilisateur vegetatif (b 4560 R. P.). *Presse Méd* 60:206–208, 1952.

Lieberman J, Johns C, Pollack S, Borenstein M, Kane J. The effects of clozapine on tardive dyskinesia. *Br J Psychiatry* 158:503–510, 1991.

Lingjaerde O. Effect of the benzodiazepine derivative estazolam in patients with auditory hallucinations. *Acta Psychiatrica Scand* 65:339–354, 1983.

Lindström H. The effect of long-term treatment with clozapine in schizophrenia: a retrospective study in 96 patients treated with clozapine for up to 13 years. *Acta Psychiatrica Scand* 77:524–529, 1988.

Lohr JB, Cadet JL, Lohr MA, Larson L, Wasli E, Wade L, Hylton R, Vidoni C, Jeste DV, Wyatt RJ. Vitamin E in the treatment of tardive dyskinesia: the possible involvement of free radical mechanisms. *Schizophr Bull* 14:291–296, 1988.

Luby ED, Gottlieb JS, Cohen BD, Rosenbaum G, Domino EF. Model psychosis and schizophrenia. *Am J Psychiatry* 119:61–65, 1962.

Marder SR, Meibach RC. Risperidone in the treatment of schizophrenia. *Am J Psychiatry* 151:825–835, 1994.

Meltzer HY. Duration of a clozapine trial in neuroleptic-resistant schizophrenia. *Arch Gen Psychiatry* 46:672, 1982.

Meltzer HY. The role of serotonin in the action of atypical antipsychotic drugs. *Psychiatr Ann* 20:571–579, 1990.

Meltzer HY, Fang VS, Young MA. Clozapine-like drugs. *Psychopharmacol Bull* 16:32–35, 1980.

Meltzer HY, Matsubara S, Lee J-C. Classification of typical and atypical antipsychotic drugs on the basis of dopamine D-1, D-2 and serotonin$_2$ pKi values. *J Pharmacol Exp Ther* 251:238–246, 1989.

Nestoros JN, Nair NPV, Pulman JR, Schwartz G, Bloom D. High doses of diazepam improve neuroleptic-resistant chronic schizophrenic patients. *Psychopharmacology* 81:42–47, 1983.

Reyntjens A, Gelders YG, Hoppenbrouwer M-LJA, van den Bussche G. Thymosthenic effects of ritanserin (R 55667), a centrally acting serotonin-S$_2$ receptor blocker. *Drug Devel Res* 8:205–211, 1986.

Rosse RB, Schwartz BL, Leighton MP, Davis RE, Deutsch SI. An open-label trial of milacemide in schizophrenia: an NMDA intervention strategy. *Clin Neuropharmacol* 13:348–354, 1990.

Skarsfeldt T. Electrophysiological profiles of the new atypical neuroleptic, sertindole, on midbrain dopamine neurons in rats: Acute and repeated treatment. *Synapse* 10:25–33, 1992.

Skarsfeld T, Perregaard J. Sertindole, a new neuroleptic with extreme selectivity on A10 versus A9 dopamine neurons in the rat. *Eur J Pharmacol* 182:613–614, 1990.

Stephenson FA, Dolphin AC. GABA and glycine neurotransmission. *Sem Neurosci* 1:115–123, 1989.

Sulser F, and Mishra R. The discovery of tricyclic antidepressants and their mode of action. In: Clark WG, del Giudice J, eds. *Principles of Psychopharmacology.* New York: Academic Press, 1983.

Tran P, Beasley C, Tollefson G, Beuzen JN, Holman S, Sanger T, Satterlee W. Olanzapine: A promising "atypical" antipsychotic agent. *European College of Neuropsychopharmacology Annual Meeting.* Jerusalem, Israel, 1994a.

Tran P, Beasley C, Tollefson G, Sanger T, Satterlee W. Clinical efficacy and safety of olanzapine: A new atypical antipsychotic agent. *American Psychiatric Association Annual Meeting.* Philadelphia, PA, 1994b.

Waziri R. Glycine therapy of schizophrenia. *Biol Psychiatry* 23:210–211, 1988.

Williams P. An open trial of ondansetron (GR38032F) in the treatment of acute schizophrenia. *Schiz Res* 3:48, 1990.

Woolley DW, Shaw E. A biochemical and pharmacological suggestion about certain mental disorders. *Proc Natl Acad Sci USA* 40:228–231, 1954.

Zukin SR, Javitt DC. The PCP/NMDA theory of schizophrenia. In: Lindenmayer J-P, Kay SR, eds. *New Biological Vistas on Schizophrenia*. New York: Bruner/Mazel Publishers, 1992.

Schizophrenia and the Self

HELLE THORNING, M.S.W., and ELLEN LUKENS, M.S.W., Ph.D.

Schizophrenia is most likely a heterogeneous illness with multiple etiologies. As evidence of neurobiological abnormalities supporting a biological disease model for schizophrenia is mounting, an understanding of the subjective experience is crucial in facilitating the individual's adaptation to living with the illness.

In this chapter we will outline the psychoanalytic and psychodynamic understanding of the *psychology of schizophrenia*. Our goal is first to synthesize the current knowledge of schizophrenia as having both neurobiological and psychological significance, and second, to move toward a more broad understanding of the impact that having a long-term mental illness has on the individual. To this end we will provide an overview of the evolution of theoretical models of the psychology of schizophrenia in an effort to examine how they differ from normal psychology. We will also present an overview of various individual treatment modalities that can be defined structurally as involving one to one contact between the patient and the therapist. Although social skills training, vocational rehabilitation, cognitive and behavioral therapies fall within this paradigm, we will primarily highlight traditional forms of dynamic or supportive individual psychotherapy among persons with schizophrenia.

LIVING WITH SCHIZOPHRENIA

Schizophrenia is a catastrophic illness best described as a traumatic assault on the self. In witnessing and talking to individuals struggling with schizophrenia one is struck by the courage and strength that is needed to combat and deal with what can be terrifying symptoms. Thought processes, perceptions, abilities to function in relationships, at work and in love can all be profoundly affected by the circumstances of the illness. This is most evident in how the individual's sense of self is affected by the illness.

Individuals suffering from schizophrenia have trouble relating "themselves" in multiple and meaningful ways both to others and to the passage of time as "the self" deteriorates. This may manifest itself in the inability to bring the traumatic experiences and the events surrounding the symptoms associated with schizophrenia into identifiable relationships with other events. The ordeal of having endured the symptoms of schizophrenia cannot easily be put into a "story" that has a smooth cause and effect progression. This has been described as similar to findings experienced by persons suffering from post-traumatic stress disorder after combat in the Vietnam war (Cromwell 1993).

Nature versus nurture

A recurring debate in schizophrenia research has been whether schizophrenia is a result of nature or nurture. The first paradigm (nature), emphasizes the biologic aspect of the disease and views schizophrenia as an illness out of the ordinary—an "accident" to (or in) the brain. In the second paradigm (nurture), schizophrenia is understood as an experience of regressive behavior along a continuum from wellness to neurotic behavior to psychosis; a psychological model of defense or a model of psychological deficit originating in the early parent-child interaction.

Brief historical perspective

The notion of schizophrenia, or *dementia praecox*, as it was first labeled by Kraepelin (1896), has undergone paradigmatic shifts since its original formulation by Kraepelin and Bleuler at the turn of the century. At that time, schizophrenia was regarded as a brain disease differing from other neurological conditions only because there was no formal evidence of any definite observable pathology found during post-mortem autopsy. The postulation of the existence of a central nervous system defect was furthered by Kraepelin and his contemporaries as they described a number of neuropathologic abnormalities in the brains of patients with schizophrenia, but at the time their findings were discredited as being either nonspecific or artifactual (Cutting and Shepherd 1978, Mesulam 1990).

A marked divergence of opinion followed concerning the nature of schizophrenia. In different countries, various schools of thought emerged contesting Kraeplin's original concept (Cutting and Shepherd 1978). As a result, there was a shift away from the biologic aspect (nature) of the illness towards an emphasis on environmental factors (nurture). This was attributed to the absence of detectable brain pathology.

Thus, the criticisms of the biologic paradigm and the success of psychodynamic approaches in many fields of mental illness forced the biologic research in schizophrenia into the background during the first half of this century. As opinions concerning the nature of schizophrenia shifted, a psychoanalytic and psychodynamic understanding of the illness emerged. The general aim of psychoanalysis was stated in terms of initiating and maintaining a process whereby repressed relationships were brought back within the organizing system of the ego so that they could be subjected to learning and adaptation (Sutherland 1994). Although this introduced a more humane approach to patients suffering from schizo-phrenia in that it focused on the experience of the illness as an integral aspect of the whole person's modus operandi, it did not lead to substantial insights into the causes of the illness. In addition, the theoretical underpinnings of the psychoanalytic concepts of developmental process and psychopathology often produced a great deal of turmoil in the affected families because of feelings of guilt and responsibilities it engendered (see chapter by Lukens and Thorning).

Despite the emergence of some efficacy of psychotropic medication, the psychological and social formulations were so influential in the 1950s and 1960s that some writers (e.g., Laing 1967) suggested that schizophrenia was an artifact, a construct to label societal misfits. By 1970, a number of societal forces brought about a focus on the plight of the mentally ill. The civil rights movement centered on the rights of patients to live in the community and influenced the federal government to push for deinstitutionalization (Langsley 1980). During the 1980s and 1990s the researchers have begun to re-examine the fact that

178

the absence of gross brain pathology by itself does not eliminate an organic basis for schizophrenia. More subtle manifestations of the disorder, exemplified by neurotransmitter abnormalities or a physiological imbalance between the activity of the two hemispheres have come to the fore and are attracting the attention of neuroscientists working in this field.

THE FOUR PSYCHOLOGIES

In spite of the renewed interest in biology, the developmental perspective is central to the discussion of the origin of this illness, providing a psychological understanding of schizophrenia either related to psychological models of regression, defenses or deficits (Cutting 1978). There is no question that the psychological disruption caused by a profound mental illness such as schizophrenia, leads to the eruption of regressive manifestations that have a fundamental impact on the experience of the self. These manifestations include primary-process thinking, expression of words and infantile impulses, loss of ego boundaries, and the disturbance of the sense of self and of the integrity of ego boundaries. Yet, as we consider the neurobiologic evidence, it is likely that manifestations of psychosis do not have a counterpart in normal development. In other words, the symptoms presented in adult schizophrenia are most likely caused by biologic abnormalities, and therefore, cannot just be considered manifestations of regression, defenses or psychological deficits. Nonetheless, we argue that psychological theories play a key role in providing a more comprehensive view of how a person experiences the illness (Willick 1990).

To address this point, a brief overview will be presented of the current dominant psychologies and their conceptualizations of schizophrenia. They will be presented in chronologic order and include Freud's drive theory, ego psychology, object-relations, and self psychology.

Drive theory

Sigmund Freud (1856–1939), the founder of psychoanalytic theory and practice, based his theory on the notion that the individual is motivated by sexual and aggressive drives and unconscious wishes and fears. Freud postulated that all behavior is strictly determined and that childhood events are critical to psychosexual development. In his voluminous work, he established the groundwork for the notion that predisposition to various kinds of illness can be traced back to fixations at specific stages of development in childhood. Thus, disposition to illness was described as an "inhibition in development," which also could be thought of as a chronologic timetable of fixation and resulting symptoms (Willick 1990). Hence the development of psychopathology was based on the symptom neurosis and neurotic characteristics, unconscious conflicts, fixations and pathological defense formations.

Freud's early formulations concerning schizophrenia were very different form Kraepelin's biologic approach. In schizophrenia, Freud postulated that the drive (libido) was exclusively directed toward the self. Thus, schizophrenia was characterized by a *decathexis* from the object world, a regression in response to intense frustration and conflict with others. While he viewed neurosis as a conflict between the ego and the id, he regarded psychosis as a conflict between the ego and the external world. Hence, Freud asserted that persons with schizophrenia were untreatable when using interventions that relied on reworking childhood trauma in an intense therapeutic relationship (Freud 1900, 1911, 1913, 1917a, 1917b).

Ego psychology

Early ego-psychologists (Hartman 1964, Lowenstein 1966, Erikson 1950) further developed Freud's notion of the ego. The main thrust of the theory was that the individual is born with an innate capacity for adaptive functioning and that both early childhood and later events and transactions are crucial.

Heinz Hartman (1950), described the ego as a substructure of personality that is defined by its functions. He stated that

"the ego organizes and controls motility and perception—perception of the outer world but probably also of the self. It also serves as a protective barrier against excessive external, and in a somewhat different sense, internal stimuli. The ego tests reality" (Hartman 1950, pp 114–115).

He continued to define psychosis as a failure of neutralization resulting in the inability of the ego to assume its organizational role and to mediate between the drives and reality. By neutralization he envisioned a process which moves both libidinal and aggressive energies from the instinctual to the non-instinctual mode, thereby making them available to the ego. When there is a failure of neutralization, the ego is unable to mediate between the drives and reality and employ defenses. The failure of this process results in psychopathology.

Individual problems in ego-functioning stem from life stages and role transitions, as well as traumatic events or stress, ego-deficits, maladaptive defenses (lack of fit between inner capacities and external resources) or conditions, or maladaptive patterns of relating. Thus, the main deficit operating in schizophrenia was seen as relating to faulty ego boundaries and organizing functions. Without this organizing function, the ego cannot exist (Blanck and Blanck 1979).

The ego functions as further detailed by Bellak (1969) are defined as follows: 1) reality testing, 2) judgement, 3) sense of reality of the world and of the self, 4) regulations and control of drives, affects and impulses, 5) object (or interpersonal relations), 6) thought processes, 7) adaptive regression in the service of the ego, 8) defensive functioning, 9) stimulus barrier, 10) autonomous functioning, 11) synthetic integrative functioning, and 12) mastery-competence. They require organization to attain meaning and purpose (Blanck and Blanck 1979). The symptoms of schizophrenia often impact directly on these functions, leaving the person struggling to organize his/her subjective experience in relation to the outer world.

Because schizophrenia is an episodic illness with variability in functional capacity, the deterioration of the ego-functions may vary as well. In schizophrenia and related states of psychosis, a disturbance in reality-testing means that the patient primarily lives in a world of delusions and hallucinations. Psychotic defects in judgement are most likely to be rooted in firm delusional systems, particularly of a paranoid nature. This disturbance of sense of reality of the world and of the self strongly interferes with one's ability to relate to others and gain a sense of identity (Bellak 1994). A disturbance in the ability to interact with others in the sphere of object relations has a particularly difficult impact on the person with schizophrenia in that relationships with family members and others suffer greatly.

Poor regulation and control of drives are probably the most frequent occurrence for hospitalization of patients with schizophrenia. Overstimulation may result in ego disorganization because of a disturbance in the stimulus barrier. Hence poor drive-control causes more social disruption than most ego-function disturbances and is more easily perceived as a threat by those surrounding the patient.

Adaptive regression in the service of the ego and the functions of defenses play an important role in the strengthening of defenses against the emergence of psychotic material. This must be particularly understood as the individuals struggle with understanding what has happened *vis a vis* their illness.

In schizophrenia and psychosis, the primary autonomous functions, such as memory, attention, movement and language are often affected. Functions that were previously taken for granted begin to deteriorate and seriously decrease one's self esteem. Thus, feelings of mastery and competence are impacted by the very nature of the illness. This is further exacerbated by common sources of stress stemming from disturbance in ego functions. These include altered perceptions, cognitive confusion, attentional deficits and impaired identity (Hatfield 1989).

Moving from drive to relational models

Harry Stack Sullivan (1892–1949) was the key figure in altering the notion that persons with schizophrenia were unreachable and "decathexed" from the outer world, as he developed interpersonal psychoanalysis, which became manifest in the late 1930s. He attempted to demonstrate that the phenomenon observed in schizophrenia were not merely random products of neurologic deteriorations, but conveyed meaning, similar to Freud's demonstration of the meaning of neurotic symptoms 20 years earlier. Furthermore, Sullivan believed that schizophrenia is not a process emerging from within the individual but rather a reaction to interactions and events taking place between the individual and the environment. Sullivan defined the environment as both the significant people with whom the individual interacts and the larger social and cultural values they transmit. He postulated that the phenomenon of schizophrenia could not be understood apart from the interpersonal context. According to Sullivan, schizophrenia reflects a fundamental disorder in the basic organization of the personality, resulting in a "disaster to self-esteem " (Sullivan 1962, Greenberg and Michell 1983).

Object relations theories

Melanie Klein served as a key transitional figure between the drive structural model and the relationship/structure model (Greenberg and Mitchell 1983). Her theory focused on interpersonal relationships and their internalization in the formation of psychic structure. In addition to Klein, the major proponents were Fairbain, Guntrip and Winnicott of the British School of Object Relations. The American School includes Mahler, Jacobson and Kernberg (Greenberg and Michell 1983). They argued that the individual is object seeking from birth and for the infant to thrive, it must have a nurturing environment to develop its innate potential. Through the developmental process, the person internalizes relationships as experienced through early attachment to others, internalization of "good" and "bad" self and object representations and their integration, the maternal holding environment and attuned parenting, and sequential stages and critical periods of development of internalized object relationships. Hence, the problems in psychopathology were seen as an internalization of "bad" self and object-representations that are split off and projected into the interpersonal world caused by either maternal deprivation or aggression.

Self-psychology

In the early 1970s, Heinz Kohut (1913–1981) introduced the concept of self-psychology. Since that time an extensive theoretical and clinical literature has evolved that has had a significant influence on clinical practice.

Kohut suggests that an infant is born with innate potentialities that form the nuclear self. The self is therefore not seen as a representation or product of the ego, but is understood as an entity unto itself. Kohut describes the self as an active agent that has basic needs requiring attuned parenting to fulfill (1977). Frustration in these basic needs causes a disturbance in the development of the self. Without parental atunement, the infant's sense of self becomes fragmented and psychopathology ensues. Psychopathology is therefore seen as a representation of persistent problems in self-cohesion and self-esteem regulation as a result of early parental empathic failures. Thus, the evolving theory of self psychology came to view all psychological problems as disorders of the self, ranging from neurotic to psychotic states, with the position on the continuum relating to the extent and degree of the unempathic response by parental figures (selfobjects) (Kohut 1971; 1977; 1984).

All of the psychoanalytic theorists based their understanding of the etiology of schizophrenia on developmental origins of psychosis and neurosis assuming an actual correlation between phases of development and specific pathology. This led to an acceptance of the idea that one can establish a chronological developmental time table of etiological phases specific for the various psychotic illnesses. Willick (1990) summarizes the psychoanalytic theory main points as follows:

" 1. If there is profound failure in the development in the first few months of life, the result will be basic defects in psychic structure, which causes autistic and symbiotic psychosis. 2. If these failures occur in the early months and up through the first year of life, failure achieving differentiation between self—and object representations will result in schizophrenia. 3. phase specificity means that the developmental failures stem primarily from deficiencies in the nurturing and caretaking environment" (Willick 1990, p.1050).

Willick's contention is that there is insufficient evidence to conclude that the etiology of the adult psychosis can be attributed to failures in development or fixations during the early years of life. Adult psychosis cannot be attributed to failure in the nurturing environment given current biological evidence.

As we have discussed, the behavior and symptoms in adult psychosis lead to regressive behavior (i.e., primary process thinking, expression of infantile behavior in verbal and nonverbal behavior, loss of ego control, disturbance in the sense of self and a disturbance in the ego-boundaries). These behaviors are probably a result of biologic disease or biologic abnormalities. Aside from the biologic factors, the focus of our attention should, therefore, be on how these organic impairments are expressed throughout development in a patient's subjective experience, as well as in his/her attempt to cope with and make sense of his or her own "story."

CHANGING ATTITUDES IN PSYCHOTHERAPY

The multiplicity of theories for understanding schizophrenia is striking. These include biologic, behavioral, cognitive-developmental, social and psychodynamic orientations. Each of these represents a particular approach and a particular way of thinking about psychopathology generally and schizophrenia in particular (Strauss 1979).

There are also a large number of methods in a variety of settings for treating schizophrenia. Within the psychosocial domain, individual psychotherapy, individual family therapy, multiple family group treatment, occupational therapy, cognitive rehabilitation (i.e., social skills training) are among the most widely used. The increase in the availability of a variety of treatment modalities, although presenting us with a large arsenal of treatment possibilities, makes it that much more confusing in our examination of what is effective and limits our ability to appropriately select among them.

In the following section we will focus on the individual interventions that can be defined structurally as one-to-one contact between patient and therapist. Mueser and Berenbaum (1990) reflect on the current relevance of dynamic psychotherapy, stating that psychodynamic therapy continues to be an important individual treatment modality for schizophrenias. But there is still no universally accepted definition of "psychologic therapies" for persons with schizophrenia.

PSYCHOLOGIC TREATMENT APPROACHES

Beginning in the 1960s a series of studies were completed that examined the role of psychotherapy in the outcome of schizophrenia. In one of the largest studies, May and his colleagues (1967) randomized 200 patients with schizophrenia to five treatments. These included psychotherapy alone, psychotherapy and medication, medication alone, electroshock therapy, and a control group receiving general treatment. The psychotherapy was described as ego-supportive with an emphasis on defining reality. The results suggested that medication plus psychotherapy was equivalent to medication alone, and both were better than either psychotherapy alone or the control milieu treatment.

In 1966, Brookhammer and his colleagues compared 14 first-break hospitalized patients treated with "direct analysis" to 37 control patients who participated in a variety of other treatments. They found no differences between the two groups. Rogers studied a mixed group of 32 acute and chronic-state hospitalized patients randomized either to client-centered psychotherapy or to no psychotherapy. Both groups received medication. Again they found there were no outcome differences between the two groups. Karon and Vadenbos (1972) randomized 36 hospitalized patients to three treatments: psychotherapy alone, psychotherapy plus drugs and drugs alone. The therapy followed an "ego-analytic" therapy model. Findings suggested that patients receiving psychotherapy with and without medication had significantly shorter hospitalization stays than the group of patients with medication alone.

By the mid-1980s, the political climate was such, and the research on psychotherapy equivocal enough, that psychotherapy as a treatment per se for schizophrenia was largely dismissed. The pendulum had swung in a new direction, focusing more on the biologic causes of the illness. With the explosion of modern technology, which enables us to look for minute details in the functioning of the brain, interest shifted away from individual psychology.

In summary, there have been few controlled trials of individual psychotherapy for persons with schizophrenia, and the nature of this therapy varies from study to study. The existing studies are generally of limited quality providing little confidence in the validity and reliability of the results. Some of the weaknesses in design include non-comparable treatment conditions, poorly defined and operationalized treatments which were often conducted by inexperienced therapists, limited outcome measures with questionable reliability, inadequate follow-up intervals, and small samples with limited power. Therefore, no firm conclusion can be drawn regarding the efficacy and effectiveness of individual psychotherapy as a treatment for persons with schizophrenia.

DRUGS ARE NOT ENOUGH

Clearly, drugs alone are insufficient treatment for this severe brain disease. This fact is complicated by the very symptoms of the illness and the side effects of the medication, both of which contribute to lack of cooperation or compliance with treatment regimens among patients. Looking to the literature about normal persons suffering from chronic medical illness provides some clues to the complexity involved in expecting such cooperation among persons with schizophrenia. As Becker and others have reported, many studies have found that in treating chronic medical disorders—essential hypertension being the classic example—noncompliance and denial are the norm rather than the exception (Glanz and School 1983, Becker 1988). Leventhal (1984), also writing about controls, describes what he calls the self-regulation model of compliance, which involves gathering data from the environment, formulating a representation of the environment, establishing behavioral goals, generating plans and responses to reach those goals, and finally, monitoring how coping reactions affect problems and self. Moos and Tsu (1977) describe the stages involved in coping behavior, again referring to the range of normal responses. These include: 1) seeking relevant information, 2) finding some meaning in the illness, 3) denying or minimizing the seriousness of crisis, 4) setting concrete and limited goals, 5) learning specific illness related procedures, 6) rehearsing alternative outcomes, and 7) requesting reassurance and emotional support.

While we explore new avenues for more effective medical treatment, we are also obligated to focus our work on understanding the human experience of living with schizophrenia and enhancing the quality of life for whom the illness has such devastating impact. To this end, we need to search for ways to understand and better manage the symptoms of schizophrenia. From this perspective, it is crucial that future research explore the origins of the alteration of the self experience and how this is processed thorough a person's mind, since this complex phenomenon is so poorly understood, and has such tremendous bearing on an individual's struggle with schizophrenia.

Given that schizophrenia is seen as an organic illness affecting the functions of the ego, a person's sense of self, and his/her relationships to others as well as the role of the family in rehabilitation, a multilevel service systems approach must be considered as central to treatment. The challenge for mental health professionals over the next decade will be to comprehensively address both the neurobiologic and psychologic aspects of this neurodevelopmental disorder in such a way that the impact on the self is not obscured.

REFERENCES

Adler D, Drake R, Berlant J, Ellison J, Carson D. Treatment of the nonpsychotic chronic patient: A problem of interactive fit. *Am J Orthopsychiatr* 57:579–586, 1987.

Avison WR, Nixon-Speechley K. The discharged psychiatric patient: A review of social, social-psychological, and psychiatric correlates of outcome. *Am J Psychiatr* 144:10–18, 1987.

Bellack A, Morrison R, Wixted J, Mueser K. An analysis of social competence in schizophrenia. *Br J Psychiatr* 156:809–818, 1990.

Bellack A, Mueser K. Psychosocial treatment for schizophrenia. *Schiz Bull* 19(2):317–336, 1993.

Bellak L, Loeb L. *The Schizophrenic Syndrome.* New York: Grune & Stratton, 1969.

Bellak L. *Crisis and Special Problems in Psychoanalysis and Psychotherapy.* Northvale, NJ: Jason Aronson Inc, 1994.

Bennett D. Psychosocial Rehabilitation. Evolution, principles, and application in combating negative symptoms. *Int J Ment Health* 16(4):46–59, 1988.

Blanck G, Blanck R. *Ego Psychology. Psychoanalytic Developmental Psychology.* New York: Columbia University Press, 1979.

Brookhammer RS, Meyer RW, Schober CC, Piotrowski AZ. A five year follow-up study of schizophrenics treated by Rosen's "direct analysis" compared with controls. *Am J Psychiat* 123:602–604, 1966.

Carpenter W. Thoughts on the treatment of schizophrenia. *Schiz Bull* 12(4):527–539, 1986.

Carpenter W, Heinrichs D, Alphs L. Treatment of negative symptoms. *Schiz Bull* 11:440–451, 1985.

Carpenter W, Heinrichs D, Wagman A. Deficit and nondeficit forms of schizophrenia: The concept. *Am J Psychiatr* 145(5):578–583, 1988.

Cromwell R, Snyder CR, eds. *Schizophrenia: Origins, Processes, Treatment, and Outcome.* New York: Oxford University Press, 1993.

Cutting J, Shepherd M, 1978, eds. *The Clinical Roots of The Schizophrenia Concept.* Translations of seminal European contributions on schizophrenia. Cambridge: Cambridge University Press, 1987.

Freud S. *The Interpretation of Dreams.* Standard Edition 4 & 5, 1900.

Freud S. *Psychoanalytic Notes on an autobiographical case of paranoia* Standard Edition, Vol 12, 1911.

Freud S. *The disposition of obsessional neurosis.* Standard Edition, Vol 12, 1913.

Freud S. *Introductory Lectures on Pschoanalysis.* Standard Edition, Vol 15, 1917a.

Freud S. *Mourning and Melanchonia.* Standard Edition, Vol 14, 1917b.

Gabbard G. Schizophrenia. In: *Psychodynamic Psychiatry in Clinical Practice* 149–176, 1990.

Gittelman M, Dubuis J. Continuity and coordination in care of the mentally ill: Adapting intervention to the course of mental illness. *Int J Ment Health* 20(3):5–11, 1991.

Glanz K, School T. Intervention strategies to improve adherance among hypertensives: Review and recommendations. *Pat Counsel & Health Ed* 1:14–28, 1983.

Goldstein M. Psychosocial issues. *Schiz Bull* 13(1):157–171, 1987.

Goldstein M. Psychosocial (nonpharmacologic) treatments for schizophrenia. *Rev Psychiatr* 10:116–137, 1987.

Greenberg J, Mitchell S. *Object Relations in Psychoanalytic Theory.* Cambridge, MA: Harvard University Press, 1983.

Hartman H. *Essays on Ego Development.* New York: International University Press, 1964.

Hatfield A. Patients' accounts of stress and coping in schizophrenia. *Hosp Commun Psychiatr* 40:1141–1144, 1989.

Herz M. Recognizing and preventing relapse in patients with schizophrenia. *Hosp Commun Psychiatr* 35:344–349, 1984.

Karon BP, VandenBos GR. The consequences of psychotherapy for schizophrenic patients. *Psychother Theory Res Prac* 12:143–148, 1972.

Kingdon D, Turkington D. A role for cognitive-behavioral strategies in schizophrenia? *Soc Psychiatr Epidemiol* 26:101–103, 1991.

Kohut H. *The Analysis of the Self.* New York: International University Press, 1971.

Kohut H. *The Restoration of the Self.* New York, International University Press, 1977.

Kohut H. *How Does Analysis Cure?* Chicago: University of Chicago Press, 1984.

Kraepelin E. *Psychiatrie.* Dementia Praecox. 5th Edition. Bart: Leipzig. In: Cutting J, Shepherd M, eds, *The Clinical Roots of The Schizophrenia Concept. Translations of seminal European Contributions on Schizophrenia.* Cambridge: Cambridge University Press, 1986, pp, 426–441.

Laing RD. *The Politics of Experience.* New York: Ballantine Books, 1967.

Langsley DG. Community Psychiatry. In: Kaplan, H, Freedman B, eds. *Comprehensive Textbook of Psychiatry.* Vol 11. Baltimore: Williams and Wilkins, 1980.

Lee P, Lieh-Mak Y, Spinks J. Coping strategies of schizophrenic patients and their relationship to outcome. *Brit J Psychiatr* 163:177–182, 1993.

Lehrman N. Effective psychotherapy of chronic schizophrenia. *Am J of Psychoanalysis* 42(2):121–131, 1982.

Lowenstein R. Heinz Hartman: Psychology of the ego. In: Alexander F, et al. eds. *Psychoanalytic Pioneers.* New York: Basic Books, 1966.

Liberman R, Corrigan P. Designing new psychosocial treatments for schizophrenia. *Psychiatry* 56:238–249, 1993.

May PRA, Tuma AH. Treatment of schizophrenia: An experimental study of five treatment methods. *Brit J Psychiat* 111:503–510, 1965.

Mesulam M. Schizophrenia and the brain. *N Engl J Med* 322:12, 1990.

Moos RH, Tsu VD. The crisis of physical illness. In: Moos RH, ed. *Coping with Physical Illness.* London: Plenum Press, 1977.

Mueser K T, Berenbaum H. Editorial: Psychodynamic treatment of schizophrenia. Is there a future? *Psychol Med* 20:253–263, 1990.

O'Connor F. Symptom monitoring for relapse prevention in schizophrenia. *Arch Psychiatr Nurs* 4:193–201, 1991.

Ruocchio P. How psychotherapy can help the schizophrenic patient. *Hosp Commun Psychiatr* 40:188–192, 1989.

Sarti P, Cournos F. Medication and psychotherapy in the treatment of chronic schizophrenia. *Psychiat Clin N Am* 13:215–228, 1990.

Schwab B, Drake R, Burghardt E. Health care of the chronically mentally ill: The culture broker model. *Commun Ment Health J* 24:174–184, 1988.

Sidley G, Smith J, Howells K. Is it ever too late to learn? Information provision to relatives of long-term schizophrenia sufferers. *Behav Psychother* 19:305–320, 1991.

Strauss J, Docherty Sledge W, Downy TW. Toward comprehensive treatment of chronic schizophrenic patients. In: *Psychotherapy of Schizophrenia.* International Congress Series 464, pp. 291–299, 1979.

Strauss J, Rakfeldt J, Harding C, Liebermann P. Psychological and social aspects of negative symptoms. *Brit J Psychiatr* 155:128–132, 1989.

Sullivan HS. *Schizophrenia As A Human Process.* New York: W.W. Norton, 1962.

Sutherland J. *The Autonomous Self.* The Work of John D. Sutherland. Scharff JS, ed. Northvale, NJ: Jason Aronson, 1994.

Tarrier N. Coping strategy enhancement (CSE) : A method of treating residual schizophrenic symptoms. *Behav Psychother* 18:283–293, 1990.

Tarrier N, Sharpe L, Beckett R, Harwood S, Baker A, Yusopoff L. A trial of two cognitive behavioral methods of treating drug-resistant residual psychotic symptoms in schizophrenic patients. *Psychiatr Epidemiol* 28:5–10, 1992.

Tessler R, Bernstein A, Rosen B, Goldman H. The chronically mentally ill in community support systems. *Hosp Commun Psychiat* 33:208–211, 1982.

Willick M. Psychoanalytic concepts of the etiology of mental illness. *J Am Psychoanal Assn* 38:1049–1081, 1990.

Schizophrenia: The Family's Experience

MARTIN S. WILLICK, M.D.

Schizophrenia, which has been estimated to affect as much as 1% of the population, is a particularly devastating illness which takes its toll not only on the person who suffers from it, but on family members as well. Advances in treatment over the last ten years, particularly in psychopharmacology, enable the majority of persons with schizophrenia to live outside of a hospital, often at home with their families. Over the course of these past ten years we have learned that family members have a vital role to play in providing the most positive atmosphere for treatment and rehabilitation.

During this time, aided by organizations such as the National Alliance for the Mentally Ill and its statewide affiliates, and by Psychiatry Departments such as Columbia, family members have made themselves as knowledgable as they can about schizophrenia—its symptoms, the medications used to treat them, and the course of the illness. They have educated themselves by reading many of the numerous publications, journals and books devoted to the study of schizophrenia. Many of these articles and books have specifically documented the enormous emotional toll that this illness takes on the close relatives of those who are affected by this illness. (See the Suggested Reading list at the end of this chapter.) In addition, groups of families often meet regularly to learn more about the illness and its treatment as well as to share experiences with others. Such meetings are of enormous value, not only in helping family members educate themselves about the illness, but in realizing that they are not alone in what they are experiencing. Along with participating actively in the treatment and rehabilitation process, family members themselves have to cope with all the difficult emotional reactions that are aroused when a close relative has schizophrenia.

This chapter will describe some of the reactions that we have learned to be normal and expected in the presence of schizophrenia in a loved one. It is written with the hope that understanding such emotional reactions to be an inevitable consequence of dealing with the tragedy of this mental illness, will enable family members to cope better with the emotional difficulties that they have to face. What we hope to accomplish over the next ten years is to make family members, along with the patients themselves, an even more valuable part of the treatment and rehabilitation process.

Because schizophrenia, despite the presence of some common features, can manifest itself in many different ways, the experience of the family will vary a great deal. For example, some persons affected with schizophrenia may have had serious problems during childhood, while others may have been relatively normal until late adolescence or early adulthood. Some manifestations of the illness may be gradual and insidious, with a slow but gradually worsening course while, in other instances, the first sign of difficulty may be an acute psychotic reaction. Some patients are primarily withdrawn and passive while others are boisterous and aggressive; some may be compliant and take their medication, while others may refuse medication and require frequent hospitalizations.

Despite these differences, schizophrenia generally manifests certain features, which although not present in each and every case, are common enough so that some generalizations can be made about the kinds of emotions and reactions aroused in members of the family. Certain kinds of emotions and reactions will be more intense in parents while others may be more characteristic of a sibling's response.

MOURNING AND LOSS

Parents and siblings always experience feelings of loss and grief because of the profound personality changes that occur in their child or sibling. They may express these feelings in various ways, such as, "He has changed so much, we hardly know him," or "She is not the same person anymore." If the person with schizophrenia has particularly severe "negative" symptoms which involve loss of feeling, lack of motivation, inability to experience pleasure, decreased speech and spontaneous movement, there results a loss of a certain kind of emotional connectedness to their ill relative. It becomes difficult for the ill child to experience previously felt affection toward his or her parents or siblings, further robbing them of a feeling of closeness and increasing their feeling of loss. When these feelings of loss are very intense, family members may have to endure long periods of grief and sadness, much like the mourning that occurs after the death of a child. Yet the child is very much alive although in an altered form, so that this mourning is often a "mourning without end."

Feelings of loss can also be compounded by the fact that it is often very difficult for the family members to talk to their ill child and sibling about his or her illness. Unlike other illnesses in which the family can cry together or talk about how awful it is to go through what is happening, the person with schizophrenia may deny for long periods of time that he or she is sick or that a real internal change has taken place. This characteristic "denial of illness" or "lack of insight" into the illness, it is now believed, may be a consequence of the organic nature of the illness itself, rather than an inability to accept psychologically that some devastating change has taken place. This lack of insight is similar to that manifested by patients who have sustained actual damage to the frontal lobes of the brain.

Parents always have to endure a significant loss of their hopes and expectations for the future of their child. A person with schizophrenia may not be able to attend or complete college, or hold a job, or eventually marry and have a family. When parents meet their child's former friends or classmates who are leading relatively normal and successful lives, they will be painfully reminded of their own dashed hopes and dreams. Siblings may have to suffer the painful awareness that they have lost a close relationship with a brother or sister—a relationship in which thay could have shared and compared the joys of a young adult's social life, and of career goals and decisions.

In some instances, the family may have to tolerate their relative turning away from them in anger, or leaving home and cutting off contact. This actual loss can be even more intense when their child harbors paranoid ideas about them, ideas that can be very difficult to counteract no matter what efforts are made.

GUILT

It is very rare nowadays that parents are blamed for their child's illness as was the case a number of years ago. Nevertheless, feelings of guilt are very common among parents, even when they understand intellectually that schizophrenia is a biological illness. Some blame themselves for possibly passing on a defective genetic trait, and others conjure up all kinds of things they might have been able to do to help prevent the illness. Still others dwell on their perceived past failures that they imagine contributed to the child's stress. They can easily feel guilty about decisions that they made or actions that they took that may have not have turned out well for their child, despite the fact that mental health professionals themselves often cannot advise family members about how to respond to each and every symptom.

Many siblings have yet another kind of guilty feeling which can be described as "survivor guilt." They suffer from feelings of guilt that their loved brother or sister is the sick one, rather than they themselves. As they proceed through life and watch their sick sibling unable to lead a normal life, these feelings can be intensified. Many siblings are of an age to leave the home and get on with their own lives when they are confronted with the fact that their sibling cannot do so. They can feel guilty that they are forming a close relationship with someone they may choose to marry because by doing so they feel they are abandoning their ill sibling. They also feel guilty that they are leaving their parents with the burden of caregiving while they themselves are urged to move on.

Feelings of guilt may not always be conscious but may take a terrible toll on siblings without their being aware of it. Feelings of depression may be a manifestation of guilt in some, while others may unconsciously not do well in their own lives. For example, some siblings may not permit themselves the happiness of marriage out of an unconscious sense of guilt toward the sibling that they are leaving behind.

ANXIETY AND FEAR

Many parents and siblings live with a great deal of anxiety and fear, frequently for a number of years, and sometimes such emotions never disappear. Anxiety and fear can be especially acute when there is a threat of suicide. It has been estimated that up to 15 % of people with schizophrenia commit suicide, and many more make at least one attempt to do so during their lifetime. There are also persistent fears of rehospitalization, especially in those case where the patient refuses to take medication. Even when the course of the illness has stablized, parents live with the constant fear that their child will not be able to take proper care of himself or herself. As parents age, these fears become more pronounced as they begin to worry about the care of their child after their death.

Some people with schizophrenia become very angry and have difficulty controlling their feelings of rage. Some family members, therefore, have to live with the fear that their child or brother or sister will attack them, if not physically, then verbally. Unfortunately, some people with schizophrenia end up being put in jail rather than being hospitalized for behavior that is out of control and misunderstood.

While siblings may experience anxiety and fear for all the same reasons as their parents, they have an additional anxiety to live with. They fear that they themselves may become schizophrenic especially when it is explained to them that there is a genetic component contributing to the cause of schizophrenia. This is especially true for younger siblings who learn that schizophrenia usually doesn't manifest itself until late adolescence or early adulthood. Epidemiological studies indicate that the risk for a sibling developing schizophrenia is less than 10%, although it is still not clear what weight to give to genetic factors in causing the illness.

Siblings experience other kinds of chronic anxieties and worries as they enter adult life. They may avoid introducing their sick sibling to their prospective spouse for fear that the latter will be made uncomfortable or have second thoughts about marriage. Once married, adult siblings live with the fear that their offspring, a niece or nephew of the affected member of the family, may develop schizophrenia. As years pass, the siblings begin to worry that the responsibility for the care of their brother or sister will fall to them when their parents die.

BEWILDERMENT, CONFUSION, AND HELPLESSNESS

Although we now have many new research tools with which to study the structural and functional impairments of the brain in schizophrenia, we do not as yet have any "test" to document the presence of the illness. We still have to rely on the history of the illness and the symptoms with which the patient presents to the physician. Unlike other illnesses which, although equally tragic, are more "explainable" or "understandable" such as cancer, infections or traumatic injury, little is known about the causes of schizophrenia. Family members often feel bewildered and confused about "what has happened." These feelings are often present whether the onset of the illness has been gradual or sudden. Uncertainty about the diagnosis itself further compounds these feelings of confusion. Often at least six months of illness must elapse before psychiatrists can make the diagnosis of schizophrenia with any degree of accuracy. Even after that much time, and for many years, there may be uncertainty as to whether one is dealing with schizophrenia or manic-depressive (bipolar) illness, or even with an intermediate group called schizoaffective illness. It is also frequently very difficult for the parents to be given a clear idea of the prognosis or future course of the illness.

As with other chronic illnesses that often do not respond sufficiently to treatment, the family experiences feelings of helplessness. These feelings may be made even more intense when mental health professionals themselves have been unable to provide effective treatment.

ANGER

Before the establishment of a firm diagnosis of schizophrenia, it is not at all unusual for parents and siblings to be angry at their ill member. However, it is also very important for family members to realize that even after the diagnosis has been made and they have accepted on an intellectual level the fact that their child and sibling suffers from an illness of the brain, they can still experience strong feelings of anger at times. The behavior of a schizophrenic may seem to indicate laziness or stubborness or worse, the complete abandonment of those activities that are to be expected of a maturing individual. The person who is developing schizophrenia may drop out of school, no longer pay attention to grooming, and be unable to get along with anyone, especially other family members.

One of the most common reasons for anger is the refusal of the patient to take medication despite all the pleas of physicians and family members. Understanding that "lack of insight" into their illness is part of the illness itself can help, but parents are often angry that their child refuses to take the very medication that has been shown to decrease his or her psychotic symptoms.

Anger can also be experienced toward those patients who use street drugs and alcohol, both of which can cause further worsening of the condition. Anger is also provoked by the schizophrenic's paranoid ideas toward the parents and siblings, including accusations that the family members are responsible for the illness itself. It may also be impossible not to respond with anger to the many delusions that people with schizophrenia have. Parents often argue and become exasperated as they try to reason with their child who is having unrealistic ideas or is hearing voices. And tragically, parents may be angry at their child for exhibiting some of the worst symptoms of the illness—the "negative" symptoms described above that, like delusions and hallucinations, are also not really under the ill person's control. These negative symptoms, especially the loss of emotion and affection, rob the parents of feeling loved, appreciated and responded to despite all their efforts to be helpful and understanding. In addition, even very loving and sympathetic parents may feel angry at their mentally ill child for the toll that his or her illness is taking on the other children in the family—how the sibling's own lives are being altered in all kinds of ways.

Parents and siblings may also feel a diffuse anger that this catastrophe has happened to their child, as well as anger and frustration toward mental health professionals who may not be able to help sufficiently. Such feelings are even more intense when mental health professionals actually are not competent or do not treat the patient and his or her family with respect. As has already been mentioned, although it is not very common now, in the past family members had to endure accusations of blame about the cause of the illness.

In addition to having the same reasons for feeling angry as do parents, there are more specific reasons for other kinds of anger that siblings may feel. Despite the fact that their hearts go out to their sick brother or sister, they often feel angry that so much attention has been directed toward their sick sibling. It may be that for many years their parents have been overwhelmingly preoccupied with the care of the sick child of the family, often robbing the healthy siblings of the attention that would normally have been directed toward them. Sometimes the family's financial resources are depleted, further provoking feelings of anger toward the sick sibling as well as toward the parents themselves.

SHAME

Much has been done by family members and the Alliance for the Mentally Ill to counteract the stigma that is still associated with mental illness. Nevertheless, even when parents and siblings know that their ill relative's behavior is not under his or her control, feelings of shame may emerge. They may occur particularly when the person with schizophrenia manifests bizarre behavior in front of strangers or even in front of friends and relatives. Shame may be also be felt over the unkempt appearance of many people with schizophrenia. They may look awkward or strange, preoccupied or withdrawn from the world around them. They may not be responsive when spoken to, especially if they are hearing voices or are otherwise tuned in to their own delusional thought processes. In such circumstances, despite the awareness that these are manifestations of the illness itself, family members may still experience shame.

HOW TO COPE

Whatever advice can be given about coping with an illness like schizophrenia in the family, it must be acknowledged that this painful experience, which lasts for so many years, can only be partly assuaged. Nevertheless, there is much that a family can do, not only to ease the pain, but to foster in themselves the strength to actually improve their lives and the life of the person afflicted with schizophrenia. There is no doubt that over the next 10 years there will continue to be a great deal of attention paid to the experience of families. Mental health professionals will come to appreciate even more the role of the family in the rehabilitation process.

Understanding that the feelings that have been described such as mourning and loss; guilt; anxiety and fear; bewilderment, confusion and helplessness; and shame are all normal and expected reactions to the presence of schizophrenia in the family, can be of enormous help in itself. It is also helpful to be able to share these feelings with other families in a formal support group or other setting so that one sees he or she is not alone in experiencing them.

Once the diagnosis has been made and it is clear that one is dealing with this chronic illness, it is very important for family members, parents and siblings alike, to tell other relatives and friends that there is a serious mental illness in the family. This is often extremely hard to do, especially because of the feelings of shame and stigma that are, unfortunately, still associated with mental illness. It is hard to imagine a family that would be unwilling to tell people close to them that their child or sibling has multiple sclerosis or a brain tumor. Yet, it is common for families to be unwilling to let others know of the particular tragedy that is schizophrenia.

Families should be willing to talk to friends and other relatives openly and without shame. They should tell people that their loved one has a different kind of biological illness that affects the functioning of the brain. If they are direct and straightforward about the illness and how it affects their ill family member, many people will be sympathetic and responsive. All too often, families of a person with schizophrenia go into a sort of "hiding," no longer going out as much, or if they do, avoiding talking about their child or sibling. Such isolation detracts from their lives, adds to their pain and unhappiness, and is not really good for the person with schizophrenia as well. As much as is possible, members of the family should try to conduct a normal life, doing those things which have always been pleasureable and important to them.

There is no doubt that making oneself as knowledgeable as possible about schizophrenia is vitally important in coping with this illness. Understanding what the symptoms are and that many of them are not really under the patient's control is very helpful. Being well informed about the latest advances in treatment enables the family to deal with the mental health professionals who are involved in the patient's care. For the most part, family members should be included in the treatment process. They are often the first ones to detect a resurgence of symptoms or a general worsening and will be the first ones to alert the patient and his or her psychiatrist that there has been a change in the condition that needs addressing. Armed with a knowledge about medications and their side effects, family members can and should actively engage psychiatrists and other mental health professionals in a discussion of the available treatment plans and options.

Parents should also explain to their other children what schizophrenia is and how their sibling has been affected. This information may have to be repeated many times, particularly for young children. It is often helpful for the entire family to meet with a knowledgeable mental health professional so that everyone can learn about the illness and discuss ways of coping with particular symptoms and behaviors. Individual psychotherapy can also be helpful, especially for those siblings who may develop strong guilt feelings, loss of self esteem and anxiety. It is important that the psychotherapist be knowledgeable about schizophrenia and its effect on family members.

Finally, it is imperative that family members retain some hope and confidence that the illness will improve over time. There is much evidence to indicate that most people with schizophrenia do begin to improve as they enter their thirties and beyond. More importantly, the new medications like clozapine and risperidone have already significantly improved the lives of many patients. Not only are other new medications on the way, but research into the causes of schizophrenia and studies of its brain abnormalities are moving along at an astonishingly rapid rate, further promoting hope that treatments will continue to improve. The next ten years will bring dramatic changes not only in our understanding of this illness but also in improvements in treatment and rehabilitation.

SUGGESTED READING

Atkinson SD. Grieving and loss in parents with a schizophrenic child. *Am J Psych* 151:1137–1139, 1994.

Deveson A. *Tell Me I'm Here: One Family's Experience of Schizophrenia.* New York: Penguin Books, 1991.

Hatfield A, Lefley H. *Families of the Mentally Ill: Coping and Adaptation.* New York: Guilford Press, 1987.

Hatfield AB, Lefley HP. *Surviving Mental Illness: Stress, Coping and Adaptation.* New York: Guilford Press, 1993.

Keefe Richard SE, Harvey Philip D. *Understanding Schizophrenia: A Guide to the New Research on Causes and Treatment.* New York: The Free Press, 1994.

Lefley H. The family's response to mental illness in a relative. New Directions in Mental Health Services No. 34. San Francisco: Jossey-Bass, 1987.

Marsh DT, et. al. Troubled journey: Siblings and children of people with mental illness. *Innov Res* 2:13–24, 1993.

Marsh DT, et. al. Anguished voices: Siblings and children of people with mental illness. *Innov Res* 2:25–34, 1993.

Miller F, et. al. A preliminary study of unresolved grief in families of seriously mentally ill patients. *Hosp Comm Psych* 41:1321–1325, 1990.

Torrey EF. *Surviving Schizophrenia: A Family Manual.* New York: Harper and Row Publishers, 1988.

Walsh M. *Schizophrenia, Straight Talk for Families and Friends.* New York: William Morrow and Company, Inc., 1985.

Willick MS. Schizophrenia: A parent's experience: Mourning without end. In Andreasen N, ed. *Schizophrenia: From Mind to Molecule.* Washington, DC: American Psychiatric Press, 1994.

Schizophrenia and the Family

ELLEN LUKENS, M.S.W., Ph.D., and HELLE THORNING, M.S.W.

Schizophrenia is a debilitating and poorly understood mental illness. Such long-term chronic illness has a devastating impact on both the person with the illness and on the family, particularly given that in the United States an estimated 60%–75% of adults currently suffering from schizophrenia reside with their families (Kuipers and Bebbington 1988). Since the family is so often the primary caregiver, questions regarding the relationship between the clinical characteristics of the person with the illness and the family environment have received significant attention in the psychosocial literature throughout this century.

This chapter will focus on the need to understand the impact of schizophrenia on the family more fully through psychosocial treatment and research, primarily as a means for improving quality of life and functioning for persons with schizophrenia, their parents, siblings and other family members. Using historical, theoretical, and clinical perspectives on schizophrenia and the family as a frame of reference, we will review the development of various models that reflect the clinical and conceptual issues and methods involved in providing comprehensive care, as well as the implications and challenges for future research.

SETTING THE STAGE: THE FIRST HALF OF THE CENTURY

The early studies on family dynamics and schizophrenia presented the family, most particularly the mother, in a negative light in relationship to onset and course of illness. Research conducted during the first half of the twentieth century on the families of patients suffering from schizophrenia provides important clues to the evolution of thinking regarding both the causes of the illness and the phenomenon of "blaming the family". In the early 1930s a series of studies were published describing the characteristics of the parents of patients suffering from schizophrenia and other disorders (Levy 1931, Kasanin et al. 1934, Despert 1937). These works reinforced the thinking of some of the early psychoanalytic theorists, that schizophrenia was a severe personality disorder with roots in a disturbed parent child relationship which emerged during the early childhood of the patient (see Chapter 11).

The focus of this early clinical research was almost solely on the mother, probably because the major responsibility for child rearing was traditionally assigned to her. Fromm-Reichman completed a key article on the treatment of patients with schizophrenia using psychoanalytic psychotherapy in 1948. This work directly attributed the causes of the illness to the interpersonal relationship between the "schizophrenogenic" mother and the patient during early childhood, and suggested approaches to treatment based on such relationship.

In reviewing Fromm-Reichman's work and other early studies on schizophrenia and the family from the perspective of current methodologic theories, the flaws in design are apparent. Some obvious weaknesses include small sample size, unclear and inconsistent diagnostic criteria for schizophrenia, either inadequate or nonexistent control groups, retrospective design, and the use of case notes as the basis for creating categorical types of personality distinction. Yet such case study approach provided the theorists and clinicians of the time a means of attempting to understand a group of baffling symptoms which seemed particularly unresponsive to known treatment. Given few alternative explanations, this early research strongly influenced the thinking of both clinicians and researchers for many decades regarding the evolution of schizophrenia in relationship to the family.

THE 1950s: EVOLVING ATTITUDES, PSYCHOTROPIC DRUGS, AND DEINSTITUTIONALIZATION

Provided with these beginnings, it is not surprising that the family therapy movement as it evolved in the 1950s became increasingly focused on the impact of family process and dynamics on the health of individual family members (Reiss and Wyatt 1975), and on how the illness of schizophrenia evolved and should be treated. Throughout this period, clinicians tended to avoid and discourage contact with the relatives of the patients. Such thinking was based on the premise that the problems and symptoms associated with schizophrenia arose from unhealthy relationships with family members and could best be alleviated by treatment through a private relationship between therapist and patient (Mishne 1993). Thus, families were often separated from their ill member during hospitalization and either directly or indirectly excluded from treatment.

By the mid-1950s however, there was increasing recognition of the apparent reciprocal influences among hospitalized patients suffering from a range of mental illnesses and their family members. In 1956, Bateson, Jackson, and their colleagues (Bateson et al. 1956) documented the effects that the treatment of patients had on their families, regardless of diagnosis or presenting symptoms. They observed that after a patient had successfully responded to psychotherapy, the spouse or other family member worsened in his or her own capacity to function. Any disruption of the preexistent equilibrium, predicated on a fit between the identified patient and other family members, caused a collapse when the balance was disrupted.

Later, Bateson and Jackson (Bateson 1961, Bateson et al. 1963) presented a somewhat different approach based on their hypothesis of the "double bind", a kind of family situation which they thought would ultimately lead to the development of schizophrenia in the offspring. They characterized this as a form of communication in which at least one parent consistently delivers one kind of verbal message to the child, while contradicting that message with posture, gesture, tone of voice, or meaningful action. Thus,

"the child is punished for discriminating accurately what [the parent] is expressing, and he is punished for discriminating inaccurately—he is caught in a double bind" (258).

In 1957, Lidz and his colleagues published an article entitled "Marital Schism and Skew" describing a series of case studies of 14 marriages, all of which included parents of adult children with schizophrenia. They observed that conflicted marriages alone would not produce a child with schizophrenia, but concluded that such relationships would surely have some impact on the development and course of the illness (Lidz et al. 1957).

These observations served to perpetuate the assumptions regarding the alleged link between family life and the development of schizophrenia. In this context family therapists continued to focus on the impact of patient change within the family. This impact was most often portrayed in a negative light vis a vis the family and its role in maintaining the status quo with regard to the identified patient's symptoms.

Other factors also contributed to perceptions of the family's role in the evolution of schizophrenia. The widespread use of the neuroleptic medications as a viable treatment for schizophrenia began in the 1950s. Moreover, the civil rights movement and the concomitant politicization of poverty had a major impact on the treatment of a range of vulnerable groups, including the mentally ill. The change emerging from both the political climate and new treatment possibilities led to the phenomenon known as deinstitutionalization, in which large numbers of patients diagnosed as chronically mentally ill were discharged from the hospitals into the community. With such change in locus of care, and with very few community resources in place, the burden of responsibility for the mentally ill was thrown onto the family. With this shift in responsibility from hospital to home, the emphasis on how family attitudes and behavior might be related to the course of treatment or cause of illness for schizophrenia received renewed attention.

It was at approximately the same point in time that work and attention began to be placed on a phenomenon described as "expressed emotion" (Brown et al. 1958, Brown and Rutter 1966, Rutter and Brown 1966). This research focussed on the idea that family members could provide an atmosphere characterized by dominance, overprotection, rejection, and contradictory messages, and that such behaviors were strongly associated with the exacerbation or relapse of the symptoms of schizophrenia, particularly among male patients. Expressed emotion has traditionally been measured by two key component variables, termed overinvolvement and criticism, which refer to the style in which a parent relates to the ill adult child. Families are characterized as *high* in expressed emotion if they express high levels of criticism, overinvolvement or both toward the patient according to ratings on an a priori scale drawn from family interview. The impact of these family variables on a core of positive symptoms in patients has been extensively examined, with emphasis on high expressed emotion as a risk factor for relapse (Brown et al. 1972, Leff et al. 1982, 1989). However, the validity of this construct as a causative variable in schizophrenia has been extensively criticized on many fronts including its ambiguous assignment as a trait or state variable, and the potentially interactive nature of the variable with patient symptoms and behaviors (Barrowclough 1984).

THE RISE OF THE FAMILY ADVOCACY MOVEMENT

Beginning in the 1960s, research on the physiologic characteristics of schizophrenia attracted renewed interest, and psychiatry began to focus on the biologic aspects of the illness. However, the work on expressed emotion continued to be a key theme in the psychosocial literature . As families became more politicized in the 1970s and the 1980s through various national self-help groups such as the Alliance for the Mentally Ill (AMI), the work on family variables became increasingly scrutinized by family lobbyists. Not surprisingly, the continued emphasis on family variables and causality triggered anger and criticism among family advocates. This controversy led to a tendency to dismiss the research on expressed emotion as a mechanism for "blaming the family", and encouraging clinicians to do the same (Hatfield et al. 1987, Kanter et al. 1987, Leff et al. 1987, Lefley 1992, Mintz et al. 1987). AMI members interpreted such studies as a distraction from what they considered the more critical biologic research regarding the causes of such a severe illness, and as yet another way to distract monies and time from the increasingly urgent needs of the patients and families for resources such as housing or social and vocational rehabilitation. As Mintz stated,

"expressed emotion has become a focus of controversy in psychiatry: parents of schizophrenic patients have resisted what appears to be a new attempt to blame them for the illness, through the concept of stress as a cause of breakdown, while professionals who view the basis of schizophrenic illness as biological have argued against the allocation of resources to the study of psychosocial factors" (Mintz et al. 1987, 314).

In this context, clinicians have been accused of both equating high expressed emotion with bad parenting and of uncritically accepting the idea that high expressed emotion is a causal factor that increases the likelihood of relapse of psychotic symptoms, and interferes with the ongoing rehabilitation of the patient (Kanter 1987, Lefley 1992). The families and their advocates have argued that high levels of involvement (i.e., overinvolvement) may be functional in trying to negotiate a less than supportive and frequently inadequate mental health system (Grunebaum 1984, Terkelsen 1983), and that little attention has been paid to a) the positive aspect of family involvement and how this might serve both family and patient (Terkelsen 1983, Grunebaum, 1984, Kanter 1987), and b) to the possible negative consequences of low expressed emotion for both family and patient (Kanter 1987, Lefley 1992). These critics also suggest that low expressed emotion is poorly understood and operationalized, that lack of either involvement or criticism could encompass a passive neglect and rejection as well as neutral detachment and that it could also serve to impede self development albeit minimizing stress (Koenigsberg et al. 1986, Kanter 1987). Others contend that the very lack of positive conditions suggested by low involvement (i.e., lack of support and stimulation) may function as a source of stress (Cassel 1976, Kanner 1978).

STRESS AND SCHIZOPHRENIA

The controversy over expressed emotion is better understood in the context of theories about stress and schizophrenia. It is well established that course, outcome, and both the positive and negative symptoms of schizophrenia are exacerbated by stress. The Stress-Diathesis model of schizophrenia (also known as the Vulnerability Stress model) posits a multifactorial relationship among a) provoking agents (stressors), b) vulnerability and symptom formation (diathesis), and c) outcome (Zubin and Spring 1977). Recently, Nicholson and Neufield (1992) extrapolated from this model to propose a dynamic vulnerability formulation of schizophrenia that suggests a transactional relationship between stress and pathology over time.

The stress-arousal model developed by Heinrichs and Carpenter (1983), provides another theoretical frame of reference. The authors contend that either excessive arousal or low levels of arousal can interfere with individual functioning on many levels. As Heinrichs and Carpenter state,

"Most individuals have learned that excessive levels of anxiety (excessive arousal) interfere with their functioning but, if they lack the fine edge that moderate anxiety provides and are too apathetic (insufficient arousal), their performance, again, is less than optimal" (1983, 269).

From this perspective, arousal characterizes both the positive symptoms of schizophrenia (psychotic and nonpsychotic), as described in the literature on symptoms (Berrios 1985), and criticism and overinvolvement, as defined in the expressed emotion literature (Brown et al. 1972, Leff and Vaughn 1985). If both high levels of positive symptoms among patients and high overinvolvement and criticism among families are assumed to represent excessive arousal, and low overinvolvement, criticism and warmth and negative symptoms are assumed to represent insufficient arousal, it follows that a very careful balance would have to be achieved if both family and patient were to function at an optimal level at any given time. In this context, the relationship between environmental factors and the symptoms and behaviors associated with schizophrenia must be considered interactive or reciprocal.

THE PAST DECADE

During the past decade, attitudes regarding the family and its role in the evolution of schizophrenia have slowly begun to change. Increasing attention has been paid to the needs of the families and how this severe illness might affect their quality of life. Clinicians and researchers have begun to focus on such areas as the burden and stress associated with providing care for a person suffering from mental illness (Fadden et al. 1987, Link 1992); issues of mourning and loss for both the relative and ill person (Struening et al. 1995); issues of stigma (Lefley 1989, Link 1992); and new and innovative methods for working with families, such as educational interventions and multiple family groups (McFarlane et al. 1995).

For example, Rolland (1987), using what he refers to as the Family Illness Paradigm, describes three-dimensional factors which shape the families response to any kind of serious illness. These include the phase of the illness (i.e., premorbid, early stages, chronic), the type of illness (i.e., gradual, acute, or episodic), and the components of family functioning. Figley (1989), and Marsh (1994) elucidate this family response further with what is referred to as the ABCX Family Stress Model. In this model, a variety of stressors are seen as contributing to the family outcome or adaptation to the reality of having a seriously ill member. From this perspective family outcome (X) includes coping effectiveness, well-being and satisfaction, as well as family distress. The contributing variables are labeled as (A) family life events, such as the occurrence of the illness itself, and both concurrent and prior life events, (B) family resources, such as family process, socioeconomic status, coping strategies and both professional and personal supports, and (C) family appraisal, including a family's understanding, perspective, and knowledge about mental illness.

THE NEXT TEN YEARS

It is clear that the creation of a healthy environment, however defined, is important for the long-term prognosis of schizophrenia, that people with schizophrenia respond to stress, and that dysfunction within a family can contribute to a stressful environment for *any* individual, whether they suffer from mental illness or not. If it is true that socially intrusive behaviors can overstimulate someone with schizophrenia to the point that a latent thought disorder becomes manifest as psychotic behavior, or if such symptoms can exacerbate the behavior of significant others or caregivers, this is key information for professionals and family members alike. Therefore, expressed emotion and a multitude of other environmental variables ultimately need to be approached and understood as blame-free phenomena that mental health professionals and family members alike can validate. Such understanding could then be used to decrease the impact of the symptoms of schizophrenia on both the individuals with the illness and their families or caregivers in a range of settings.

The past decade has witnessed significant change in theory, research and practice concerned with families of people with serious mental illness. The new models are based on collaborative partnerships, designed to build on the strengths and expertise of all parties; respecting the needs, desires, concerns and priorities of families; enabling families to play an active role in decision making along with mental health professionals; and establishing mutual goals. Attribution and understanding among family members not only influence patient outcome but are modifiable by education and social support. It would not be surprising if family attitudes and behavior also influenced patients' levels of insight into their illness. The family serves as an important frame of reference for a patient and can directly or indirectly influence a patient's knowledge about his or her illness. As such, family education may be critical to the development of increased insight and cooperation with treatment among the individuals who suffer from the illness.

Moving from the assumption that the family milieu can confer protection or stress on any family member regardless of mental status, identifying and titrating personal and environmental protective factors is probably as important for the mental health of the family as for the patient. The goal for the next 10 years should be to continue to move away from the preoccupation with family variables as a causal factor in the relapse of the psychotic symptoms per se. This would allow more rigorous exploration of the reciprocal model among family variables and the symptoms of the illness as proposed by Strachan, Goldstein and others (Miklowitz et al. 1989, Strachan et al. 1989). It would also encourage clinicians and families to more actively acknowledge, accept, and address the complex interplay among various groups of patient symptoms, family and sibling characteristics and other environmental variables, and how these interact with the course of schizophrenia over time.

REFERENCES

Anderson C, Hogarty G, Reiss D. Family treatment of adult schizophrenic patients: A psychoeducational approach. *Schiz Bull* 6:490–505, 1980.

Anderson C, Reiss D, Hogarty G. *Schizophrenia and the Family: A Practitioners Guide to Psychoeducation and Management*. New York: Guilford Press, 1986.

Barrowclough C, Tarrier N. Psychosocial interventions with families and their effects on the course of schizophrenia: A review. *Psychol Med* 14:629–642, 1984.

Bateson G, Jackson D, Haley J, Weakland J. Toward a theory of schizophrenia. *Behav Sci* 1:251–264, 1956.

Bateson G. The biosocial integration of behavior in the schizophrenic family. In: Ackerman NW, Beatman FL, Sanford S, eds, *Exploring the Base for Family Therapy*. New York: Family Service Assoc, 1961.

Bateson G, Jackson DD, Haley J, Weakland JH. A note on the double bind—1962. *Fam Proc* 2:154–161, 1963.

Becker L. Family systems and compliance with medical regimens. In: Ramsey CN, ed, *Family Systems in Medicine*. New York: The Guilford Press, 1989, pp. 1–33.

Birchwood MJ. Families coping with schizophrenia: Coping styles, their origins and correlates. *Psychol Med* 20:857–865, 1990.

Birchwood MJ, Smith J. Schizophrenia and the family. In: Orford J, ed, *Coping with Disorder in the Family*. Kent: Croom Helm. 1987, pp 7–38.

Brown GW, Monck EM, Carstairs GM, Wing JK. Influence of family life on the course of schizophrenic illness. *Brit J Soc Med* 16:55–68, 1958.

Brown GW, Rutter M. The measurement of family activities and relationships. *Hum Relat* 19:241–263, 1966.

Brown GW, Birley JLT, Wing JK. Influence of family life on the course of schizophrenic disorders: A replication. *Brit J Psychiatr* 121:241–258, 1972.

Cassell J. The contribution of the social environment to host resistance. *Am J Epidemiol* 104:107–123, 1976.

Corrigan PW, Liberman RP, Engel JD. From noncompliance to collaboration in the treatment of schizophrenia. *Hosp Comm Psychiatr* 41(11):1203–1211, 1990.

Doane JA, Falloon IRH, Goldstein MJ, Mintz J. Parental affective style and the treatment of schizophrenia. *Arch Gen Psychiatr* 42:34–42, 1985.

Doane JA, West KL, Goldstein MJ, Rodnick EH, Jones JE. Parental communication deviance and affective style. *Arch Gen Psychiatr* 38:679–685, 1981.

Domenici N, Griffin-Francell C. The role of family education. *J Clin Psychiatr* 54(3):31–34, 1993.

Drake R, Osher F. Using family psychoeducation when there is no family. *Hosp Comm Psychiatr* 38:274–277, 1987.

Drake R, Sederer L. Inpatient psychosocial treatment of chronic schizophrenia: Negative effects and current guidelines. *Hosp Comm Psychiatr* 37:897–901, 1986.

Engel G. The clinical application of the biopsychosocial model. *Am J Psychiatr* 137:535–544, 1980.

Estroff SE. Self, identity, and subjective experience of schizophrenia: In search of the subject. *Schiz Bull* 15:186–189, 1989.

Evans J, Goldstein M, Rodnick E. Premorbid adjustment, paranoid diagnosis, and remission. *Arch Gen Psychiatr* 28:666–672, 1973.

Fadden G, Bebbington P, Kuipers L. The burden of care: The impact of functional psychiatric illness on the patient's family. *Brit J Psychiat* 150:285–292, 1987.

Falloon I, Boyd J, McGill C. *Family care of schizophrenia*. New York: Guilford Press, 1984.

Figley CR. *Helping Traumatized Families*. San Francisco: Jossey-Bass, 1989.

Fromm-Reichmann F. Notes on the development of treatment of schizophrenics by psychoanalytic psychotherapy. *Psychiatry* 2:263–273, 1948.

Glynn S, Liberman R. Functioning of relatives and patients facing severe mental illness. In: Lefley HP, Johnson DL, eds, *Families as Allies in the Treatment of the Mentally Ill:*

New Directions for Mental Health Professionals. Washington, DC: American Psychiatric Press, 1990, pp. 255–266.

Grunebaum H. Parenting and children at risk. In: Grinspoon L, ed, *Psychiatry Update*, Vol. III. Washington, DC: American Psychiatric Press, 1984.

Hatfield A. Coping and adaptation: A conceptual framework for understanding families. In: Hatfield AB, Lefley HP, eds, *Families of the Mentally Ill: Coping and Adaptation.* New York: Guilford Press, 1987, pp. 60–84.

Hatfield A. Families as caregivers: A historical perspective. In: Hatfield AB, Lefley HP, eds, *Families of the Mentally Ill: Coping and Adaptation.* New York: Guilford Press, 1987, pp. 3–29.

Hatfield A. Taking issue: The expressed emotion theory: Why families object. *Hosp Comm Psychiatr* 38(4):341, 1987.

Hatfield A. Issues in psychoeducation for families of the mentally ill. *Int J Ment Health* 17(1):48–64, 1988.

Heinrichs D, Carpenter W. The coordination of family therapy with other treatment modalities. In: McFarlane WR, ed, *Family Therapy in Schizophrenia.* New York: Guilford Press, 1983.

Hemsley D, Zawada S. Filtering and the cognitive deficit in schizophrenia. *Brit J Psychiatr* 128:456–461, 1976.

Hirschber W. Social isolation among psychiatric outpatients. *Soc Psychiatr* 20:171–178, 1985.

Hogarty G, Anderson C, Reiss D, Kornblith S, Greenwald D, Javna C, Madonia M. Family psychoeducation, social skills training, and maintenance chemotherapy in the aftercare treatment of schizophrenia. *Arch Gen Psychiatr* 43:633–642, 1986.

Hogarty G, Anderson C, Reiss D. Family psychoeducation, social skills training, and medication in schizophrenia: The long and the short of it. *Psychopharmacol Bull* 23:12–13, 1987.

Hogarty G, Anderson C, Reiss V, Kornblith S. Family psychoeducation, social skills training, and maintenance chemotherapy in the aftercare treatment of schizophrenia. *Arch Gen Psychiatr* 48:340–347, 1991.

Johnson D. The family's experience of living with mental illness. In: Lefley HP, Johnson DL, eds, *Families as Allies in Treatment of the Mentally Ill: New Directions for Mental Health Professionals.* Washington, DC: American Psychiatric Press, 1990, pp. 31–65.

Kaplan H. Psychological distress in sociological context: Toward a general theory of psychosocial stress. In: Kaplan HP, ed, *Psychosocial Stress: Trends in Theory and Research.* New York: Academic Press, 1983, pp. 195–264.

Kasanin J, Knight E, Sage P. The parent-child relationship in schizophrenia. *J Nerv Ment Dis* 79:249–263, 1934.

Leff J, Vaughn C. *Expressed Emotion in Families: Its Significance for Mental Illness.* New York: Guilford Press, 1985.

Lefley H. Families of the mentally ill: Meeting the challenges. In: Hatfield AB, ed, *New Directions for Mental Health Services.* San Francisco: Josey-Bass, 1987.

Lefley HP. Family burden and family stigma in major mental illness. *Am Psychol* 44:556–560, 1989.

Lefley H. Research directions for a new conceptualization of families. In: Lefley HP, Johnson DL, eds, *Families as Allies in Treatment of the Mentally Ill: New Directions for*

Mental Health Professionals. Washington, DC: American Psychiatric Press, 1990, pp. 127–162.

Liberman R. Coping and competence as protective factors in the vulnerability-stress model of schizophrenia. In: Goldstein MJ, Hand I, Hahlweg K, eds, *Treatment of Schizophrenia: Family Assessment and Intervention*. Berlin: Springer, 1986, pp. 201–216.

Lidz T, Cornelison AR, Fleck S, Terry D. The intrafamilial environment of the schizophrenic patient. II. Marital schism and marital skew. *Am J Psychiatr* 114:241–248, 1957.

Lidz T, Cornelison AR, Singer MT, et. al. The mothers of schizophrenic patients. In: Lidz T, Fleck S, Cornelison AR, eds, *Schizophrenia and the Family*. New York: International Universities Press, 1964.

Link B. The consequences of stigma for persons with mental illness: Evidence from the social sciences. In: Fink P, Tasmin A, eds, *Stigma and Mental Illness*. Washington, DC: American Psychiatric Association Press, 1992.

Marsh D. The psychodynamic model and services for families: Issues and strategies. In: Lefley H, Wasow M, eds, *Helping Families Cope with Mental Illness*. Chur, Switzerland: Harwood Academic Publishers, 1994.

MacGregor P. Grief: The unrecognized parental response to mental illness in a child. *Social Work* 39:160–166, 1994.

McFarlane WR. *Family Therapy in Schizophrenia*. New York: The Guilford Press, 1983.

McFarlane W, Lukens E. Systems theory revisited: Research on family expressed emotion and communication deviance. In: Lefley H, Wasow M, eds, *Helping Families Cope with Mental Illness*. Chur, Switzerland: Harwood Academic Publishers, 1994.

McGlashan T. Predictors of the shorter-, medium- and longer-term outcome in schizophrenia. *Am J Psychiatr* 143:50–55, 1986.

McGlashan T. Recovery style from mental illness and long-term outcome. *J Nerv Ment Dis* 175(11):681–685, 1987.

McKeown JE. The behavior of parents of schizophrenic, neurotic, and normal children. *Am J Sociol* 56:175–179, 1950.

Miklowitz D, Goldstein M, Doane J, Neuchterlein K, Strachan A, Synder K, Magana-Amato A. Is expressed emotion an index of a transactional process? I. Parent's affective style. *Fam Proc* 28:153–156, 1989.

Mishne JM. *The Evolution and Application of Clinical Theory*. New York: Free Press, 1993.

Nicholson IR, Neufeld WJ. A dynamic vulnerability perspective on stress and schizophrenia. *Am Orthopsychiat Assoc* 62:117–130, 1992.

Nuechterlein K, Dawson M. A heuristic vulnerability-stress model of schizophrenic episodes. *Schiz Bull* 10:300–312, 1984.

Owens D, Johnstone E. The disabilities of chronic schizophrenia: Their nature and the factors contributing to their development. *Br J Psychiatr* 136:384–395, 1980.

Pearlin L. Role strains and personal stress. In: Kaplan HB, ed, *Psychosocial Stress: Trends in Theory and Research*. New York: Academic Press, 1983, pp. 3–32.

Reiss D, Wyatt RJ. Family and biologic variables in the same etiologic studies of schizophrenia: A proposal. *Schiz Bull* 1:64–81, 1975.

Rolland JS. Family illness paradigms: Evolution and significance. *Fam Sys Med* 5:467–486, 1987.

Runions J, Prudo R. Problem behaviors encountered by families living with a schizophrenic member. *Canad J Psychiatr* 28: 382–386, 1983.

Rutter M, Brown G. The reliability and validity of measures of family life and relationships in families containing a psychiatric patient. *Soc Psychiatr* 1(1):38–53, 1966.

Smith J, Birchwood M. Specific and non-specific effects of educational intervention with families living with schizophrenic relative. *Brit J Psychiatr* 150:645–652, 1987.

Smith J, Birchwood M. Relatives and patients as partners in the management of schizophrenia: the development of a service model. *Brit J Psychiatr* 156:654–660, 1990.

Sommer R. Family advocacy and the mental health system : The recent rise of the Alliance for the Mentally Ill. *Psychiatr Quart* 61:205–221, 1990.

Strachan A. Family intervention for the rehabilitation of schizophrenia. *Schiz Bull* 12:678–698, 1986.

Struening EL, Stueve A, Vine P, Kreisman DE, Link BG, Herman DB. Factors associated with grief and depressive symptoms in caregivers of people with serious mental illness. *Res Comm Ment Health* 8:91–124, 1995.

Teague G, Drake R, Bartels S. Stress and illness. *Stress Med* 5:153–165, 1989.

Tennant C. Stress and schizophrenia: A review. *Integr Psychiatr* 3:248–261, 1985.

Terkelsen KG. Schizophrenia and the family. II. Adverse effects on family therapy. *Fam Proc* 22:191–200, 1983.

Zubin J, Spring B. Vulnerability: A new view of schizophrenia. *J Abn Psychol* 86:103–126, 1977.

The Neurobiology of Schizophrenia and Its Implications for the Mentally Ill Homeless

SCOTT C. CLARK, M.D., and CHARLES A. KAUFMANN, M.D.

The origins of homelessness are myriad. Economic and social factors such as unemployment, unavailability of low-cost housing, and mass deinstitutionalization combine with interpersonal stressors—loss of income, eviction, withdrawal of family support, and lack of aftercare in biologically and psychologically vulnerable individuals (Baxter and Hopper 1981). In this chapter, we discuss the role individual vulnerability plays in this formula for disenfranchisement, and focus on the most prevalent of severe and chronic psychiatric illnesses, schizophrenia. Many who suffer from schizophrenia are vulnerable to repeated episodes of illness and chronic disability, which set the stage for impoverishment, social isolation, economic instability and homelessness.

We also focus only on biologic aspects of the disorder, while recognizing that this approach has inherent limitations. Our aim is not to be overly reductionistic, nor is it to deemphasize the role psychosocial, environmental, political and financial factors play in determining the fate of those vulnerable to homelessness. We recognize that the problems of the homeless are multidimensional, are not easily isolated one from another, and are not readily separable based on degree of simplicity or complexity. Nonetheless the consequences of abnormal brain structure and function are clearly important as, ultimately, all behavior and experience are mediated by the central nervous system.

While we briefly consider the acute aspects of schizophrenia (e.g., paranoia, thought disorder, perceptual disturbance), with their acknowledged disruptive effects on social functioning, we focus on what are often the less well recognized intermorbid aspects of this illness. The behavioral and cognitive deficits that we maintain are less reversible (spontaneously or with treatment) are more highly correlated with chronicity and poor outcome, and are thus more relevant to the lot of the severely mentally ill who are numbered among the homeless.

Many individuals with schizophrenia suffer from a poor outcome which can be attributed to dysfuntion of the prefrontal cortex. We consider this persistent "prefrontal syndrome" and discuss the psychological deficits and behavioral vulnerability it produces.

Schizophrenia is not a unitary disease but a syndrome (Kety 1980). It refers to a group of disorders characterized by onset in late adolescence or early adulthood, psychosis, and a frequently chronic, deteriorating course. The latter two aspects have played a fundamental role in shaping diagnostic thinking since Kraeplin in 1919 first separated patients with "dementia praecox" from those with manic-depressive illness based on prognosis. For Bleuler (1911), who focused on phenomenology in his diagnostic thinking, the crucial distinction was between what he called the primary or fundamental aspects of the illness (emotional flattening, poor motivation, ambivalence and dissociated thinking) and the accessory symptoms (delusions, hallucinations, and catatonia). The advent of neuroleptic medications resulted in a great deal of attention being paid to the acute symptoms that were found to be treatable with these agents. It is likely, however, that it is the symptoms less affected by drugs, those that persist and yet are often more subtle, that impact more strongly on the course of schizophrenia and may have more profound effects on individual vulnerability. Let us look more closely at these groups of symptoms.

SYMPTOMATOLOGY OF SCHIZOPHRENIA: THE ROLE OF NEGATIVE SYMPTOMS

The recognition of different kinds of symptoms in both psychiatric and neurologic disorders dates to 19th century British physicians and their attempts to explain their patients behavior (Berrios 1985). Their thinking contributed to J. Hughling Jackson's hierarchical model of the nervous system, which attempted to explain the difference between observed symptoms as arising from different sources. By this model, negative symptoms were caused by a paralysis of some level of nervous function; this resulted in a loss of inhibition of a lower level of the nervous system, from which emanated positive symptoms. While this model has probably outlived its usefulness, the current conceptualizations of positive and negative symptoms bear striking similarity to their historical antecedents. Thus Crow (1980) describes positive symptoms as representing behavior or function that is normally not pres-ent in the individual, while negative symptoms represent similar phenomena that normally would be present. Another conceptualization, that of Frith (1992), refers to positive symptoms as abnormal perceptions, and negative symptoms as abnormal behavior. Several frameworks for explaining the origin and progression of positive and negative symptoms have been offered.

Crow went on to hypothesize positive symptoms (delusions, hallucinations, thought disorder) as resulting from an excess of dopamine activity, causing a reversible state that is responsive to pharmacotherapy and that characterizes a group of patients whose outcome is relatively good. Negative symptoms, on the other hand, define a group with a relatively poor prognosis who often suffer impairment in cognitive faculties. More resistant to neuroleptic medication, these symptoms (poverty of speech, blunted affect, diminished motivation and drive) are enduring, often intractable, and seen as resulting from structural changes in the brain, specifically, loss of tissue and perhaps aberrancy in the connections formed between different brain regions. In contrast to this view of two independent pathologic processes accounting for observed symptoms is that of Andreasen and Olsen (1982), who see positive and negative symptoms as representing the extremes of a continuum, that is, a single dimension of pathology. There is some evidence that the pattern of occurrence of these two kinds of symptoms in patients better supports the dual dimension hypothesis of Strauss (1974) and Crow (see Lenzenweger et al. 1989).

Carpenter (1988) has refined the idea of negative symptomatology by recognizing that many symptoms called negative may have causes other than the underlying disease process. He proposes a broad use of the term negative and the more specific use of "deficit" to describe behavior that is clearly not due to factors other than the schizophrenia itself. Such "primary" symptoms should be enduring factors of the illness that are present independent of neuroleptic treatment side effects and degree of positive symptomatology.

Differentiating these primary defect symptoms from those secondary to other causes is a challenge for the researcher and clinician. By this we mean acknowledging the anergia that may result from drug treatment of positive symptoms, the social withdrawal that may accompany paranoid delusions, and the retreat from stimulating environments that may be an appropriate response to loss of internal organization of thinking and the sense of self. Depression, which in chronic schizophrenic patients exceeds the rate in the general population (Breier 1991), may add to negative symptom burden and must also be differentiated from the deficit state. There is certainly therapeutic utility in distinguishing primary from secondary symptoms, with resolution of the latter often providing a substantial lessening of illness burden for this population. Although positive and negative symptoms are not restricted to those with schizophrenia, true deficit symptoms may prove to be more specific, and further research may underscore the pathogenetic utility of the deficit concept. It should be noted that a distinction between primary and secondary negative symptoms has not been made in most earlier studies.

In comparison to positive symptoms, true deficit symptoms appear to be more specific to schizophrenia. Moreover, unlike positive symptoms, these negative symptoms seem to be associated not only with personality deterioration but with intellectual decline. Thus patients without positive symptoms and, even more strikingly, patients with negative symptoms show impairment on such measures as orientation, serial 7's, digit span, memory, and paired-associate learning (Johnstone et al. 1978b). In another group of patients tested an average of two weeks after hospital admission, those with prominent negative symptom ratings showed poorer performance on tests measuring visual-motor and visual-spatial skills (Green and Walker 1985). Breier (1991), studying previously hospitalized patients an average of 13 years after discharge, found a significant relationship between negative symptoms and performance on frontal lobe tests, which Perlick (1992) replicated in female patients with chronic schizophrenia. In both studies, a lack of association of frontal test performance with positive symptoms was demonstrated. The specific intellectual deficits and particular vulnerability of patients with chronic schizophrenia will be discussed below.

Positive and negative symptoms have different courses: positive symptoms are often present early in the course of the disease and are frequently the reason patients are first brought to medical attention (Pfohl and Winokur 1982). In chronically hospitalized individuals with schizophrenia such symptoms may be less frequent after the first decade (Bridge et al. 1978), while flat affect can develop late and persist (Pfohl and Winokur 1982). In addition, negative symptoms were found to be relatively more stable over a four-year period than positive symptoms in a study of chronically hospitalized patients (Johnstone et al. 1986). Thus, while positive symptoms may remit or progress, it seems less likely that deficit symptoms, once present, will resolve (Crow et al. 1982).

Persistent negative symptoms probably play an important role in the prognosis of schizophrenia. With associated intellectual impairment, they may be better predictors of poor long-term outcome than positive symptoms (Crow et al. 1982, Tsuang 1982). Breier (1991) found negative symptoms to be significantly associated with poorer social and work functioning when examined after more than a decade of illness. Positive symptoms did not predict outcome in this study. Patients with the deficit syndrome were found to be at high-risk for poor outcome and long-term disability by Fenton and McGlashan (1994) when they examined outcome an average of 19 years after admission to hospital. Furthermore, neuroleptic treatment appears to have a greater effect on short-term than long-term prognosis (Pritchard 1967, Scarpiti et al. 1964), suggesting that prognosis is related to a relatively treatment-insensitive aspect of the disease. As discussed below, negative symptoms may be less responsive than positive symptoms to neuroleptic treatment and may thus constitute this treatment-refractory aspect.

Neuroleptic treatment is overwhelmingly more effective than placebo in both the treatment of schizophrenic symptoms (Klein and Davis 1969) and preventing relapse (Davis 1975). Hallucinations, paranoid ideation, and incoherent speech seem especially responsive to neuroleptic treatment (National Institute of Mental Health 1964). Angrist and others (1980) found that positive symptoms, not negative symptoms, account for most of the change seen in Brief Psychiatric Rating Scale scores for acute and chronic schizophrenic patients after one to six weeks of neuroleptic treatment. In fact, the dramatic response, mostly of positive symptoms, observed by the first users of antipsychotic medications resulted in the hypothesis that increased dopamine function, whether resulting from increased transmitter availability, enhanced receptor sensitivity, or altered feedback regulation (or some combination of these) might underlie psychotic symptoms. This led researchers to uncover a principal action of neuroleptic drugs—antagonism of dopamine receptors (Carlsson and Lindqvist 1963).

The chronic use of haloperidol has also been found to reduce dopamine release in nigrostriatal and mesocortical systems as measured by DOPAC, a major metabolite of dopamine that can be measured by microdialysis in vivo. While the effectiveness of neuroleptics in treating schizophrenia is without doubt, a number of patients (perhaps as many as 35%) will nonetheless inadequately respond to conventional antipsychotics, some because of continued psychosis. Neuroleptic efficacy for positive symptoms has been relatively easy to document; their usefulness in the treatment of negative symptoms is more problematic.

For example, Johnstone and others (1978a) showed that positive symptoms (incoherence, hallucinations, and delusions) but not negative symptoms (flattening of affect and poverty of speech) improved with administration of the active neuroleptic alpha-fluphenthixol in comparison with its inactive isomer, beta-fluphenthixol, or with placebo. Cognitive deficits associated with negative symptoms also may be unresponsive to neuroleptics, as Depue and others (1975) found; the NIMH collaborative study (1964) likewise showed little effect of neuroleptics on symptoms like disorientation and memory deficit. This is an important finding to which we will return later.

A study by Weinberger and others (1980) provides additional evidence that deficit symptoms may be *relatively* neuroleptic-refractory. They found that only ventricular enlargement, a feature associated with negative symptoms, could discriminate neuroleptic responders from nonresponders among 20 patients with chronic schizophrenia well matched for age, duration of illness, drug dose, and plasma level and treated for two months. Further evidence exists that neuroleptics have less effect on the symptoms of chronically ill than of acutely ill patients (Prein and Klett 1972). Similarly, studies have shown that neuroleptics may offer little to some chronic patients. Hughes and Little (1967) discontinued in a blinded fashion the phenothiazine medication being taken by a group of hospitalized chronic patients, substituting a placebo. Patients were restarted on medication if their clinical condition warranted, but only 19% of subjects were placed back on medications after 18 months of observation.

The reintroduction of clozapine in the early 1990s has heralded several insights into the mechanism of action of these drugs. It has also resulted in the improved treatment of both positive and negative symptoms in schizophrenia. Called atypical in part because of the relative lack of neurologic side effects resulting from its use, clozapine has other features that distinguish it from its predecessors. Chief among these are the fundamental differences in receptor activity, and the probable specificity for mesolimbic over nigrostriatal dopamine systems. Studies have shown clozapine is not only superior for the treatment of positive symptoms (compared to typical neuroleptics), it also appears to have a beneficial effect on negative symptoms that has not been convincingly demonstrated with other medications. Pickar (1992) demonstrated superior improvement in both symptom types in a crossover study comparing clozapine to fluphenazine. Symptomatic improvement was predicted by high levels of extrapyramidal side effects during prior treatment with fluphenazine, a finding noted in other studies that suggests clozapine efficacy is tied to its unique lack of nigrostriatal effects. Breier and colleagues (1994) compared haloperidol to clozapine in outpatients. Clozapine was the better treatment for both positive and negative symptoms, but improvement in the latter was limited to *secondary* negative symptoms. Patients with primary "deficit" negative symptoms did not see them improve. Thus the deficit syndrome, as discussed above, may constitute a less reversible, more enduring condition that, it can be hypothesized, is related to frontal lobe dysfunction. The source of negative symptoms is discussed more fully below.

PATHOPHYSIOLOGY OF NEGATIVE SYMPTOMS

Recent research findings suggest that both structural and functional aberrations in the brain may be implicated in the production of negative symptoms. There is evidence for both diffuse impairment and specific damage to the prefrontal cortex. Evidence for diffuse damage ranges from postmortem neuropathologic studies through in vivo studies of brain structure (by pneumoencephalography, computerized axial tomography, and magnetic resonance imaging) and brain function (by electroencephalography and the presence of neurologic soft signs). Evidence for localized damage comes from clinical similarities between patients with frontal lobe injuries and those with schizophrenia. Further evidence appeared with the advent of topographic imaging techniques of brain function (regional cerebral blood flow, positron emission tomography, and brain electrical activity mapping). We will briefly review some of these findings.

Evidence for diffuse CNS damage

Neuropathology

The most consistent neuropathologic finding in schizophrenia is cerebral atrophy (Colon 1972, Tatetsu 1964). Factors such as diet, institutionalization, and therapy (neuroleptics and convulsive therapy) might artifactually produce such atrophy (Trimble and Kingsley 1978); however, the presence of cortical abnormalities in patients who never received somatic treatment and their absence in patients who had various convulsive therapies (Tatetsu 1964) argue against atrophy as merely an artifact of previous treatment. Supporting an atrophic process are findings of gliosis in the periventricular structures of the diencephalon, the basal forebrain (Stevens 1982), and the brainstem (Fisman 1975) of schizophrenics. Postmortem findings of a reduction of GABA uptake sites (Reynolds 1990) and of the neuropeptides, cholecystokinin (CCK) and somatostatin, (Ferrier et al 1983) in limbic regions and decreased binding of CCK in frontal cortex (Farmery 1985) of the brains of schizophrenic patients further support an atrophic process.

Neuroimaging

Techniques which have aided researchers in their study of normal and abnormal brain structure include pneumoencephalography (PEG), computerized axial tomography (CT), and nuclear magnetic resonance imaging (MRI). PEG was one of the first ways of visualizing structures within the brain itself; CT and MRI continue to provide valuable information for researchers and clinicians alike. Pneumoencephalography is a radiographic technique involving injection of air into the ventricular system.

Numerous PEG studies have disclosed abnormalities in the brains of schizophrenic individuals. Findings of cortical atrophy and ventricular enlargement are highest among the most severely and persistently ill groups studied (Weinberger et al. 1979), i.e., those who require frequent or prolonged hospitalization and who may represent a group particularly vulnerable to homelessness. As many as 75% of these patients have such abnormalities. The degree of intellectual and personality disintegration (i.e., negative symptoms) correlates with the severity of atrophy, especially of the ventricular system (Haug 1962). Likewise, the degree of overall adaptive, social, and work impairment may correlate with PEG-assessed ventricular size (Seidman 1983).

CT scan, another radiologic technique, uses a radiographic source that rotates in a horizontal plane and scans a thin cross-section of the head in combination with a computer that constructs an image ("slice") representing the distribution of radiodensities within the cross-section. It represents a vast improvement over PEG as it is noninvasive and provides better resolution; it can discriminate structures down to 0.3 mm.

Twenty-six of 35 CT scan studies of schizophrenic patients and controls have disclosed enlarged ventricles, while 14 of 20 have disclosed cortical atrophy (Shelton and Weinberger 1986). Other abnormalities have included cerebellar atrophy and reversed cerebral asymmetry (Seidman 1983). Ventricular enlargement is the most common abnormality, with significant enlargement occurring in 20%–35% of patients. The finding that the entire distribution of ventricular sizes in schizophrenic patients is shifted upward in relation to controls suggests that the abnormality is not the province of a distinct subgroup. Moreover, the finding that 20% of first-episode patients demonstrate ventricular enlargement argues against it being an exclusive characteristic of chronic, deficit syndrome patients (Weinberger et al. 1982). Nonetheless, it would appear that an especially high incidence of CT scan abnormalities, approaching 50%, occurs in chronic inpatients with substantial neuropsychological deficits (Donnelly et al. 1980, Golden et al. 1980, Johnstone et al. 1976) and with a predominance of negative symptoms such as alogia, affective flattening, avolition, and anhedonia (Andreasen et al. 1982). Ventricular enlargement seems to be associated with a poor response to neuroleptic drug treatment (Weinberger et al. 1980).

MRI has the advantage over CT of providing better resolution, especially in distinguishing grey and white matter structures, without the use of ionizing radiation. Instead, electromagnetic forces are passed through the body, exciting hydrogen atoms and causing the release of measurable signals that, with the aid of a computer, can be reconstructed into detailed pictures representing, as with CT, slices of the brain. MRI has begun to further document the structural abnormalities found with CT. Andreasen has found smaller frontal lobes, cerebrums and craniums (1986), and increased ventricular volume (1990) in two studies comparing schizophrenic patients with control subjects. In the latter study, the increased ventricular size was accounted for almost entirely by the males in the group. Negative symptoms correlated with most of the structural abnormalities found, and impaired cognitive testing correlated with decreased cranial and cerebral size. Schizophrenic males have significantly larger temporal ventricular horns in comparison with bipolar and normal subjects (Johnstone 1989), and Suddath (1989) has inversely correlated volume of temporal lobe grey matter with lateral ventricular volume, suggesting cellular loss in the temporal cortex.

In an interesting study, scans of monozygotic twins discordant for schizophrenia were visually compared by an investigator blind to which twin had the illness; in 12 of 15 pairs, the schizophrenic twin could be distinguished from the unaffected twin by the increased size of cerebrospinal spaces alone (Suddath 1990). This last finding suggests that structural differences in the schizophrenic brain are consistent features of the illness that are at least partially due to nongenetic factors.

Electroencephalography (EEG)

EEG and other neurophysiologic measures like sensory evoked potentials have been used in hundreds of studies of schizophrenic patients. About 25% of the patients show EEG abnormalities, even in studies with careful diagnosis that control for treatment effects and rigorously quantify EEG interpretation (Itil 1977, Seidman 1983). Although a variety of nonspecific EEG abnormalities have been found, Mirsky (1969) has noted diffuse slowing, poor response to light stimulation, and little or no alpha activity in patients with a predominance of negative symptoms. Pandurangi (1986) found EEG abnormalities more prevalent in patients with enlarged ventricles.

An association between ventricular enlargement and lowered alpha activity has been sought by those who note that the periventricular regions are believed to be the source of alpha discharge. One group has found such an association (Karson 1988), while another has not (Gambini 1990). Fenton and others (1980) noted increased delta slowing in hospitalized patients with chronic schizophrenia compared to similarly characterized outpatients, acute schizophrenics, and controls; one might assume the inpatients had a predominance of deficit symptoms. Ambulatory EEG studies have also demonstrated greater delta slow wave activity in schizophrenics (Stevens et al. 1982). This unresponsive "hyperstable" EEG record is associated with poor prognosis (Pincus and Tucker 1978). Furthermore, Ganguli (1987) found a strong association between negative symptoms and decreased slow-wave sleep in a small group of never-medicated schizophrenic patients.

Neurologic signs

Ever since Kennard (1960) reported an increased incidence of often subtle but persistent neurologic findings in a group of disturbed children, there has been interest in the significance of neurologic findings in psychiatric disorders, particularly schizophrenia. Though called "soft" signs because often they do not localize a putative lesion, these findings nonetheless represent a deviant neurologic process, thought by Pincus and Tucker (1978) to be a diffuse rather than specific dysfunction of the nervous system. Signs such as astereognosis, extinction on double simultaneous stimulation, abnormal finger-nose test and impersistence of gaze occur significantly more often in schizophrenic individuals than controls (Buchanan and Heinrichs 1989), and several studies have confirmed a higher rate in schizophrenic patients relative to those with affective and other nonpsychotic psychiatric disorders. Neurologic signs may be more prevalent in patients with negative symptoms (Rochford et al. 1970), and correlate with poor performance on neuropsychologic testing and premorbid asociality (Quitkin et al. 1976), history of developmental abnormalities (Kolakowska 1985), and chronicity (Torrey 1980). Negative symptoms have correlated with neurologic signs referable to the frontal (Merriam 1990, Cox and Ludwig 1979) and parietal (Buchanan et al. 1990) lobes of the brain. As currently conceptualized (Heinrichs and Buchanan 1988), schizophrenic patients are seen as suffering difficulties in the more broadly defined areas of sensory integration, motor coordination, and complex motor acts. Studies examining the relationship of neurologic signs with functional and structural abnormalities are needed to assess the meaning of these abnormalities.

Evidence for localized prefrontal damage

Regional cerebral blood flow (CBF)

Regional cerebral blood flow in the brain correlates highly with local metabolism (glucose and oxygen consumption) and function (Sokoloff 1977). Changes in regional CBF can therefore be used as an index of specific neuronal activity. To monitor the flow, the movement of radioactive xenon 133, an inert gas that has been injected intra-arterially or inhaled, is followed with gamma detectors on the surface of the head, and "functional landscapes" of hemispheric blood flow are constructed.

Studies comparing regional CBF of schizophrenics and controls have disclosed significant reductions in frontal blood flow in the former (Ingvar 1976). Schizophrenic patients at rest were found to have a relative decrease in frontal blood flow that correlated with impaired performance on neuropsychological measures including the Wisconsin Card Sort (WCS) and the Luria-Nebraska Battery. Blood flow to temporal and posterior portions of the brain was increased in these patients, resulting in an overall increase in whole brain blood flow that was correlated with positive symptoms (Paulman et al. 1990). In patients undergoing a simple motor activity, those with predominantly positive symptoms tended to elevate blood flow diffusely; negative symptom patients did not (Guenther et al. 1989). Moreover, a hypofrontal response to visual stimulation has also been noted in older schizophrenic patients, with a predominance of negative symptoms. Individuals with schizophrenia may actually suppress frontal blood flow when performing cognitive activities that ordinarily activate blood flow in normals (Berman et al. 1984). One example is the WCS; while performing this task, schizophrenic patients failed to activate dorsolateral prefrontal cortex compared to controls (Weinberger 1986).

Positron emission tomography (PET scan)

As noted, local glucose use in the brain closely parallels neuronal activity. Deoxyglucose, an analog of glucose, is labeled with a positron-emitting radioisotope, 18/F; extracranial detection of positron emission and computer reconstruction depicts regional differences in glucose metabolism and thus neuronal function. PET scan studies of schizophrenic patients, although preliminary, again suggest lower (dorsolateral) frontal activity in relation to controls (Buchsbaum et al. 1982, Farkas et al. 1980). It has also been shown that patients with more negative symptoms show less of an increase in frontal metabolism (when performing an activating task) when compared to other schizophrenic patients and to controls

(Volkow 1987). Recent studies, however, have been inconsistent (Weinberger 1988). Researchers continue to be intensely interested in studying cerebral metabolic hypofrontality, for, as Weinberger and Berman have pointed out (1988), this particular finding may represent evidence of a significant neurophysiologic mechanism underlying some of the symptoms of schizophrenia.

Evidence for selective hypofunctionality of dopaminergic systems

In addition to gross damage to the prefrontal cortex, a growing body of evidence indicates that chronic, deficit syndrome schizophrenics have selective damage to dopamine containing neurons (Chouinard and Jones 1978, Lecrubier et al. 1980, Wyatt 1983). Such selective damage may be related to more general findings of prefrontal dysfunction, as this region has the highest dopamine concentrations of all cortical areas (Berger 1981) and is the major terminus for mesocortical dopamine neurons. Evidence for selective hypofunctionality of dopaminergic systems comes from clinical, neurochemical, and neuropharmacologic studies. Moreover, added support is provided by preclinical studies of selective dopamine lesions in laboratory animals.

Clinical evidence

Deficit symptoms of schizophrenia strongly resemble the apathy, lack of spontaneity, and impaired concept formation seen in Parkinson's disease (Javoy-Agid and Agid 1980), a disorder in part related to brain dopamine deficit. Negative symptoms also are similar to the "psychic torpor" seen as a sequel to encephalitis lethargica (Economo 1931), a disorder marked by profound (20-fold) loss of dopaminergic nerve cell bodies in the mesencephalon (Bogerts et al. 1983). Neuroleptic-induced dopamine blockade, discussed earlier, frequently produces an anergic and bradykinetic state that can compound existing deficit symptoms. Nonmotor behaviors may also be affected, resulting in apathy, lack of goal-directedness, and alogia (Klein et al. 1980).

Neurochemical evidence

Bowers (1974) found lower accumulation of the dopamine metabolite homovanillic acid (HVA) in the cerebrospinal fluid (CSF) of poor-prognosis schizophrenic patients. van Kammen and others (1983) have found decreased HVA concentrations in CSF of drug-free schizophrenic patients with ventricular enlargement and cortical atrophy, linking hypodopaminergia with a prevalent structural abnormality, while Weinberger and colleagues (1991) found CSF HVA to predict prefrontal activation measured by rCBF in patients performing a frontally-specific behavioral task. Similarly, Kaufmann and others (1984) have found decreased concentrations of another metabolite, dopamine sulfate, in CSF of treatment-refractory chronic schizophrenic patients, while lowered plasma HVA has been linked to the presence of deficit symptoms in a group of chronically hospitalized schizophrenic patients (Davidson and Davis, 1988).

Neuropharmacologic evidence

Preliminary data for the effectiveness of dopamine agonists and precursors in the treatment of certain negative symptoms, discussed above, support the existence of a hypodopaminergic substrate for such symptoms. Administration of apomorphine and amphetamine has also been shown to increase frontal blood flow, and in the case of amphetamine, correlate with improvement on the Wisconsin Card Sorting Test, a measure of frontal performance (Davis 1991). Improvement in cognitive measures might be expected to parallel negative symptom change in such circumstances, and would point to a common pathophysiology for negative symptoms and cognitive abnormality. Further evidence comes from the relative resistance of large-ventricle patients to the psychosis-exacerbating effects of apomorphine (Jeste et al. 1983).

Preclinical studies

Several animal models for the cognitive deficits that accompany gross lesions of the prefrontal cortex have been developed. Delayed-response tasks are particularly sensitive to such lesions. In rhesus monkeys not only surgical removal of dorsolateral prefrontal cortex but selective depletion of dopamine with the neurotoxin, 6-hydroxydopamine, impairs delayed-response performance. This behavioral deficit can be reversed by the dopamine precursor levodopa and the dopamine agonist apomorphine (Brozoski et al. 1979). The prefrontal cortex receives dense reciprocal projections from diencephalic structures (like the mediodorsal thalamic nucleus and anterior striatum), which in turn receive projections from mesencephalic dopaminergic (A10) neurons. Six-hydroxydopamine injections in rat striatum (Dunnett and Iversen 1979) or mesencephalon (Simon et al. 1980) also disrupt delayed-response tasks.

In rats with experimentally induced lesions of prefrontal cortex, exploratory activity is usually unaffected. When "stressed" with a substance that enhances dopamine turnover and lowers exploratory behavior even in unlesioned rats, prefrontally lesioned rats exhibited significantly greater reduction in this behavior than unlesioned rats. These findings suggest that prefrontal cortex may play an important role in coordinating cognitive coping processes and that inhibited behavioral responses to stress may result from dysfunction of prefrontal dopamine systems (Jaskiw and Weinberger 1990). Thus a growing body of data supports the idea that selective loss of *function* at critical stations in dopaminergic pathways can produce the characteristic cognitive disturbances associated with prefrontal dysfunction.

Summary

Schizophrenia appears to be a heterogeneous disorder, characterized at various times or in various individuals by a predominance of productive symptoms (hallucinations, delusions, thought disorder) or deficit symptoms (flat affect, alogia, avolition, anhedonia, and cognitive deficits). While the former symptoms may be neuroleptic-responsive, the latter are relatively refractory to typical neuroleptic treatment (may even be exacerbated through side effects like akinesia) and are associated with poor prognosis and social decline. Epidemiologic studies among the mentally ill homeless have not specifically addressed the prevalence of positive versus negative symptoms, or of cognitive disruption; such studies are clearly necessary. Nonetheless, anecdotal accounts suggest that deficit symptoms predominate.

Evidence from the fields of clinical brain imaging, neuropathology, neurophysiology, neurochemistry, and neuropharmacology support the view that frontal lobe dysfunction is an important factor in chronic schizophrenia. *Pre*frontal dysfunction results in a specific constellation of behavioral and cognitive disturbance that renders the chronic schizophrenic individual vulnerable to stress-induced exacerbations of illness (Zubin 1980; Weinberger 1987). There is a loss of ability to process novel and complex information, to filter distractions, and to plan. These deficits persist in the absence of more florid symptoms, and are associated with a poor prognosis.

THE PREFRONTAL SYNDROME

The prefrontal cortex, while phylogenetically recent, represents more than 25% of the mass of the human cerebrum. It may be divided, on the basis of connections and functions, into two major components, lying dorsolaterally and ventromedially. The prefrontal cortex receives a variety of inputs related to the general drive state or arousal of the organism, to its internal needs, and to the motivational significance of external stimuli in gratifying those needs. In turn, it is responsible for forming cohesive behavioral schemes to obtain these goals.

Studies suggest that simple, well-established behavioral patterns can be executed without the prefrontal cortex. More complex, novel behaviors, especially those discontinuous over time (that is, with long delays interposed) demand the involvement of the prefrontal cortex: the prefrontal cortex is necessary to bind individual elemental behaviors into a gestalt, an organized whole whose meaning transcends that of its component behaviors, to include the relation of these elements one to another (their timing and order) and to the overall goal.

In forming temporal gestalts, the prefrontal cortex embraces four functions, two apparently localized in its dorsolateral and two in its ventromedial (orbital) components. The dorsolateral prefrontal cortex is involved in the prospective function of anticipation or foresight, preparing the sensory and motor apparatus for a range of possible environmental cues relevant to the goal, thereby optimizing reception and compensating for expected movement. It is also involved in the retrospective function of provisional memory, allowing for the referral of any event in a behavioral sequence to preceding events or to the original scheme. The ventromedial prefrontal cortex is involved in supressing interference, be it irrelevant external stimuli or internal drives or affects (Fuster 1980). It may also be involved in maintaining cortical tone (Luria 1973), evident in the vasodilation of cerebral blood vessels and increase in EEG fast-wave activity (desychronization) that accompany voluntary attention. Lesions to the prefrontal cortex result in characteristic deficits in motor, language, cognitive, and affective functioning, as well as impairment in executive functioning and awareness.

Mattson and Levin (1990) in a review of frontal lobe dysfunction have noted that behaviors of patients with lesions (such as atrophy, tumors or surgical excision) of the dorsolateral frontal cortex include loss of initiative, withdrawal, impaired attention, inability to plan ahead, loss of social awareness and social restraints, and difficulty with a variety of cognitive tasks, findings which are similar to the negative symptoms and their correlates that we have been discussing in regard to schizophrenia. While linking cognitive impairment firmly with localized frontal lobe injury is problematic because of the difficulty in ruling out diffuse effects of head injury, some findings do suggest that victims of frontal lobe injury suffer greater impairment of metacognitive tasks, including self-assessment of abilities, impulse regulation and planning (Levin 1987).

Further evidence that frontal lesions are associated with schizophrenia-like symptoms comes from studies of elderly patients with nonAlzheimer's dementia. These individuals have frontal atrophy which can be documented with CT or single photon emission computed tomography (SPECT), and absence of posterior cerebral abnormality (as would be expected in Alzheimer's disease). In a series of such patients reported by Neary (1988), apathy, neglect of personal hygiene, lack of motivation and denial of illness were frequent findings. Personality change, "social breakdown" and a marked unawareness of difficulty resulting in profound self-neglect characterize these patients (Orrell 1989).

Specific motor disorders follow lesions to the dorsolateral PFC and affect the spontaneity and purposefulness of behavior. Severe lesions result in what Luria has called the "apathico-akinetico-abulic syndrome": behavior is not initiated but can be provoked. Less extensive lesions result in varying degrees of breakdown of complex behaviors and loss of a goal-oriented scheme. Perseverative responses to external cues are also frequent.

Similarly, language deficits vary depending on the magnitude and location of the lesion. Severe lesions result in poverty of content: speech lacks spontaneity in what Luria has called "frontal dynamic aphasia" (Luria 1970). Posterior lesions, near Broca's area, affect the syntactic component of language, governing the relation between words (e.g., subject, verb, and object). More anterior lesions affect the discourse component of language, governing the manner in which sentences are combined to construct an idea or story. This latter component appears to be especially disrupted in schizophrenia (Andreasen 1982). Furthermore, as dorsolateral lesions interfere with provisional memory, language loses its primacy over behavior. The individual may recall instructions and intend to comply with them but lack the capacity to compare ongoing actions with these instructions. The capacity to verify actions, to check them against the original cognitive scheme and notice mistakes, is lost.

Ventromedial lesions result in characteristic cognitive disturbances: an inability to sustain attention and to suppress irrelevant stimuli. Deficient "directed" attention (Stuss and Benson 1986) would result in disorders of complex behavior, e.g., where monitoring, feedback, and goal-selection were required. Impulsivity, distracibility, and rapid alternation of attention adversely affect the ability to analyze complex stimuli. Random behaviors break through, disrupting the intended gestalt. Considered interpretations are replaced by impulsive, fragmentary guesses based on irrelevant details.

Attention deficits can be measured by continuous-performance tasks (CPTs). CPT deficits have been most thoroughly investigated in patients with schizophrenia (Chapman 1979). Such deficits are frequently present in patients with schizophrenia, and as noted earlier, more often in those with prominent negative symptoms. Deficits often persist despite clinical remission (Wohlberg and Kornetsky 1973).

Damage to the prefrontal cortex may produce specific disorders of affect and emotion. Dorsolateral lesions result in profound apathy and indifference, blunted affect, and lack of drive and emotional reactivity. Ventromedial lesions reduce inhibition of instinctual drives, resulting in euphoria, impaired judgement, inappropriate social behavior, restlessness and disinhibition of sexual or aggressive impulses (Stuss and Benson, 1986).

Impaired awareness in brain-injured patients often refers to their inability to attend to a part of their body, or a lack of appreciation of some neurologically based deficit. Thus, in the syndrome of unilateral neglect, when presented with stimuli to both sides of the body, patients only recognize the stimulus on one side. While multiple brain regions are probably involved in unawareness and neglect, the complex and abstract nature of deficits in self-awareness, judgement and understanding probably gain a role for the higher order functions thought to reside in the frontal lobe. There is evidence that in neurologic patients, frontal deficits akin to those we have been discussing above are implicated in lack of awareness of one's difficulties and limitations (Neary 1988), and others have suggested, based on a review of all the syndromes wherein abnormal awareness occurs, that some malfunction of the frontal lobe must play a part in this perception (Stuss and Benson 1984).

Awareness of illness is often lacking or severely impaired in psychiatric patients, resulting in resistance to treatment and increased morbidity. Among hospitalized, acute schizophrenic patients, a wide variation in level of awareness has been found using a structured interview, although average scores tend to be poor (McEvoy 1989). Whether schizophrenic patients evidence poorer insight into their illness than do otherwise mentally ill individuals is largely an unsettled, because sparsely studied, issue (Amador et al. 1991). Lack of acceptance or appreciation of illness and the need for treatment presents a great challenge for those working to improve the care of the severely mentally ill, and can greatly complicate the treatment of the homeless.

TREATMENT

The homeless are not all mentally ill, and the mentally ill homeless do not all suffer from chronic diseases. Certainly many do, and any effective treatment approach must be sensitive to their unique vulnerability and needs. But if our clinical descriptions have shown anything, it is the heterogeneity of symptoms, treatment responses, and outcomes among the chronically psychiatrically ill.

First and foremost, treatment of this patient group must be flexible. Such flexibility depends on accurate diagnostic assessment, not only of manifest psychopathology but of more subtle neuropsychologic deficits. We have seen that measures of cognitive impairment have significant prognostic value; they should be an integral part of epidemiologic surveys as well as individual evaluations. Beyond diagnosis, treatment of the mentally ill homeless may involve environmental interventions, rehabilitation, psychosocial approaches, and, particularly in the case of schizophrenia, pharmacotherapy (see chapter by Felix et al.)

The "prosthetic environment"

Individuals with persistent prefrontal dysfunctions have a need for ongoing compensatory interventions, what Lindsley (1970) has called a "prosthetic environment." Difficulties with anticipation and planning suggest the importance of active case management (Lamb 1980) and aggressive outreach. Without these, the symptoms of the mentally ill and their lack of goal-directedness will deny them continuous access to the very treatment they need.

Stein and Test (1980) have reported the beneficial effects of an intensive community-based treatment program, providing ongoing and close monitoring and assistance to help patients live and work independantly. Their finding that improvements in employment status, living situation, and productive symptomatology did not persist one year after the aggressive community program was replaced by more traditional programming suggests that ongoing, active involvement was necessary to compensate for the persisting deficit (prefrontal) symptoms.

Deficits in filtering stimuli suggest the importance of individualized treatment. Vast public shelters are disruptive for neurologically intact individuals, let alone for the psychiatrically ill with impairments in sustaining attention. Intensive sociotherapy in the absence of medication may present comparable risk. A failure to control disruptive stimuli may ac-

219

count for the high relapse rate among neuroleptic-free chronic schizophrenics who receive intensive social casework (Hogarty et al. 1974a) as well as among those who return to over-involved families with a high level of expressed emotion (Vaughn and Leff 1976).

Social withdrawal, a prominent difficulty faced by the chronically ill and the clinicians who work with them, may also result if not already present. This complicates access to care and limits the acquisition of contacts needed to thrive in the community. Social skills training and environmental interventions aimed at restoring social networks are clearly needed. Family work based on education and support may help some individuals, especially relatively early in the course of illness. Others may benefit from drop-in centers, which provide accessible, "supported" social groups—persisting even without individual initiative—and which tolerate optimal social distance. The building of larger social networks helps patients feel more satisfied and function better, especially if social contacts are casual and unintrusive (Lehmann 1980).

Individual and family psychotherapy may also have important roles in the treatment of the chronic mentally ill. Each may contribute to the development of a therapeutic alliance, usually crucial to good outcome, as well as providing an opportunity for education about prodromal signs, which, when monitored and addressed in a timely way, may help prevent relapse. Hogarty and others (1974a, 1974b) found that individual "major role" therapy, a problem-solving, psychosocial technique, reduced relapse rates and improved social adjustment in neuroleptic-maintained patients at 2-year follow-up. Similarly, Leff (1979) has advocated working with families of medicated schizophrenics in multifamily groups, giving parents the opprotunity to learn about the illness and share problem-solving experiences. McFarlane et al. (1995) found such treatment provided significant protection from relapse and improved outcomes for patients whose families joined this psychoeducationally based approach.

Rehabilitation and psychosocial approaches

We have referred to the relative tenacity of cognitive deficits and associated symptoms of the prefrontal syndrome. There is growing evidence from the field of "cognitive retraining" suggesting that impaired individuals can, with extensive practice, be taught new strategies for performing psychological tasks. In a controlled study by Goldberg (1987), schizophrenic patients receiving continuous instruction were able to adequately perform the Wisconsin Card Sort, a neuropsychologic measure that was mentioned earlier as a relatively specific measure of frontal lobe functioning. Once the instructor ceased his or her assistance, however, the patients reverted to their pre-taught levels of markedly poor performance. In an interesting follow-up to this report, another group found that if patients were both instructed and rewarded (for correct answers), some were able not only to perform well but also could maintain their improved performance even after instruction was withdrawn (Green 1990). While the WCST cannot be accepted as a benchmark for problem-solving and community-living skills, it seems likely that some cognitive deficits may be remediable with focused intervention. Workers in the field of neuropsychologic rehabilitation propose a number of such interventions aimed at disorders of motivation, reasoning and concept formation, cue utilization, and productive thinking. The psychiatric rehabilitative techniques of Anthony and Liberman (1992) similarly strive to train and develop atrophied skills and coping behaviors in chronically ill individuals. We can hope that, as the field develops, such cognitive retraining will come to supplement environmental interventions in the rehabilitation of the severely mentally ill.

The need for tolerance and flexibility combined with continuity of care and caretakers is discussed in Thorning and Lukens chapter. For a discussion of the importance of an individualized approach and attention to dynamic factors in treatment of the mentally ill homeless (see chapter 15).

Medication

The use of neuroleptic medication in the treatment of schizophrenia is also developing in response to new findings and drugs. Antipsychotics remain a fundamental part of treatment for this disorder, both for control of positive symptoms and for prevention of relapse. Still, upwards of 30% of patients will relapse even with good medication compliance (Schooler et al. 1980). A similar number may never adequately respond to conventional drugs at all. And for those that do respond, continuous neuroleptic exposure presents an increasing risk of tardive dyskinesia, which for some may be irreversible. Clearly, alternate drug treatment strategies are needed.

One such strategy, low-dose treatment (1.25–5 mg of fluphenazine decanoate biweekly), apparently results in a high relapse rate, but does not preclude rapid restabilization in the community (Kane 1983). Moreover, relatively young schizophrenics treated with this regimen appear less withdrawn and demonstrate fewer signs of dyskinesia. It should be emphasized that these patients received intensive follow-up. Nonetheless, if such follow-up can be provided, low-dose treatment may afford a reasonable approach to maintaining patients in the community while minimizing cumulative neuroleptic dose (Kane 1983).

A second strategy, intermittent or targeted treatment, involves follow-up of drug-free patients until prodromal signs of impending relapse appear. Medication is then provided to abort the impending episode, and discontinued after restabilization. Patients receiving targeted medication fare no worse, in terms of psychopathology ratings, number of hospitalizations, or days in hospital, than those receiving continuous drug treatment; moreover, cumulative neuroleptic exposure is diminished by 60 percent (Carpenter and Heinrichs 1983). Once again, it bears mentioning that in part, the success of this approach is intensive follow-up—with individual, group, and family therapies and, when necessary, active environmental manipulation to reduce stress.

Clozapine offers a measure of hope to those with poor response to typical neuroleptics, and those with severe tardive dyskinesia. Essentially free of extrapyramidal side effects, and better at treating a wider range of psychotic and deficit symptoms, the 1% risk of developing potentially fatal agranulocytosis disappointingly limits a wider use of this drug. Studies have begun to document advantageous effects in work and social functioning in clozapine responders. Meltzer et al. (1990), for example, report better outcome in interpersonal relationships and instrumental roles after six months of clozapine treatment. Breier (1994) found role functioning to be highly correlated with degree of negative symptoms in his long-term study of outcome, suggesting that if clozapine is more effective than other drugs in treating these symptoms, it may lead to a more productive and satisfying life for those with schizophrenia.

CONCLUSIONS

The homeless mentally ill suffer from diverse disorders of varying severity that call for a flexible approach to treatment. Neuropsychologic impairments, when present, require environmental interventions including active case management, outreach, and stimulus reduction. Recent studies suggest that some impairments may be partly reversible with cognitive retraining. Neuroleptic medication, of limited value by itself, plays an integral role in the comprehensive treatment of schizophrenia. Newer treatment strategies, including low- and intermittent-dosing with conventional neuroleptics, as well as introduction of atypical neuroleptics, may provide adequate prophylaxis against relapse of productive symptoms while minimizing deficit symptoms and cumulative drug exposure. These pharmacologic approaches are most successful when combined with psychosocial interventions. Only through such individualized, comprehensive treatment can the needs of this highly vulnerable population be met.

REFERENCES

Amador XF, et al. Awareness of illness in schizophrenia. *Schiz Bull* 17:113–132, 1991.

Andreasen N, et al. Magnetic resonance imaging of the brain in schizophrenia: The pathophysiologic significance of structural abnormalities. *Arch Gen Psych* 47:35–44, 1990.

Andreasen N, et al. Structural Abnormalities in the frontal system in schizophrenia: A magnetic resonance imaging study. *Arch Gen Psych* 43:136–144, 1986.

Andreasen NC, Olsen S. Negative vs. positive schizophrenia: Definition and validation. *Arch Gen Psych* 39:789–794, 1982.

Angrist B, Peselow E, Rubinstein M, et al. Partial improvement in negative schizophrenic symptoms after amphetamine. *Psychopharmacology* 78:128–130, 1982.

Angrist B, Rotrosen J, Gershon S. Differential effects of amphetamine and neuroleptics on negative versus positive symptoms in schizophrenia. *Psychopharmacology* 72:17–19, 1980.

Baxter E, Hopper K. *Private Lives/Public Spaces: Homeless Adults on the Streets of New York City.* New York: Community Service Society, 1981.

Berger PA. Biochemistry in schizophrenia: Old concepts and new hypotheses. *J Nerv Ment Dis* 169:90–99, 1981.

Berman KF, Zec RF, Weinberger DR. Impaired frontal cortical function in schizophrenia, I: rCBF evidence, in Abstracts, 39th Annual Meeting, Society of Biological Psychiatry, Los Angeles, 1984.

Berrios GE. Positive and negative symptoms and Jackson. *Arch Gen Psych* 42:95–97, 1985.

Bleuler E. *Dementia praecox or the group of schizophrenias (1911).* New York: International Universities Press, 1950.

Bogerts B, Hantsch J, Herzer M. A morphometric study of the dopamine-containing cell groups in the mesencephalon of normals, Parkinson's patients, and schizophrenics. *Biol Psychiat* 18:951–969, 1983.

Bowers NB. Central dopamine turnover in schizophrenic syndromes. *Arch Gen Psych* 31:50–54, 1974.

Breier A, et al. National Institute of Mental Health longitudinal study of chronic schizophrenia. *Arch Gen Psych* 48:239–246, 1991.

Breier A, et al. Effects of clozapine on positive and negative symptoms in outpatients with schizophrenia. *Am J Psychiat* 151:20–26, 1994.

Bridge TP, Cannon HE, Wyatt RJ. Burned-out schizophrenia: evidence for age effects on schizophrenic symptomatology. *J Gerontol* 33:835–839, 1978.

Brozoski TJ, Brown RM, Rosvold HE, et al. Cognitive deficits caused by regional depletion of dopamine in prefrontal cortex of rhesus monkey. *Science* 205:929–932, 1979.

Buchanan RW, Heinrichs DW. The neurological evaluation scale: A structured instrument for the assessment of neurological signs in schizophrenia. *Psych Res* 27:335–350, 1989.

Buchanan RW, et al. Clinical correlates of the deficit syndrome in schizophrenia. *Am J Psychiat* 147:290–294, 1990.

Buchsbaum MS, Ingvar DH, Kessler R, et al. Cerebral glucography with positron tomography: use in normal subjects and patients with schizophrenia. *Arch Gen Psychiat* 39:251–259, 1982.

Carlsson A, Lindqvist M. Effect of chlorpromazine and haloperidol on formation of 3-methoxy-tyramine and normetanephrine in mouse brain. *Acta Pharmacol Toxicol* 20:140–144, 1963.

Carpenter WT Jr, Heinrichs DW. Early intervention, time-limited, targeted pharmacotherapy of schizophrenia. *Schizophr Bull* 9:533–542, 1983.

Carpenter WT, et al. Deficit and non-deficit forms of schizophrenia: The concept. *Am J Psychiat* 145:578–583, 1988.

Chapman LJ. Recent advances in the study of schizophrenic cognition. *Schiz Bull* 5:568–580, 1979.

Chouinard G, Jones BD. Schizophrenia as dopamine deficiency disease. *Lancet* 2:99–100,1978.

Colon EJ. Quantitative cytoarchitectonics of the human cerebral cortex in schizophrenic dementia. *Acta Neuropathol* 20:1–10,1972.

Crow TJ. Molecular pathology of schizophrenia: More than one disease process? *Br Med J* 280:66–68, 1980.

Crow TJ, Cross AJ, Johnstone EC, et al. Two syndromes in schizophrenia and their pathogenesis. In: Henn FA, Nasrallah AH, eds, *Schizophrenia as a Brain Disease*. New York: Oxford University Press, 1982.

Davidson M, Davis KL. A comparison of plasma homovanillic acid concentrations in schizophrenic patients and normal controls. *Arch Gen Psych* 45:561–563, 1988.

Davis JM. Overview: maintenance therapy in psychiatry, I: Schizophrenia. *Am J Psychiat* 132:1237–1245, 1975.

Davis KL, et al. Dopamine in schizophrenia: A review and reconceptualization. *Am J Psychiat* 148:1474–1486, 1991.

Depue RA, Dupicki MD, McCarthy T. Differential recovery of intellectual, associational, and physiological functioning in withdrawn and active schizophrenics. *J Abnorm Psychol* 84:325–330, 1975.

Donnelly EF, Weinberger DR, Waldman IN. Cognitive impairment associated with morphological brain abnormalities on computed tomography in chronic schizophrenic patients. *J Nerv Ment Dis* 168:305–308, 1980.

Dunnett SB, Iversen SD. Selective kainic acid (HA) and 6-hydroxydo-pamine (6-OHDA) induced caudate lesions in the rat: Some behavioral consequences. *Neurosci Lett* 3(Suppl):207, 1979.

Economo CF. *Encephalitis Lethargica: Its Sequelae and Treatment*. Neuman KO, ed. London: Oxford University Press, 1931.

Farkas T, Reivich M, Alavi A, et al. The application of 18F-deoxy-glucose and positron emission tomography in the study of psychiatric conditions. In: Passonneau JV, Hawkins RA, Lust WD, et al, eds. *Cerebral Metabolism and Neural Function*. Baltimore: Williams & Wilkins, 1980.

Farmery SM, et al. Reduced high affinity choleycystokinin binding in hippocampus and frontal cortex of schizophrenic patients. *Life Sci* 36:473–477, 1985.

Fenton GW, Fenwick PBC, Dollimore J. EEG spectral analysis in schizophrenia. *Br J Psychiat* 136:445–455, 1980.

Fenton WS, McGlashan TH. Natural history of schizophrenia subtypes II: positive and negative symptoms and long-term course. *Arch Gen Psych* 48:978–986, 1991.

Ferrier IN, Roberts GW, Crow TJ, et al. Reduced cholecystokinin-like and somatostatin-like immunoreactivity in limbic lobe is associated with negative symptoms in schizophrenia. *Life Sci* 33:475–482, 1983.

Frith CD. *The Cognitive Neuropsychology of Schizophrenia*. Hove, UK: Lawrence Erlbaum Associates Ltd, 1992.

Fuster JM. *The Prefrontal Cortex: Anatomy, Physiology, and NeuropPsychology of the Frontal Lobe*. New York: Raven Press, 1980.

Gambini O, et al. EEG power spectrum profile and structural CNS characteristics in schizophrenia. *Biol Psychiat* 27:1331–1334, 1990.

Ganguli R, et al. Electroencephalographic sleep in young, never-medicated schizophrenics. *Arch Gen Psych* 44:36–44, 1987.

Goldberg TE, et al. Further evidence for dementia of the prefrontal type in schizophrenia? *Arch Gen Psych* 44:1008–1014, 1987.

Goldberg SC, Schooler NR, Mattsson N. Paranoid and withdrawal symptoms in schizophrenia: differential symptom reduction over time. *J Nerv Ment Dis* 145:158–162, 1967.

Golden CJ, Moses JA, Zelazowski MA, et al. Cerebral ventricular size and neuropsychological impairment in young chronic schizophrenics: Measurement by the standardized Luria-Nebraska Neuropsychological Battery. *Arch Gen Psych* 37:619–623, 1980.

Goldstein MJ, Roddick EH, Evans JR, et al. Drug and family therapy in aftercare of acute schizophrenics. *Arch Gen Psych* 35:1169–1177, 1978.

Green MF, et al. Teaching the Wisconsin Card Sorting Test to schizophrenic patients (letter). *Arch Gen Psych* 47:91–92, 1990.

Green M, Walker E. Neuropsychological performance and positive and negative symptoms in schizophrenia. *J Abnorm Psych* 94:460–469, 1985.

Grinspoon L, Ewalt JR, Shader RI. *Schizophrenia: Pharmacotherapy and Psychotherapy*. Baltimore: Williams & Wilkins, 1972.

Guenther W, et al. Pathological cerebral blood flow and corpus callosum abnormalities in schizophrenia: Relations to EEG mapping and PET data. *Psychiat Res* 29:453–455, 1989.

Hammer M. Social supports, social networks, and schizophrenia. *Schiz Bull* 7:45–57, 1981.

Harrow M. et al. Positive thought disorder in schizophrenia: Its importance, its longitudinal course, and impaired perspective as a contributing factor. In: Harvey P, Walker E, eds. *Positive and Negative Symptoms in Psychosis*. Hillsdale: NJ, 1987.

Haug JO. Pneumoencephalographic studies in mental disease. *Acta Psychiatr Scand* 38(suppl 165):1–104, 1962.

Heinrichs DW, Buchanan RW. Significance and meaning of neurological signs in schizophrenia. *Am J Psychiatry* 145:11–18, 1988.

Hempel K.-J, Treff WM. Be steht eine korrelation zwischen nervenzel-lausfall und den schwundzellveranderungen bei der katatonie? *J Hirn-forsch* 4:479–485, 1960.

Hogarty GE, Goldberg SC, Schooler NR, et al. Drug and sociotherapy in the aftercare of schizophrenic patients, II: Two year relapse rates. *Arch Gen Psychiatry* 31:603–608, 1974a.

Hogarty GE, Goldberg SC, Schooler NR, et al. Drug and sociotherapy in the aftercare of schizophrenic patients, III: Adjustment of non-relapsed patients. *Arch Gen Psychiatry* 31:609–618, 1974b.

Holzman PS, Levy DL. Smooth pursuit eye movements and functional psychoses: A review. *Schizophr Bull* 3:15–27, 1977.

Holzman PS, Proctor LR, Hughes DW. Eye tracking patterns in schizophrenia. *Science* 181:179–181, 1973.

Hughes JS, Little JC. An appraisal of the continuing practice of prescribing tranquilizing drugs for long-stay psychiatic patients. *Br J Psychiatry* 113:867–873, 1967.

Ingvar DH. Functional landscapes of the dominant hemisphere. *Brain Res* 107:181–197, 1976.

Ingvar DH, Sjolund B, Ardo A. Correlation between dominant EEG frequency, cerebral oxygen uptake, and blood flow. *Electroencephalogr Clin Neurophysiol* 41:268–276, 1976.

Itil TM. Qualitative and quantitative EEG findings in schizophrenia. *Schizophr Bull* 3:61–79, 1977.

Jaskiw GE, Weinberger DR. Ibotenic acid lesions of the medial prefrontal cortex potentiate FG-7142-induced attenuation of exploratory activity in the rat. *Pharmacol Biochem Behav* 36:695–697, 1990.

Javoy-Agid F, Agid Y. Is the mesocortical dopamine system involved in Parkinson's disease? *Neurology* 30:1326–1330, 1980.

Jeste DV, Zalcman S, Weinberger DR, et al. Apomorphine response and subtyping of schizophrenia. *Prog Neuropsychopharmacol* 7:83–88, 1983.

Johnstone EC, et al. The relative stability of positive and negative features in schizophrenia. *Br J Psychiat* 150:60–64, 1986.

Johnstone EC, et al. Temporal lobe structure as determined by nuclear magnetic resonance in schizophrenia and bipolar affective disorder. *J Neurol Neurosurg Psychiat* 52:736–741, 1989.

Johnstone EC, et al. Institutionalization and the outcome of functional psychoses. *Br J Psychiat* 146:36–44, 1985.

Johnstone EC, Crow TJ, Frith CD, et al. Cerebral ventricular size and cognitive impairment in chronic schizophrenia. *Lancet* 2:924–926, 1976.

Johnstone EC, Crow TJ, Frith CD, et al. Mechanism of the anti-psychotic effect in the treatment of acute schizophrenia. *Lancet* 1:848–851, 1978a.

Johnstone EC, et al. The dementia of dementia praecox. *Acta Psychiatr Scand* 57:305–324, 1978b.

Kane JM. Low-dose medication strategies in the maintenance treatment of schizophrenia. *Schizophr Bull* 9:528–532, 1983.

Karson CN, et al. Alpha frequency in schizophrenia: An association with enlarged cerebral ventricles. *Am J Psychiat* 145:861–864, 1988.

Kaufmann CA, Weinberger DR, Linnoila M, et al. CSF monoamines and schizophrenic subtypes, in Abstracts, 39th Annual Meeting, Society of Biological Psychiatry, Los Angeles, 1984.

Kay SR, Singh MM. The positive negative distinction in drug-free schizophrenic patients. *Arch Gen Psych* 46:711–718, 1989.

Kay SR. Longitudinal course of negative symptoms in schizophrenia. In: Greden JF, Tandon R, eds, *Negative Schizophrenic Symptoms: Pathophysiology and Clinical Implications.* Washington, DC: American Psychiatric Press, 1991.

Kennard MA. Value of equivocal signs in neurologic diagnosis. *Neurology* 10:753–764, 1960.

Kety SS. The syndrome of schizophrenia: Unresolved questions and opportunities for research (the 52nd Maudsley lecture). *Br J Psychiat* 136:421–436, 1980.

Klein DF, Davis JM. *Diagnosis and Drug Treatment of Psychiatric Disorders.* Baltimore: Williams & Wilkins, 1969.

Klein DF, Gittelman R, Quitkin A, eds. *Diagnosis and Drug Treatment of Psychiatric Disorders: Adults and Children.* Baltimore: Williams & Wilkins, 1980.

Kolakowska T, et al. Schizophrenia with good and poor outcome, III: Neurological "soft signs", cognitive impairment and their clinical significance. *Br J Psychiat* 146:348–357, 1985.

Kornetsky C. Hyporesponsivity of chronic schizophrenic patients to dextroamphetamine. *Arch Gen Psychiat* 33:1425–1428, 1976.

Kornetsky C, Orzack MH. Physiological and behavioral correlates of attention dysfunction in schizophrenic patients. *J Psychiatr Res* 14:69–79, 1978.

Kraepelin E. Dementia Praecox and Paraphrenia (1919) Translated by Barclay, RM, Robertson, S.M. New York: Krieger, 1971.

Lamb HB. Therapist-case managers: More than brokers of service. *Hosp Commun Psychiat* 31:762–764, 1980.

Lecrubier Y, Puech AJ, Widlocher D, et al. Schizophrenia: A bipolar dopaminergic hypothesis. In: Proceeding of the 12th CINP Congress, Goteburg. *Prog Neuropsychopharmacol* (supplement), 1980.

Leff JP. Developments in family therapy of schizophrenia. *Psychiatr Q* 51:216–232, 1979.

Lehmann S. The social ecology of natural supports. In: Jeger A, Slotnich RW. *Community Mental Health: A Behavior-Ecological Perspective.* New York: Plenum Press, 1980.

Lenzenweger MF, Dworkin RH, Wethington E. Models of positive and negative symptoms in schizophrenia: An empirical evaluation of latent structures. *Abnor Psychol* 98;62–70, 1989.

Letemendia FJJ, Harris AD. Chlorpromazine and the untreated chronic schizophrenic: A long term trial *Br J Psychiat* 113:950–958, 1967.

Levin HS. The neurobehavioral rating scale: Assessment of the behavioral sequelae of head injury by the clinician. *J Neurol Neurosurg Psychiat* 50:183–193, 1987.

Lindsley OR. Geriatric behavioral prosthetics. In: Kastenbaum RJ. *New Thoughts on Old Age.* New York: Springer, 1970.

Lipton FR, Cohen CI, Fischer E, et al. Schizophrenia: A network crisis. *Scizophr Bull* 7:144–151, 1981.

Luria AR. *Restoration of Function After Brain Injury:* London: Pergamon Press, 1963.

Luria AR. *The Working Brain: An Introduction to Neuropsychology.* New York: Basic Books, 1973.

Luria AR. *Traumatic Aphasia:* The Hague: Mouton, 1970.

Mattson AJ, Levin HS. Frontal lobe dysfunction following closed head injury: A review of the literature. *J Nerv Ment Dis* 178:282–291, 1990.

Mayazumi K, Tsutsui J. Abnormalities of pursuit eye movement and visual field in hemispherical brain damage. *Acta Soc Ophthalmol Jap* 78:1059–1065, 1974.

McEvoy JP, et al. Insight in schizophrenia. Its relationship to acute psychopathology. *J Nerv Ment Dis* 177:43–47, 1989.

Meltzer HY, et al. The effect of neuroleptics and other psychotropic drugs on negative symptoms in schizophrenia. *J Clin Psychopharmacol* 6:329–337, 1986.

Meltzer HY, et al. A prospective study of clozapine in treatment-resistant schizophrenic patients. *Psychopharmacology* 99:S68–S72, 1989.

Meltzer HY, et al. Effects of six months of clozapine treatment on the quality of life of chronic schizophrenic patients. *Hosp Comm Psychiat* 41:892–897, 1990.

Merriam AE, et al. Neurological signs and the positive-negative dimension in schizophrenia. *Biol Psychiat* 28:181–192, 1990.

Mirsky AF. Neuropsychological bases of schizophrenia. *Ann Rev Psychol* 20:321–348, 1969.

National Institute of Mental Health, Psychopharmacology Service Center, Collaborative Study Group: Phenothiazine treatment in acute schizophrenia: Effectiveness. *Arch Gen Psych* 10:246–261, 1964.

Neary D, et al. Dementia of frontal lobe type. *J Neurol Neurosurg Psych* 51:353–361, 1988.

Ogura C, Kishimoto A, Nakao T. Clinical effect of L-dopa on schizophrenia. *Curr Therap Res* 20:308–318,1976.

Orrell MW, et al. Self-neglect and frontal lobe dysfunction. *Brit J Psych* 155:101–105,1989.

Orzack MH, Kornetsky C. Attention dysfunction in chronic schizophrenia. *Arch Gen Psych* 4:323–326, 1966.

Pandurangi AK. A comprehensive study of chronic schizophrenic patients: II. Biological, neuropsychological, and clinical correlates of CT abnormality. *Acta Psychiat Scand* 73(2):161–171, 1986.

Paulman RG, et al. Hypofrontality and cognitive impairment in schizophrenia: Dynamic single-photon tomography and neuropsychological assessment of schizophrenic brain function. *Biol Psychiat* 27:377–399, 1990.

Perlick D, et al. Negative symptoms are related to both frontal and nonfrontal neuropsychological measures in chronic schizophrenia. *Arch Gen Psych* 49:245–246, 1992.

Pfohl B, Winokur S. The evolution of symptoms in institutionalized hebrephrenic catatonic schizophrenics. *Brit J Psychiat* 141:567–572, 1982.

Pickar D, et al. Clinical and biologic response to clozapine in patients with schizophrenia. *Arch Gen Psych* 49:345–353, 1992.

Pincus JH, Tucker GJ. Behavioral Neurology. New York: Oxford University Press, 1978.

Prien RF, Cole JO. High-dose chlorpromazine therapy in chronic schizophrenia. *Arch Gen Psych* 18:482–495, 1968.

Prien RF, Klett JC. An appraisal of the long-term use of tranquilizing medication with hospitalized schizophrenics: A review of the drug discontinuation literature. *Schiz Bull* 5:64–73, 1972.

Prien RF, Levine J, Cole JO. High-dose trifluoperazine therapy in chronic schizophrenia. *Am J Psychiat* 126:305–313, 1969.

Pritchard M. Prognosis of schizophrenia before and after pharmacotherapy. *Br J Psychiat* 113:1345–1359, 1967.

Quitkin F, Rifkin A, Klein DF. Neurological soft signs in schizophrenia and character disorders: organicity in schizophrenia with premorbid asociality and emotionally unstable character disorders. *Arch Gen Psych* 33:845–853, 1976.

Reynolds GP, et al. Deficit and hemispheric asymmetry of GABA-uptake sites in the hippocampus in schizophrenia. *Biol Psychiat* 27:1038–1044, 1990.

Rochford JM, et al. Neuropsychological impairments in functional psychiatric diseases. *Arch Gen Psych* 22:114–119, 1970.

Rylander G. *Personality Changes after Operations on the Frontal Lobes*. London: Oxford University Press, 1939.

Scarpiti FR, Lefton M, Dinitz S, et al. Problems in a homecare study for schizophrenia. *Arch Gen Psych* 10:143–154, 1964.

Schooler NR, Levine JR, Brauzer D, et al. Prevention of relapse in schizophrenia: An evaluation of fluphenazine decanoate. *Arch Gen Psychiat* 37:16–24, 1980.

Seidman LJ. Schizophrenia and brain dysfunction: An integration of recent neurodiagnostic findings. *Psychol Bull* 94:195–238, 1983.

Shakow D. Segmental set: a theory of the formal psychological deficit in schizophrenia. *Arch Gen Psych* 6:1–17, 1962.

Simon H, Scatton B, LeMoal M. Dopaminergic A10 neurones are involved in cognitive functions. *Nature* 286:170–171, 1980.

Sokoloff L. Relation between physiologic function and energy metabolism in the central nervous system. *J Neurochem* 29:13.26, 1977.

Sokolovsky J, Cohen C, Berger D, et al. Personal networks of ex-mental patients in a Manhattan SRO hotel. *Hum Organiz* 37:5–15, 1978.

Stein LI, Test MA. Alternative to mental hospital treatment, I: Conceptual model, treatment program, and clinical evaluation. *Arch Gen Psych* 37:392–397, 1980.

Stevens JR, Livermore A. Telemetered EEG in schizophrenia: Spectral analysis during abnormal behavior episodes. *J Neurol Neurosurg Psych* 45:385–395, 1982.

Strauss JS, et al. The diagnosis and understanding of schizophrenia: Part III. Speculations on the processes that underlie schizophrenic signs and symptoms. *Schiz Bull* 11:61–69, 1974.

Stuss DT, Benson FD. Neuropsychological studies of the frontal lobes. *Psychol Bull* 95:3–28, 1984.

Stuss DT, Benson FD. *The Frontal Lobes*, Raven Press: New York, 1986.

Suddath RL, et al. Temporal lobe pathology in schizophrenia: A quantitative magnetic resonance imaging study. *Am J Psychiat* 146:464–472, 1989.

Suddath RL, et al. Anatomical abnormalities in the brains of monozygotic twins disordant for schizophrenia. *N Engl J Med* 322:789–794, 1990.

Susser E, et al. Psychiatric problems in homeless men: Lifetime psychosis, substance use, and current distress in new arrivals at New York City shelters. *Arch Gen Psychiat* 46:845–850, 1989.

Tatetsu S. A contribution to the morphological background of schizophrenia with special reference to the findings in the telencephalon. *Acta Neuropathol* 3:558–571, 1964.

Test MA, Stein LI. Practical guidelines for the community treatment of markedly impaired patients. *Commun Ment Health* 112:72–82, 1976.

Torrey EF. Neurological abnormalities in schizophrenic patients. *Biol Psychiat* 15:381–388, 1980.

Trimble M, Kingsley D. Cerebral ventricular size in chronic schizophrenia *Lancet* 1:278–279, 1978.

Tsuang MT. Schizophrenic syndromes: The search for subgroups in schizophrenia with brain dysfunction. In: Henn FA, Nasrallah HA, eds. *Schizophrenia as a Brain Disease*. New York: Oxford University Press, 1982.

Van Kammen DP, Mann LS, Sternberg DE, et al. Dopamine-beta-hydroxylase activity and homovanillic acid in spinal fluid of schizophrenics with brain atrophy. *Science* 220:974–976, 1983.

Vaughn CE, Leff JP. The influence of family and social factors on the course of psychiatric illness. *Brit J Psychiat* 129:125–137, 1976.

Venables PH. Input dysfunction in schizophrenia. *Prog Exp Pers Res* 1:1–47, 1964.

Volkow ND, et al. Phenomenological correlates of metabolic activity in 18 outpatients with chronic schizophrenia. *Am J Psych* 144:151–158, 1987.

Weinberger DR, Berman KF. Speculation on the meaning of cerebral metabolic hypofrontality in schizophrenia. *Schiz Bull* 14:157–168, 1988.

Weinberger DR, Wyatt RJ. Cerebral ventricular size: A biological marker for subtyping chronic schizophrenia. In: Hanin PI, Usdin E, eds. *Biological Markers in Psychiatry and Neurology.* New York: Pergamon Press, 1982.

Weinberger DR, Torrey EF, Neophytides AN, et al. Lateral cerebral ventricular enlargement in chronic schizophrenia. *Arch Gen Psych* 6:735–739, 1979.

Weinberger DR, Bigelow LB, Klein JE, et al. Cerebral ventricular enlargement in chronic schizophrenia: Association with poor response to treatment. *Arch Gen Psych* 37:11–14, 1980.

Weinberger DR, DeLisi LE, Perman GP, et al. Computed tomography in schizophreniform disorder and other acute psychiatric disorders. *Arch Gen Psych* 39:778–783, 1982b.

Weinberger DR, et al. Physiologic dysfunction of dorsolateral prefrontal cortex in schizophrenia: I. Regional cerebral blood flow evidence. *Arch Gen Psych* 43:114–124, 1986.

Weinberger DR. Implications of normal brain development for the pathogenesis of schizophrenia. *Arch Gen Psych* 44:660–669, 1987.

Weinberger DR, Berman KF, Daniel DG. Prefrontal cortex dysfunction in schizophrenia. In: Levin HS, Eisenberg HM, Benton AL, eds. *Frontal Lobe Function and Dysfunction.* New York: Oxford University Press, 1991.

Weisbrod BA, Test MA, Stein LI. Alternative to mental hospital treatment, II: economic benefit-cost analysis. *Arch Gen Psych* 37:400–405, 1980.

Wohlberg GW, Kornetsky C. Sustained attention in remitted schizophrenics. *Arch Gen Psych* 28:533–537, 1973.

Wyatt RJ. The dopamine hypothesis: Variations on a theme. Presented at the American College of Psychiatrists, New Orleans, 1983.

Zubin J. Chronic schizophrenia from the standpoint of vulnerability. In: Baxter C, Melnechuk T, eds. *Perspectives Schizophrenia Research.* New York: Elsevier Science Publishers, 1980.

Back to the Future: The Role of the Psychiatrist in Treating Mentally Ill Individuals Who Are Homeless

ALAN FELIX, M.D., ELIE VALENCIA, J.D., M.A.,
and EZRA S. SUSSER, M.D., Dr.P.H.

INTRODUCTION

There have been wide-ranging estimates of the number of homeless individuals in the United States, but a recent study found that the extent of the problem may be much greater than previously realized (Link et al. 1994). According to that study, 7.4% of the current U.S. population, or 13.5 million people, have experienced literal homelessness (defined as sleeping in shelters, abandoned buildings, and public spaces) at some point during their lifetimes.

Persons with chronic mental illness are at 5–10 times the risk of becoming homeless than the general population (Susser et al. 1994) and approximately 5% of all persons with severe mental illness in the U.S. are homeless at any time (Federal Task Force on Homelessness and Severe Mental Illness 1992). The sad fact is that the streets of our cities, and some rural areas, have become increasingly populated with mentally ill individuals during the past two decades.

In our current times of high-tech biologic therapies and treatment guidelines tailored for disorders, not individuals, psychiatrists run the risk of neglecting important aspects of patient care. In general, psychiatrists are trained in the medical model where the aim is to elicit symptoms, make a diagnosis, and prescribe appropriate treatment. This model of care has led to important advances, but when applied too narrowly, it has serious limitations, especially with the homeless mentally ill.

Before the advent of psychotropic medications, psychiatrists who treated severely mentally ill patients relied on their understanding of a patient's relationship to them to bring about clinical change (Searles 1965, Federn 1952). From our current perspective, we recognize the great limitations faced by our predecessors who struggled to help severe and persistently mentally ill individuals without the benefits of effective medications. Yet while current medications may significantly alleviate symptoms, we should not neglect the non-pharmacologic perspectives of our predecessors.

The negative consequences of an over-reliance on pharmacologic treatments accompanied by an underestimation of the psychosocial aspects of treatment is illustrated most clearly by the deinstitutionalization movement during the past three decades. First, we observed the "revolving door" phenomenon as the community mental health system failed to meet the needs of the chronically mentally ill (Torrey 1988). Then, in the 1970s, we witnessed the increase of homelessness among the mentally ill as the economy and housing market changed (Hopper et al. 1985). While the effort to end homelessness among the severe and persistent mentally ill continues, we see the growing numbers of this population inhabiting our jails and prisons (Lehman 1995).

In the sections to follow, we describe the nonpharmacologic techniques that are thought to be crucial in the treatment of the homeless mentally ill and how they can set the stage for incorporating state-of-the-art medical model treatments into the overall treatment plan. Thus, in combining the wisdom of our predecessors with the latest somatic therapies, we take you back to the future.

We will break down treatment into three phases: engagement, treatment proper, and transition to housing. More emphasis will be placed on the first and last phases, when we feel that nonpharmacologic techniques are especially important. We will stress the importance of understanding a homeless patient's material, physical and emotional needs in the overall assessment process. Consistent with this perspective, we will also argue for the importance of a treatment that is comprehensive and continuous over time, especially during periods of residential transition.

In addition to discussing interventions on the clinical level, we will discuss recently developed programs and policies that incorporate these techniques and provide effective care to the severe and persistent mentally ill. We will conclude with suggestions for future developments that aim at minimizing homelessness and hospitalization while maximizing stability and quality of life in the community.

ENGAGEMENT

A psychiatrist's role in engagement frequently diverges from the traditional medical model. There are two aspects to the engagement phase of treatment with mentally ill individuals who are homeless. First, because patients often do not seek treatment, outreach is necessary. Second, an assessment of a patient's problems, strengths, and needs is required.

Outreach

The initial assessment by a psychiatrist treating the homeless mentally ill usually takes place under adverse conditions. Typically, some form of outreach is being done whereby a team of providers have come to the patient, rather than the reverse. When patients come willingly, such as in a shelter or drop-in center, they more often want housing or employment, not psychiatric treatment.

Outreach techniques have been well described elsewhere (Susser and Gounis 1990, McQuistion et al. 1991, Susser et al. 1992a, Valencia et al. in press). Here, we will emphasize how a psychiatrist might prioritize an evaluation of a new patient when the initial goal is engagement with a treatment team, rather than the provision of medical treatment (Susser et al. 1990, Susser 1992, Valencia et al. in press).

When meeting a patient in a shelter or street setting, the psychiatrist must first evaluate safety. A nonintrusive, nonclinical, friendly approach works best, especially when combined with offering food, cigarettes, a blanket or clothing. Assuming the patient demonstrates no obvious behaviors that present a danger to him or herself or others, the psychiatrist must then ask, "To what degree is this patient willing to let me intrude into his/her world?" The patient's responses to the initial approach, verbally and nonverbally, will determine the answer to this question. However, one must constantly readdress this question throughout the interview.

While there are some patients who have the capacity to rapidly form trusting relationships with a psychiatrist, others take months or years. Outreach with the latter population may consist of saying "hello" for a year to someone who is withdrawn into a corner of a shelter, and "Nice to see you" for another year as the patient moves his/her station near the mental health program, before finally saying, "Come on in and have a cup of coffee."

We offer an example of this approach. A psychiatrist for an on-site mental health program, in a large New York City shelter (Kass et al. 1992, Caton et al. 1990, Valencia et al. 1994), approaches a homeless person in the shelter:

Psychiatrist: How are you doing? Anything you need help with?
Patient: Yeah, I want to get out of this place before these X-rays kill me. (He points to the ventilation system, explaining that the government is pumping X-rays in through the ducts).
Psychiatrist: Our program can help you get out of this place. We'll find you a nice place to live and we'll have a doctor check your health if you want.
Patient: I want my own apartment, but I don't like doctors and I won't take medication. I'm allergic to it. I just take vitamins.
Psychiatrist: Great. I don't think you need medication right now, but we'll start a housing application and we have a nurse who will give you vitamins. Come in for a cup of coffee and I'll show you around our program.

This brief dialogue illustrates several points about engagement. The patient is addressed with his/her needs in mind, without the psychiatrist imposing his/her own agenda. Delusions are not challenged and the patient's disdain for medication is respected. However, by offering vitamins, the psychiatrist knows the patient will begin the process of accepting medication from the program nurse. Later, after some trust is established and the patient begins to show signs of attachment to the staff by coming to the program regularly and asking the staff for help, the importance of medication can be introduced.

A psychiatrist is in a unique position to evaluate all the factors that determine decisions not only about involuntary commitment, but also more subtle choices about how aggressively one should pursue medication compliance and when to begin to set limits, such as refusing to give tokens. Obtaining a history or providing medication must often take a back seat. In fact, in some situations, engagement can be fostered by siding with the patient's refusal to take medication. While this may sound outrageous, it is sometimes the only way to engage a leery patient to enter treatment and maintain any hope of his taking medication at a later date. The decision to wait before offering medication to a severely psychotic patient is a difficult one, but in some cases, the mere mention of medication may lead a patient to literally run out the door.

As a general rule, it is best to proceed cautiously during outreach, avoiding confrontation of a patient's denial or lack of insight. Demonstrating an understanding of a patient's perspective is a more useful way to foster engagement. The road to forming a treatment al-

233

liance might start with avoiding any questions about symptoms, problems, hospitalizations, medication history, etc. Discussing a patient's interests and strengths will boost his/her self-esteem and engender trust in the provider. Gradually, more stressful areas of inquiry can be introduced, each time evaluating the patient's response, backing off or moving deeper, based on the patient's cues. The psychiatrist who doggedly pursues a complete psychiatric assessment in the early phases of outreach runs the risk of losing the patient.

Initial assessment. Once a patient has agreed to further contact, a more comprehensive assessment of the patient's needs can begin. However, we propose that the needs assessment performed by the psychiatrist or other members of the treatment team, under the supervision of the psychiatrist, should differ from the usual one conducted in the medical model of care. The usual psychiatric approach to the chronic mentally ill patient prioritizes the patient's biologic needs and may or may not consider psychologic needs (e.g., the need for support, structure and limits, or confrontation). The psychiatrist's perspective is often, "What can *I* do to convince the patient he or she needs what *I* am offering?"

We propose a client-centered perspective wherein the needs assessment emphasizes aspects of a patient's life that are immediate and meaningful *to the patient.* Thus, we initially address the patient's material, physical, and emotional needs as the patient defines them. While the biologic and psychologic needs as defined by the psychiatrist are important and related to these other needs, they must be introduced gradually, only after a treatment alliance has formed and the patient is ready to acknowledge them.

Material needs: In the standard psychiatric assessment, the chief complaint concerns psychiatric symptoms such as depression, anxiety, or hallucinations. However, from the homeless patient's perspective, the chief complaint is typically, "I want a place of my own" or "I need a job." It might be even more basic, such as "I need a cigarette," "I'm hungry," or "I'm cold." By attending first to a patient's material needs, the chance of establishing a treatment alliance increases.

During the process of assessing the patient's material needs and formulating a plan to meet them, it is important to recognize the emotional effects of gratifying or frustrating these needs. Many of the homeless come from backgrounds of deprivation and their experience with the mental health service system and other authorities is similar to their past. They are denied access to public spaces, they are often denied treatment, and they might be denied entitlements. When a request for housing is met by a psychiatrist's a statement about the patient's medication needs or when a case worker who over-vigilantly guards against feeling manipulated denies a request for transportation tokens, the patient may react with a transferential rage that leads to the patient or staff ending the treatment.

Material goods, as gifts, may play an important role in treatment. Typically, during their training, psychiatrists are dissuaded from giving gifts to, or accepting them from, patients. However, inanimate objects, as noted by Searles some 35 years ago (Searles 1960), may serve to satisfy emotional needs unfulfilled by the schizophrenic's impoverished interpersonal world. We believe that the inanimate object itself partly fulfills this function, but the act of meeting the patient's need also paves the way to an interpersonal bond between patient and provider. Thus, cigarettes, coffee, transit tokens, and other gifts may be used not only as reinforcers of positive behaviors as in token economies, but to develop positive interpersonal relationships as well.

For example, Mr. A, who suffered from a psychotic depression, revealed that he once loved playing the trumpet. By coincidence, his psychiatrist shared this passion and happened to have an extra trumpet that was collecting dust. Upon giving it to the patient, a noticeable improvement in Mr. A's mood could be observed. Furthermore, Mr. A received great satisfaction playing in a talent show in the shelter. The trumpet provided a link to a healthier past and it helped motivate the patient to move into housing. The act of gift-giving served to strengthen Mr. A's attachment to the program staff and to other patients who enjoyed his playing.

Another patient, Mr. B, was psychotic and unkempt. He initially refused mental health services, but kept asking for a yellow legal pad. Acting on the hunch that Mr. B would derive satisfaction of a grandiose wish, the psychiatrist provided him with the pads. He took interest in Mr. B's writings which contained disorganized notes about obtaining a job and apartment. Finally, after sensing that Mr. B was beginning to trust him, the psychiatrist informed Mr. B that he could only use the pads in the mental health program. The patient agreed, although he frequently tested this limit. Mr. B ultimately agreed to take medication and later acknowledged that he had held the delusional belief that he was an important attorney.

Had the psychiatrist refused Mr. B's request, challenging his delusion or pushing medication too soon, the patient likely would have fled. Not until the later stages of the treatment, after a treatment alliance was solidified, was the promise of fulfilling the patient's material needs (e.g., housing and benefit procurement) linked to his taking medication and participating in substance abuse treatment groups. With these treatments, Mr. B improved to the point that he obtained his much desired apartment and job, albeit both in supportive settings.

Physical needs: Despite their medical training, psychiatrists frequently overlook their patients' physical needs. Again, as with material needs, the *patient's* perspective of *his/her* physical needs is often missed in favor of a medical model approach to "ruling out organic causes" of mental illness. While such a medical approach may be indicated as one component of the assessment, it runs the risk of missing essential concerns of the patient when applied exclusively.

While it goes without saying that it is essential to diagnose the major medical disorders to which the homeless are vulnerable (e.g., TB, HIV and other STDs, hepatitis, pneumonia, peripheral vascular disease), it is important to recognize that a homeless person might have physical concerns that seem insignificant to the psychiatrist, but are important to the patient. Once again, meeting the patient's needs can foster the engagement process. Thus, providing relief from cold symptoms, curing a case of scabies, or relieving the neuroleptic-induced extrapyramidal side effects of a recently hospitalized patient are all ways of addressing a patient's immediate physical concerns.

As mentioned in the section on material needs, addressing a patient's physical needs simultaneously addresses emotional and relationship needs. We only need to recall the magic of a mother's kiss on a child's "boo boo" to appreciate this point. Later we will take a more detailed look at the crucial activity of assessing a homeless patient's emotional needs.

Sexual needs: Ironically, psychiatrists treating the chronic mentally ill have a tendency to neglect an important aspect of patient life—sex. Despite the tradition of emphasizing the sexual derivation of conflict, psychiatrists tend to overlook the present-day sexual needs, attitudes, and behaviors of chronic mentally ill patients (Cournos et al. 1993, Cournos et al. 1994, Susser et al. 1995). We believe that attending to these areas of sexuality have several important outcomes.

First, by acknowledging a patient's sexuality, the psychiatrist opens an avenue that very often deepens empathy for the patient. The patient, moreover, feels that he/she is understood as a person, and not simply a cluster of symptoms. Understanding a patient's sexual attitudes and behaviors helps in the treatment of drug abuse and in money management. Some of the homeless depend on the exchange of crack for sex, or they use their disability benefits to obtain sex from prostitutes (Susser et al. 1995). These behaviors jeopardize the chances of obtaining and sustaining housing.

Secondly, attending to the sexual attitudes and behaviors of the homeless mentally ill permits interventions that may reduce the risk of contracting and transmitting HIV infection. This is a population at high-risk for HIV infection. We documented the rate of HIV seroprevalence among homeless mentally ill in a large NYC municipal shelter to be at an alarmingly high 19% (Susser et al. 1993). Yet, knowledge about preventive measures in this population remains scant. Currently, there is only one intervention to reduce HIV risk behaviors being tested with this population (Susser et al. 1994, Valencia et al. in press).

Emotional needs: Engagement is always the most important phase of psychiatric treatment and it is often the most challenging. This is especially true when treating the homeless mentally ill. Homeless persons frequently distrust the medical "establishment" due to the perception that they will be harmed by its treatments. For example, street- or shelter-dwellers fear being sedated because they will be more prone to victimization. Other patients have bad memories of being committed or forcibly restrained in treatment settings. The formation of a treatment alliance also requires special emphasis with this population because many homeless mentally ill individuals come from backgrounds of out-of-home placements and shifting caretakers (Susser et al. 1991, Caton et al. 1994).

Thus, as introduced previously in our discussion of assessing material needs, there is a high risk for reenactments of past pathologic relationships. For example, a patient may act in ways that cause the provider to withdraw from or punish the patient. The patient who acts aggressively, intrusively, manipulatively, or demandingly, may contribute to turning the provider into another reluctant caregiver.

One role of the psychiatrist is to recognize these transference and countertransference reactions and clarify them for the outreach team and/or case manager before the treatment is irreparably damaged. Then, limits can be set in the context of greater understanding of and empathy for the patient, rather than in a punitive manner driven by anger and fear.

Sometimes, the transference and countertransferences are difficult to recognize, displayed less by acting out than by more subtle forms of resistance and defense. Furthermore, certain providers who are perhaps rigid, out of touch with their own emotions, or who harbor rescue fantasies, are prone to missing these important aspects of the clinical relationship. Our extensive clinical experience working with this population strongly suggests that outreach mental health programs should encourage a low-demand, need gratifying approach in order to facilitate a positive transference and treatment alliance (Gounis and Susser 1990, Susser et al. 1992A, Valencia et al. in press).

However, we recognize that this approach will not eradicate the patient's underlying anger towards or distrust of parental transference figures. On the contrary, we try to anticipate through the assessment of the patient's emotional needs (see below) which patients are likely to undermine the bonds they form with treatment providers—for example by cashing in a couple of subway tokens (intended for travel to an Narcotics Anonymous (NA) meeting) to buy a hit of crack. We look at these enactments as an opportunity to point out to patients how their "getting over" is really a self-defeating misplacement of their anger. While acknowledging the anger and tracing its sources to their difficult, if not traumatic past experiences, we try to show patients how they are destroying the opportunity for trust-worthy, helpful relationships with staff.

The psychiatrist must appreciate that the homeless mentally ill person's sense of self is dually threatened by the presence of mental illness and by homelessness. The homeless patient often has lost most of his/her possessions, including the most basic of all—a home. Relationships with family and friends are commonly lost or strained. To preserve even a thin veneer of integrity, homeless mentally ill patients, like Mr. B, mentioned in a vignette above, may employ grandiose defenses and denial. These defenses need reinforcement initially. Any implication that the patient is "ill" or in need of treatment might threaten the patient to the point that he/she must avoid treatment to save face.

Some patients seem compliant initially, only to later refuse services or relapse into pathologic patterns (drug use, medication non-compliance, and regressive wishes to remain living in a shelter). A psychiatrist with a psychodynamic perspective is able to anticipate and understand this behavior. For example, some patients never successfully negotiated the separation-individuation phases of development (Mahler 1972) and therefore undermine efforts to obtain housing in order to preserve their attachment to current providers. Other patients harbor unconscious guilt which motivates self-defeating behavior in the form of maintaining their status as a member of the homeless subculture. It is crucial to understand the dynamics of these resistances to change to help the patient progress toward housing.

In summary, a psychiatrist is called upon to evaluate the needs of a homeless patient in ways that often go beyond his or her training and usual experience. The provision of treatment must be viewed broadly, including understanding patients' perspectives of their needs while establishing a trustworthy, need-satisfying role for patients. While attending to the more pressing physical, sexual, material and emotional needs of a patient, a solid relationship can be established, opening the way to more mainstream psychiatric treatment.

COMPREHENSIVE ASSESSMENT AND TREATMENT

Through careful assessment of the quality of a patient's relationship with staff, the psychiatrist can determine when it is time to move to the next phase of treatment. For example, a patient might exhibit improved modulation of his affect, greater honesty and openness with staff, and an overall increase in motivation for treatment. The latter may be evident in obvious ways, such as the patient who begins to attend a treatment program daily or who asks for medication. But it may be evident in more subtle ways, as in the patient who begins to sit outside the program, rather than remaining secluded in the shelter's hallways, or who asks for help in ways apparently unrelated to treatment, such as requesting to use a case worker's phone.

Some patients express their readiness for treatment by sitting behind the desk of a case worker, a behavior that might offend an uninformed provider. Motivated by anger, the case worker then punishes the patient by prematurely establishing boundaries and limits, rather than acknowledging the patient's need for the case worker's presence which could lead to a deepening of the treatment relationship. While there is no substitute for a comprehensive understanding of the patient, we do recognize the role of the intuitive "feel" that grows with experience and helps inform treatment decisions, such as when to introduce more intensive treatment.

When a patient is engaged in treatment, many of the traditional roles of the psychiatrist can be assumed. The psychiatrist performs diagnostic assessments, including a mental status exam and treatment plan. However, the route from engagement to housing is rarely a direct one. Typically, expectations must be introduced gradually, taking into account that the patient will have setbacks in progress toward more independent living.

Treatment may include addressing needs not fully acknowledged by the patient. For example, groups that use peer input, including peer counseling, help ready the patient for more independent and permanent housing. We emphasize addressing the areas that are most clearly linked with homelessness and relapse, including medication compliance, substance abuse treatment, money management, housing readiness, preventing HIV infection, crisis management and developing activities of daily living.

There are many functions that a psychiatrist can serve when treating the homeless mentally ill, but only if enough time is dedicated to the task. In most treatment settings for the homeless mentally ill, a psychiatrist, if present at all, is in a part-time or even volunteer position. We believe this supposedly "cost-effective" approach can be quite costly. By contrast, a full-time psychiatrist has the advantage of taking part in the engagement process, psychotherapy, and family therapy, roles which often boost a psychiatrist's more traditional functions as medication prescriber and supervisor of staff.

It can be extremely helpful to be aware of the transference throughout the treatment course of a homeless individual. Patience, flexibility, empathy, and creativity go a long way to-ward establishing a positive transference and help contain acting out of negative transference/countertransference binds.

For example, one case worker was finding that his tolerance for a patient's eccentric behavior, drug use, and poor hygiene was wearing thin. One day, the case worker watched and listened carefully as the patient, a Haitian man, applied lipstick and spoke French to his reflection in a mirror. The worker came over and gently asked, "Who are you talking with?" To the case worker's surprise, the patient replied that he was speaking with a favorite relative, his grandmother. A long conversation about her followed. This prompted the case worker to contact an elderly woman who ran a successful group home. The patient met her, they hit it off, and he is currently in his second year of residence in her home. We cannot think of a better example of using the transference to achieve a positive clinical outcome.

Finally, and perhaps this is the key to working with this population, we believe it is critical to find something likeable or interesting about a patient. Our experience has taught us that even the angriest, most help-rejecting patient still wants some form of human contact. During the course of treatment it is incumbent on the psychiatrist to find the help-seeking part of the patient, to cultivate it, and bring it to the attention of the other members of the treatment team.

TRANSITION TO COMMUNITY LIVING

In traditional settings, such as hospital inpatient units, emergency departments, and community mental health centers, treatment is confined within the walls of that particular setting. A territorial machismo may even develop, as depicted in the novel, *House of God* (Shem 1988). Within one setting a team approach may be lacking, but more likely, there is no cooperation among treatment teams in different settings. Patients are "turfed" to other sites with no one taking responsibility for longer-term care.

Discharges usually look good on paper, but they are not implemented and, in actuality, the patient suffers. Sadly, the homeless are most vulnerable to these practices. Prescriptions that require unobtained Medicaid cards go unfilled, appointments at clinics that require bus fare are not kept. The importance of housing in maintaining mental and physical health is often overlooked due to inexperience or pressures to discharge patients after short stays.

Based on experiences in shelters, we recognized that the homeless mentally ill who underwent day treatment in a shelter experienced a loss of supports when they moved into community housing. Even after New York State began a program of supportive housing for the homeless mentally ill (NY State Office of Mental Health 1990), patients struggled to adapt to their new settings and frequently became homeless again (Caton et al. 1990, Caton et al. 1993, Valencia et al. 1994). Just when they need the most support, they lose everything they struggled to establish with their previous caregivers. To address those patients who slipped through the cracks, we designed a treatment that specifically focused on patients' vulnerabilities during the transition from a shelter to housing. We called it the "Critical Time Intervention (CTI) for Homeless Mentally Ill Individuals in Transition from Shelter to the Community" (Valencia et al. 1994, Valencia et al. in press).

CTI revolves around a case manager who is familiar with the patient from the shelter, initially providing direct services with the support of a multidisciplinary team (including a psychiatrist and psychiatric nurse), but gradually transferring care to community-based resources. Services focus on preventing homelessness and relapse: substance abuse rehabilitation, medication compliance, money mangement, family psychoeducation, and resolution of housing-related crises. Within this context, we describe the unique role of psychiatrists in providing continuity of care to homeless mentally ill patients in the period of transition to community living, using the CTI model as a reference.

A psychiatrist who provides ongoing treatment as a patient moves from one setting to another is able to offer critical benefits to the patient and the new providers. Sharing records and experiences with a new treatment team not only improves the overall quality of care, but it may help in a more specific way. When a patient acts out shortly after being place in supportive housing, he/she runs a high risk of becoming homeless again. However, a psychiatrist familiar with the patient might recognize the underlying motivation for the behavior, point out that it is specific to the anxiety-provoking transitional phase of treatment, and relieve the anxieties of both the patient and the new providers.

When necessary, typically in the first 3 months after community placement, the psychiatrist may be called on to provide direct care during the transition phase. A patient missing an appointment with a new psychiatrist should not be denied medication out of fear of reinforcing regressive behavior. Rather, treatment should be given and the patient's behavior should be addressed by both the new and old psychiatrist. Our experience has been that providing ongoing treatment in this manner helps stabilize the patient and preserve housing. Furthermore, most patients are able to make the transition to a new treatment setting within 3 months, and ongoing treatment by the CTI team did not extend beyond 9 months, although the benefits of reduced risk of homelessness persisted for up to 18 months (See Valencia et al. 1994 for preliminary results).

In the last phase of the CTI intervention, as the patient becomes established with comprehensive community-based supports, the psychiatrist plays a less central, but not less important, role. He or she may be called on to intervene with the new providers if a crisis arises or to participate in assessing the family's role in a patient's life in permanent housing.

The overriding and guiding role of the psychiatrist in the CTI model is to coordinate the continuity of care and comprehensiveness of the treatment during the period of transition. Based on a comprehensive understanding of the patient's material, physical, and emotional needs through the various stages of treatment, the psychiatrist offers recommendations that shape the process of continuity of care carried out by the CTI team's community-based work.

CONCLUSION

The introduction of psychotropic medication was a major advance in the field of medicine. Too often, however, valuable lessons from the premedication era about engagement and treatment of chronic mentally ill patients are forgotten. We see this as "throwing out the baby with the bath water," especially in the strict adherence of some psychiatrists to the medical model of treatment.

The psychiatrist's role in our approach to treating chronic mentally ill patients who are homeless combines a comprehensive assessment of needs from the patient's perspective and continuous care through the various stages of treatment and across settings. Interventions at all stages are informed by an understanding of the patient's dynamics, particularly as they manifest themselves in the transference, countertransference, resistance, and acting out behaviors. The psychiatrist may perform these functions directly, or indirectly, providing a treatment team with a guiding perspective that is both comprehensive and continuous.

We begin with a heavily patient-centered, low-demand, highly gratifying approach in the outreach phase. Only after seeing evidence of a treatment alliance do we move into the assessment and treatment phases, recognizing that premature introduction of medication causes many patients to flee treatment.

Finally, the psychiatrist retains his/her role as supervisor of the team and direct provider of care, if necessary, after the patient moves into housing. The psychiatrist's understanding of the emotional stresses wrought by changes during the transition to a new living setting and from one treatment team to another is crucial to preventing relapses into both illness and homelessness. We contrast this approach to the usual "buff and turf" attitude that pervades a variety of treatment settings, from emergency departments to inpatient units to prison mental health units.

As we look to the future, we hope to see an expansion of programs that have demonstrated their effectiveness, such as Assertive Community Treatment (Santos et al. 1995, Burns and Santos 1995) and our own Critical Time Intervention (Valencia et al. 1994, Valenica et al. in press), that use comprehensive team approaches to treating the severe and persistent mentally ill, incorporating the treatment principles outlined in this chapter. We especially believe that by focusing on the difficulties of making the transition to community living, we can overcome the obstacles faced by the mentally ill individuals who continue to inhabit our streets, shelters, state hospitals, and prisons. While this paper draws on our experience with chronic mentally ill patients who are homeless, many aspects of our approach could improve care and prevent homelessness in all persons with chronic mental illness.

ACKNOWLEDGMENTS

We thank the staff of the Critical Time Intervention Mental Health Program for the Homeless, Columbia-Presbyterian Medical Center, at the Fort Washington Shelter for Men, New York City, for their contribution to this article. In particular, we acknowledge the contributions of Julio Torres, M.Div. and Sarah Conover, M.P.H. We also thank Bibiana Marquez for her assistance. This work was supported in part by NIMH grant R18MH 48041.

REFERENCES

Burns BJ, Santos AB. Assertive community treatment: An update of randomized trials. *Psychiat Serv* 46:7, 669–675, 1995.

Caton CLM, Wyatt RJ, Grunberg J. An evaluation of a mental health program for homeless men. *Am J Psych* 147:286–289, 1990.

Caton CLM, Wyatt RJ, Felix A, Grunberg J, Dominguez B. Follow-up of chronically homeless mentally ill men. *Am J Psychiat* 150:1639–1642, 1993.

Caton CLM, Shrout P, Eagle PF, Opler LA, Felix A. Correlates of Co-disorders in homeless and never-homeless indigent schizophrenic men. *Psychol Med* 24:681–688, 1994.

Cournos F, McKinnon K, Meyer-Bahlburg H, Guido JR, Meyer I. HIV risk activity among the severely mentally ill: Preliminary findings. *Hosp Commun Psychiat* 44:1104–1106, 1993.

Cournos F, Satriano J, Herman R, Kaplan M. HIV Risk Reduction Groups for People with Serious Mental Illness. *Psychosoc Rehab J,* 1994.

Federn P. *Ego Psychology and the Psychoses.* New York: Basic Books, 1952.

Gounis K, Susser E. Shelterization and it's implications for mental health services. In: Cohen N, ed. *Psychiatry Takes to the Streets.* New York: Guilford Press. 1990.

Hopper K, Susser E, Conover S. Economies of makeshift: Deindustrialization and homelessness in New York City. *Urb Anthro* 14:183–236, 1985.

Kass F, Kahn D, Felix A. Day treatment in a shelter: A setting for assessment and treatment. In: Lamb HR, Bachrach LL, Kass F, eds. *Treating the Homeless Mentally Ill.* Washington, DC: American Psychiatric Press, 1992.

Lehman C. States begin to address tragedy of mentally ill prisoners. *Psychiatr News* 5, 1995.

Link BG, Susser E, Stueve A, Phelan J, Moore R. Lifetime and five-year prevalence of homelessness in the United States. *Am J Pub Health* 84:1907–1912, 1994.

Mahler M. On the first three subphases of the separation-individuation process. *Int J Psychoan* 53:333–338, 1972.

McQuistion HL, D'Ercole A, Kopelson E. Clinical principals to steer the system. In: Cohen NL, ed. *Psychiatric Outreach to the Mentally Ill. New Directions for Mental Health Services.* No. 52. San Francisco: Jossey-Bass, 1991.

New York State Office of Mental Health. *NY/NY Housing and Support Program for the Homeless Mentally Ill: Fact Sheet,* 1990.

Outcasts on Main Street. Report of the Federal Task Force on Homelessness and Severe Mental Illness. United States Department of Health and Human Services. 1992.

Santos AB, Henggeler SW, Burns BJ, Arana GW, Meisler N. Research on field-based services: Models for reform in the delivery of mental health care to population with complex clinical problems. *Am J Psych* 152:8, 1111–1123, 1995.

Searles HF. *The Non-Human Environment in Normal Development and in Schizophrenia.* New York: International Universities Press, 1960.

Searles HF. *Collected Papers on Schizophrenia and Related Subjects.* London: Hogarth Press, 1965.

Shem S. *House of God.* New York: Dell Publishing, 1988.

Susser E. Working with people who are homeless and mentally ill: The role of a psychiatrist. In: Jahiel R, ed. *Homelessness: A Preventive Approach.* Baltimore: Johns Hopkins University Press, 1990.

Susser E, Valencia E, Miller M, Meyer-Bahlburg H, Tsai W, Conover S. Sexual Behaviors of Homeless Mentally Ill Men at Risk for HIV. *Am J Psychiat* 152:583–588, 1995.

Susser E, White A, Goldfinger S. Some clinical approaches to the homeless mentally ill. *Comm Ment Health J* 26:459–476, 1990.

Susser E, Struening EL, Conover S. Homelessness in mental patients: Lifetime prevalence and childhood antecedents. *Am J Psychiat* 144:1599–1601, 1991.

Susser E, Valencia E, Goldfinger S. Clinical care of the homeless mentally ill: Strategies and adaptations. In: Lamb HR, Bachrach L, Kass F, eds. *Treating the Homeless Mentally Ill.* Washington DC: American Psychiatric Association Press, 1992.

Susser E, Valencia E, Conover S. Prevalence of HIV Infection Among Psychiatric Patients in a New York City Men's Shelter. *Am J Pub Health* 83:568–570, 1993.

Susser E, Moore R, Link B. Risk Factors For Homelessness. *Epidem Rev* 151:421–427, 1994.

Susser E, Valencia E, Miller M, Meyer-Bahlburg H, Tsai W, Conover S. Sexual behaviors of homeless mentally ill men at risk for HIV. *Am J Psych* 4:583–587, 1995.

Torrey EF. *Nowhere To Go: The Tragic Odyssey of the Homeless Mentally Ill.* New York: Harper & Row, 1988.

Valencia E, Susser E, Caton C, Felix A, Colson P. The New York City Critical Time Intervention Project: Guiding the Transition to Independent Living. In: *Making a Difference: Interim Status Report of the McKinney Demonstration Program for Homeless Adults with Serious Mental Illness.* Center for Mental Health Services, U.S. Department of Health and Human Services. Rockville, MD, 1994.

Valencia E, Susser E, Torres J, Felix A, Conover S. Critical time intervention for homeless mentally ill in transition from shelter to community. In: Breakey W, Thompson J, eds. *Innovative Programs for the Homeless Mentally Ill.* Switzerland: Harwood Academic Publishers. (in press)

Valencia E, Torres J, Susser E. HIV prevention work with homeless mentally ill individuals. In: Cournos F, Bakalar N, eds. *HIV/AIDS and Severe Mental Illness.* New Haven, CT: Yale University Press. (in press)

Appendix A
Psychopharmacologic Agents*

Drug	Company	Indication	U.S. Development Status
aripiprazole (OPC-14597)	Otsuka America Pharmaceutical (Rockville, MD)	schizophrenia	Phase II
CI-1007	Warner-Lambert (Morris Plains, NJ)	psychosis	Phase I
iloperidone	Hoechst Marion Roussel (Kansas City, MO)	schizophrenia	Phase III
MAR 327	Sandoz Pharmaceuticals (East Hanover, NJ)	schizophrenia	Phase II
mazapertine	Janssen Pharmaceutica (Titusville, NJ)	schizophrenia	Phase II
MDL 100,907	Hoechst Marion Roussel (Kansas City, MO)	schizophrenia	Phase II
NGD 94-1	Neurogen (Branford, CT)	schizophrenia	Phase I
ORG-5222	Organon (West Orange, NJ)	psychosis	Phase II
pramipexole	Boehringer Ingelheim Pharmaceuticals (Ridgefield, CT) Pharmacia & Upjohn (Kalamazoo, MI)	schizophrenia (see also mood disorders)	Phase I/II
RP 62203 fananserin	Rhone-Poulenc Rorer (Collegeville, PA)	schizophrenia	Phase II
Seroquel dibenzothiazepine	Zeneca Pharmaceuticals (Wilmington, DE)	schizophrenia	Phase III
sertindole	Abbott Laboratories (Abbott Park, IL)	psychosis	application submitted
SR 27897	Sanofi (New York, NY)	psychosis	Phase II
SR 31742	Sanofi (New York, NY)	psychosis	Phase I
U-101387	Pharmacia & Upjohn (Kalamazoo, MI)	schizophrenia	Phase II
ziprasidone (CP-88,059)	Pfizer (New York, NY)	schizophrenia	Phase III
Zyprex® olanzapine	Eli Lilly and Company (Indianapolis, IN)	schizophrenia	application submitted

*This table is adapted from a 1996 survey prepared by the Pharmaceutical Research and Manufacturers of America (PhRMA). Of the 17 new drugs under development, 3 are in Phase I (studies of 20–80 healthy volunteers, lasting approximately 1 year, aimed at determining drug safety and dosage); 9 are in Phase II (studies of 100–300 patient volunteers, lasting approximately 2 years, aimed at evaluating drug effectiveness and side effects); 3 are in Phase III (studies of 1,000–3,000 patient volunteers, lasting approximately 3 years, aimed at verifying drug effectiveness and monitoring adverse reactions associated with long-term use); and 2 (Seroquel® [dibenzothiazepine] and Zyprex® [olanzapine]) are awaiting FDA review of a New Drug Application (NDA), a process which ordinarily takes from 1.6–2.5 years.

Appendix B
Clinical Resources for the Study of
Schizophrenia

Following is a listing of clinical centers for the study of schizophrenia currently funded by the National Institute of Mental Health. The listing provides the names of center directors, and the names, addresses, and telephone numbers of each center.

Director	Clinical center	Address	Telephone number
Andreasen, Nancy, M.D., Ph.D.	MH-CRC: Neurobiology and Phenomenology of the Major Psychoses	Iowa City, IA	319-356-4720
Carpenter, William T., Jr., M.D.	CRC: Classification and Course of the Schizophrenias	Baltimore, MD	301-455-7666
Cloninger, C. Robert, M.D.	Diagnostic Center for Psychiatric Linkage Studies (Schizophrenia)	St. Louis, MO	314-362-7005
Friedhoff, Arnold J., M.D.	MHCRC for Organic, Affective & Schizophrenia Disorders	New York, NY	212-263-5717
Gorman, Jack, M.D.	Developing Clinical Research Center for the Study of Schizophrenia	New York, NY	212-960-2371
Gur, Raquel E., M.D., Ph.D.	MHCRC - Regional Brain Function in Schizophrenia	Philadelphia, PA	215-662-2826
Kaufmann, Charles A., M.D.	Diagnostic Center for Psychiatric Linkage Studies (Schizophrenia)	New York, NY	212-960-2211
Liberman, Robert P., M.D.	Clinical Research Center for the Study of Schizophrenia	Camarillo, CA	805-484-5663
Pfefferbaum, Adolf, M.D.	MHCRC to Study Biological Correlates of Psychopathology	Palo Alto, CA	415-852-3456
Tsuang, Ming T., M.D., Ph.D., Dsc.	Diagnostic Center for Psychiatric Linkage Studies (Schizophrenia)	Brockton, MA	508-583-4500 x3723

Index

INDEX

INDEX